A Short History of the Liberal

GW00374806

WITHDRAWN

Also by Chris Cook

* THE AGE OF ALIGNMENT: ELECTORAL POLITICS IN BRITAIN, 1922–29
* SOURCES IN BRITISH POLITICAL HISTORY, 1900–51 *(6 vols, with Philip Jones et al.)*
  THE SLUMP: BRITAIN IN THE GREAT DEPRESSION *(with John Stevenson)*
  BY-ELECTIONS IN BRITISH POLITICS *(ed. with John Ramsden)*
* EUROPEAN POLITICAL FACTS OF THE TWENTIETH-CENTURY *(with John Paxton)*
* BRITISH HISTORICAL FACTS, 1830–1900 *(with Brendan Keith)*
* THE POLITICS OF REAPPRAISAL, 1918–39 *(ed. with Gillian Peele)*
* CRISIS AND CONTROVERSY: ESSAYS IN HONOUR OF A.J.P. TAYLOR *(ed. with Alan Sked)*
  POST-WAR BRITAIN: A POLITICAL HISTORY *(with Alan Sked)*
  THE LONGMAN HANDBOOK OF MODERN BRITISH HISTORY, 1714–2001
  (with John Stevenson)
  THE LABOUR PARTY *(ed. with Ian Taylor)*
* AFRICAN POLITICAL FACTS SINCE 1945 *(with David Killingray)*
  THE LONGMAN COMPANION TO BRITAIN SINCE 1945 *(with John Stevenson)*
  THE LONGMAN HANDBOOK OF MODERN AMERICAN HISTORY, 1763–1996
  (with David Waller)
  WHAT HAPPENED WHERE *(with Diccon Bewes)*
* A DICTIONARY OF HISTORICAL TERMS
  THE ROUTLEDGE COMPANION TO BRITAIN IN THE NINETEENTH CENTURY, 1815–1914
  THE ROUTLEDGE GUIDE TO BRITISH POLITICAL ARCHIVES
  THE ROUTLEDGE COMPANION TO EUROPEAN HISTORY SINCE 1763
  (with John Stevenson)
  THE ROUTLEDGE COMPANION TO WORLD HISTORY SINCE 1914 *(with John Stevenson)*

* Also published by Palgrave

A Short History of the Liberal Party
The Road back to Power

Chris Cook

First edition 1976
Second edition 1984
Third edition 1989
Fourth edition 1993
Fifth edition 1998
Sixth edition 2002
This edition published 2010 by
PALGRAVE MACMILLAN

Palgrave Macmillan in the UK is an imprint of Macmillan Publishers Limited,
registered in England, company number 785998, of Houndmills, Basingstoke,
Hampshire RG21 6XS.

Palgrave Macmillan in the US is a division of St Martin's Press LLC,
175 Fifth Avenue, New York, NY 10010.

Palgrave Macmillan is the global academic imprint of the above companies
and has companies and representatives throughout the world.

Palgrave® and Macmillan® are registered trademarks in the United States,
the United Kingdom, Europe and other countries

ISBN   978–0–230–21043–1   hardback
ISBN   978–0–230–21044–8   paperback

This book is printed on paper suitable for recycling and made from fully
managed and sustained forest sources. Logging, pulping and manufacturing
processes are expected to conform to the environmental regulations of the
country of origin.

A catalogue record for this book is available from the British Library.

A catalog record for this book is available from the Library of Congress.

10   9   8   7   6   5   4   3   2   1
19 18 17 16 15 14 13 12 11 10

Printed and bound in Great Britain by
CPI Antony Rowe, Chippenham and Eastbourne

Contents

Introduction and Acknowledgements		vii
1	The Liberal Tradition	1
2	Liberalism in Eclipse	19
3	The Liberals in Opposition: 1900–1906	30
4	The Liberal Ascendancy: 1906–1910	41
5	The Crisis of Liberalism: 1910–1914	51
6	Liberals at War: 1914–1918	62
7	A Party Divided: 1918–1923	76
8	Revival and Decline: 1923–1926	90
9	Lloyd George Again: 1926–1931	105
10	Dissension and Decline: 1931–1945	117
11	A Party in the Wilderness: 1945–1956	129
12	The Sound of Gunfire: 1956–1967	136
13	The Thorpe Leadership: 1967–1976	147
14	Pacts and Alliances: 1976–1983	163
15	A Tale of Two Leaders: 1983–1987	175
16	Merger Most Foul: 1987–1988	188
17	A New Agenda: 1988–1992	201
18	Voting for Change: 1992–1997	213
19	Living with Labour: 1997–2001	238
20	An Effective Opposition: 2001–2005	260
21	From Kennedy to Clegg: 2005–2010	279
22	Voting for Deadlock: The General Election of May 2010	309
23	Consenting Adults: The Liberal–Conservative Coalition	317

Appendix I   *Major Holders of Liberal Party Office, 1900–1988*   327
         II   *Major Holders of Liberal Democrat Office, 1988–2010*   330
        III   *The Liberal Vote, 1918–2010*   331
         IV   *Liberal By-Election Victories since 1945*   332
          V   *Liberal Democrat Seats (after May 2010)*   333
         VI   *The Continuing Liberal Party*   335
Bibliographical Note   336
Notes   341
Index   356

Introduction and Acknowledgements

This volume attempts a relatively short survey of the fortunes of the Liberal Party and its successor, the Liberal Democrats, during the period since 1900. Since the history of the party during these years must be seen in the context of the Victorian era, the first two chapters of the book are devoted to a brief survey of the main events of that period.

No person writing on the history of the Liberal Party can fail to be indebted to the important studies produced by Roy Douglas and Trevor Wilson.* This book incorporates new material and more recent published studies, but its original debt to both authors remains high.

In producing a short survey, many episodes have necessarily to be passed over briefly. In particular, the halcyon years of Liberalism from 1906 to 1914, together with the First World War, have been only briefly surveyed here, for they have both been extensively written about elsewhere. For other periods (such as 1945 to 1956) the story is short because very little of lasting importance happened to the depleted Liberal ranks.

This book has been written in the hope that students both of history and of politics will find it of use. In addition, in the changed political climate in Britain, it is hoped that the facts and figures given here on the fortunes of the Liberal Democrats since their birth in 1988 and their recent performance in the May 2010 general election will be of relevance both to the specialist and to the general reader.

Much of the research for the seventh edition of this book was done at the London School of Economics. A particular debt is owed to colleagues and friends there who helped at various stages in its production. Much of the typing for the current edition of this book was done with unfailing energy and kindness by Linda Hollingworth. I must also thank James Robinson and John Stevenson for their help and support in preparing this edition. Finally, my continued thanks are due to the publishers, Palgrave Macmillan, for encouraging a seventh edition of this book – over thirty years after the original edition first appeared.

---

* See R. Douglas, *The History of the Liberal Party, 1895–1970* (1971) and T. Wilson, *The Downfall of the Liberal Party* (1966). For the Victorian period, the brilliant study by John Vincent, *The Formation of the Liberal Party, 1857–1868* (1966), is indispensable.

1
The Liberal Tradition

Over a century has now passed since the Liberal electoral landslide of 1906. Likewise over ninety years have gone by since Lloyd George supplanted Asquith as Prime Minister in December 1916. For over eighty years, since the electoral debacle of October 1924, the Liberal Party has been the Cinderella of British politics. During this period the party has endured repeated dissension and decline.

Yet despite the oft-repeated forecasts of politicians and historians, the party still remains. Its fighting spirit is still very much in evidence. In 1962, with a sensational by-election victory in suburban Orpington, the party achieved a major, if temporary, revival. Again, in 1973, a remarkable series of electoral victories brought the party into the forefront of British politics. In the subsequent general election of February 1974 the party polled over 6 million votes. In the 1980s, the Alliance of Liberal and Social Democrats in the June 1987 election preceded the birth in March 1988 of the Social and Liberal Democratic Party. Under the leadership of Ashdown and Kennedy the new party grew in strength. After the election of May 2010 it was back in government.

It is with the varying fortunes of the party since 1900 that this book is concerned. But the fate of the party in this period can only be seen in perspective against the background of Victorian politics in which the Liberal Party grew up so successfully.

In the confused and changing period of British politics between the Reform Acts of 1832 and 1867 the Liberal Party of the Victorian era gradually took shape. However, there is no single satisfactory moment when the Liberal Party can be said to have been born. The nearest is, perhaps June 1859. On this occasion, at the famous meeting in Willis's rooms, the Whig, Peelite and Radical leaders in Parliament combined together to oust the minority Government of Disraeli and Derby.

However, although 1859 marks an important stage in the evolution of the party, the new government of Palmerston, which included for the first time both Gladstone and Lord John Russell and which survived until Palmerston's death in October 1865, was less a 'Liberal' ministry than a reconstituted Whig Government. The decisive date at which the Victorian Liberal Party came of age was 1868. In the general election of that year, following the Second Reform Bill, a definite Liberal victory heralded the formation of Gladstone's first administration.

The Parliamentary Liberal Party which slowly took shape in the decade after 1859 was almost unrecognisable from the unified, disciplined parties of the twentieth century. It was less a party in the modern sense than a loose alliance of groups of many shades of political opinion and widely differing social background. From the beginning, the Liberal Party was an uneasy coalition. The most divergent shades of opinion within the Liberal ranks were represented by the Whigs and the Radicals. It was this division which constituted the most obvious potential split within the political coalition that made up mid-nineteenth-century Liberalism.

The division of Whigs and Radicals was one of both social background and political ideology. The great Whig family groupings – such names as Portland, Argyll and Devonshire – formed the traditional aristocratic core of the party. The Liberalism of these great landowners was much more the product of tradition, loyalty and history rather than of any very specific programme or set of principles. However, despite their innate conservatism, the Whig grandees played a crucial part in nineteenth-century Liberalism – even after successive Reform Acts in 1832 and 1867 had reduced their influence in the Commons. Their importance lay neither in their numbers (although they formed a large and important group in the House of Lords) nor in their immense wealth, but rather in their domination of the key posts in Liberal ministries. It was the Whigs much more than the Radicals who held the vital offices in Gladstone's Cabinet.

Their political programme was extremely limited. Such interest as they possessed in moderate reform rapidly waned in the field of parliamentary and electoral reform. Here, their own political vested interests were deeply affected, since any measure of reform would inevitably strike at Whig influence in the surviving small boroughs. Within the Liberal ranks the Whigs constituted an exclusive caste in the upper reaches of political society. Thus the leadership of Lord John Russell, despite his close association with parliamentary reform, was acceptable partly because he came from the same social stratum as the Grosvenors, Cavendishes and Fitzwilliams.

Gladstone, on the other hand, represented a break with the past. Socially, he always remained outside the powerful inner circle of Whig society which Palmerston had successfully manipulated. Politically,

Gladstone was suspect both as a former Peelite and a known advocate of reform. In this respect, Gladstone was more in sympathy with the opposite end of the Liberal political spectrum, the Radicals.

Standing in marked contrast to the passivity of the Whigs, the Radicals provided the party with its main areas of growth and with its most advanced political ideas. The Radicals themselves were a diverse group. Whilst they included in their ranks such intellectuals as Henry Fawcett or John Stuart Mill, their most important element was the Nonconformist manufacturing interest. Such men as Samuel Morley, William Rathbone and John Bright were representative of this group. It was from constituencies in Lancashire, Yorkshire and the industrial Midland counties that these Radical dissenters and businessmen were chiefly returned. And it was from this group that there came the strongest demands for radical reform – for extension of the franchise, the secret ballot, the extension of state education and the abolition of church rates.

This Radical group was the one section of the party firmly committed to challenging the established order both in Church and State. Their great obstacle to reform was not the conservatism of the Whig hierarchy but the inertia of the mass of moderate Liberals who constituted the bulk of the parliamentary party. These moderate Liberals, often landowners, lawyers and army and naval officers, were distrustful of Radical enthusiasm. To this extent they tended to be a conservative force within the party, although usually willing to follow the lead of the Liberal front bench.

It was these three elements – Whigs, Radicals and the mass of moderates – which made up the Parliamentary Liberal Party. However, just as important as these developments within the party at Westminster was the evolution of the party at the grassroots in the constituencies. The development of the Parliamentary party coincided with, and was indeed linked with, important new social forces at work in the country.

Three particular factors were at work which helped mould Liberalism. The first was the growth of the cheap daily provincial press. Helped by the repeal of the stamp and paper duties between 1855 and 1861, the numbers and circulation of the provincial press leaped forward. Many of these new papers were dominated by Liberal families – the Baines family with the *Leeds Mercury* or the Cowens' *Newcastle Chronicle*. This rapidly expanding provincial press helped build up an articulate, radical, self-conscious provincial Liberalism which became one of the pillars of the new Liberal Party.

A second source of Liberal strength lay in militant Nonconformity. Traditionally, the Nonconformists had always looked to the old Whig Party as their natural allies against the Anglican Tories. For the Nonconformists, the Liberal Party seemed the best instrument to realise the religious and educational reforms they so much desired. However, by 1868 the Nonconformists were no longer willing to act as the 'poor relation' of the Whigs. Mid-century militant Nonconformity now constituted a vocal force in its own right.

The rise of the new working-class voters in the mid-nineteenth century was another phenomenon closely allied to the evolution of the Liberal Party. As with the Nonconformists, the working class looked to the Liberal Party, not merely for reform in such areas as trade union rights, wages and hours of work, franchise extension and social reform, but in a much more significant way. Their political emancipation was symbolised by supporting and voting for the Liberal Party.

In the ten years after 1859, by being able to harness both militant Nonconformity and a rising working-class political consciousness to their party, as well as having a prime voice in the new provincial press, the Liberal Party became of major political importance. It was a party which, because it had established links with new and dynamic forces at work in the country, stood to be the party of the future.

The person who turned this potential into reality was W.E. Gladstone. And the period which marked the heyday of political Liberalism was the years of the two great ministries he headed: 1868 to 1874, and 1880 to 1885. In 1867, Gladstone was 58. He had begun his political life as a reactionary Tory and High Churchman, having become MP for Newark in 1832. However, the great determinant in Gladstone's future political career was his religion. Gladstone was a fervent believer that politics must be a field for Christian action. A corollary of this was his concept of 'freedom'. For Gladstone, the struggle of a nation fighting to be free – whether Bulgaria in 1876 or Ireland a decade later – just as the freedom of people to pursue the ideal of self-fulfilment and moral development – was a moral cause which overruled all else. This passionate moralism, plus his dominating personality, his brilliant administrative gifts and his supreme oratory, were Gladstone's strength – and weakness – in politics. Indeed, Gladstone was often a bad party leader and manager, tactless and awkward with many of his colleagues, and neglecting vital issues both of policy and organisation in order to pursue, ruthlessly and relentlessly, his personal crusades.

In 1867, however, Gladstone's years as Premier lay ahead. A more immediate issue had arisen which showed the extent to which the Liberal Party could be divided even by an issue which had never lacked prominent Liberal advocates. The occasion was the struggles which preceded the passing of the Second Reform Bill. The most notable Liberal opponents of parliamentary reform were the Adullamite 'cave' of Whig politicians. Centring on Robert Lowe, Lord Grosvenor, Lord Clanricarde and Lord Elcho, they never numbered more than twelve in any organised form.[1] But they were able to attract the support of dissident Radical industrialists and rural Liberals, as well as the inevitable Whigs. Thus, when the Russell Reform Bill was defeated in June 1866, 44 Liberals voted in the majority against the government. It was Disraeli's subsequent advocacy of household suffrage which made the 'cave' less dangerous by depriving it of a Conservative refuge. Indeed, Gladstone admitted that he and many Liberals were 'bowled over' by Disraeli's proposals since they were still thinking in terms of a limited borough franchise. As an attempt to control the Liberal leadership the 'cave' had its Radical counterpart in John Bright and his followers, who were dedicated to the removal of the reactionary Whigs from their political ascendancy and to the introduction of a wide measure of parliamentary reform – an endeavour where he, too, was 'trumped' by Disraeli.[2]

It was against this background that the Liberals fought the general election of December 1868. As Professor Hanham has correctly written, the outcome of the election did not involve great speculation. It was widely believed that the minority Conservative Government would, in fact, suffer defeat at the polls. However, though Gladstone and the Liberals achieved an important victory in 1868, the size of this Conservative defeat was in many ways less than had been expected. Partly, this was a consequence of Gladstone's declaration in favour of the disestablishment of the Irish Church.

Gladstone's proposals for a comprehensive programme for the disestablishment and disendowment of the Irish Church, together with the ending of the Maynooth grant, not only alarmed certain sections of public opinion, but also created unease within the Parliamentary Liberal Party. Two groups, in particular, were apprehensive about disestablishment. John Bright, together with other Radicals, would have preferred to give priority to the land question, disregarding the views of such people as Cardinal Manning who regarded the Irish establishment as the root of bitterness in Ireland. However, whilst Bright was hardly likely to desert Gladstone on this question, this was not the case with those Whig landowners in the counties who thoroughly disapproved of Gladstone and all his Irish works. Several influential Whigs either deliberately refused to play an active part in the election or positively encouraged their tenants to vote Conservative in order to teach the Liberals a sharp lesson.

The outcome, overall, was to return Gladstone to power with a majority of over 100, an increase of 40 over 1865. The counties, however, produced a different result. Maurice Cowling has calculated that, in the counties affected by the 1867 Reform Bill, there had been 32 Liberals and 34 Conservatives elected in 1865. In 1868 the figures were 30 Liberals and 57 Conservatives.[3] Much of this Liberal failure to advance in the counties can be attributed to opposition to disestablishment. Certainly, the inactivity of Whig patrons in such constituencies as South Shropshire and West Surrey cost the party dearly.[4]

At the same time, certain working-class areas in which the Liberals had previously done well came out as decisively as the Whigs against disestablishment. This was particularly noticeable in Lancashire, where traditional anti-Irish feeling had recently been reinforced by Fenian terrorism in Manchester. Not only Gladstone himself, but such other leading Liberals as Milner-Gibson and Hartington, were all defeated in Lancashire partly because of Protestant-Conservative revulsion over Ireland. Gladstone, after his defeat in South West Lancashire, was returned for Greenwich. As Sir Charles Dilke drily remarked, Gladstone was much more likely to become a democratic leader now he sat for a big town.

These defections from Liberalism in Lancashire, together with the Conservative advance in the counties, were easily offset by the Liberal gains in the large cities and by the substantial Liberal majorities in Wales, Scotland and Ireland. As Professor Vincent has observed, these Liberal majorities in Wales and Scotland, gained with very little overt electioneering, were often for causes for which the Liberal leadership was indifferent or even hostile.[5]

However, despite the various disturbing features of the election returns – most particularly, signs that the Radicals had reached their peak too soon in urban England – the outlook for the Liberal Party after December 1868 seemed set fair. More united and more popular than it was to be again, the Liberals seemed set for a constructive and full term in office.

With Gladstone's own personal ascendancy unchallenged, the Liberal leader set out to construct his Cabinet. Its personnel reflected the changed composition of the parliamentary party and the diverse supply of capable men now thought appropriate for the important ministerial posts. Unlike the almost wholly Whig Cabinets of Palmerston and Russell, it contained only five members who could definitely be classified as Whigs: de Grey, Clarendon, Granville, Hartington and Chichester Fortescue. Against this, there were seven 'new men', all of them commoners, with a varying degree of commitment to reform: Robert Lowe (Chancellor of the Exchequer), H.A. Bruce (Home Secretary), H.C.E. Childers (First

Lord of the Admiralty), John Bright (President of the Board of Trade) and G.J. Goschen (President of the Poor Law Board). Two members of the Cabinet, apart from Gladstone, are best described as Peelites: the Duke of Argyll (Secretary for India) and Edward Cardwell (Secretary for War). The followers of Peel, long departed from the Tory fold, still retained a strong sense of their own identity as a separate group among the Liberals and, for this reason, were likely to act as a moderating and cohesive element among the Whigs and Radicals of this composite Cabinet.

The new ministry had lacked neither talent nor leadership. Yet within five years the reforming enthusiasm of the government was spent and the party was deeply divided and disarrayed. Indeed, much of Gladstone's energy was absorbed in dealing with the dissension and opposition from within the ranks of his own party.

The heart of the problem was not difficult to discover. The Liberals were still a party composed of so many differing factions and interest groups – social, political and religious – that it was almost impossible for the government to undertake the kind of reforms it envisaged without mortally offending one of its own constituent sections. Gladstone was himself unable to attract the constant confidence and unfailing support of any group: he was always distrusted by the Whigs; his views on Ireland already alarmed the moderates; his moderation in reforming measures was to disillusion the dissenters, Catholics and Radicals.

The issue above all others on which the party was to flounder was Ireland, the province which Gladstone had proclaimed it was his mission to pacify. The uneasiness of the Whigs over Ireland first manifested itself in 1869 over the Bill to disestablish and disendow the Irish Church. This was eventually carried in the form that Gladstone desired, with endowments being converted 'mainly for the relief of unavoidable calamity and suffering'.[6] But the Whigs in the Lords felt that this was too sweeping a move and one not necessarily guaranteed to bring religious or social peace. For some time they argued in vain for a scheme of concurrent endowment, giving both the Catholic and Protestant priests a house and land. The Irish Land Bill of the following year, surprisingly, earned the ideological disapproval of Bright and Lowe rather than the opposition of the Whigs. The Bill aimed to 'prevent the landlord from using the terrible weapon of undue and unjust eviction by so framing the handle that it shall cut his hands with the sharp edge of pecuniary damages'.[7] This was in fact an extension to the rest of Ireland of the Ulster system of 'tenant right'. It was opposed by Bright on the grounds that what was needed in Ireland was a wholesale transfer of land ownership from the present owners to the downtrodden occupiers. It was attacked by Lowe as an invidious extension of state intervention. But most of the Whig landowners concentrated in the Lords seem to have agreed with Chichester Fortescue that 'this Bill will limit my power as a landlord but only when that power is unjustly abused'.[8]

This increasing Whig disillusion with the Liberals was aggravated by three other measures unconnected with Ireland. Each provided a further milestone in the steady drift of the Whigs towards Conservatism. First, Cardwell initiated in 1871 the abolition by Royal Warrant of the system of purchasing commissions in the Army. Secondly, in 1870 Lowe secured open competition for entry to the Civil Service – where the Minister at the head of the department approved. (This was accepted by all the Ministers except Clarendon at the Foreign Office.) Thirdly, open voting was ended by the Ballot Act of 1872. The first two reforms radically altered the long-established apparatus for advancement which had benefited Whig families. The third abolished a system which many of the older Whigs still held to be an integral and worthy part of the constitution.

Meanwhile, Gladstone's administration faced not only rumblings from the right but a damaging and open split with the Nonconformists over W.E. Forster's Education Bill in 1870. The Nonconformists were 'the largest, most active and most high-principled section of the party. As such they seemed to be in a position to claim the redress of their grievances.'[9] The Education Bill, however, failed to end sectarian education, as demanded by Joseph Chamberlain and Robert Dale, founders of the National Education League in 1869, and by Edward Miall, a veteran champion of dissent. Instead it gave a privileged position to the Church of England: denominational schools were to continue where they were working efficiently; elsewhere they were to be supplemented by school boards, who were given religious liberty. John Morley, later to be Gladstone's biographer, pointed out the irony of the circumstances surrounding this measure: 'Mr Disraeli had the distinction of dishing the Whigs, who were his enemies. Mr Gladstone on the other hand dished the Dissenters, who were his friends. Unfortunately, he omitted one element of prime importance in those rather nice transactions. He forgot to educate his party.'[10] Although Miall declared that 'it was a lover's quarrel, and nothing more need be said about it', the Act led to a long period of Nonconformist anti-government agitation and to the most virulent attacks on Forster, and finally shattered the illusion that the Liberal Party would become 'the mouth-piece of the Nonconformists'.[11]

This was not the only religious interest group that Gladstone offended. In 1871 the University Test Act abolished the need for entrants to Oxford and Cambridge to subscribe to the 39 Articles and thus alarmed many

Anglicans. In 1873 a misguided desire for compromise led to a plan for a new university in Ireland, which failed to gain the support of either Anglicans or Catholics. Gladstone had in fact proposed to set up a university insulated from Ireland's religious strife by an absence of teaching in theology, modern history or moral and mental philosophy. This idea was immediately attacked by disappointed Catholics as a proposal for a 'godless college', and when it was defeated in the Commons (by 287 to 284) 35 Irish Liberals voted against it.

The Irish University Bill was not the only Liberal measure to alienate two possible sources of support at one blow. Bruce's Liquor Licensing Bill of 1872 was strongly opposed by the Temperance Liberals of the United Kingdom Alliance who, like the members of the National Education League, had vainly hoped for better things from their own Government. It also started the flight of the drink trade, caught between the twin evils of Liberal Temperance societies and the new restraints of Liberal legislation, towards the Conservatives.

The Liberals could take comfort that dissenters at least could find no acceptable home outside the Liberal Party. But a number of minor measures, inept decisions and misfortunes combined to accelerate the progress of the Government down the precipice of its own unpopularity with the more uncommitted voters in the country. Lowe's proposal to tax matches brought out the match factory workers to rouse public opinion against the government. The final settlement of the *Alabama* claims at $15 million was seen as a humiliation for Britain that contrasted strongly with the results of Palmerston's policy in the previous decade; the same was felt over British acquiescence over the abrogation by Russia of the demilitarisation of the Black Sea. The Collier and Ewelme cases focused disproportionate public attention on the government's possible misuse of its right to certain judicial and ecclesiastical appointments.

Much more fundamental than these minor problems was the Trade Unionist agitation against the 1871 Trade Union Act, the Liberal legislation which followed the Royal Commission on Trade Unions set up in 1867. The 1871 Act, although giving the unions full legal recognition, took from them the right of 'peaceful picketing'. This was done by passing a separate Criminal Law Amendment Act which in fact reinforced the old 1825 Act making unions liable to prosecution. This legislation from the Liberal Government was bitterly resented by the unions – a resentment which grew in intensity by the way in which the law was applied.

The net result of all these factors was that the unity and purpose which had brought the party to power was split. By 1873 the party was deeply divided, its legislative zeal gone completely and its popularity faded.

The whole process of loss of popularity was given added momentum by the vivid campaigning speeches of Disraeli, and by the fact that the government's inexorable decline was regularly made obvious in frequent by-elections. The culmination of this demoralisation came when Disraeli refused to form a minority government after Gladstone's defeat in 1873.

Against this political background, it was not surprising that by the beginning of 1874 Gladstone had decided to dissolve Parliament and go to the country on a campaign to repeal Income Tax. To Gladstone, this was the popular issue which would unite the party and ensure success at the polls. Gladstone's course of action was accelerated by the refusal of Cardwell and Goschen to accept the proposed reductions in their estimates. Accordingly, the dissolution was announced on 24 January 1874. The news caught not only such bodies as the National Education League unprepared, but took the country by surprise.

Gladstone's calculated plans, however, soon went astray. During the campaign Disraeli was able, in his famous phrase, to deride the Liberals as a 'range of exhausted volcanoes'. The outcome of the 1874 election was an overall majority of 50 for the Conservatives. Among the Liberal casualties was Joseph Chamberlain at Sheffield. In England the most noticeable loss of support occurred among the middle classes in the boroughs, where the Liberals lost 32 seats. This was partly due to the appeal of Disraelian Conservatism, and partly to the failure of Liberal organisers either to supply strong central support and direction, or to keep in touch with those local associations which had aided them in 1868. As a result, many such associations had either ceased to exist or had been alienated from giving whole-hearted support to the party through lack of understanding of Liberal policies. Though Gladstone declared that the party had been 'borne down in a torrent of gin and beer', loss of working-class support together with the reaction of the middle-class voter in suburban England, in response to the increasing manifestations of working-class power, had been more responsible for the defeat.

The only comfort that Liberals could derive from the election was that a spell in opposition would give the party a chance to reorganise itself in decent obscurity. Furthermore, many of those sections of the party which had caused trouble during the life of the government in fact rallied back to the Liberal flag at the election. This was particularly true of the dissenters, who probably accounted for the fact that the Liberals won back in 1874 ten of the seats that they had lost in recent by-elections. But this could not obscure the fact that many energetic party workers now preferred to work for a particular pressure group rather than for the party, and that Liberal support was now more than ever confined to a hard core in the boroughs, with declining support in the counties, Wales and Scotland. Even more ominous for the future of Liberalism were the results from Ireland. There 58 of the 105 members returned were Home Rulers, wiping out the semi-permanent Liberal majority in Ireland overnight, and reducing orthodox Liberal representation in Ireland to a mere 12 members.

The period immediately after the 1874 defeat was one of confusion among the Liberal leadership. Gladstone was anxious to retire. He wanted, as Morley wrote, 'an interval between Parliament and the grave'. He also felt himself out of sympathy with the tumultuous politics of the new generation of mainly Radical Liberals, particularly on the questions of education and religion. Perhaps more important, he could discern 'no great positive aim' in contemporary politics that might have given him personal satisfaction. Dispossessed of the initiative of office, the party itself also lacked a sense of direction or purpose. Both were to be supplied within the next few years – but not by the official leadership in Parliament.

When Gladstone finally announced his withdrawal from the leadership in January 1875, there was no very obvious successor. Forster, the man best qualified to succeed to the leadership in the Commons, was ruled out by the Nonconformist campaign against him. The post eventually fell to the Marquis of Hartington, a Whig of rather more limited political ability, who was considered adequate for what promised to be a dull Parliament. His position was made somewhat easier by the departure of Disraeli to the Lords in 1876, leaving Sir Stafford Northcote to lead the Conservatives in the Commons. Hartington's task was, however, complicated in the first place by muffled rumblings of dissatisfaction from the Radicals – principally Chamberlain, Dilke and Morley – who had lost, in Gladstone, the most respected advocate of reform, and were now forced to exist under Whig leadership and to watch a growing series of mild Conservative reforming measures. Secondly, Hartington was easily overshadowed by Gladstone whenever the latter chose to take part in a debate, and indeed was almost totally eclipsed by him, though still nominal leader, when Gladstone erupted back to prominence.

Although the Liberal Party was in opposition from 1874 to 1880, these six years were a period of great importance in the evolution of the party, most particularly in the creation and development of party organisation following the founding at Birmingham, in 1877, of the National Liberal Federation.

Prior to 1877, the structure of party organisation differed very little from that of the Conservatives at this date. At the centre, the work was divided between the Whips and the Liberal Registration Association, formed by the Whips and a small body of Liberal MPs in 1861. The Whips looked after candidatures, party funds and political patronage, whilst the Liberal Registration Association attempted to supervise and coordinate the work of the constituency Liberal associations. These local associations looked after the task of local registration (a process at which the political parties had become more adept than the official overseers) and organised the election campaigns, often working with a local part-time paid agent.

In theory, the Liberal machine was adequate. In practice, however, it suffered a series of defects which rendered it less efficient than that of the Conservatives. After the retirement of the principal agent, Drake, in 1865, the party lacked a replacement for twenty years, despite the obvious importance of the post. The work was divided between the Whips (already over-worked and under-staffed), the Liberal Registration Association and the party's local agents.[12] At the same time, the officials of the Liberal Registration Association were frequently able to make little impression upon those urban areas where very efficient local Liberal organisations were in control, and where such local managers as Edward Baines in Leeds were extremely unlikely to admit any outside interference. The problem was not confined to the boroughs. In the counties the party was equally incapable of inducing the Whigs, who controlled these county associations, into greater activity. Thus, until the coming of the National Liberal Federation in 1877, and with it a more influential and efficient central party organisation, the Liberals in the constituencies were often allowed to rest in Whig-induced lethargy or to waste their efforts and votes on duplicating candidatures.

Prior to the Reform Bills of 1867 and 1868 these deficiencies of organisation, though important, were not vital. However, the remodelling of the franchise (adding approximately 938,000 new electors to an existing electorate of 1,057,000 in England and Wales, with corresponding increases in Scotland and Ireland) and the Redistribution Bill brought about vast changes, not only in the structure of parliamentary representation but also, over the longer term, in the whole response of both political parties to the possibilities of more democratic participation in the choice of governments and in their policies.

The overall effect of the 1867 Reform Act was to introduce household franchise in the towns and the £12 occupancy franchise in the counties. The fact that Disraeli had been manoeuvred into accepting the Hodgkinson amendment which abolished compounding (i.e. the payment of rates by tenants through their landlords) enabled large numbers of tenants to become enfranchised as rate-paying occupiers. The accompanying Redistribution Bill for England and Wales took away 45 seats from boroughs with a population of under 10,000. Sometimes (as in the case of Thetford) the borough was disfranchised completely. Elsewhere (as in the case of Devizes) representation was reduced from two members to one. Whig acquiescence in these changes was partly explained because 25 additional seats were given to the counties.

An interesting experiment introduced by the Act affected the double-member constituencies of Manchester, Leeds, Liverpool and Birmingham. A third member was added to each of these cities, although each elector could exercise only two votes. It was hoped that, by this device, minority interests would gain representation. In fact, the capture of all seats in such towns as Birmingham rapidly became one of the supreme tests of party organisation.

All these developments, coupled with the defeat of 1874, impressed on Liberals the need for more efficient organisation. The lead in this field came from Birmingham. There, the 'caucus' of Radical Liberal politicians had been well known since 1868 for its victories at general elections and for the constant attention it paid to furthering Liberal candidates in municipal elections.[13]

The foundation of the National Liberal Federation grew out of the desire of Birmingham's Liberal leaders to supply from their own experience the kind of political organisation which the party lacked, and to provide from a Radical starting-point that cohesion and sense of purpose among Liberal associations that the Whig leaders at the centre were unwilling or unable to provide. More immediately, the NLF hierarchy grew from the personnel of the Birmingham Liberal Association and the National Education League, a Birmingham-based dissenting pressure group whose members, led by Chamberlain, felt the need for wider horizons and shared the general desire of former rebels to aid the party from within after the defeat of 1874. Thus the NLF centred at the start on Birmingham politicians of national and local note – Chamberlain, Jesse Collings and J.S. Wright. Its first secretary, Francis Schnadhorst, remained secretary of the Birmingham Liberal Association until 1884.

Delegates from 95 local Liberal associations accepted invitations to the first conference of the NLF in May 1877.[14] Chamberlain was elected president and an administrative General Committee appointed which would provide continuous organisation and summon an Annual Council: 46 local associations joined the NLF during the first month of its existence. At this stage the general aim of the NLF was to 'reflect Liberalism in the country'. As McGill has pointed out,[15] the NLF was basically an organisational machine rather than a means whereby the provincial Radicals could dictate party policy. However, Hartington, the party Whips and the managers of the Liberal Central Association in London were bound to see it as a challenge to the power of the centre. Although Gladstone visited the first conference at Birmingham, Hartington withheld approval of the scheme. The main activities of the NLF and its affiliated associations in the early stages were the dissemination of party propaganda, the arrangement of *ad hoc* political meetings, particularly in support of Gladstone's campaigns, and the gradual repair of the vast gaps in Liberal organisation in the counties.[16]

A variety of other Liberal organisations followed in the wake of the National Liberal Federation. The Women's Liberal Federation was founded in February 1887. In Scotland, the North and East of Scotland Association was founded in 1880, followed shortly after by the Glasgow-based Scottish Liberal Federation. In 1887 the two united. Other developments included the establishment in 1887 of the Liberal Publication Department and the inauguration in 1893 of the *Liberal Magazine* under the editorship of Charles Geake. Meanwhile, by the 1890s regional organisations had been set up in such areas as the Home Counties, the Midlands and the West Country.

The restructuring of Liberal organisation after 1877 coincided with two important political events: the re-entry of Gladstone into active politics and the increasing unpopularity of Disraeli's government.

Gladstone's re-entry into politics, with his campaign against the Eastern policy of the government after 1876, marked the moment when the Liberals first regained their vigour and sense of purpose after the defeat of 1874. Gladstone broke his political silence with the pamphlet *The Bulgarian Horrors and the Question of the East*. In this tract, Disraeli was bitterly attacked for condoning Turkish atrocities against the Slav Christians of Montenegro and Serbia, then in revolt against Ottoman rule.

Despite the fact that, in using Turkey as an ally against Tsarist Russia, Disraeli was only pursuing traditional British diplomacy, the fervour and sincerity of Gladstone's attack soon had a decisive impact on public opinion. In Parliament, his Commons resolutions of 1877 were extraordinary in that they did not have the support of Hartington and other Whig leaders. Despite this, and despite Disraeli's return to popularity after the Congress of Berlin in 1878, Gladstone's initiative had given the whole Liberal Party a policy, and had given life and vigour to a somnolent opposition.

Meanwhile the economic depression of the 1870s was eating into the government's popularity. The Farmers' Alliance, founded by James Howard in 1879, rallied the support of many farmers behind the Liberals in the hope that they would make the Land Laws more flexible, and give the tenant farmers more protection during a depression.[17] In addition, the government's reputation in foreign affairs was damaged by the disasters to its 'prancing proconsuls' of empire, defeated at Isandhlwana and Kabul in 1879.

The latter events gave Gladstone an opportunity to attack anew the government's foreign policy during his campaign in Midlothian. This extraordinary progress, undertaken against the Tory Earl of Dalkeith in the winter of 1879, even before the Queen had dissolved Parliament, set a precedent for future election campaigns.[18] Together with the Bulgarian agitation, it also gave the Liberals an example of innovation in political communications to set beside the NLF. Moreover, it gave the Liberals in the constituencies the political fighting spirit which the Whigs in nominal control of the party were quite unable to match, and in destroying the Conservative record it had a material effect upon Liberal confidence and upon the result. In Ireland alone the general trend towards Liberalism was upset. There the 37 moderate Home Rule Liberals and 16 Liberals saw emerge a far more potent force, the 24 members of Parnell's militant Home Rule party, dangerous to both Liberals and Conservatives in their desire to use, but not to support, either party.

In the election of 1880, the Liberals gained an overall majority of 54, making inroads into the Conservative preserves in the counties, and winning back many of the urban seats lost in 1874. Wales and Scotland returned 9 Conservatives and 78 Liberals. The NLF, whose total of affiliated associations reached 97 in 1880, was bound to claim the credit for much of this victory.[19]

When the result of the 1880 election was known, the immediate problem for the Liberals was to decide the leadership. Gladstone's resumption of political activity and the wide support he had gained for himself and the party in the Midlothian campaign meant that his claim to be Premier, although not explicitly stated, could not be ignored. Hartington and Granville both acknowledged to the Queen the practical impossibility of forming a government and maintaining it in power without Gladstone's active participation and support. Thus Gladstone's lukewarm promises of independent support for a Hartington administration ultimately guided the Queen's choice in his direction, and he took office at the end of April 1880.

Post-election euphoria was felt in many sections of the party. Gladstone's exclamation, 'The outlook is tremendous', was echoed among young Liberals of Asquith's generation, who saw this as the beginning of an era of promise, and among many Radicals, who hoped that their say in the party's Parliamentary future would now be increased in proportion to their contribution to the Liberal victory. General expectations of Liberal reforming activity were soon shattered by the obstructionist tactics of Parnell and the Irish Nationalists, who eventually succeeded in concentrating Liberal energies upon the Irish question and thus in bringing the party into a new and this time irretrievable schism.

The more specific hopes of the Radicals were immediately shaken by the composition of Gladstone's Cabinet. This contained only two Radicals, John Bright and Joseph Chamberlain, and was otherwise of a far more Whiggish character than that of 1868, and still included Lord Granville as Foreign Secretary, Sir William Harcourt as Home Secretary and Lord Hartington as Secretary for India.

For a variety of reasons, the high hopes the Radicals entertained of Gladstone's second ministry were rapidly disillusioned. Nor was this attributable solely to the marked Whig dominance in the Cabinet. The disruptive tactics of Parnell, the whole issue of Ireland, together with the activities of the 'Fourth Party', hindered the ministry. More than this, however, was the personal failing of Gladstone's leadership. Certainly, the 1880 Liberal Cabinet needed a stronger control by the Prime Minister than Gladstone cared to exercise.

For whatever reasons, historians have not been charitable on the achievements of Gladstone's second ministry. According to Ensor, never in the modern era had a triumphant majority in the Commons achieved so little. There was truth in this verdict. Four years after the triumph of 1880, the reforms dreamed of by the Radicals remained unfulfilled. Partly this failure after 1880 was due, as after 1868, to factional disputes within the government. All this was aggravated, however, by a series of incidents at home and abroad which served to discredit the government. In colonial affairs, Gladstone's second ministry faced vexing problems in the Transvaal (including a British defeat at Majuba Hill), the revolt of Arabi Pasha in Egypt and a series of tragic mistakes in the Sudan culminating in Gordon's death at Khartoum. At home, the Bradlaugh case, Radical dissent at the lack of social reform, growing electoral unpopularity, but above all the problem of Ireland, overshadowed the ministry.

It was apparent from the start that on the question of Ireland the government would be under pressure from two different directions. The Nationalists under Parnell were unsure of Liberal sincerity over land reform and realised that, however many minor reforming palliatives were directed towards Ireland, it was only by constant agitation that Ireland could remain as a permanent problem for which the politicians at Westminster would have to arrive at a permanent solution. The main opposition to Gladstone's policy of reforming the major causes of Irish discontent came from among the Whigs, but so wide was the disparity of views within the party that when the government fell back upon a policy of coercion in 1882 , an equally sizeable opposition to this policy came from the Radicals, led by Chamberlain and Bright. For the Liberal Party the tragedy was that when Home Rule was put forward as the Liberal solution it at once united men from these formerly quite distinct and different factions in opposition to the policy of the leadership.

The first intimation of the obstacles in the way of Gladstone's policy came in 1880 with the Irish Compensation for Disturbance Bill, empowering County Courts to award compensation to tenants evicted for non-payment of rent. This was thrown out by the Lords, thus precipitating a renewal of outrages against landlords and agents in Ireland. The Land Bill of the following year was more successful, partly because it contained some safeguards for landlords in the form of an accompanying Coercion Bill. The Land Bill promised Irish tenants fair rents, free sale and fixity of tenure and, once the Lords showed signs of delaying its passage, was the occasion for one of the first mass demonstrations organised by the NLF in support of the government's policy. However sincere Gladstone's intentions towards Ireland, as shown in the Land Bill and other measures, it seemed to many Liberals that his policies were playing into the hands of Parnell.

Events seemed to justify these fears. The Kilmainham Treaty (in April 1882) brought Parnell a definite Arrears Bill and the government an indefinite promise of Irish cooperation. Forster, the Chief Secretary and Lord Cowper, the Viceroy, both resigned over this. The murder of Lord Frederick Cavendish, the new Chief Secretary, and T.H. Burke, the Under-Secretary, together with the Nationalist-organised 'boycott' not only of landlords but also of the government's new Land Courts, justified those who were suspicious of Irish sincerity.

The Whig opposition to the Irish measures of 1881–2 (Hartington had refused to give the Land Bill his active support) came at a time when their political and social position was already under attack from members of their own party, in Parliament and in the country. In Parliament they fought in vain against the repeal of the malt tax and against the Game Bill. Although Chamberlain's 1883 attack on the House of Lords, 'who toil not neither do they spin', was primarily directed against the permanent Conservative majority in the Lords, it was seen by many Radicals to apply equally well to the more reactionary members of the Liberal Party. In the country, new Liberal candidates, mainly farmers, were being endorsed by the Farmers' Alliance, and with the promise of popular support were easily able to supplant previous Whig candidates and managers. The organisational drive of the NLF in the counties was inevitably tending to have the same effect.

The most important result of Radical agitation and the most important blow to the Whigs' political future came in 1884 with the Franchise Bill. This was a measure strongly advocated by Chamberlain, Dilke and George Trevelyan, and by Gladstone: it was reluctantly accepted as inevitable by Hartington.

But however strong the delight among Radicals and moderate Liberals at the Bill's passing, the Whigs were appalled by the measure and especially by the calculating Radicalism of the Conservative negotiator, Sir Michael Hicks Beach, on whose supposed reactionary ideas they may have been tempted to rely.[20] The Bill meant the end of Whig political power as it had contrived to continue in Parliament and the country after 1832. The increased electorate and the departure of the small boroughs deprived them of the sources of their power; the 1883 Corrupt Practices Act deprived them of the means whereby they might still have been able to manipulate their way to victory; the single-member seats meant the end of the Liberal practice of running a Whig and a Radical in 'double harness'. It was a sign of the end of the Whig hegemony at the centre that in 1884 Chamberlain prevailed upon Gladstone to reform the Whig-dominated LCA, under the Chief Whip, Lord Robert Grosvenor.[21]

By 1885, despite the Franchise Act and Irish legislation, the government seemed as much a spent force as it had in 1873. Within the Cabinet, factional feeling was heightened by the rejection of Chamberlain's scheme for Irish County Boards and a national council. In the country at large, the mistakes leading to the death of Gordon had reduced the government's popularity yet further. However, the actual defeat of the government in June 1885 on the Budget was to result, not in an immediate general election but in a short administration by the 3rd Marquis of Salisbury.

2
Liberalism in Eclipse

The resignation of Gladstone and the subsequent minority Salisbury Government (a caretaker administration until December 1885, when an election could be held on the revised electoral register) inaugurated a period of intense political turmoil culminating in the defeat of Gladstone's Home Rule Bill in 1886. There ensued a period of two decades in which the Liberal Party was firmly eclipsed by the Conservatives.

An important event in the period before the December 1885 election was the launching of Chamberlain's 'unauthorised programme'. In this he advocated free primary education, land reform ('free land') to secure the multiplication of ownership, a revision of taxation to close the gap between excessive wealth and extreme poverty, and the creation of county councils and national councils in Dublin and Edinburgh. Chamberlain claimed that 'about two thirds of the Liberal Party' fought the election on this programme in 1885. Not surprisingly the 'unauthorised programme' bitterly antagonised the Whigs. This cleavage spilt over into the election campaign. The fact that the quarrel took place in the open, and during an election campaign, was a symbolic landmark. It represented a Radical offensive against the established bases of power in the Liberal Party, with the object of creating a truly democratic party in tune with the coming democratic age. During this bitter quarrel Gladstone, still the head of the party, remained aloof. Retirement was in the air, and no doubt Chamberlain saw himself as the successor to the mantle of the GOM. Chamberlain's campaign was not so much a direct attack on Gladstone's leadership of the party as an attempt to secure the type of Liberal Party in which Chamberlain would be the natural heir. Thus, during the 1885 campaign, the Irish issue was secondary to the far more important dispute within the Liberal Party itself, and if the party fought on any programme it was not the pledge to Home Rule (only some six Liberal candidates were returned on this issue), but rather the domestic reforms advocated by Chamberlain.

Despite these divisions within the Liberal ranks, there was a general feeling that, even after the stormy events of the previous five years, the enlarged electorate would return Gladstone to power. Not for the first time the verdict of the electorate came as a surprise. The result of the election gave the Liberals 335 seats, the Conservatives 249 and the Irish Nationalists 86. Parnell was left in the crucial position of holding the balance of power. To this extent, the decisive element in the results was not the election programme of Chamberlain or Gladstone, but the edict from Parnell to the Irish in England to vote Conservative. Although the efforts of the National Liberal Federation and the Farmers' Alliance in the rural seats did result in a Liberal total of 133, against 54 in 1880, in the boroughs the Liberals lost heavily, the Tories winning 118 of the 238 seats, against only 85 of the 287 seats in 1880. No Liberals at all were returned for Ireland.[1]

Despite the success of Chamberlain and Collings, on balance, however, the result was a blow for the Chamberlainites. The promise of free education had proved counter-productive, and the new Liberal Party depended for its majority on men who owed little to the influence of the NLF on their constituencies, and to whom the political reputation of Gladstone was a far more tangible thing than that of Chamberlain. The appeal to the principles of 'progress', as conceived by the Birmingham school, had failed to sweep the country, and the balance in the next Parliament was to be held by Parnell's 86 Irish who were concerned simply and solely with obtaining Home Rule and did not greatly care whether it came from Conservatives, Whigs or Radical Liberals.

It was against this peculiarly indeterminate election result that the political bombshell of the 'Hawarden Kite' burst on to the scene. This leak, by Herbert Gladstone, of Gladstone's conversion to the cause of Home Rule, also signalled the return of Gladstone to the active leadership of the Liberal Party. Prior to the 1885 election, an open 'Home Rule' commitment would have been unthinkable, but in the circumstances of December 1885 Gladstone's action could be seen as an attempt to ensure a working majority for the next reforming Liberal Government – and so many Radicals chose to view it. But the 'Hawarden Kite' served another purpose also, insofar as it thwarted Chamberlain's hopes for an immediate capture of the Party by himself and his followers. Even if the Whigs could no longer be kept within the party fold, Gladstone was unwilling that the party he had done so much to create should fall into the hands of a man for whom he felt so much personal antipathy and whose style and conception of politics were so different from his own.

The effect of the 'Hawarden Kite' at Westminster was immediate. The Conservatives severed their tenuous links with Parnell (which had brought them a small number of seats at the December 1885 election). Parnell, likewise, moved to support the Liberals. The result was the rapid demise of the Salisbury Government. The Conservatives were turned out on Collings' amendment to the Address, advocating the creation of smallholdings, a commitment on which the majority of the party was clear.

The defeat of the Salisbury administration on this amendment paved the way for the formation of Gladstone's third ministry. It was, however, a government formed against an unpropitious background. To begin with, the Liberal Party was far from solid in its support of Gladstone. As Hamer has written: '...by the end of 1885, Liberals seemed no longer to have a clear agreed understanding as to what made them all Liberals, or what they ought to be doing together in politics'.[2] This statement was no exaggeration. The Whigs, who had abstained on the Collings motion, refused to take office in Gladstone's Cabinet. Whilst Hartington refused at the outset, such Radicals as Chamberlain and Trevelyan agreed to join but later resigned when Gladstone produced his Home Rule Bill and Land Purchase Bill.

The split of Gladstone and Chamberlain over the issue of Home Rule was one of the cardinal political events of late nineteenth century political development. It reflected a basic and fundamental division between the two men. Chamberlain believed that a truly democratic reform in the domestic sphere would solve the Irish question without the need for political dismemberment of the United Kingdom, while Gladstone and his followers maintained that by returning 86 Parnellites (and, incidentally, eradicating the Liberal representation in Ireland) Ireland had won the right to fulfilment of its Home Rule demands. In fact, however, the differences in outlook on the Irish question were involved with the whole question of the future of the Liberal Party itself, the question being whether the party was to stand for a clear programme of domestic reforms carefully calculated to win electoral support, or to retain its faith in the pursuance of the politics of moral enthusiasm in the tradition of Gladstone. From January until June 1886 Chamberlain was engaged in a tactical battle to persuade the party that he, and not Gladstone, could provide the Liberal Party with the key to the solution of the Irish question that would leave the Liberal Party with a secure future.

The point at which the differences between Gladstone and Chamberlain came to a head was in May 1886, when he resigned from the Cabinet when Gladstone made known the details of his proposed Bill. The only member who left with him was Trevelyan. Chamberlain was forced to base his objections to Gladstone's proposals on specific principles, objecting to the removal of the Irish MPs from Westminster. What was even more crucial was the fact that although he could win a declaration of support from the Birmingham Liberals for his own plan for 'Home Rule All Round', Schnadhorst and the rest of the National Liberal Federation had gone over to the support of Gladstone.

This decision of the NLF was crucially important. At the meeting of the General Committee in May 1886 it expressed overwhelming support for the idea of Irish self-government. At this Chamberlain withdrew and six members of the General Committee resigned. But there was no general exodus: indeed 70 Liberal MPs not previously connected with the NLF expressed support for it. No local Liberal associations withdrew but 50 new ones requested affiliation.[3] Apart from his Birmingham base, Chamberlain was almost isolated in the Liberal Party. The NLF, the symbol of the mass of moderate and Radical Liberal support for Gladstone in the country, parted company with its founders.

Despite the loyalty of the NLF to Gladstone, the secession of many Whigs, led by Hartington, Goschen and Sir Henry James, on the Home Rule issue was the more important in Parliament since it gave the Conservatives complete superiority in the Lords. The secession of a small group of Radicals into the Liberal Unionist refuge was also important since it gave strength to the idea that Liberal Unionism was a microcosm of the Liberal Party. It was this secessionist Radical group, led by Chamberlain and faithful to the distant and ambiguous dictates of Bright, which eventually nullified the efforts of Gladstone and Russell and led to the defeat of the Home Rule Bill on its second reading by 343 to 313. A total of 93 Liberals voted against Gladstone.

The struggle over Home Rule between Gladstone and Chamberlain had been fought out among the parliamentary leadership, in the party organisation, and openly in some of the constituencies during the 1886 election. The revealing fact was the totality of the Gladstonian victory, and the ease with which Gladstone was able to split up the potential forces which were apparently secure behind the Radical leader in 1885. Morley declared himself behind Gladstone in December 1885, and when it came to the crisis men like Sir William Harcourt and Henry Labouchère put their faith in Gladstone's political instinct rather than in the potential appeals of Birmingham radicalism. Even extreme Radicals could see reason in the Gladstonian argument that the total removal of the Irish problem would leave the field open for a comprehensive reform of domestic institutions, all the more possible now that the recalcitrant

Whigs had removed themselves from the rest of the party. Eventually, the numbers Chamberlain was able to carry into the lobby against the Home Rule Bill were small. A section of the hostile vote was made up of 'Hartingtonians' and Conservatives as well as committed 'Radical Unionists'.

Isolated from the bulk of Liberals, Chamberlain now began to establish his own independent organisation in Birmingham, the National Radical Union. Cut off from the party organisation, Chamberlain found himself moving closer to the Hartingtonians, and a large number of those with whom Chamberlain had opposed the Home Rule Bill in the Commons were men who stood closer to Hartington and his 'Committee for the Preservation of the Union' than the Radical politics of the Birmingham Unionist leader.

Meanwhile, despite the failure of the Home Rule Bill, Gladstone (and Schnadhorst) felt confident enough for electoral success to ask for a dissolution on the morrow of defeat. It was not the future of the Liberal Party, but the personal future of Chamberlain, that was in doubt as the 1886 election campaign was waged, The election which followed gave the Conservatives 316 seats and the secessionist Liberal Unionists 78. The Gladstonian Liberals secured 191 and the Irish Nationalists 85, giving the Conservatives an overall majority of 118. Liberal anti-Home Rule candidates had not been bothered by Conservative opponents. In the counties, where the Liberal vote had risen in 1885, the labourers were often moved by dislike of migrant Irish labour to follow Collings and Chamberlain against Gladstone. But the agricultural seats were not the only areas of disaster. In all, the Liberals suffered their largest ever defeat in terms of loss of seats (144 net loss), and the failure of the reversal of the Irish vote in non-Irish constituencies to swing seats to the Liberals, together with the sharp decline in the number of Liberal-held agricultural constituencies, were major features of the result. The reverse was in part due to the demoralisation caused by the defection of Chamberlain, but probably much more to the defects on the party machine caused by the withdrawal of Whig support.

In many respects, the defeat of 1886 marked a divide in the evolution of the party. Despite the loss of office, political Liberalism from 1886 to 1892 was far from static and far from demoralised.[4] A steady tide of by-election successes from 1886 to 1891, and very clear signs that the Conservative–Liberal Unionist alliance was a troubled one, gave hope to Gladstonians that they would soon see the victory of their cause.

The party, however, could not afford to stand still and wait. The 1886 defeat implied the need to develop appeals that went beyond the cry of 'Justice for Ireland'. While the party was to make valuable political capital out of the unpopularity of Balfour's repressive Irish policy, and the popularity that Parnell won out of his vindication by the Commission set up to investigate *The Times* articles (which had suggested that he condoned the Phoenix Park murders), Liberals were concerned to maintain their image as the party of progressive reform on a wider front – and in ways with which the GOM was not always wholly in sympathy.

The development of a Radical programme was in some ways aided by the events of 1885–6 insofar as the hesitant Whig element had withdrawn from the party, and the promulgation of plans for domestic reform served to cut the ground from beneath Chamberlain, isolating him from the party on the *principle* of Home Rule for Ireland rather than the *tactics* by which domestic reform was to be pursued. With Chamberlain personally there could be no reconciliation while Gladstone remained the Liberal Leader. So much was clear from the failure of the 'Round Table' conferences on the possibility of Liberal reunion in 1887, but the party could still try to win over those who supported Unionism for the sake of Chamberlain's reputation as the leader of the Radical movement.

Hence, after 1886 the progressive image was cultivated to the extent of defending those accused after the 'Bloody Sunday' affair in Trafalgar Square, and inserting a commitment to an Employers' Liability Bill in the party programme. The Liberals ran many working-class candidates where conditions favoured this (notably in Birmingham by-elections against Chamberlainite Unionists), and by 1892 were calling for the payment of MPs to allow further working-class representation in the House. If the withdrawal of the Whigs allowed a resurgence of radicalism in the Party, it also had another interesting consequence: it encouraged the rise of younger men through the party in a most un-Gladstonian fashion. It was during this period of opposition that Asquith, Campbell-Bannerman and R.B. Haldane emerged as competent political figures. These younger politicians were often far more concerned with the issues of social reform than with the traditional Gladstonian Liberal shibboleths. The shake-up given to the party leadership in 1885–6 had done much to speed up their rise within the Liberal Party hierarchy.

However, the most distinctive feature of the internal development of the Liberal Party after 1886 was the growth in influence within the party of the National Liberal Federation, whose offices moved to London in October 1886. Having given important support to Gladstone against Chamberlain in 1886, the Federation saw itself as a power to be reckoned with – a trend which culminated in the declaration of the 'Newcastle Programme' in 1891. This consisted of a series of resolutions advocating measures which the next Liberal Government might pursue. Both Celtic and Nonconformist enthusiasm were apparent in the motions in support of Welsh and Scottish disestablishment and a 'direct and popular veto on the Liquor Trade'. But the programme was most significant as a clear statement of Radical demands for democratic reforms (as in the one man, one vote principle, and the 'mending or ending' of the House of Lords). In addition, the Newcastle Programme stressed the need to reform the Land Laws, extend the Factory Acts, and remodel taxation and rating systems. On the Home Rule issue the party looked 'with unshaken confidence to Mr Gladstone' to get through a measure which would leave Parliament 'free to attend to the pressing claims of Great Britain for its own reforms'. The Newcastle Programme was thus a bold attempt to commit the Liberal Party to a designated plan of reform proposed and supported by the 'grassroots' of the party, and constructed with an eye to electoral advantage. The tone of the programme, and its apparent acceptance by the party leadership, indicated that Gladstone's personal obsession with Home Rule had not restricted the instincts of the party for domestic reform. Never before in British politics had the lower echelons of an organised political party claimed such a positive role in policy-making with such apparently effective results.

Insofar as the 1891 Newcastle Programme was the platform on which the party fought the 1892 election, the high number of contested elections (outside Ireland only 23 Conservatives and seven Liberal Unionists were returned unopposed) testified to the enthusiasm for the programme within the party. However, the Liberals were already suffering from financial shortages, and the leadership was well aware of the need to mollify the demands of the party faithful in the pre-election period. Significantly, Gladstone himself never fully endorsed the Newcastle Programme.

Prior to the campaign of 1892, the political scene was temporarily galvanised as the news of the Parnell divorce hit Britain. Massive Nonconformist pressure from both within the Liberal Party and outside culminated in Gladstone's repudiation of Parnell. Despite the crisis blow of the O'Shea divorce the Liberal Party remained confident, and was eager for the election, which they felt would bring a Home Rule majority of at least 100. However, the result failed to live up to Gladstone's expectations. The Liberals, with full Irish and Labour support, had a majority of 40 over the combined strength of 268 Conservatives and 47 Liberal Unionists. The tenacity of Liberal Unionism in Scotland and the West Midlands had stemmed the tide of Liberal recovery. The result thus left Gladstone with an unstable majority with which to redeem the electoral pledges of the previous six years.

The election of 1892 was to usher in a period of confusion within the Liberal Party that was to last at least until the turn of the century. Several factors compounded the difficulties facing the 1892–5 Liberal Government. Firstly, the cause of Home Rule had a priority over domestic reform, at least as long as Gladstone was at the head of the party. This determination at least had the advantage of securing Irish support for the government, and thus allowing it to continue in office; but the dependence on Irish goodwill was constricting and humiliating. While the Home Rule Bill passed the Commons, the Lords rejected it in September 1893, and the futility inherent in the position of a Liberal Government, facing a hostile Upper Chamber, while unable to muster popular enthusiasm for its controversial measures, soon became apparent. Elements in the party who were more interested in reform in a domestic context resented the concentration of the party's legislative effort on the Home Rule issue, and were unwilling to countenance a possible dissolution after the Lords' rejection of the Bill. The electoral appeal of Gladstonian Home Rule could justifiably be questioned after the experiences of 1886 and 1892.

Secondly, it was apparent that the leadership of the party were personally antagonistic towards one another. Stansky's study of this period reveals the almost oriental intrigues that dominated Cabinet decision-making during the administrations of both Gladstone and Rosebery.[5] One basic conflict was between Harcourt and Rosebery. It was a real divergence of principle over the policy of Imperialism and the foreign policy that a Liberal Government ought to pursue. Many members of the Cabinet, however, showed themselves all too eager to conduct their disputes on the lines of personal vendetta. The conflicts that followed the resignation of Gladstone early in 1893 were, in the words of Morley, 'an episode that no one of the prominent actors...can pretend to look back upon with unalloyed satisfaction'. The divisions in the Cabinet became worse after the removal of Gladstone, loyalty to whom had at least been a common agreement in the post-1886 party. Thus, while Harcourt objected to the government's handling of diplomatic conflicts over the Sudan, the Armenian massacres of 1895 and the Nicaraguan dispute, Rosebery disliked the death duties which Harcourt made the central feature of his 1894 Budget. By the later stages of the administration the leaders were hardly on speaking terms with one another, and any hope for a concerted policy on which to fight the 1895 election had been abandoned. Each of the leaders went his own way – Harcourt to press the claims of Local Option, Morley those of Home Rule, while Rosebery sought to build the Liberal campaign on the issue of reforming the House of Lords. By 1895 the chief figures in the Liberal Party felt that they had been betrayed by one or another of their colleagues, and an air of personal recrimination and bitterness was not one which fostered productive legislation or electoral success.

In addition the government found that the Newcastle Programme was frustrated by the tactics of the House of Lords, which rejected or seriously amended government Bills to deal with the liquor trade and education. The antagonism of the Lords over these Bills seriously demoralised the party. But popular enthusiasm for an anti-Lords campaign (mooted by Gladstone in 1893, and openly advocated by Rosebery after October 1894) proved impossible to raise. The NLF had no clear policy on the reform plans to be pursued. The record of by-elections fought when Rosebery was pressing this proposal was not encouraging. Such a programme of legislation undertaken by a government with a slim and declining majority (by December 1894 by-election defeats and withdrawals from the party had reduced the Liberal majority from 40 to 32) in the face of the hostility of the Parnellite section of the Irish, who had gone into open opposition to the government when it refused to press Home Rule after the 1893 defeat, proved unprofitable. It served only to highlight the impotence of the Liberal Government.

Finally, the Cabinet seemed to have lost touch with its supporters. Dissent was rife within the party, most particularly among the Celtic Radicals at Westminster who were bitterly disappointed at the seeming inactivity of the administration over reforms for Scotland and Wales. In 1893 one Scottish MP resigned his seat (subsequently lost to a Liberal Unionist candidate) in protest against the government's failure to introduce legislation to protect the crofters. In 1894 Lloyd George, already the most vocal of the Welsh Radicals, resigned the Liberal whip along with three of his colleagues. Meanwhile other Radicals, such as Labouchère, did not hesitate to make trouble for Rosebery after he had become Prime Minister. Nor were relations between the Cabinet and the National Liberal Federation very close. Indeed, when the Cabinet chose to resign in June 1895, it was against the clearly expressed advice of the NLF secretary to carry on 'by hook or by crook'.

All these difficulties were aggravated by the loss of working-class support for the Liberals. The handling of the Featherstone strike, together with the low priority given to industrial legislation at a time of worsening industrial relations, all served to alienate the trade union and working-class supporters within the party. It was, perhaps, symbolic that Keir Hardie's Independent Labour Party was formed in 1893.

It was hardly surprising, against this background both in Parliament and in the country, that Rosebery's administration was short-lived. When, due to a ruse by the opposition Whips, the government was defeated in the Commons (early in 1895) over the Campbell-Bannerman army reforms, it was with a certain sense of relief that the Cabinet determined to leave office.

Whilst the Liberals could point to some successful legislation – the establishment of parish councils, Harcourt's important fiscal innovation of graduated death duties, Henry Fowler's Indian legislation, together with the competent records of Asquith at the Home Office and Rosebery at the Foreign Office – the overall state of the party was one of confusion and disunity. The party lacked both finance and enthusiasm, with the result that in the election of 1895 many Conservative-held seats went uncontested. In addition, the party lacked anything resembling a coherent unified policy.

The outcome of the election was a crushing Liberal defeat. The Conservatives, with 341 seats, gained a majority of 152. The Liberals were reduced to 177. In addition, there were 70 Liberal Unionists and 82 Irish Nationalists. The extent of the Liberal disaster was evident when both Harcourt and Morley were defeated in their own constituencies. It was a defeat which took the Liberals, in an atmosphere of bitter mutual recrimination, into a period in opposition which was to last for ten years.

The 1895 election in fact marked a watershed in the development of the Liberal Party. Not only did it lead to a decade of opposition, but it also marked quite firmly the end of the Gladstone era. In a different way, the 1895 defeat also marked the beginning of a reaction against the power of the National Liberal Federation.

The departure of Gladstone from political life had a double impact on the party. It deprived the Liberals of his political acumen and his immense reputation, but at the same time prepared the way for the party to shed the more constricting, negative elements of the Gladstonian creed. These years saw the growing influence of a more 'constructivist' Liberal philosophy, represented by such people as C.T. Ritchie. In due course these ideas provided the basis for the programme of social reform of the 1905 to 1914 era.

The reaction to the power of the National Liberal Federation which set in after 1895 was hardly unexpected. By 1898 the NLF was ready to disavow any claim to be the policy-making centre of the party. Its resolutions recognised that the Federation was not to 'interfere with the time or order in which questions are taken up'. Similarly, the Federation agreed that its relationship with the official leadership was purely advisory. There were no more 'omnibus' resolutions proposing specific measures for a Liberal Government to undertake. The heyday of the caucus was over.

Although the Liberals had been soundly defeated in the 1895 election, the party remained a potent force at Westminster. Despite the crippling divisions among the party leaders, the Liberals were able to prevent the Conservatives getting their education proposals through the Commons. At the same time, however, there were optimistic signs of reviving Liberal fortunes in a series of by-election victories in such seats as Southampton and Reading after 1895.

Overshadowing these encouraging signs, however, were the changes and struggles within the leadership of the party. As Stansky has appropriately labelled the period, it was an age of ambition and strategy. Rosebery resigned as leader of the party in November 1896. Harcourt stayed as leader of the Liberals in the Commons, with Lord Kimberley becoming leader in the Lords. It was an unhappy arrangement. Harcourt rapidly encountered difficulties, most particularly from within the party at his failure to condemn the government more vigorously during the inquiry into the Jameson Raid. This, in fact, was one element which caused Harcourt to resign in 1899. The party, divided and in opposition, was once again faced with the necessity to select a leader of the Liberal Party within the House of Commons. It was in this situation that Sir Henry Campbell-Bannerman became leader of the party. With Campbell-Bannerman as leader, the Liberal Party was to enter the new century.

3
The Liberals in Opposition: 1900–1906

Campbell-Bannerman became leader of the Liberal Party in the Commons in February 1899. He was hardly the most obvious candidate to be leader of a party – indeed, in 1895 he had nearly become Speaker of the House, a post which would have removed him from active party politics. Nor had Campbell-Bannerman many of the characteristics of charisma or dynamism likely to set him as an obvious leader. Although he had first experienced Cabinet office in 1886, and had been Secretary of State for War under both Gladstone and Rosebery, his ministerial experience was relatively narrow. Yet Campbell-Bannerman had qualifications much needed by the party: good-humoured, upright, a man of character and principle, he had just the temperament required to hold the party together. Indeed, the many difficulties facing the new leader were soon to be greatly compounded by a serious division within the Liberal ranks over the situation in South Africa. From early 1899 onwards, the position grew increasingly tense as conflict with the Boers appeared nearer. Appropriations were increased for the Army in Cape Colony and plans were under way to send out additional troops. These appropriations were criticised by Campbell-Bannerman on 21 April in the Commons. By June, the Liberal leader's criticism of British intentions had significantly increased.

Speaking at Ilford on 17 June, in the most effective speech Campbell-Bannerman had made since becoming leader, he made a forceful plea for a peaceful settlement between Britain and the Transvaal. Three days later, on 20 June, Joseph Chamberlain assured Campbell-Bannerman that war was not intended, but that the military plans for the Cape were merely to reinforce the diplomacy of the Colonial Office. Clearly, Chamberlain wanted the support of the Liberals to remove the issue above party politics. After consulting his colleagues, Campbell-Bannerman refused to agree to Chamberlain's request. From this time on, the Colonial Secretary increasingly began to use the theme which dominated the political debate over the next years – namely, that the government's critics were in fact the enemies of peace and friends of the Boer enemy.

It was unwise that, against a deteriorating situation, Campbell-Bannerman went on vacation to Marienbad in mid-summer, ignoring the bad news which followed him from England. The net result was that, by September, the Liberal front bench was taking widely divergent lines over the issue of Kruger and the Transvaal. There had always been considerable tensions within the party between the ardent 'Little Englanders' and those who looked with favour on a humanitarian and benevolent Imperialism. This conflict had been a feature of the 1892–5 government. During the 1890s these fundamental divisions widened further as the prospect of conflict with the Boer Republics grew. The outbreak of war, following the ultimatum from Kruger and the invasion of Natal and Cape Colony, brought these divisions to a head.

Stanhope's motion of October 1899, censuring the government, split the Liberal Party forces. While Campbell-Bannerman, Asquith, Haldane and Sir Edward Grey abstained, 186 Liberals went into the opposition lobby. The crisis became more serious when Rosebery (together, with Asquith, a member of the Imperial Federation League) seemed to be emerging from retirement in order to mount a campaign that would unite the pro-Imperialist elements in a breakaway party. In July 1900 some 41 Liberal MPs actually voted with the Unionists against the 29 members of their own party who supported Sir Wilfrid Lawson's 'pro-Boer' amendment. The Liberal Imperialists gained control of the *Daily Chronicle* from anti-war Liberals, and there was a clear division between the *Manchester Guardian* and *Westminster Gazette* (anti-war) and those Liberal newspapers which followed a more Imperialist line (e.g. the Roseberyite *Daily News*).

Campbell-Bannerman's own position was sympathetic to the Radicals. He had all along been convinced that the conflict had been unnecessarily provoked, both by Chamberlain and the Cape Government. He accepted the war, declaring that he would not in any way hinder the efforts of British arms, but also repeated that he would not withdraw any of his previous criticisms of British policy. As the war progressed, Campbell-Bannerman increasingly leaned to the Radical position, especially after he learned of the civilian concentration camps being used in the Transvaal.

On the right of the party, a powerful minority of leading Liberals, including Asquith, Grey, Haldane and Fowler, were in support of Rosebery's Imperialist position. They urged Liberals to forget past events and join whole-heartedly with the government in full support of the war. At the opposite extreme of the party were the Radicals such as John Morley and David Lloyd George, for whom the war was a clear case of the rights of a small nation against the power of an aggressive empire. Although the actual outbreak of war made the anti-Imperialist position difficult to sustain (for it was Kruger who had invaded Natal, not Britain the Transvaal), as the war progressed support for the pro-Boer position in the party rose.

The divisions in the Liberal ranks were soon followed by a sharp reversal of Liberal by-election performances. Prior to the outbreak of war, Liberals had secured several by-election gains from the government. In the first two by-elections of the war (at Bow and Bromley and at Exeter) Liberals performed extremely badly. In both seats the government increased its majority.

With these obvious divisions in the Liberal ranks, and with public opinion strongly on the side of the government, the Conservatives under Salisbury took advantage of the opportunity to call an election for July 1900. Shortly before the dissolution, a Liberal Imperial Council had been formed with Lord Brassey as chairman. This organisation subsequently began 'approving' Liberal candidates whose attitudes were certainly not in line with the views propounded by Campbell-Bannerman. There were signs that, once again, the party might be faced with a breakaway group.

With so many advantages on the Conservative side, under difficult circumstances the Liberals made a better fight than many expected in July 1900. Partly they were helped by the Conservative campaign which attempted to brand all Liberals as 'pro-Boer' (which was ludicrously untrue) rather than concentrate on the real and undeniable divisions within the party. The outcome of the July 1900 'Khaki election' was a triumph for Salisbury. The Conservatives secured 402 seats to the 186 of the Liberals. The Liberals had thus improved their position very marginally compared with 1895, although their representation was less than when Parliament had been dissolved. The Liberals lost ground in the English counties and in Scotland, but improved their position in Wales, where opposition to the war in South Africa was strongest. Scotland and the large cities showed most enthusiasm for the war.

The result was of little comfort for Campbell-Bannerman, who now found himself in the unenviable position of an opposition leader who had led his party to a crushing electoral defeat, and whose most able colleagues openly followed the lead of a rival statesman. And yet, although the election had exposed Liberal divisions, curiously the result of the election was to make the chances of a real breakaway from the party less likely. Both Chamberlain and Salisbury had sought to brand the entire party with the pro-Boer label; yet the Liberals had not lost ground in terms of their parliamentary representation. The electoral assets of Liberal Imperialism were still dubious, and in some constituencies it had proved a distinct disadvantage (as it did at Merthyr where Keir Hardie was returned against a Liberal who had supported the government in its conduct). The election of July 1900 had effectively demonstrated that a reunion of the forces of 1885, of which Rosebery was thinking, was not a viable programme.

With Chamberlain himself uninterested in a cross-party alliance, Liberal Imperialism did not have enough strength to stand on its own, a fact which was appreciated by Asquith if not by Rosebery. As long as Campbell-Bannerman held the centre of the party and the National Liberal Federation behind him there was little chance of an internal *coup d'état*. Indeed, in July 1901 the official leader was able to secure a unanimous vote of confidence at a meeting of the parliamentary party.

Such an apparent display of unanimity, however, did not end the conflict within the party. Most obvious was the antagonism between Rosebery and Campbell-Bannerman which was displayed quite openly. In his Chesterfield speech of 15 December 1901, Rosebery came out with an appeal for a total revision of the objects of the party. Instead of the 'fly-blown phylacteries' of the old Liberal creed (notably the commitment to Home Rule, but by implication extending to the rest of the Gladstonian programme) the party must build up a new programme from a 'clean slate'. Rosebery talked of a government based on 'national efficiency', and an ending of the old party antagonisms. The Liberal League, formed in 1902 and involving Rosebery (as president), Asquith, Fowler, Haldane and Grey (as vice-presidents), served to maintain these divisions, but the younger Imperialists saw its function as an internal pressure group within the party rather than as a separatist body.

By May 1902, however, the Treaty of Vereeniging ended the war. At home the tide of public opinion began to swing more noticeably against the government. Liberal criticism of the government's handling of the conflict (Campbell-Bannerman's 'methods of barbarism' had proved a telling phrase) became a viable political platform, and the Liberals were able to capitalise on the criticisms put forward by the Commission of Inquiry into the war.

Meanwhile, other events were to aid the reviving fortunes of the Liberal Party. The most important was the Education Act of 1902. This legislation was to provide the first glimmering of a Liberal dawn. It not only opened up divisions within the Unionist Cabinet (Chamberlain found the approach adopted by the government particularly unpalatable), but also roused the grassroots of the Liberal Party in defence of the control of primary education by the school boards. Nonconformist anger was brought to a level not seen since the Bulgarian atrocities. Both Campbell-Bannerman and Asquith sank their differences over the Boer War in defence of the Liberal principles now under attack. The Education Act of 1902, followed by the argument over the tax on the importation of corn and later by the 1904 Licensing Act, represented attacks on Liberal principles that had been part of the party's heritage. In the face of these measures the party found a new unity. Rosebery's call for a review of the basic philosophy of the party could be forgotten. Liberal enthusiasm to fight in defence of its old principles was rekindled. By mid-1903 only a handful of constituencies lacked Liberal candidates eager to give battle on the 1902 Education Act.

From 1901 onwards, the effect of the government's growing unpopularity was revealed in successive by-election reverses. It rapidly became clear that this was something more than the 'swing of the pendulum'. When, in January 1903, the Newmarket constituency was lost, the seventh by-election defeat since the passing of the Education Act, it was perhaps understandable that the Liberals believed the long winter of their discontent was drawing to an end.

The unpopularity of the government, however, was not the only lesson of the by-elections. Liberals were attracting not merely Nonconformists outraged by the Education Act, but also gaining support from the political wing of the Labour movement, now indignant at the outcome of the Taff Vale decision. By turning the interest of the Labour movement to events in Parliament, the Taff Vale decision acted as a much-needed fillip for the Labour Representation Committee. Since its birth in February 1900 the LRC had hardly been a triumphant success. Only two 'Labour' candidates (R. Bell and Keir Hardie) had been elected in July 1900, whilst the trade unions had often been difficult to interest in parliamentary action. Taff Vale dramatically changed that attitude.

By 1903 both the LRC and the Liberals were united in opposition to the government. Given that past relations between the Liberals and the Trades Union Congress had been good (Henry Broadhurst, the TUC General Secretary, had been a Liberal candidate in 1895), and given that neither group had found much advantage in their lack of unity during the 1895 and 1900 elections, there were powerful figures on both sides who saw the considerable advantages that might come from some sort of accommodation.

Early in 1903, significant moves towards an 'entente' between Labour and Liberals were made. Speaking at Belmont on 2 January, Campbell-

Bannerman expressed his keen sympathy for more Labour representatives in the Commons. A month later, Lord Tweedmouth, the chairman of the Council of the Scottish Liberal Federation, told the Edinburgh annual general meeting that a Liberal–Labour alliance was greatly to be desired. In fact, it was Ramsay MacDonald who made the first approach to the Liberals through George Cadbury, by pointing out to Gladstone's secretary, Jesse Herbert, the dangers that the Liberals would face by opposing any LRC candidates. MacDonald went on to promise that, on almost every issue, LRC members would support a Liberal Government, but that given hostility by the Liberal Party, the LRC would oppose Liberal candidates throughout the country.

This threat soon became more meaningful when, on 21 February 1903, the fourth LRC annual conference at Newcastle passed a resolution providing for a Parliamentary Fund for Labour candidates, to be raised by contributions from affiliated societies at the annual rate of one penny per annum. This, together with the 'Newcastle Resolution', had important consequences for the negotiations. The Parliamentary Fund gave the LRC a decisive power for electoral action which it had not previously possessed. Meanwhile, a month later, on 11 March 1903, Labour won the Woolwich constituency, a seat in which in 1900 a Conservative had been returned unopposed. Will Crooks owed much of his victory to the support of the local Liberal association and the by-election seemed yet further proof of the advantages to be gained by cooperation.

Against this background, Jesse Herbert strongly warned Herbert Gladstone of the advantages of cooperation with Labour, most particularly since he believed the LRC could 'influence the votes of nearly a million men'. Herbert feared that, if the LRC vote went against the Liberals, the party would be trounced in the boroughs, and in the county divisions of Lancashire and Yorkshire. In addition, there was the important consideration that any entente which provided for straight LRC–Conservative contests in 35 constituencies would not only save the Liberal Party £15,000 but win ten seats from the Conservatives. After detailed discussion and negotiation between Herbert Gladstone and Ramsay MacDonald, by March 1903 the agreement was settled. On 13 March, Gladstone provided Campbell-Bannerman with a detailed memorandum outlining the terms of the secret alliance.[1] An agreed number of Labour candidates were to fight the next election with Liberal support. In return, Labour would not contest Liberal-held seats.

On one point, however, Gladstone had been insistent: the local constituency Liberal associations must retain freedom of choice. This clause was subsequently to provide a constant thorn in the side of the entente, causing some rival by-election candidates. Thus in the Barnard Castle contest in July 1903, the local Liberal association refused to allow Arthur Henderson, the LRC candidate, a straight fight with the Conservative. Despite pressure from Headquarters, a Liberal candidate was fielded, although Henderson subsequently went on to win by 47 votes over the Conservative, with the Liberal a poor third.[2]

A further example of the lack of goodwill at constituency level was displayed in the Norwich by-election of January 1904. G.H. Roberts, the Socialist-sponsored candidate, refused to stand aside and, although finishing at the foot of the poll, took 2,444 votes, not sufficient to deny the Liberals victory, but nonetheless a strong showing. Although both by-elections had demonstrated the dangers of splitting the progressive vote, local Liberal associations often continued reluctant to accede to outside pressure to come to a local accommodation with Labour – particularly in Scotland, South Wales and the industrial North East.

Fortified by the opposition to the Education Act, and with the Gladstone–MacDonald entente securing the flank against Labour, the Liberals were already, by 1903, well on the road to recovery. Meanwhile the greatest blow to the government came from a different quarter. On 15 May 1903 Joseph Chamberlain launched his campaign for Tariff Reform and Imperial Preference in a speech at Birmingham. It was a rallying-cry from which the Liberal Party never looked back.

The raising of the issue of Tariff Reform brought all Liberals together in defence of Free Trade. With the exception of Rosebery, who became increasingly isolated from the Liberal leadership, Free Trade acted as a tonic to party unity. Asquith was brought into close cooperation with Campbell-Bannerman. During 1903, as Liberals attacked the Chamberlain heresy, something of the old Gladstonian crusading spirit returned to the party. The tone of Asquith's speeches moved the Liberals firmly towards a policy of social reform. The party was on the march again.

The impact of Tariff Reform on Conservative fortunes was disastrous. Chamberlain, who had split the Liberal ranks in 1885, split the Conservative Cabinet in 1903. The Free Traders led by the Duke of Devonshire, were in revolt. A small group of backbenchers, including Winston Churchill and Sir John Dickson-Poynder defected to the Liberals. In Parliament, Free Trade Conservatives voted with the Liberals against the Address in 1904. For a time, it seemed that the government might collapse and an election be imminent. The Liberals, in fact, were to be disappointed, both in their expectation of an early general election and in their hopes of an alliance with the Conservative Free Traders. Although negotiations took place between Devonshire, Earl Spencer and Asquith in December 1903 and January 1904, they eventually collapsed over the vexed question of the 1902 Education Act.

But though Liberals were disappointed in their hope of an early general election, the by-elections continued to bring them fresh victories. A severe government defeat at Norwich was followed by similar catastrophes at Gateshead in January 1904 (a Labour gain) and Oswestry, normally regarded as safe Conservative territory, in June 1904 (won by the Liberals). The nadir of the government's fortunes came in March 1905, when Buteshire was lost, followed a month later by Brighton.

During 1905, however, Balfour began a counter-offensive aimed at what appeared to be the Liberal's weakest points: the Liberal League and Ireland. The Liberal League (formed in February 1902 as the official organisation of the Liberal Imperialists) was still, despite Campbell-Bannerman's hostility, a potentially powerful organisation. But Balfour's attempts to woo the League, and thereby reopen the party split, came to nothing. If for no other reason, the Liberal Imperialists realised that their best hope of office remained with the Liberal Party.

Balfour's failure with the Liberal Imperialists seemed as if it might be offset by a revival of Liberal divisions over Home Rule. On 14 November, at a breakfast meeting with John Redmond and T.P. O'Connor, Campbell-Bannerman convinced the Irish leaders that he was still strongly committed to Home Rule. He promised to outline, in his next major speech, a policy committing Liberals to Home Rule in gradual stages. In a carefully-worded speech at Stirling on 23 November 1905, Campbell-Bannerman fulfilled his pledge. Two days later, in a speech at Bodmin, Rosebery made a strong attack on Campbell-Bannerman's 'Stirling Declaration'. Most Liberals decried Rosebery's attack, whilst Asquith calmed the situation. A potentially divisive issue then subsided, but before it was totally quietened, Balfour took the opportunity to resign. On 4 December, Balfour offered his resignation, no doubt hoping to embarrass the Liberals.

In fact, Balfour's hope of creating disunity in the Liberals over taking office was soon doused. On 24 November, when rumours of Balfour's impending resignation were circulating, Herbert Gladstone wrote to Campbell-Bannerman arguing that, on tactical grounds, he should refuse office. Gladstone was supported in this argument by Asquith, Grey and the editors of the *Westminster Gazette* and *Spectator*. However, the thought that swayed Campbell-Bannerman was the danger of who the King might ask to form a government. The Marquis of Ripon warned Campbell-Bannerman of this on 28 November. The prospect of the Marquis of Lansdowne, Joseph Chamberlain or, worse still, Rosebery forming a government decided the issue. The net result was that when King Edward sent for Campbell-Bannerman on 5 December the offer was speedily accepted.

The one problem that remained on 5 December concerned whether it should be Asquith or Campbell-Bannerman who led the party in the House of Commons. This had already been the subject of intrigue by Asquith, Grey and Haldane at a meeting at Relugas (Grey's fishing lodge in north-east Scotland) as early as September 1905. It had been agreed at this meeting that Asquith would become Chancellor of the Exchequer, and would lead the party in the Commons. Campbell-Bannerman, although Premier, would be removed to the House of Lords. In this plan, which effectively removed Campbell-Bannerman from the real seat of power, Haldane would become Lord Chancellor, and Grey Foreign Secretary. Events, however, failed to materialise in this way. Campbell-Bannerman stood firm in his resolve to stay in the Commons. Grey and Haldane, despite earlier protestations to the contrary, accepted the position and the Relugas compact collapsed.

The main task facing Campbell-Bannerman's administration was to prepare for victory in the forthcoming general election. With the party machine, under Herbert Gladstone, very much in preparedness, and with Campbell-Bannerman's own position both in the party and in the country very much stronger than in 1900, Liberals prepared for the election in a mood of confidence. Although the campaign proper did not begin until after Christmas, the opening broadside was delivered by Campbell-Bannerman in a speech at the Albert Hall on 22 December. Its contents were fairly predictable, with the emphasis on Free Trade, but also references to trade union law reform, land, the question of the Chinese coolies in South Africa and payment of members of the House of Commons. Other proposed reforms included site value taxation, smallholdings legislation, modernisation of the Poor Law, relief of overcrowding and action to end 'sweated' labour. In a later speech at Stirling, although again stressing Free Trade, Campbell-Bannerman promised 'a course of strenuous legislation and administration, to secure those social and economic reforms which have been too long delayed'. The message, or so it appeared, was that the Liberals were to be the party firmly committed to social reform. However, on the details of this forthcoming social legislation, Campbell-Bannerman was fairly silent. Instead, the bulk of the Liberal offensive was directed at the record of the Balfour administration, the obvious divisions of the Conservatives on the fiscal question and the potential dangers if Chamberlain were returned to power.[3]

Liberal enthusiasm for the battle was apparent in the nominations. Only a few avowed Conservative Free Traders were allowed an unopposed return. Except for two seats (Oxford University and Mid-Cumberland), every constituency was contested by a Free Trader, whether Liberal or Labour. Liberals contested 121 more seats than in 1900. The Liberal press enjoyed the support of such Conservative Free Trade journals as the *Spectator*. Meanwhile, with the exception of Scotland, the MacDonald–Gladstone pact worked extremely well; and outside Scotland only two Liberal-held seats were attacked by Labour.

Though many factors combined to favour the Liberals, the landslide victory of the election came as a stunning surprise. On 12 January the Liberals gained their first victory in Ipswich. The following day Arthur Balfour lost Manchester East.

The defeat of Balfour was the prelude to a Liberal landslide in industrial Lancashire. Even the staunchest of Conservative citadels, in the hitherto safe rural shires, fell to the Liberals. In all, 1906 was a landslide comparable only with the victory of the 'coupon' candidates in 1918, or the National candidates in 1931 and Labour in 1945. The full results are shown in Table 3.1.

Table 3.1

	Seats	Total Votes	% of Total
Unionist	157	2,463,606	43.7
Liberal	375	2,583,132	45.9
Labour	54	528,797	9.4
Nationalist	83	35,109	0.6
Others	–	21,557	0.4

Few Conservative seats escaped the landslide of 1906. The only important exceptions were West Lancashire, the stronghold of Birmingham and Sheffield. Even the south-east of England, usually a Conservative monopoly, saw normally safe seats fall to Liberals. Although a few rural seats in the West Midlands, Lincolnshire and the East Riding stayed Conservative, the electoral map of Britain had been almost totally redrawn.

The greatest single disaster for the Conservatives came in the textile districts of East Lancashire and the West Riding, where 29 of the 30 seats won in 1900 were lost. In Wales 28 of the 34 constituencies returned Liberals; only one Conservative survived, while in Scotland, for the 70 seats, only six Conservatives and five Liberal Unionists survived against 57 Liberals.

The Liberals had a further reason for elation at the results of 1906. For the election had seemed a total vindication of the Gladstone–MacDonald entente. In virtually all the English constituencies, Liberal–Labour cooperation had worked well. Such Liberal organisers as Jesse Herbert were delighted at the results.[4] A major exception, however, was to be found in Scotland. Here, the pact was not operated since the Scottish Liberal Federation, considerably to the right of English Liberalism, refused any compromise with Labour. North of the border, no Labour candidate enjoyed a straight fight against a Conservative. In ten constituencies, three-cornered contests occurred. Significantly, in these ten contests, while Labour only won two, the Liberals forfeited six seats they might otherwise have won.

Outside Scotland, however, in only five constituencies did Liberals contest recognised Labour seats, with Labour taking four of them nonetheless. It was a tribute to the working of the pact that in only two constituencies were Liberal seats lost as a result of Labour candidates. In all, 29 LRC representatives were elected and almost all were dependent on Liberal votes.

With the Liberal election triumph, the almost unrelieved Conservative massacre, and the harmonious working of the Gladstone–MacDonald pact, 1906 saw the Liberal Party at its zenith. The euphoria of the results had now to be translated into the reality of government.

4
The Liberal Ascendancy: 1906–1910

With the triumph of the election behind him, Campbell-Bannerman found himself in a position of strength unequalled by any Liberal leader in recent history. He was head of the largest anti-Conservative majority for over eighty years. If the Liberal back-benches were filled with men new to Parliament, there was no lack of capable and indeed brilliant men seeking the higher positions of office. Hence the Cabinet chosen by Campbell-Bannerman proved to be one of the strongest and most gifted of any peacetime administration. It was a blend of the outstanding intellectual power of Asquith, who became Chancellor of the Exchequer, Haldane at the War Office, Augustine Birrell as President of the Board of Education and James Bryce as Chief Secretary for Ireland, together with the dynamism and drive of Lloyd George at the Board of Trade and Winston Churchill as Under-Secretary at the Colonial Office. The Foreign Office was entrusted to the much respected Sir Edward Grey.

Despite the inclusion of such obvious young Radicals as Lloyd George, the Cabinet retained a strongly Gladstonian flavour. Such men as Lord Loreburn, the Lord Chancellor, Morley, Herbert Gladstone, Bryce and Ripon all belonged to the Gladstonian tradition. In addition, Lord Crewe as Lord President of the Council, Lord Tweedmouth as First Lord of the Admiralty and Lord Elgin as Colonial Secretary were all moderates unlikely to ruffle the placid waters of Whitehall.

It was hardly surprising, armed with such a massive majority and with a Cabinet of undoubted strength, that Radicals had high hopes of reforms to come. The early days of the new government lent strength to these Radical hopes. There were persistent rumours that Campbell-Bannerman was moving increasingly to the Left. The King's Speech, in February 1906, tended to reinforce this optimism. It promised a reduction in armaments and a major legislative programme of 22 Bills for the new session.

However, despite so many factors in its favour, the Campbell-Bannerman administration never really fulfilled the high hopes of the early days of 1906. What, then, had gone wrong? Partly the explanation was to be found in the personality of the new Premier. For whilst Campbell-Bannerman soon established an undisputed command over the Commons, proving himself an able parliamentarian, he was a weak leader of a government. His policy was to allow each Minister to care for the problems of his own department. At no time did Campbell-Bannerman play the part of a leader or Prime Minister. Indeed, as his private secretary recorded, 'he was continually forgetting that he *was* Prime Minister'.[1] Hence, lacking leadership, the Liberal Party lacked also both impetus and direction.

A second factor in the equation lay in the character of the Parliamentary Liberal Party elected in the 1906 landslide. An analysis of the 377 Liberals in the new Parliament soon dispels the myth that the Liberals represented left-wing reforming radicalism. The occupational background (by group) was: barristers, 64; service officers, 22; 'gentlemen', 69; established businessmen, 80; self-made businessmen, 74; solicitors, 21; writers and journalists, 25. The remaining 22 were made up of nine teachers, eight trade unionists and five doctors. Thus the Parliamentary Liberal Party was not composed of the wild Radicals that its enemies sometimes supposed. Politically, the party was dominated by 'centre' Liberals. Its social composition was preponderantly middle-aged men from the commercial and professional middle class. The real Radicals were few and far between: 'The dangerous element does not amount to a dozen', reported Herbert Gladstone to Campbell-Bannerman early in 1906 with undisguised relief.[2]

Compared with the Conservative opposition, the relative strength of barristers, solicitors, writers and businessmen was greater in the Liberal Party. The officers and country gentlemen were less numerous than in the Conservative opposition. The Liberals were still not a party catering to any significant degree to the parliamentary ambitions of working men: on the contrary, 125 of the 377 Liberals were public-school educated, 135 had attended Oxford or Cambridge and more than one in four were men of great wealth. Not surprisingly, the social composition and political outlook of the parliamentary party acted as no great spur to radical reform.

Apart from this restraining force among the Liberals themselves, part of the failure of the Campbell-Bannerman administration to achieve even greater measures of social reform lay with the House of Lords. Balfour had already declared, in his Nottingham speech, his intention of blocking social reform in the Upper House. The Lords faithfully carried out that pledge. During 1906 the Lords destroyed Birrell's Education Bill, designed to remove Nonconformist objections to the 1902 Education Act. A Bill to abolish plural voting met a similar fate. During 1907 a variety of land reform measures were similarly blocked, including the Small Holdings Bill, the Evicted Tenants (Ireland) Bill, the Small Landowners (Scotland) Bill and the Land Values (Scotland) Bill. By mid-1907 it was already clear that Balfour and Lansdowne intended to use the power of the Lords for purely party-political purposes – although it was noticeable that the hostility of the Lords to Liberal legislation was tempered by the electoral popularity (or otherwise) of the Bill concerned. Thus it was significant that the Lords were careful to avoid blocking the Trade Disputes Act.

1907 was thus a year of frustration and anger for Liberals. The outcome of the government's legislative programme in 1907 was minimal. There was truth in Lloyd George's reference to a bundle of sapless faggots fit only for the fire. Of the nine major Bills which the Liberals had hoped to carry, only the Territorial Army Act, the Small Holdings and Allotments Act and the Patents Act became law.

Meanwhile other factors, in addition to the wrecking tactics of the House of Lords, were helping to undermine the popularity and esteem of the government as the euphoria of 1906 died away. By 1907 the economic prosperity of the previous year had given way to a worldwide trade recession. Nor had the Liberals any cause for optimism on the electoral front. The party lost three of the 16 contested by-elections during 1907, while in the municipal elections of November 1906 there had been heavy losses to the Conservatives.

Two of the by-elections, at Colne Valley and at Jarrow, were both significant for the increased support shown for Labour. In the Colne Valley, Victor Grayson, an avowed Socialist who in fact refused to join the Labour Party, won the seat despite Liberal and Conservative opposition. In the Jarrow division, the death of the Liberal member produced a four-cornered by-election in July 1907. The result was a triumph for Labour, whose candidate, the trade unionist Peter Curran, topped the poll with 4,698, compared with the 3,930 of the Conservative, 3,474 for the Liberal and 2,122 for the Nationalist. It was significant that the Liberal polled only half the 1906 total.

The advent of 1908 brought new electoral setbacks. Three more Liberal seats were gained by Conservatives early in 1908. The municipal election results were equally depressing, with such traditional Liberal council strongholds as Coventry and Nottingham falling to Conservatives. Added to these electoral difficulties was the rapid decline in the health of the Prime Minister. The strain of office, and the illness and death of his wife, proved too much for Campbell-Bannerman. From the spring of 1908, ill-health confined him to his home at 10 Downing Street. On 6 April 1908 he resigned; he died later the same month.

The administration that had begun with such high hopes in 1906 was over. With its demise, the feeling was one of disillusion. For although Campbell-Bannerman's two years in office were in many ways important and constructive, his ministry as a whole never really constituted a real success. Whilst it had brought self-government to South Africa, initiated far-reaching Army reforms, pursued a successful detente with Russia and repaired the damage done by the Taff Vale decision, it was open to fundamental criticism. Essentially, the ministry had been concerned with the issues of the past, not of the future. It had been repairing the damage and omissions of the previous decade, not preparing new or enlightened attitudes towards the social problems of the future.

Yet Campbell-Bannerman's administration had achieved a success of a different kind. It had given experience and office to men who were to prove themselves in later years. Indeed, the administrative success of many of the individual Ministers in the Campbell-Bannerman ministry was remarkable. This was particularly true of Haldane, the Secretary of State for War. He created not only the General Staff, but by the Territorial and Reserve Forces Act of 1907 revised the whole organisation of the Army. Haldane's energy was at least equalled by the dynamism of Lloyd George at the Board of Trade. His most constructive achievements were the Merchant Shipping Act of 1906 and the Port of London Authority Act which, although it did not become law until Lloyd George had moved to the Treasury, had been prepared by him. A third source of energy came from Winston Churchill, the Under-Secretary at the Colonial Office. Churchill's abilities were given greater scope than usual because Elgin, the Secretary of State, was among the weakest members of the government. Churchill's achievements at the Colonial Office included the establishment of self-government in the Transvaal, followed by similar status immediately afterwards for the Orange Free State.

The departure of Campbell-Bannerman from the political scene marked a significant event in the evolution of the Liberal Party. With his disappearance, John Morley warned, 'will arrive a critical hour for our Party and our Principles'. And so it proved.

The successor to Campbell-Bannerman as Prime Minister was Herbert Asquith. At 56, Asquith was a natural choice. He had been in Parliament for twenty years, and had served both Gladstone and Rosebery as Home Secretary, before becoming Campbell-Bannerman's Chancellor of the Exchequer. Although, late in 1907, there had been talk of a move to draft Sir Edward Grey, the Foreign Secretary, no one challenged Asquith's succession in 1908.

The new Premier entered office with two important advantages. He was, as one early biographer wrote, outstanding among Liberal statesmen as the one politician who most united the party.[3] Secondly, he inherited from his predecessor an exceptionally talented ministry. Indeed, Asquith's first act was to strengthen the team even further. Elgin was replaced at the Colonial Office by Lord Crewe. Tweedmouth, whose faculties were fast fading, was removed from the Admiralty to the less onerous position of Lord President of the Council. Much the most significant appointment, however, was the advancement of David Lloyd George to be Chancellor of the Exchequer. It was an appointment that changed the course of the ministry and indeed the history of the country.

Born in Manchester in 1863, Lloyd George's upbringing and background were rooted in Welsh radicalism. In 1890, at the age of 27, he had won a dramatic victory by 18 votes in a by-election at Caernarvon Boroughs, the constituency he was to retain at 13 successive general elections. Lloyd George's preoccupation in his first years in the Commons was with the objectives of Welsh radicalism – the need to attack and destroy the established church, the destruction of the power of landlords, the creation of a University of Wales and the establishment of a Welsh Parliament.

Lloyd George was above all, though, the champion of conscience; he was the voice of the underprivileged. And his oratory was, perhaps, unsurpassed in modern British politics; it was the oratory to move men and inspire movements. In 1900 his outspoken sympathy with the Boers had made him a Radical hero. His period at the Board of Trade after 1906 showed his administrative ability. By 1908 Lloyd George's journey into Liberal politics had brought him from the mists and hills of North Wales to 11 Downing Street.

The reconstructed ministry under Asquith faced a troubled political outlook. In the last days of the Campbell-Bannerman Government, the party had suffered a severe blow in the Peckham by-election on 24 March 1908, when a Liberal majority of 2,300 was easily overturned. The popularity of the government seemed to be ebbing fast, and the advent of Asquith failed to halt this trend.

The elevation of Churchill to the Presidency of the Board of Trade necessitated a by-election in Manchester North West. When polling took place on 24 April, Churchill lost the seat to the Conservatives by 29 votes. Churchill had subsequently to be moved to the safer territory of Dundee, where he was returned to Westminster on 9 May despite Conservative and Labour opposition. The result in Manchester North West, if the most dramatic, was not isolated. Of the 15 Liberal-held seats which saw by-elections in 1908, the Liberals retained only nine.

Against this electoral background, 1908 saw the introduction of an important Liberal social reform. The 1908 Budget, prepared by Asquith as Chancellor and introduced by him as Prime Minister, provided old-age pensions at 8s. per week for married couples.

The winter of 1908–9 found the Liberal Government at the nadir of its fortunes. The by-elections were still running strongly against it. The government's legislative programme had been mutilated by the Lords. Powerful interests had been alienated by its attempts at reform. A deepening trade recession gripped the country. Moreover, the party itself had been torn by a back-bench rebellion over naval expenditure which forced Tweedmouth to reduce the estimates by £400,000.[4]

These difficulties, though important, were part of a more fundamental weakness. In 1908, as in 1906, the Liberals had still to formulate a policy of social reform that would move the party away from nineteenth-century political Liberalism – the mixture of the freedom of the individual, the absolute necessity of free trade, an acceptance of capitalist economics and a somewhat vague and haphazard social empiricism – on which the party was still living. The Liberals had yet to find the policies to tackle the grave social problems in the country that had been highlighted by Charles Booth's study of London and Seebohm Rowntree's survey of York. It was against this background that the 'New Liberalism' was born. At the centre of this movement were a group of writers centred round the *Nation*, including J.L. Hammond, Henry Brailsford, L.T. Hobhouse, C.F.G. Masterman and J.A. Hobson. An articulate spokesman of the new creed was Winston Churchill, whose agile brain was already devising schemes for labour exchanges, wage boards, and a 'Committee of National Organisation' to counter fluctuations in unemployment. To this extent, Churchill was singling out for attack the issues which aroused the *Nation* group – casual labour, unemployment, undernourishment and poverty.

Within this new radicalism, Asquith was never really at home. As Hazlehurst has written: 'Although he continued the work of social reform begun under Campbell-Bannerman, Asquith's radicalism went little deeper than that of his predecessor. His speeches on the constitutional crisis in 1910 and 1911 were a revelatory reminder of his own fundamental conservatism.'[5] Asquith, indeed, though assenting to the new departures, gave them neither inspiration nor passion and remained lukewarm about state intervention. Yet despite Asquith's lack of zeal for social reform, the new Liberalism made rapid and tremendous strides. By 1910 the Liberal Government had put on to the statute book measures creating wage boards, labour exchanges, public provision for the development of natural resources, old-age pensions, new measures to control town planning and major policies to develop smallholdings. Even such enthusiasts of the new Liberalism as J.A. Hobson were impressed. To Hobson, the new legislation constituted 'an organic plan of social progress, which implies a new consciousness of Liberal statecraft'.[6]

As if to crown these measures of social reform, there came the introduction of Lloyd George's 'People's Budget'. But there were some ironical features of this measure. The Budget that Lloyd George claimed was a 'War Budget' to wage implacable war against poverty and squalidness was also to pay to construct the Dreadnoughts; the Budget that was eventually to provoke the peers towards constitutional rebellion was introduced as virtually the only radical measure not likely to be rejected by the Lords.

These things aside, the text of Lloyd George's speech on 29 April 1909 to the Commons saw his radicalism at its most perfect. He ended his peroration by looking to 'that good time when poverty, wretchedness and the human degradation which always follows in its camp will be as remote to the people of this country as the wolves which once infested its forests'.

Faced with the need to raise an additional £16 million in revenue, Lloyd George produced proposals which to his opponents seemed little short of revolutionary. Income tax was raised from 1s. to 1s 2d. in the pound, while for those with incomes over £5,000 a supertax of 6d. in the pound was introduced. The tobacco duty was increased by ½d. an ounce, whisky duty was up 6d. a bottle (a measure that not unnaturally was strongly opposed by the government's Irish Nationalist allies). New taxes were introduced on cars and petrol, with the pledge that the revenue raised was to be devoted to road-building. The proposals that produced most political apoplexy, the land taxes, were strangely enough to survive only a few years, and were abolished by Lloyd George when Prime Minister.

The full realisation of the radical nature of the Budget dawned on the Conservative benches only slowly. When it did, the parliamentary battle commenced: in all, 70 parliamentary days and no fewer than 554 divisions were needed to push the Budget through the Commons – Lloyd George himself voting in 462 of them, Asquith in only 202.

Outside Parliament, an equally vehement debate raged in the country – a debate memorable for Lloyd George's outspoken speech at Limehouse, a speech which actually provoked the King so far as to dispatch a letter of rebuke. In a less restrained manner, the Duke of Beaufort declared that he would like to see Lloyd George (and Winston Churchill for that matter) put in the middle of twenty couple of dog-hounds.

Despite the outcry of the peers, the tide of public opinion was flowing in support of the Budget by August 1909. The High Peak by-election (of July 1909) had been a comforting result for the Government. Meanwhile, the Budget Protest League was increasingly seen to be ineffective. At the same time, the issue was rapidly switching from the fiscal merits of the Budget proposals to the much more dangerous ground of whether the peers were entitled to reject a Finance Bill – an event that had not occurred for 250 years.

Before July, such a possibility was hardly mentioned; now the crisis of the Budget had become a crisis of the Constitution. Through the folly of his opponents Lloyd George saw his wish fulfilled: the implacable war against poverty had extended to war against that most obvious target of political reform, the Lords.

Speaking at Birmingham in September, Asquith had warned the peers, in the vein of a Victorian headmaster, of the perils of rejection. Only a bold man, declared Asquith, could forecast or foresee the consequences. Lloyd George was by now well aware of the obvious advantages of an outright rebellion by the peers. At Newcastle-upon-Tyne on 9 October Lloyd George waxed lyrical, asking of his audience 'who ordained that a few should have the land of Britain as a perquisite; who made 10,000 people owners of the soil, and the rest of us trespassers in the land of our birth?'

These were radical, challenging speeches. The Lords, in their anger, fell into the trap Lloyd George had prepared. At the beginning of November Asquith had warned the King that rejection of the Budget by the Lords was now probable. On 30 November his warning was fulfilled. The Finance Bill was rejected by the Lords by 350 votes to 75. Two days later, a resolution moved by Asquith was carried in the Commons declaring that the action of the House of Lords was a 'breach of the constitution and a usurpation of the rights of the Commons'. The following day Parliament was dissolved; the general election was fixed for polling to begin on 14 January 1910.

The election found the Liberals in confident mood. At last, the party had an issue on which to fight, and an issue on which public opinion seemed on the side of the government. The Liberals were entering the battle as a united party, but the Conservative ranks were still divided between the Tariff Reformers and the Tory Free Traders grouped as the 'Centre Party'.

The Liberal campaign also started well. Asquith's major opening speech was delivered at the Albert Hall on the 10 December. His most significant theme, apart from repeating the need of the Commons for absolute control over finance, the maintenance of Free Trade and the curtailment of the legislative powers of the House of Lords, was his declaration of future strategy. Asquith declared:

> I tell you quite plainly, and I tell my fellow countrymen outside, that neither I nor any other Liberal Minister supported by a majority of the House of Commons is going to submit again to the rebuffs and the humiliation of the last four years. We shall not assume office, and we shall not hold office, unless we can secure the safeguards which experience shows to be necessary for the legislative utility and honour of the party of progress.[7]

These were attacking words. Yet it was by no means certain that the electorate would follow Asquith's call. Indeed, the first results, showing 18 Conservative gains on the first day, suggested hope for the Opposition. It soon became clear, however, that whilst the Conservatives had recovered some lost ground, the Liberals, with Labour and Irish Nationalist support, would easily retain office.

The returns in January 1910, with the 1906 figures in parentheses, are shown in Table 4.1. Compared with the 1906 election, the Liberals had lost over 100 seats, with corresponding Conservative successes. At the same time, the Liberals recovered most of the by-election losses they had suffered (regaining Churchill's old constituency of Manchester North West, and recapturing the Colne Valley seat lost in 1908 to Victor Grayson). Most of the Liberal losses were in the areas won in the landslide of 1906, particularly in the agricultural seats of the South Midlands, in the suburbs of London and in the usually Conservative strongholds of Surrey, Kent and Sussex.[8]

Table 4.1

	MPs		Votes	%
Liberal	275	(377)	2,880,581	43.2
Unionist	273	(157)	3,127,887	46.9
Labour	40	(53)	505,657	7.6
Nationalist	82	(83)	124,586	1.9
Others	0	(0)	28,693	0.4
Total	670	(670)	6,667,404	100.0

The Conservatives made no net gains either in Wales or Scotland, both areas returning to the pattern of 1885. Nor did Conservatives make many gains in the textile areas of East Lancashire or in West Yorkshire, whilst the North East remained equally strongly Liberal.

Far more than the landslide victory of 1906, the results in January 1910 were a fair representation of the geographical areas of Liberal strength in the Edwardian period. Generally, the Liberals were weakest in the major cities, but strongest in rural Scotland and Wales and in the mining regions. The Liberals were weakest of all in the four largest cities, namely Glasgow, Birmingham, Liverpool and London. In January 1910, for example, the party won none of the seven seats in Birmingham and only one of the nine in Liverpool. The exceptions to this general rule were such cities as Edinburgh, Leeds, Bradford and Bristol. The Liberals were also weak where the middle-class suburban vote was strongest, most particular in Kent, Surrey and parts of Middlesex.

Although the mining constituencies constituted a solid base of Liberal support, there were indications as early as 1910 that this loyalty was to some extent being eroded by Labour. Labour were making definite headway in South Wales and West Yorkshire and to a lesser extent in the North East, although the Liberals still remained entrenched in the Derbyshire–Nottinghamshire coalfield.

Liberal support in the rural areas varied from region to region. Wales was an impregnable stronghold; eastern Scotland was equally secure. Both East Anglia and the West Country had strong Liberal representation, while the party won most of the West Yorkshire seats. On the other hand, the Liberals never dislodged the Conservatives from their local strongholds around York, Exeter, the South Coast and parts of Kesteven.

Given the controversial measures of the 1906–10 government, the Liberals had cause to be pleased with the 1910 results. But the January 1910 election was, in fact, to be the prelude to a period of peculiar difficulty and grave crisis in Liberal history.

5
The Crisis of Liberalism: 1910–1914

The election of January 1910 had returned Asquith to power. In this sense, it was a Liberal victory. But Asquith had won a battle, not a war. In the four years after 1910, the Liberals were to endure crisis after crisis, as the problems of Ireland, the suffragettes, industrial militancy, relations with the Labour Party, and above all the gathering world storm, loomed over a minority Liberal Government.

In January 1910, however, the most immediate problem lay in the conflict with the Lords. On this question, Liberal confidence had suffered a somewhat severe blow. For, prior to the January 1910 election, Asquith had given the impression that he had a guarantee from the King to create sufficient peers to pass the Budget into law. When it was revealed that no such assurance had been given, disappointment and frustration among Liberal supporters went very deep.

Both in the constituencies and in the back-benches, there was considerable disillusion. Many constituency associations were faced with the resignations of senior officials; backbenchers, so confident in the January campaign, found they had much explaining to do. At Westminster, Asquith seemed totally to have lost his nerve and there were rumours that, if the situation were not saved promptly, Churchill and Lloyd George might be tempted to resign and lead a party revolt.[1] By April, however, the government had recovered its nerve; the main lines of the Liberal attack had been drawn up. In mid-April, three resolutions were submitted to Parliament. These three resolutions proposed:

- that the Lords should no longer have the power to reject or amend a money Bill;
- that Bills passed by the Commons in three successive sessions of Parliament should become law despite the opposition of the Lords; and

- that the maximum length of Parliament should be reduced from seven years to five.

On 14 April a Parliament Bill containing these proposals duly received its first reading. Meanwhile the Budget passed the Commons on 27 April. The following day it passed the Lords without a division.

It was at this stage, with the Budget now passed and the wider constitutional battle about to begin, that the death of King Edward VII occurred on 6 May. This further complicated an already delicate position. The ensuing Constitutional Conference, an attempt to agree on a compromise solution and reduce the pressure on George V, eventually collapsed in failure in November.

However, at times it had come nearer to success than was then realised. Lloyd George, one of the four Liberal delegates at the conference, had gone so far as to propose the establishment of a full party coalition to settle the major political issues. It would seem that this idea (not of course, known to the general public) was at first sympathetically received by several leading Conservatives and by such Liberals as Sir Edward Grey and Lord Crewe. However, the Conservatives rapidly abandoned the idea. The prospect of coalition, like the conference itself, collapsed.

On the day the conference finally collapsed (10 November 1910) Asquith asked the King for an immediate dissolution. The King refused to grant this request until the outcome of the House of Lords vote on the Parliament Bill was known. Since the Lords then promptly proceeded to adopt the Rosebery proposals in place of the government's recommendations, the dissolution of Parliament was only delayed until 28 November.

For the second time within a year the country was again faced with a general election. For the Liberal Party, the contest was a regrettable necessity. The main lines of the Liberal election campaign were laid down by Asquith in a speech at the National Liberal Club on 19 November. The Liberals would fight on the issue that the Lords had systematically thwarted the wishes of the House of Commons elected in 1906.

To a large degree, the election of December 1910 was a repeat performance. And as such, the argument and appeal had to some extent already been heard before. But the Liberals still possessed a major advantage: they were able to face the electorate as a united party. The Conservatives still remained with the millstone of Tariff Reform round their necks.

From the first results, it became clear that whilst the Conservatives were picking up the occasional seat, they would not gain the necessary

62 seats to ensure them a majority. Indeed, the final results showed little overall change from January (see Table 5.1).

Table 5.1

	Total Votes	%	Seats
Unionist	2,426,625	46.4	274
Liberal	2,290,020	43.8	270
Labour	374,409	7.1	42
Nationalist	131,720	2.5	84
Others	11,509	0.2	–
Total	5,234,283	100.0	670

The small net turnover in seats in fact disguised considerable real changes. In two areas, the North West and the extreme South West, the Conservatives made substantial gains, whilst the Liberals improved their position in the agricultural constituencies of the South Midlands. Wales and Scotland remained the stoniest of soil for the Unionists. Only three of the 34 Welsh seats, and nine of the 70 Scottish constituencies, returned Unionists or Liberal Unionists.

The Liberals also benefited to some extent, in such seats as Whitehaven and Cockermouth, by local arrangements with Labour.[2] In all however, though the trends of the December 1910 election indicated that a few parts of the country were moving away from the Liberals, the verdict of the electors was as clear as in January. The Liberal Government was to continue. But though Asquith was to continue in power, the election had not diminished the number of problems facing the party.

The immediate task for the government following the verdict of the December 1910 election was to settle the question of the House of Lords. The election itself had not solved the passage of the Parliament Bill. It still remained possible that it would be necessary to create a sufficiently large number of peers to overcome a recalcitrant House of Lords. In fact, George V had given a secret pledge prior to the December election to create the necessary peers if Asquith so requested him. The pledge was reluctant – but definite. In July 1911, when it seemed that the Conservative majority in the Lords would try to make serious amendments to the Bill, Asquith formally informed Balfour of the King's pledge. In the face of this threat, the Unionist leaders backed down. Landsdowne, the leader of the Unionist peers, advised his followers to abstain.

The position was, however, gravely complicated by the revolt of the die-hard peers, headed by Lord Halsbury. The seriousness of the revolt lay in the fact that it was soon clear that the diehards would outnumber the Liberal peers, even with the Lansdowne moderates abstaining. Once again, the prospect of a mass creation of Liberal peers seemed very likely. In the event, after delicate negotiations between Lord Crewe and Lord Cromer, the government narrowly won on 10 August 1911, with a majority of 17. The Liberals, aided by the votes of a variety of cross-bench peers together with 37 Conservative peers, had very narrowly scraped home. Eight days later the Parliament Bill received the royal assent.

The struggle with the Lords, though ending with a triumph for the Commons after a bitter struggle, did not end the conflict. Subsequent controversial Liberal legislation was to suffer under the terms of the Parliament Act. Two such measures concerned Welsh Church disestablishment and the abolition of plural voting. The Welsh Church Disestablishment Bill, introduced into the Commons in April 1912, was twice rejected by the Lords. In 1914, when the Bill again passed through the Commons, the Parliament Act was invoked. By this time, however, the outbreak of war led to the suspension of the operation of the Parliament Act. A very similar fate befell the Plural Voting Bill.[3]

Meanwhile, the most important Liberal legislative achievement of the 1910–14 period was the National Insurance Act of 1911, aimed at providing state insurance against both sickness and unemployment. Although the Bill provoked much outcry in the country, the Conservative opposition did not seriously question the principle of the legislation whilst the Lords let the Bill through without a debate.

The Government's Franchise Bill, introduced in June 1912 against a background of mounting suffragette militancy, met a less happy fate. Although the aims of the Bill were confined to universal male suffrage, the abolition of plural voting and the abolition of university constituencies, the Bill would have provided the opportunity to allow the Commons to extend the vote to women if it so wished. Three different amendments were proposed at committee stage to this end. These plans seriously miscarried when the Speaker (much to Asquith's annoyance) ruled these amendments out of order.

The Bill was then withdrawn and a Private Member's Bill introduced shortly afterwards. Whilst this would have enfranchised many women, it would not have given them equal franchise. This was lost by 292 votes to 245. It was opposed by Asquith, Churchill and Herbert Samuel and supported by Grey, Lloyd George and Walter Runciman.

These divisions (on a free vote) over women's suffrage were not the only evidence of a growing lack of unity in the parliamentary party. There was evidence of a growing disquiet over defence policy. In March 1911,

37 Liberal MPs voted for a reduction of military and naval expenditure. In July 1912, 23 voted against the Naval Supplementary Estimates and a further back-bench revolt occurred in March 1913. Although these radical critics of the government's foreign policy never constituted a serious threat to the government, even at the peak of their influence, they were evidence of the strains the party was later to face during the war.

An equally embarrassing issue for the government arose over the 'Marconi' affair, in which allegations were made that both Lloyd George and Sir Rufus Isaacs had derived a personal gain from certain government dealings with the British Marconi Company. These allegations were later modified so that the issue centred round whether the two Ministers should have disclosed certain private transactions to Parliament. The Marconi affair, itself very much a small storm in a large teacup, was of more interest in revealing the degree of party bitterness existing in 1912.

This party bitterness was itself a reflection of the climate in the country. The strikes of 1912, centred round the 'Triple Alliance' of railwaymen, miners and dockers, were evidence of the new dimensions of industrial militancy. The violence of the suffragettes and the militancy of the strikers seemed to contemporaries and historians alike to mark the beginning of the end of the old era of politics.

But overshadowing events in England lay the growing menace of civil war in Ulster. With the passing of the Parliament Act, a new element was introduced into the question of Ireland. No longer could the opposition rest assured that, whatever the Liberal Government might attempt, the Lords would inevitably veto it. By 1912 the opponents of Home Rule, faced with the prospect of Home Rule within the lifetime of a single Parliament, had become increasingly desperate. And at the head of the Conservative opposition was Andrew Bonar Law, himself a man with strong Ulster connections.

In 1912 the House of Commons saw the introduction of the Government of Ireland Bill, providing for an Irish Parliament which would legislate on most Irish affairs, but with overriding power vested in Westminster, in which a reduced contingent of Irish MPs would sit. The Bill passed the Commons; almost inevitably, it was then rejected by the Lords. The next session of the Commons again passed the Bill; once again the Lords duly rejected it. The Bill, now being prepared for submission to Parliament once again, would become law whatever action the Lords might take.

At this juncture, an attempted compromise was introduced. On 9 March 1914 Asquith proposed an amendment whereby Protestant Ulster could opt out of Home Rule for a six-year period, a proposal bitterly attacked by the opposition as a 'delay in execution'. This attempted compromise was followed shortly afterwards by the 'Curragh Mutiny'. This in turn led to the resignation of J.E.B. Seely, the Secretary for War, a position which Asquith himself took on.

Asquith continued attempts at compromise, including a Buckingham Palace conference with representatives from each party – a move which caused much anger among the Liberal rank-and-file who saw the government's prestige and authority visibly disintegrating. On 25 June 1914 the conference collapsed, confirming that events in Ulster were passing out of the control of the politicians. The growth of the Ulster Volunteers and, in the South, the National Volunteers was unmistakably clear evidence. The problem of Ireland, so near to explosion in July 1914, was itself to be engulfed in a wider and more devastating event. On 28 June the Archduke Franz Ferdinand was assassinated at Sarajevo; the approaching civil war in Ulster was overshadowed by a world becoming engulfed in war.

By the summer of 1914, the Liberal Party had entered a very different political climate from the *annus mirabilis* of 1906. The crises on the industrial front, suffragette militancy and deep Cabinet divisions had all shaken the party. Equally, the by-election record of the government, especially in such seats as Leith and Midlothian, was depressing in the extreme. And yet there were signs of hope. Liberal organisers, such as Herbert Gladstone, were optimistic that opposition to the Insurance Act was fading. Lloyd George and Percy Illingworth, the Chief Whip, received glowing reports of the reception of the Land Programme. That there were signs of decay at the grassroots, and increasing divisions at the top, were undeniable. Yet it was far from certain that the Liberals would not be able to fight back in time for the next general election, most particularly as the Conservatives remained deeply divided, both over Tariff Reform and the party's leadership.

There was, however, a fundamental problem facing the Liberals which would not disappear – the question of the party's relations with Labour. Whether, as Trevor Wilson has written, this was the most menacing problem facing the Liberal Party before 1914 is at least debatable.[4] But that the problem was there is undeniable. And it was an issue which deeply divided the party. On the one side were the Radicals who favoured cooperation with Labour. They had firmly supported Herbert Gladstone's policy of accommodation in the years before 1906, and welcomed the new Labour representatives in Parliament as the allies of a vigorous Liberalism. At the opposite extreme was the right of the party, the industrialists and businessmen, who wanted no dealings with Socialism at any level.

The 1910 election had demonstrated the fact that the Liberal Party was not prepared to make concessions for any further Labour expansion beyond the mark already established in the 1906 election. Most of the by-election clashes in the period from 1911 to 1914 were fought in this context. Between the general election of December 1910, and the outbreak of war in 1914, Liberals suffered a depressing series of by-election reverses. As Table 5.2 indicates, no fewer than 15 Liberal-held seats were lost to the Conservatives. At the same time Labour lost four seats, two to the Liberals (Hanley, 13 July 1912; Chesterfield, 20 August 1913) and two to the Conservatives (Bow and Bromley, 26 November 1912; North East Derbyshire, 20 May 1914).

Table 5.2

Date of By-election		Constituency	From	To
28 Apr.	1911	Cheltenham	Lib.	Con.
13 Nov.	1911	Oldham	Lib.	Con.
21 Nov.	1911	S. Somerset	Lib.	Con.
20 Dec.	1911	N. Ayrshire	Lib.	Con.
5 Mar.	1912	Manchester S	Lib.	Con.
13 July	1912	Hanley	Lab.	Lib.
26 July	1912	Crewe	Lib.	Con.
8 Aug.	1912	Manchester NW	Lib.	Con.
10 Sept.	1912	Midlothian	Lib.	Con.
26 Nov.	1912	Bow & Bromley	Lab.	Con.
30 Jan.	1913	Londonderry	Con.	Lib.
18 Mar.	1913	S. Westmorland	Con.	Ind. Con
16 May	1913	Newmarket	Lib.	Con.
20 Aug.	1913	Chesterfield	Lab.	Lib.
8 Nov.	1913	Reading	Lib.	Con.
12 Dec.	1913	S. Lanarkshire	Lib.	Con.
19 Feb.	1914	Bethnal Green SW	Lib.	Con.
26 Feb.	1914	Leith	Lib.	Con.
20 May	1914	NE Derbyshire	Lab.	Con.
23 May	1914	Ipswich	Lib.	Con.

Although such Liberal seats as Cheltenham, North Ayrshire, South Somerset and Newmarket were lost in straight fights with Conservatives, and although these straight fights showed a fairly consistent swing away from the Liberals, much the most serious feature was the effect of the intervention of Labour candidates at other by-elections. In no fewer than 11 formerly safe Liberal seats, Labour candidates intervened in by-elections, causing five seats to fall to the Conservatives. These Liberal losses as a result of Labour's intervention comprised Oldham (13

November 1911), Crewe (26 July 1912), Midlothian (10 September 1912), South Lanarkshire (12 December 1913) and Leith (26 February 1914). Not only had the Liberal vote in these seats collapsed but, even more alarmingly, the Conservative vote had held steady or even increased.

Though bitterly frustrating to Liberals, these Labour candidates had hardly provided convincing evidence of Labour's popularity. All had come bottom of the poll; none had obtained over 30 per cent of the votes cast. Nor had Labour fought any rural or residential seats; its candidates had come forward only in such areas as Durham, industrial Scotland or industrial towns such as Crewe, Oldham and Keighley. Yet this is not to deny that in some areas Labour's advance was both definite and impressive.

Of these parliamentary by-elections, the position has been admirably summarised by McKibbin:

> In all these constituencies the Labour vote had increased compared with the last contest. In Holmfirth it was much more than doubled; in Crewe it was nearly doubled. In N.E. Lanarkshire and Leith the Labour vote rose absolutely in reduced total polls. In Keighley it was static. Plainly Labour was not doing worse than in 1910, let alone faring abysmally.[5]

Though Labour had not gained a seat, its advance in industrial areas seemed to many contemporary observers one of the most noticeable features of these by-elections. These contests, however, were important in a different way, for Labour's intervention had raised the whole question of Liberal–Labour relations. If Labour intervention in such seats as Leith or Midlothian had embittered the Liberals, equal anger had been caused by Liberal intervention in three particular contests: Hanley in July 1912; Chesterfield in August 1913; and North East Derbyshire in May 1914. These three by-elections highlighted the problems of Liberal–Labour relations. The Hanley contest was particularly significant for it threatened, more than any contest since 1906, the whole working of the Lib–Lab entente.

In the summer of 1912 Enoch Edwards, the 'Lib–Lab' miners' leader and MP for Hanley, died. Despite having signed the Labour Party Constitution in 1909, Edwards had continued to work with the local Liberals; the miners' money continued to be placed, as of old, at the disposal of the Liberals.[6] From the start, both sides claimed the seat as their own. And both adopted candidates. As the campaign developed, the relations between the two parties became even more bitter. In the event, the Liberals retained the seat, Labour came second and the Conservatives third.

The Hanley by-election was followed a year later by a by-election in Chesterfield caused by the death of James Haslam in July 1913. Haslam had in fact announced his retirement in April, with the result that the local Labour Party set about finding a successor. Barnet Kenyon, the Assistant Secretary of the Derbyshire Miners' Association, seemed the most likely choice. The real problem here arose over Kenyon's close links with the Liberals. Kenyon had attempted to find a position acceptable to both sides, by assuring Labour men that he would support the Labour Party and by letting the Liberals know that he remained essentially a Liberal. This stance was not acceptable to Labour. On 12 August the National Executive of the Labour Party refused to endorse his candidature; the Miners' Federation of Great Britain retracted its support.

Kenyon's subsequent campaign, using a Liberal agent and the Liberal organisation, proved embarrassing. Whilst many miners' MPs spoke during his campaign, MacDonald denounced as 'ridiculously absurd' the idea that he should give platform assistance. Although Kenyon won at Chesterfield, the incident had demonstrated again that the miners' links with political Liberalism were becoming more and more tenuous. And no sooner had the rancour at Chesterfield died away, than a by-election in North East Derbyshire raised the whole problem again.[7] The significance of these by-elections was not lost on progressives: as the *Nation* warned, on 23 May 1914, the real fight in the constituencies was coming to be more and more a contest between Liberalism and Labour. Even in areas of the country where Liberal–Labour relations had previously been warm, a new hostility was arising.

Other by-elections revealed the same situation. Thus, the Holmfirth by-election of June 1912 had led to the final severing of the once-close links between the Yorkshire Miners' Association and the Liberal Party.[8] A similar conflict between Liberal and Labour occurred in the summer of 1912 when the Master of Elibank's elevation to the English peerage occasioned a by-election in the strongly Liberal citadel of Midlothian.[9]

Not surprisingly, by the spring of 1914 the problem of Liberal–Labour relations had reached serious dimensions. Speaking at Ladybank on 4 April 1914, Asquith bemoaned the fact that virtually every by-election lost during the previous two years was the result of three-cornered contests. This was a theme taken up two months later by Lloyd George, in the wake of C.F.G. Masterman's defeat in the Ipswich by-election where once again the progressive vote had been split.

The problem of Liberal–Labour relations, highlighted in this rather dismal Liberal by-election performance, was repeated in the municipal elections of this period. After the sweeping municipal successes of the years up to 1905, the period after 1906 saw the Liberals not merely on the defensive, but suffering some severe reverses. Thus in 1908 Liberals suffered heavy losses throughout Lancashire as well as losing control of a variety of provincial boroughs, including Sheffield, Nottingham and Leicester. These were serious defections, for Leicester had been in Radical control since 1835, Nottingham for forty years. They were joined by others: in 1909 Coventry fell to the Conservatives for the first time in twenty years. In 1911 Burnley was won by the Conservatives for the first time in its history, whilst in 1912 Liberals lost control of Bradford.

At the same time that these former Radical citadels were falling to Conservative control, Labour appeared to be increasing its council base each year. The party registered net gains in each year up to the outbreak of war. Certainly, by 1914 Liberal strength in the major provincial boroughs had been considerably eroded. In such towns as Liverpool or Birmingham, Liberalism was already a much depleted force. In London, the Progressives (the name the Liberals used to contest local elections) were in marked decline. In some of the working-class wards in such towns as Leeds and Bradford, Liberals were already beginning to form anti-Labour alliances with the Conservatives.

The evidence of both the by-elections and the municipal elections shows clearly that the Liberals were in electoral difficulties prior to 1914. Yet, as we have seen, many of their senior organisers remained confident of the prospects for the next general election. The Land Programme, in particular, was seen as a potential vote-catcher.

If the Liberals were in difficulties prior to 1914, neither MacDonald nor the Labour Party was facing the future with any great confidence. Certainly, MacDonald was only too aware in 1913 of Labour's electoral weakness. As McKibbin has written, MacDonald was very probably keen to maintain the electoral alliance with the Liberals and was under no illusions of Labour's weakness in the country.[10] Nor was MacDonald alone in his pessimism – or political realism. Philip Snowden was realist enough to calculate that Labour could win only 'half a dozen' seats on its own account.[11] The events of Sarajevo meant that Labour's resolve was never put to the test. To that extent, the Liberal fate in the general election of 1915 will never be known.

But of the debate on the downfall of Liberalism a few points can be said. In 1914 the Liberal Party was certainly not dead, nor indeed dying, despite the arguments propounded by George Dangerfield, who saw in the political and industrial crisis prior to 1914 symptoms of the oncoming 'Strange Death of Liberal England'.[12] As McKibbin has aptly stated, in a short but impeccably devastating phrase, Dangerfield's work is a literary confection which does not attempt serious analysis.[13]

In short, a breakdown of the Gladstone–MacDonald pact for 1915 would have meant probable major reverses for the Liberals and the possible total elimination of independent Labour representation. For the evidence of 1910–14 is conclusive on one point: Liberals and Labour had either to hang together or they would hang separately. In the event, however, the most direct threat to the Liberals once war was declared came not from the external threat of Labour, but from internal factors. For the First World War was to put to the ultimate test not only the conscience of Liberalism but also the leadership of Asquith.

6
Liberals at War: 1914–1918

The coming of war in August 1914 transformed the political climate in the country. Indeed, the decision to go to war produced severe strains in the Liberal Cabinet. On 2 August the Cabinet decided that any substantial violation of Belgian neutrality would compel the British Government to take action. The same day, Germany issued her ultimatum to Belgium, demanding passage for her troops into France.

On 3 August the British Cabinet took its fateful decision to enter the war. The decision was not unanimous. Morley, John Burns, Sir John Simon and Lord Beauchamp were all reported to have offered their resignations. In the event, Asquith was able to win over Simon and Beauchamp. Only Morley and Burns resigned from the Cabinet. Among the junior Ministers, they were joined by C.P. Trevelyan.

These resignations were symptoms of a deeper concern within the Liberal ranks in Parliament. Only after Sir Edward Grey's speech to the Commons on 3 August did the majority of the party acquiesce reluctantly in the decision taken by their leaders in the Cabinet. Only one Liberal voice was raised in support of the war in that debate, whilst there was a group of some thirty 'pacifists', mainly left-wing Radicals, who bitterly attacked Grey in the debate and remained critical opponents of the government throughout the war.

The coming of war affected the parties in varying degrees. Whilst both Conservatives and Irish Nationalists pledged full support for the war, the Labour ranks were split, with Ramsay MacDonald (chairman of the Parliamentary Labour Party) heading the pacifist opposition. It was within the Liberal Party, however, that the dilemma was greatest. By tradition, the Liberals contained a strong and powerful Nonconformist and pacifist wing that might be expected to create problems. Again – and much more fundamental – the Liberals' philosophy was likely, even where it could support war, to stop short of the methods of waging total war. On such issues as conscription the Liberal conscience was likely to be put on the rack. This is not to say that the Liberal Party could not have successfully fought a war, but it would have been a war waged with aversion. As it was, the very totality of the First World War had a profound and disastrous impact on the party. For whatever reasons, the Liberal Party was never again to be the same after 1914 as it had been before.

In August 1914, however, this dark future still lay mercifully hidden. The most immediate impact of the war was the electoral truce between the parties and the run-down in Liberal organisation. The party's most able administrators moved to other causes. Thus Sir Robert Hudson was to become chairman of the Joint War Finance Committee and Sir Jesse Herbert devoted much energy to the Parliamentary Recruiting Committee. Far more significant, in the longer term, was the suspension at constituency level of even a skeleton organisation.

Although the Liberals entered the war relatively united, the first months of war soon proved an unhappy time. This was particularly so for the intellectuals within the party. As Joseph Henry of Leeds wrote to Herbert Gladstone, the 'war lords' were vermin, the war itself was a dreadful thing, but the whole thing had to be seen through.[1] Before very long, it became apparent that the Liberals would indeed find that the war was to test their conscience on a variety of issues. The Liberals had soon to fight to preserve a whole gamut of established and cherished ideals: 'Free Trade'; individual freedom of conscience; freedom of the press; the voluntary principle of recruitment. For the party faithful, these were the very constituents of their political philosophy, and many Liberals were determined that these must not be violated, even in the cause of national victory.

At the opposite extreme was the hawkish group of Liberals, men such as Henry Cowan, Sir Henry Dalziel and F.G. Kellaway, who formed a 'ginger group' for a more vigorous prosecution of the war. During late 1914 and early 1915, as general dissatisfaction with the war developed, these men led the growing right-wing criticism of the government over such issues as lax treatment of enemy aliens, inefficiency in government contracting for war supplies and the need for a Ministry of Munitions. These divisions and doubts within the party were important and significant.

But they were less important than the cardinal result of entry into war: namely, that the fortunes of British Liberalism were to be placed for the duration of the conflict in the hands of the Conservative Party.

These wider implications of the war, however, were not the thoughts uppermost in the minds of politicians as the first year of the war ended. The most significant development was the rise of public disquiet and discontent at the conduct of the war. The generals, the politicians and the press were at loggerheads, the people bitterly frustrated with the bloody stalemate on the Western Front following the Battle of the Aisne. Meanwhile, the government suffered a heavy personal blow with the death of Percy Illingworth, the highly respected Chief Whip, of whom all sections of the party approved.

This discontent with the progress of the war was to have vital and far-reaching consequences. Whilst there had been no demand at the beginning of the war for a Coalition, as 1915 progressed, calls to change to a Coalition intensified. It became increasingly clear that, without a more broadly-based government there would be damaging public controversies in Parliament and a lack of confidence in the country. The resignation of Lord Fisher, the First Sea Lord, at the same time as a parliamentary storm gathered over the alleged shell shortage, made it impossible for the Conservative leaders to keep their followers in check. Open attacks on the government, and especially the running of the Admiralty, developed. With reluctance, Asquith agreed with Bonar Law and Lloyd George that a Coalition was imperative, however much they disliked the prospect. On the evening of 17 May 1915, Asquith wrote to Lord Stamfordham, the King's private secretary: 'After much reflection and consultation today with Lloyd George and Bonar Law, I have come decidedly to the conclusion that, for the successful prosecution of the war, the Government must be reconstructed on a broad and non-party basis.'[2] Two days later, on 19 May, Bonar Law formally signified his agreement. The last Liberal Government had ended.

In the political circumstances of May 1915, a more broadly based Coalition was probably inevitable. Yet the secrecy with which it was born caused both anger and dismay among Liberals. Asquith, very typically, took the onus of the decision on reconstruction himself. Crewe, for example, later complained that 'with no preliminary discussion with one of us, even the most intimate and influential... he decided on reconstruction'.

Whatever the secrecy surrounding the birth, the new infant was not welcomed by Liberals. The Coalition appeared to be a disguised concession to Toryism. Back in 1914, Simon had felt that a Coalition would be 'the grave of Liberalism'.[3] Provincial Liberal sentiment, voiced by such spokesmen as Joseph Henry, warned of the dangers of embracing the tainted Conservative Party. Not all, perhaps, echoed Margot Asquith's degree of bitterness (she referred to 'this d——d Coalition which I loathe') but there was considerable disquiet as to the future.

Despite much Liberal resistance to the formation of a Coalition, it was overborne by Asquith. Both Conservatives and Labour joined the new government, although there was no Irish representation. The filling of the new Cabinet posts was a matter of some delicacy. Both Churchill and Haldane had to be sacrificed to placate Bonar Law. Lloyd George agreed to move to the Ministry of Munitions, a newly-created office. On Liberal insistence that a member of their ranks should be Chancellor, Reginald McKenna was allocated the office. Eight Conservatives joined the Cabinet, with Bonar Law as Colonial Secretary. Arthur Henderson, the sole Labour member of the new Cabinet (and the first member of the party to hold Cabinet office) became President of the Board of Education.

The formation of the Coalition in May 1915 was only the first of a series of tribulations that was sorely to try Liberal sentiment. For as 1915 progressed, the issue of compulsory service (which had seemed remote in January 1915) assumed more and more attention. By the summer, alarm in the Liberal ranks was widespread. At the end of May, one Liberal went so far as to warn Lloyd George that such a step would break up both the Liberal and Labour Parties and wreck progress for a generation.[4]

In fact, the whole conscription crisis was a perfect example of a virtually hidebound Liberal Party forced to follow the Conservative lead. To begin with, Conservative pressure for conscription was largely channelled into spurring on the efforts of Lloyd George at the Ministry of Munitions – the Ministry in closest touch with the recruitment problem. But by August, as Lord Curzon, the Conservative Lord Privy Seal, wrote to Lloyd George, it was apparent that the Cabinet could not continue to evade the subject.

But before the conscription crisis came to a head, another issue had arisen which bitterly divided Liberals. This was the McKenna Budget of September 1915. Its proposal for a 33⅓ per cent *ad valorem* tariff on a wide-ranging variety of luxury goods, roused the wrath of Free Trade Liberal backbenchers. Although McKenna was able to defeat a substantial Liberal revolt, some thirty Liberal and Labour backbenchers opposed the government. It was an ominous sign of the storms about to break over conscription. As the autumn of 1915 progressed, the foremost Liberal advocates of the compulsory conscription campaign were such back-bench figures as F.E. Guest, Sir Alfred Mond and Ellis Griffith. Lloyd George and Churchill were the two Liberals in the Cabinet most in favour. But the Cabinet, however, was itself deeply divided. Asquith was personally opposed to compulsion, but was prepared, so Lloyd George informed C.P. Scott, editor of the *Manchester Guardian*, to accept it as a last resort to maintain his position. Those lining up against conscription included such leading figures as Sir John Simon, the Home Secretary (who resigned over the issue), McKenna at the Exchequer and Walter Runciman at the Board of Trade. Their opposition centred not merely on their attachment to individualism but because they believed the economy could not take the strain.

The failure of Lord Derby's scheme of voluntary enlistment finally decided the issue in favour of compulsion. At the beginning of January 1916 the Conscription Bill was introduced to the Commons. Within the Cabinet, Sir John Simon had already resigned as Home Secretary. Only strong persuasion from Asquith halted other departures from the Cabinet. McKenna, Birrell, Walter Runciman and even Sir Edward Grey were all reluctant to accept conscription.

If Asquith contained the rebellion in the Cabinet, he was less successful with the Liberal backbenchers in the Commons; 35 Liberals, 13 Labour members and 59 Irish Nationalists voted against the government. The debate in the Commons fully revealed the bitterness felt within the Liberal ranks. Simon, in his resignation speech, attacked the government for imitating one of the most hateful institutions of Prussian militarism, whilst Liberal backbenchers argued that it was a violation of England's tradition of liberty.

The significance of the conscription issue cannot be underestimated. It had tested the conscience of the party severely. It had nearly brought about the disintegration of the government. Even after the crisis of December 1915 had passed, Asquith still seriously feared a split in the Cabinet. And it had confirmed deep divisions at the highest level in the Cabinet.

The conscription issue was important for another reason. It demonstrated that, by the beginning of 1916, two very distinct camps were emerging within the Parliamentary Liberal Party: there were the doves, unhappy about the Coalition from the beginning, but now also increasingly unhappy about the many fundamental Liberal beliefs that were being attacked and eroded. To these, conscription was the negation of all they believed in. At the opposite extreme were those Liberals, increasingly a clearly defined group, to whom the winning of the war exceeded all else. To these, old shibboleths might have to be abandoned in the new covenant of total war.

Already, this split was a portent of things to come. As Hankey succinctly observed in his diary, the people who wanted compulsory service did not want Asquith, whilst the supporters of Asquith did not want conscription. Here was the genesis of the great Asquith–Lloyd George split of December 1916. Meanwhile, during 1916, the advocates of a more rigorous prosecution of the war gained ground steadily. This movement was to some extent mirrored in the formation of the Liberal War Committee in January 1916. This growing cleavage in the Liberal ranks was further widened by the events of the Easter Week rising in Dublin, which was to produce the resignation of Augustine Birrell as Chief Secretary for Ireland and the politically disastrous executions in Dublin. These events persuaded Asquith to pay a personal visit. On his return, Lloyd George was given the delicate task of negotiating a solution.[5] Meanwhile, the divisions within the Liberal ranks were exposed once again in May 1916 when the government proposed to extend conscription to married men. Another back-bench revolt ensued, with 28 Liberals voting against the second reading. These divisions over conscription were themselves forced into the background when another crisis faced the government. On 5 June 1916 Lord Kitchener, the Secretary of State for War, was drowned when the *Hampshire* struck a mine shortly after leaving for Russia.

Asquith had clearly to offer the vacant War Office to Lloyd George, once an attempt had failed to persuade Bonar Law to accept the office. Yet Lloyd George (whose acceptance Asquith *had* to secure) was naturally reluctant to accept an office under the conditions which had so limited his predecessor. In this battle for power, Lloyd George was the clear victor. On 6 July Lloyd George finally accepted the post of Secretary of State for War virtually on his own terms. Asquith's position was becoming more and more untenable.

It was against this background that the great split of December 1916 between Asquith and Lloyd George must be seen. However, the crash of 5 December 1916 did not come without some warning. Long before Asquith resigned, powerful pressures had been building up within the Asquith–Unionist Coalition for a reconstruction of the government.

The two issues most affecting the stability of the government concerned, firstly, the relations of the Unionist backbenchers with their party leaders in the Cabinet and, secondly, Lloyd George's relations with the generals. This latter issue had become acute since July 1916, when Lloyd George had gone to the War Office and subsequently been locked in conflict with General Sir William Robertson.

In November 1916 the famous Nigeria debate clearly exposed the marked dissatisfaction of many Unionist MPs not only with Bonar Law but with the Coalition generally. The outcome was to spur Unionist Ministers into pressing more vigorously their demands for a reconstruction of the Government. The climax of the growing opposition to Asquith was not long delayed. Asquith resigned as Prime Minister on the evening of 5 December, the day after the critical leading article in *The Times* and the same day that Bonar Law informed him that he was unwilling to continue in the government unless the War Committee proposal, as agreed earlier, was adopted. Since Asquith knew that other Conservatives would not serve in an administration without Lloyd George or Bonar Law, the King asked Bonar Law to form a government.

The following day, 6 December, was a crucial time. Amid numerous political discussions on this day, the Liberal members of the old Cabinet (without, of course, Lloyd George) agreed that Asquith should not accept a subordinate position under Bonar Law. Consequently, Bonar Law abandoned his attempt to form a government, and Lloyd George was asked to form one. On 7 December, Lloyd George became Prime Minister.

The destruction of the last Liberal Government, leading as it did to the fatal split in the party, rapidly produced a wealth of historical mythology, most notably in the conspiracy theory which lay most of the blame at Lloyd George's hands. Some historians have changed the parameters of the debate. A.J.P. Taylor has argued that, rather than being manoeuvred out of office, Asquith deliberately resigned office as a manoeuvre to rout his critics.[6] A different view has been put forward by Hazlehurst, who has argued that, essentially, the destruction of the last Liberal Government and the fall of Asquith was the outcome, not of the machinations of Lloyd George, but of a Tory Party crisis. In their desire to prosecute the war more efficiently, the aims of the Conservatives coincided with those of Lloyd George. This did not mean that Lloyd George necessarily went over to the Tories, nor indeed that he intrigued with them to *oust* Asquith, but that Lloyd George, in company with Bonar Law and Sir Edward Carson, worked together to persuade Asquith to change the political direction of the war. As Dr Hazlehurst rightly argues, neither of the two prime movers, Bonar Law or Lloyd George, had any desire to remove Asquith from the Premiership. Indeed, the replacement of Asquith was not considered as a practical proposition by those later accused of conspiracy.

Why, then, did the crisis of December 1916 end with the resignation of Asquith and Lloyd George's assumption of the Premiership? It is now clear that this was the result of something akin to a nervous breakdown on Asquith's part after the compromise agreement of 3 December. By this compromise, it was agreed that Lloyd George should head a small three- or four-man War Commission under the supreme, though not immediate, control of Asquith, to whom all disputed decisions would be referred. This compromise in fact marked a very wide area of agreement. Henceforth, Lloyd George would have borne daily responsibility for the conduct of the war, without the supreme authority to force through decisions.

There was no need, following this agreement, for anything that called for Asquith to resign. However, it was Asquith himself who, in a brief moment of mental and emotional exhaustion, lost the will to go on ruling. A combination of a deterioration in Asquith's relations with Lloyd

George, at a moment of great nervous strain, propelled the Premier into a temporary capitulation. By the time Asquith had recovered his balance, it was too late.[7]

Lloyd George's first task as Prime Minister was the construction of a Cabinet. At least in terms of those Liberals to be included, it was a difficult task. Asquith had made it clear he would not serve under him. Other Liberals followed Asquith's lead. Although Christopher Addison agreed to serve as Minister of Munitions, no senior Liberals joined the new administration, whilst Churchill, who was keen to serve, was kept out by Conservative opposition.[8] The key posts in the new Coalition were thus filled by Conservatives. Lloyd George had thus become Prime Minister on 7 December 1916 in the most difficult circumstances. Equally as serious were the problems now facing the divided Liberal Party. As Trevor Wilson has written: 'During the last two years of the war, the difficulties facing the Liberal Party moved to a climax. Threatened by disruption within and attack on two fronts from without, the party wilted visibly before the dangers encompassing it.'[9]

In these last years of war, the Asquithian Liberals' policy towards the conflict seemed to be less positive or coherent than ever before. The party was divided over Lloyd George's struggle with the generals and equally split over Lansdowne's plea for a negotiated peace. Not only on issues of policy, however, were the Asquithian ranks divided: their position vis-à-vis the new Lloyd George Coalition was hopelessly unclear. Since they had not joined the government, they clearly did not fully support the new administration. Yet did this mean they were its outright opponents? Or, expressed differently, was there still a single Liberal Party, or had it split into two separate and hostile wings?

In a sense, after December 1916, the party had already split. One group of Liberals sat on the government benches, another on the opposition front bench. There were also two sets of Whips: one serving Lloyd George, the other Asquith. Yet the lines of division were still blurred. The respective Whips still canvassed *all* Liberals, not distinct groups of Liberals, whilst in the *Liberal Magazine* Asquith announced that, far from being an opposition leader, he would offer the government 'organised support'.[10] However, though these official platitudes tried to conceal the bitterness which the events of December had created, the divisions in the party grew more obvious. In the Derby by-election, following the resignation of Sir Thomas Roe on 21 December 1916, Asquithian resentment at the choice of Joseph Davies, a leading Lloyd Georgeite, led to the personal intervention of Geoffrey Howard, the Liberal Whip, to secure a different candidate.

In Parliament, however, the bitterness of the two ranks was muted by Asquith's refusal to oppose the government and his adoption of a nebulous policy of 'general support from the outside'. Such a policy, however idealistic it might appear, left the mass of Asquithian backbenchers politically impotent.

With Asquith providing no leadership, the parliamentary debates assumed a somewhat unreal appearance. Such back-bench Liberals as J.M. Hogge, William Pringle and Leif Jones would bitterly denounce the Lloyd George Government. But the opposition front bench would be deserted and silent.[11]

However, as 1917 progressed, a series of divisions in the Commons showed that the ranks of the respective Lloyd George and Asquithian supporters were becoming more clearly defined. One such division occurred in March 1917, when the government altered the established duties on Indian cotton goods, an action regarded by many Liberals as a move to a protectionist tariff. Despite Asquith's failure to give any lead, 46 Liberals opposed the government and 59 followed the Coalition whip. The Liberal divisions were hardening. As Haldane wrote to his sister, the Liberal Party was already 'much disintegrated'.[12]

A further split in the Liberal ranks occurred later in 1917 in divisions over the Representation of the People Bill. Many of the more extreme Coalitionists sought to retain the system of plural voting in borough constituencies and to disfranchise conscientious objectors. Both proposals offended Liberal tradition, with the result that Herbert Samuel, who led the opposition, was able to take 106 Liberals into the opposition lobby. A later debate on the disfranchisement of conscientious objectors (on 21 November) was carried on a free vote only by 209 votes to 171. This debate again demonstrated how a hard-core of unrelenting 'war to the finish' Coalitionists was developing. Their ranks included Ellis Griffith, Frederick Crawley, Sir John Cory, F.G. Kellaway, Sir Alfred Mond and Sir Courtney Warner.

By mid-1917, Liberal backbenchers were up in arms against the Lloyd George Coalition. Yet the reticence of Asquith and the Liberal front bench to oppose Lloyd George was a constant irritant. It was hardly surprising that frustrated Liberal MPs were becoming more exasperated with Asquith and his colleagues for their apathy than with Lloyd George, despite the error of his ways. Indeed, Asquith's apathy led him to fail even to oppose the Irish conscription measure in April 1918. The extent of his protest was merely to head a mass abstention by the Liberal Party on the second reading of the Military Service Bill.[13]

The significance of these bitter debates, as far as the Liberal Party was concerned, lay in the crystallisation of the supporters and opponents of the Government. The line of demarcation was steadily becoming clearer. The respective supporters of Asquith and Lloyd George fell rather distinctly into two camps. Lloyd George's support among the backbenchers had owed much to the unstinted work of Christopher Addison and David Davies during the summer and autumn of 1916. On the evening that Lloyd George was commissioned by the King to form a government, Addison made his famous statement that there were 49 out-and-out supporters of Lloyd George and a further 125 who would support him if he could form a government. After December 1916, a definite Lloyd George group of Liberals grew up. In the main, Lloyd George drew his support from those Liberals who were willing to sacrifice everything in order to win the war. It was no coincidence that 30 of the 40 Liberals who served on the Liberal War Committee followed Lloyd George. If analysed by class and wealth, by and large these Lloyd George supporters were self-made Radical Nonconformists, men in wool or engineering who were also doing well out of the war. Asquith, on the other hand, can almost be said to have taken with him the Liberal conscience.

The divisions over the Military Service Bill had confirmed these main divisions between the followers of Asquith and Lloyd George. On 9 May 1918, a further important event took place, the now famous Maurice debate. The significance of the Maurice debate was not that it was an isolated example of Liberals dividing against the Government – for it most certainly was not – but rather that it was the only occasion on which Asquith gave the division his official blessing.

The Maurice debate was occasioned when, in May 1918, Major-General Frederick Maurice, former Director of Military Operations at the War Office, had alleged in the press that Government statements concerning the numbers of British troops in France were untrue. Asquith, always ready to take issue with Lloyd George over interference in the control of military strategy, refused Bonar Law's offer of a two-man judicial inquiry and instead demanded the establishment of a Select Committee of the House of Commons. Asquith insisted his motion was not a vote of censure. Lloyd George, however, treated the issue as a vote of confidence. On the vote the Government won by 295 votes to 108 – a much larger majority than had appeared likely at the time. Some 71 Liberals had supported the Government, but 98 had voted against.

The Maurice debate, though hardly a vote on a vital point of Liberal principle, marked a significant stage in the growing separation and hostility of the two Liberal sections. And it came at a time when the prospect of a general election was coming nearer. Before the spring of 1918, Lloyd George had no compelling need to make plans for an election, nor had he particular need to contact and conciliate the Conservative Central Office.

However, the passing of the Representation of the People Bill on 6 February 1918, with its extension of the franchise and major redistribution of seats, provided an urgent reason for proceeding with an election. Lloyd George, by this time, also had special reasons for an electoral arrangement with the Conservatives, for by 1918 many Lloyd George Liberals were far from happy at the support they would obtain in their own constituencies. The advantages of an electoral understanding with the Conservatives, and the formation of a separate Coalition Liberal Party, increased steadily. Prior to the setting up of a separate party, Lloyd George's support, as we have seen, was limited to the forty or so members of Sir Frederick Crawley's 'Liberal War Committee', together with other shifting blocks of supporters. As late as the end of 1917, the Coalition Liberal Whip (Guest) advised against the formation of a separate Lloyd George Liberal Party. At that time, hopes of reunion were still alive and there was considerable sympathy for Asquith. By 1918 the position had changed. On 12 July a number of Lloyd George's supporters, at a meeting chaired by Addison, discussed the question of an election and the programme the party might adopt. The following day, Guest wrote to Lloyd George urging an agreement with Bonar Law over candidates and policy. By September, Lloyd George had decided on an election in harness with the Conservatives, although he was still negotiating with Asquith (via an intermediary, Lord Murray) for the former leader to return as Lord Chancellor, an offer Asquith duly rejected.

By October the essential arrangements over the famous 'coupon' had been made (this was the nickname given to the letter jointly signed by Bonar Law and Lloyd George stating that the holder was the officially recognised Government candidate). Under the agreement, despite much pressure from Lloyd George, it was agreed that only some 150 seats would be allocated to 'couponed' Liberals; elsewhere, Liberals would support Coalition Conservatives. For those Liberals without the coupon, the electoral prospects were likely to be bleak. On 14 November a formal announcement of the dissolution was made; on 22 November the Coalition manifesto was issued.

As part of a deliberate policy, Lloyd George not only sent many of his former Liberal Cabinet colleagues and backbenchers to face a highly uncertain electoral future, but even found it impossible to reward all the loyal followers of his own wing. Faithful supporters such as George

Lambert, the veteran member for South Molton, were denied the coupon, while others such as Colonel Josiah Wedgwood, later to join the Labour Party, received the coupon, even though they protested that they had no wish to have it.

Clearly, the deciding factor in these allocations was not personal loyalty, nor was it the voting record on the night of the famous Maurice debate of 9 May 1918: the essential and crucial factor was the limit of 150 Liberals who were to receive the coupon as arranged in the alliance with Bonar Law and Sir George Younger, the chairman of the Conservative Party organisation. In the event, 541 coupons were eventually issued, the Liberals receiving 159, the Conservatives the lion's share with 364, while 18 were allocated to the ephemeral National Democratic Party.

The 'coupon' election of 1918 was fought both on different constituencies and with a much enlarged electorate from the previous general election in December 1910. Under the Representation of the People Act, which became law in February 1918, the electorate had risen to 21,392,322. The 'coupon' election of 1918 was thus the first election in this country fought on the basis of universal adult male suffrage for those over 21.

This very important extension of the franchise in 1918 was accompanied by an equally far-reaching redistribution of constituencies. Such a redistribution – the first since 1885 – was long overdue. This redistribution, however, was mainly to the advantage of the Conservatives. The areas of greatest population growth after 1885 were the urban centres of London, Birmingham, Liverpool and Glasgow – areas in which the Conservatives were relatively strong compared with the Liberals. Meanwhile the areas of relative population decline had been rural Scotland and Wales (where the Liberals were entrenched) and Southern Ireland (by now solid Nationalist territory). Any redistribution was therefore of direct benefit to the Conservatives. It has been calculated that if the election of December 1910 had been fought on the redistributed constituencies of 1918, the Conservatives would have gained between 25 and 30 seats. This bonus enjoyed by the Conservatives at the 'coupon' election was one factor – albeit slight – in the Coalition landslide.

The election results of December 1918 were nothing short of a complete triumph.[14] It was a Coalition landslide greater than the Liberal victory of 1906 and as sweeping a success as the National Government in 1931. No fewer than 332 'couponed' Conservatives, together with 127 Coalition Liberals, were returned. Together with four Coalition Labour MPs and nine National Democratic supporters, the full strength of the Coalition numbered 472. In addition to this total, a further 47 uncouponed

Conservatives and three Ulster Unionists gave the Coalition general support. In contrast, the opposition benches presented a sorry state of disarray. The largest group, the 73 Sinn Fein members, never took their seats. Labour could muster only 60. The remnant of 'Wee Free' Liberals numbered a mere 36, while a further 17 assorted 'Independents' also generally voted against the Government.

The landslide of 1918 was quickly attributed by the Independent Liberals to the allocation of the coupon. This judgement was mistaken. The overwhelming success of the couponed candidates (472 out of 541 were returned) has disguised the exact nature of the Coalition victory. The idea that success was due to the coupon was in fact mistaken. The 1918 victory was essentially a victory of the right, and couponed Liberals were successful, not so much because they possessed the Coupon, but because they were guaranteed no Conservative opposition. Thus, in such areas as Liverpool and Manchester, even uncouponed Conservatives gained easy and substantial victories.

Even this explanation is only half correct. The paradox of 1918 was that, at a time when the electors were in an unusually radical mood, Lloyd George and his Conservative allies, by exploiting the wave of patriotic sentiment that followed the end of the war, persuaded them to return a massive majority of Conservatives and Coalition Liberals to Parliament.[15]

The circumstances of the 'coupon election' disguised the true electoral strength of the Lloyd George Liberals in December 1918. Of the 127 Coalition Liberal seats secured in 1918, many were concentrated in industrial working-class areas that would be highly vulnerable to any Labour advance. They had been won in 1918 on a patriotic campaign in the absence of Conservative opposition. By 1922 one – and sometimes both – of these factors had been removed. Except for rural North Wales, and to a lesser extent parts of East Anglia, Devon and Cornwall and some London seats, the Coalition Liberals were dependent on Conservative votes. This was most true in such areas of Coalition Liberal strength as industrial West Yorkshire, the North East, South Wales, the mining seats in Derbyshire and North Staffordshire.

If the strength of the Coalition Liberals was less than it appeared, for the Independent Liberals led by Asquith the results were both a rout and a humiliation on a scale almost unparalleled in British politics. A mere 36 uncouponed Liberals had survived the massacre. Virtually all the leaders of the pre-1914 party were defeated. Asquith, Sir John Simon, Walter Runciman, Reginald McKenna, Herbert Samuel and the Chief Whip, J.W. Gulland, all failed to return to Westminster. Two ex-Ministers, Sir Charles Hobhouse in Bristol East and T. McKinnon Wood in the St Rollox division of Glasgow, both suffered the added humility of a lost deposit at the foot of the poll in a three-cornered contest. McKenna, Runciman, Samuel and H.J. Tennant were all similarly placed in three-cornered contests.

Fewer than twenty Asquithians defeated a Coalition opponent. Fewer still had withstood a three-cornered contest, whilst the Liberal pacifists were totally obliterated. Even the most traditional of Liberal strongholds fell before the onslaught. In Frome, the sitting member, who had represented the division since 1892, obtained less than 9 per cent of the total votes. Nor were the 36 survivors of the election based on any firm regional or geographical basis. Indeed, as Roy Douglas has written, even among the tattered band who did scramble home, good luck played a large part.

Within the space of a single election, the unity and strength of the pre-war Liberal Party had been shattered.

7
A Party Divided: 1918–1923

The 'coupon' election of December 1918 had given Lloyd George his triumph. Or so, at least, it appeared on the surface. What the results of 1918 disguised was the shallowness of both Lloyd George's own personal position and that of his party. For his party (as is discussed on pp. 78–9) lacked real roots or any established power base.

In December 1918, however, these problems still lay in the future. Lloyd George's immediate task centred on the policy of reconstruction which the country so desperately needed. Although the most senior posts in the Cabinet were in Conservative hands, the Liberals retained a remarkably strong voice. In the reconstituted Cabinet of October 1919 they possessed seven members, apart from Lloyd George himself. Among these were Ronald Munro at the Scottish Office, Edward Shortt at the Home Office and Edwin Montagu at the India Office. Only two of the Coalition Liberal Ministers, however, can be said to have been near the centre of power: Winston Churchill and H.A.L. Fisher. However, outside the Cabinet there were other proponents of Liberalism, as well as the Prime Minister's own secretariat or 'Garden Suburb'.

Despite all this, the influence of the Coalition Liberal party on post-war events was far from unimportant. To begin with, they were largely responsible for the government's imaginative new departures in social reform. Despite the mismanagement of finance, Christopher Addison supplied much of the momentum behind the housing programme. T.J. Macnamara played an important part in combating unemployment, whilst Mond also pressed for employment policies. In education, H.A.L. Fisher, together with his Welsh colleague Herbert Lewis, fought a long battle to save such items as teachers salary scales from drastic economies. The important extension of national insurance in 1920 was also to their credit, whilst Edwin Montagu introduced important reforms over India.

It was significant that, when the Geddes recommendations threatened almost the entire social policy of the government, it was the Liberal

Ministers, headed by Fisher, Mond, Montagu and Churchill, who led the counter-attack in the Cabinet – although the battle they fought was largely lost and the government's social policies were left in ruins.

Over Ireland, the Coalition Liberals again acted as the voice of protest – however ineffective – against the atrocities of the Black and Tans. Such Ministers as Shortt, Addison and Fisher fought hard in 1919 for a more moderate policy – a battle again lost with the arrival of Hamar Greenwood at the Irish Office in April 1920.

Whilst the Coalition Liberals' front benches possessed a variety of talent, with such figures as Montagu, Addison and Hilton Young, the great failing of the Coalition Liberals was their anomalous political position.

Throughout 1919 and 1920, Lloyd George's political objective was the creation of a 'Centre Party' which would, by uniting the Coalition Liberals and Conservatives at all levels, provide a permanent base to fight off Socialism. The idea had been mooted with H.A.L. Fisher and Christopher Addison as early as September 1919. At that time, Lloyd George believed it would be the Unionists who would provide the main obstacle. However, after some persuasion both Bonar Law and Younger agreed. Lloyd George took the acceptance of his own party for granted.

In this, however, Lloyd George was to be rudely awakened. Whilst such Liberal Ministers as Churchill and Addison were enthusiastic for fusion – although for different reasons – they were isolated voices. When, on 16 March 1920, Lloyd George faced his Liberal colleagues at a crucial meeting intended to be the preliminary to public fusion with the Conservatives, he met firm opposition. The net result was that when Lloyd George met the Coalition back-bench MPs two days later, he made only vague appeals for 'closer cooperation' in the constituencies, rather than demanding fusion. Even this mild appeal met angry criticism.

The result was that, unable to deliver his party's own support, Lloyd George could clearly not approach the Unionists. As Morgan has written, the Coalition Liberals remained Liberals still and, whether he liked it or not, so did Lloyd George.[1]

The decision to create a Coalition Liberal Party, which became necessary after the 1920 Leamington conference (see p. 79) never really became translated into political reality. The Coalition Liberals always remained an organisation of too many Chiefs and too few Indians. The further away one came from Downing Street, the more peripheral was the influence of the Coalition Liberal Party. This weakness centred round two vital factors; the party lacked (as was seen earlier) a secure electoral base and, perhaps even more crucially, lacked organisation at the grassroots.

After the Leamington conference, the Coalition Liberals began the creation of a separate party organisation in the constituencies and federations. Despite lavish expenditure from the Lloyd George Fund, the party organisation never really provided the Coalition Liberals with firm roots. Although, in name at least, some 224 constituency Lloyd George Associations were established, few of these maintained an active existence.[2] Most had a mere propaganda value and lacked real local activity. Certainly, nothing resembling a comprehensive constituency network ever existed, and even in such areas as Scotland or Wales little constituency activity took place.[3]

The precarious electoral base of the Coalition Liberals was increasingly revealed in the by-elections from 1918 to 1922. During 1919, Coalition Liberals lost a variety of seats to Labour; and this continued during 1920 on an even greater scale. When Labour won Dartford on 27 March and South Norfolk on 27 July, the scale of the rot was obvious to all. The loss of South Norfolk produced considerable despair among Conservative supporters of the Coalition at the fate of their Liberal allies. Sir George Younger, the party chairman, wrote to Bonar Law:

This constant loss of C(oalition) L(iberal) seats becomes serious and I see no chance of any improvement. With poor candidates and no organisation of their own, the attrition is bound to go on and the indecision of the Downing Street staff does no good. They arrive, spend money lavishly, but cut little ice.[4]

With each by-election disaster, dreary reports came in of the lack of any Coalition Liberal organisation. In a general review of the dismal Coalition Liberal performance at by-elections, F.E. Guest wrote to Lloyd George: 'New methods will have to be adopted, and many of our old methods will have to be scrapped, if the new and vast electorate is to be got at.'

However, if the Coalition Liberals faced severe problems, they were relatively light compared to the difficulties facing the Asquithian Liberals. For this forlorn group, led by Sir Donald Maclean until Asquith returned to Parliament in the Paisley by-election of February 1920, the political future seemed doubtful and uncertain.

And yet some Liberals were able to put a brave face on the events of 1918. There were exceptional factors about the election – the electoral pact, the low turnout, the inadequate register, the emotional tone of the campaign – which helped explain the disaster. One defeated Liberal candidate wrote to his constituency secretary that there was no need for undue Liberal depression, since in 1918 'conditions were so peculiar that it cannot be regarded as representing the normal views of the electorate'. These views were possible consolations for the disaster of the 'coupon' election. No such comforting explanations were possible, however, as the continued party split after 1918 revealed just how much damage the party had suffered.

In fact, the Asquithian Liberals were slow to realise that Lloyd George intended a permanent separation. During 1919, however, as Lloyd George continued to employ the 'coupon' in by-elections, the nature of his intentions became clearer. The defeat of Sir John Simon in Spen Valley marked an important step in this process of separation. The final break – and the establishment of a separate Coalition Liberal organisation – came with the failure of Lloyd George's attempts to create a 'Centre Party' by fusing the two wings of the Coalition.

This attempt at fusion, though it ended in failure, had important consequences. In March 1920 the Asquithian Liberal Party declared war on the Coalition Liberals. This declaration was echoed from constituency to constituency, as Liberal Associations passed resolutions condemning both the Coalition and the policy of close cooperation with the Conservatives.

This growing animosity came to a head at the general meeting of the National Liberal Federation at Leamington in May 1920. Several Coalition Liberal MPs attended the gathering. However, when the Coalition case was argued from the platform, interruptions steadily mounted. T.J. Macnamara, who had spoken against Simon in the Spen Valley by-election, received a rowdy reception. This was nothing, however, compared with the general pandemonium which occurred when F.G. Kellaway declared that during the Boer War Asquith had been unfaithful to Liberalism. As tempers mounted Sir Gordon Hewart, the Attorney-General, stated that, in protest at these unruly proceedings, the Coalition Liberals would withdraw. Amid loud cheers, they did. The divisions in the party had become finalised; and it was at the constituency level that they were often felt most disastrously. After 1918, many local Liberal Associations suffered an almost total collapse of organisation, membership and activities.

The gravity of the situation facing the local Liberal Associations in the constituencies after 1918 was not lost on leading members of the party. Herbert Gladstone, the director of Liberal headquarters, had no illusions. He was later to write of the position after the debacle of the 'Coupon':

...The result of 1918 broke the party, not only in the House of Commons but in the country. Local associations perished or maintained a nominal existence. Masses of our best men passed away to Labour. Others gravitated to Conservatism or independence...

As Gladstone continued, the remnants in the constituencies neither held meetings nor maintained even elementary electoral organisation.

Nor was Gladstone alone in his pessimism. Thus the secretary of the Midland Liberal Federation reported after the 1922 general election that 'the most dreadful feature of our work during the past four years had been the difficulty of arousing any interest whatsoever'. Constituencies were left without agents; local branches withered away; propaganda lapsed entirely. Perhaps even more significantly, Liberals failed to field a major challenge in municipal elections.

In the decade after 1918, the Liberals never fielded a full team of municipal candidates. Only 19 per cent of those seeking election in 1921 were Liberals, while 35 per cent were Labour. By 1929, less than one in eight of those fighting provincial borough elections were Liberal.

In the first post-war municipal elections, in November 1919, Liberals suffered a major reverse at the hands of Labour. In radical towns with a Liberal tradition, such as Bradford, Leicester, Nottingham and Wolverhampton, formerly secure Liberal wards fell to Labour. The debacle of 1919 not only greatly increased Labour representation, but also precipitated the formation of numerous Liberal–Conservative 'anti-Socialist' municipal pacts. Examples of these, which in some cases lasted for the whole inter-war period, were Sheffield (where the two parties combined to form the Sheffield Citizens' Association), Bristol, Derby and Wolverhampton.

This Liberal decline at local level was most marked on the London County Council. Here, the decline of the Progressive Party had already been strongly in evidence before the First World War.[5] From 83 representatives on a Council of 118 in 1904, the Progressive strength had been reduced to 50 by 1913. In 1919, Progressive representation was reduced to a mere 40; by 1925, with only six representatives, the party had virtually disappeared as an independent force in London politics. Indeed, there were no Progressives at all after the 1934 elections.

Partly cause, partly a consequence of this collapse of local Liberal organisation at the grassroots was the disastrous by-election record of the Asquithian wing of the party from 1918 to the fall of the Coalition in 1922. Ironically, the first by-elections after the Coupon Election seemed to suggest better things. Asquithians won Leyton West (1 March 1919), Hull Central (29 March) and Central Aberdeenshire and Kincardine (16

April). Of these results, J.M. Kenworthy's victory in Hull Central on a swing of 32.9 per cent was the most sensational.

These results, however, proved to be a false dawn. After April 1919 the by-elections suddenly, but consistently, showed that the initiative in the constituencies had passed from the Liberals to Labour. During the remainder of 1919, in the three contests fought by Conservative, Liberal and Labour, the Liberals came bottom in all three. Up to the 1922 general election the Independent Liberals won only two other by-elections. These were in Louth, a traditional rural Nonconformist seat that had returned a Liberal at virtually every election since 1885, and Bodmin, a similarly traditional Liberal West Country stronghold.

The greatest disappointment for the Independent Liberals came in three-cornered contests. In such constituencies as Manchester Rusholme, Plymouth Sutton and Ilford, Labour forced Liberals into third place. In the 24 three-cornered by-election contests between 1918 and 1922, the Independent Liberals could poll only 24.8 per cent of votes cast, compared to 35.1 per cent for Labour and 40.1 per cent for the Coalition. Indeed, much the most significant feature of the by-elections during the lifetime of the Coalition was the advance of Labour, whose victories against both Coalition Liberal and Conservatives were often dramatic.[6] In the longer term, however, the significance of the by-elections was the extent to which (outside the old Nonconformist rural areas) protest votes were finding their home with Labour rather than with the Asquithian Liberals. In part this was due to the large number of seats left uncontested by Independent Liberals at by-elections. No Independent Liberals were brought forward at by-elections in such seats as Bromley, Woodbridge, Dover or Taunton.

The disintegration of Liberal organisation and morale at constituency level was a reflection of a wider malaise in the party. For after 1918, the Independent Liberals lacked two crucial weapons: distinctive policies and effective leadership. After 1918, it was difficult to determine even in broad terms what the Liberal Party stood for. Was it a party of radicals? Or anti-Socialists? Or had it become a loose Free Trade moderate centre party? The Asquithian Liberals had made few attempts to answer that question. The first – and basic – task for the Liberal Party was to decide where it stood in relation to Labour. This, in the six years after 1918, Asquith and his supporters never established. As Kinnear has written, Asquith himself declared that he was 'not in the least alarmed by the Red Spectre', whilst Simon (not even on the left wing of the Party) had stated that Labour ought not to be treated as the common enemy.[7] Yet these declarations were oddly at variance with the *Liberal Magazine* (the official

Asquithian journal) which had stated that 'under socialism, individual freedom would practically disappear' and that the Labour Party 'is a morbid political coalition held together by insincerity'.

These basic contradictions in the philosophy of the party were exposed whenever fairly advanced radical ideas were discussed. Thus, when some Liberals toyed with the idea of nationalisation early in 1920, the party immediately witnessed yet another split. A 'Liberal anti-nationalisation committee' (consisting largely of the wealthier Liberal industrialists) ran a scare campaign. As Kinnear comments, such internal disputes over economic policy would not, in normal times, have greatly hurt the party – they were indeed a healthy sign of intellectual debate – but occurring as they did in a divided and leaderless party they assumed an importance out of all proportion. It was doubly ironic that the party's failure to adopt a distinct policy and programme coincided with the institution of the Liberal Summer Schools, an important inter-war development in Liberal education. Under the inspiration of Ramsay Muir and Walter Layton, the first Summer School was held at Grasmere in 1921. Subsequent Summer Schools were held annually either at Oxford or Cambridge.

One common denominator in the Liberal misfortunes after 1918 lay in leadership; or rather the lack of it. And, in large measure, the blame lay with Asquith. In the period after the Paisley by-election of 12 February 1920 and the Leamington conference of May 1920, vital years went by (particularly in the run-up to the 1922 election) with the Liberal leader giving neither lead, direction nor policy. Asquith, who was 70 in 1922, was becoming a shadow of his former self.

Lack of positive leadership over policy from Asquith was clearly one factor. Another – allied with it – was the fact that, even before 1918, dissident radical Liberals could now look for an alternative party in Labour. This process had begun during the war; several Liberal MPs and candidates, including such figures as C.P. Trevelyan and Charles Roden Buxton had already joined Labour. Some of these seceders might have returned to the Liberal fold if Asquith had adopted a constructive and radical programme. As it was, the long-term effect was to siphon off the many advanced social reformers and make the party perhaps less open to radical ideas than before.

Whilst the Independent Liberals faced serious problems of policy, organisation and leadership, the Coalition Liberals faced problems of a different order. The Coalition Liberals were finding their political world beginning to crumble about them. Lloyd George himself was becoming the most unloved of politicians. His own personal position was becoming increasingly difficult. Coalition Liberal discontent was rife, yet Lloyd

George did little about it. The Liberal backbenchers were treated with complete indifference. With the exception of Churchill, Lloyd George's main colleagues and confidants were all Conservatives. Those Liberals left in the government were becoming increasingly isolated.

Meanwhile, in the Conservative constituency associations, the movement to sever the Coalition links was rapidly rising. On 2 June 1922, 11 Conservative peers and 30 MPs published a manifesto in the press declaring that 'to drift further with ever-changing policies must quickly produce chaos, disaster and ruin'. The signs of revolt were becoming more evident.

With all these portents, it was remarkable that it was not until August 1922, when an imminent general election seemed likely, that Lloyd George set up a committee, consisting of Mond, Kellaway and Macnamara, to investigate the Coalition Liberal Party Machine.

By the autumn of 1922, against a long background of by-election reverses, Coalition Liberal morale had all but disappeared. Lloyd George's bellicose handling of the Chanak affair did nothing to calm the party. It was the political crisis of autumn 1922, which, by threatening the Coalition with a new rebellion anyway, decided the Cabinet to take the plunge and hold an immediate election.

Meanwhile, the Conservative MPs were summoned to the Carlton Club by Austen Chamberlain, in an effort to secure their consent to fight the election as a Coalition. The meeting at the Carlton Club resolved that the Conservatives would not be the allies of the Coalition Liberals at the next election; it thereby destroyed the Coalition.

Lloyd George resigned as Prime Minister the same afternoon. On Monday 23 October, Bonar Law was unanimously elected leader of the Conservative Party to succeed Austen Chamberlain – who had himself replaced Bonar Law only 19 months previously. Three days later, Parliament was dissolved. The date of the general election was fixed for 15 November.

The fall of the Coalition left both Lloyd George and his Liberal supporters without a power base. Despite a plea by Mond that the Coalition Liberals should fight during the subsequent election as Liberals desiring a reunited party, the bulk of the Coalition Liberals decided to act with any sympathetic Conservatives during the campaign.

With the fall of the Coalition, Lloyd George was left without any clear direction in which to try to lead his followers. In a speech at Leeds on 21 October, he was palpably engaged in an exercise to buy himself time. He offered no positive programme, and he carefully avoided defining his relations with the other parties. A similar lack of positive policy was again apparent when he spoke at the Hotel Victoria on 26 October. For once, Lloyd George was in the rare and unhappy position of a leader with nothing to say.

Indeed, to some extent he was also a leader with nothing to lead. For, with the fall of the Coalition, the Lloyd George Liberals now discovered what had long been a political fact: they were a party without roots. The coming of the election meant that they must fend for themselves. Such electoral arrangements as they could make with other parties would have to be at constituency level.

Apart from North Wales, where Coalition Liberalism was strong in its own right, the most fortunate were the Lloyd George Liberals in Scotland. Feeling in the Scottish Unionist ranks was strongly in favour of a continued Coalition. As it was, the Eastern Division of the Scottish Unionist Association formally decided not to oppose sitting National Liberal Members. In return, the Scottish National Liberals agreed not to oppose sitting Conservatives. Apart from such isolated constituencies as Perth and Glasgow Cathcart, the National Liberals in Scotland enjoyed a Coalition in 1922.

South of the border, however, Coalition Liberals were forced to make such arrangements as they could to secure local Conservative support. So, in London, Macnamara in Camberwell North West, as well as Arthur Lever in Hackney Central and Lt-Col. M. Alexander in Southwark South East, received official Conservative support only after they had given specific pledges of support to a Bonar Law Ministry. Others were less fortunate. Despite repeated attempts to secure Conservative support in Sunderland, Sir Hamar Greenwood was faced with two Conservative opponents in this double-member constituency.

The rapid increase in the number of Conservatives coming forward to attack Coalition Liberal seats was likely to produce electoral disaster for Lloyd George's supporters. Yet Lloyd George was powerless to prevent it. His threat to bring forward candidates against sitting Conservatives was hardly practical politics. Though urged to adopt this course by Mond and Rothermere, nothing came of the 'phantom host' of candidates promised by C.A. McCurdy, the Chief Whip. As Churchill rightly observed, nothing was to be gained, and much would be lost, by spreading the war.

In the event, moderation prevailed. Only 144 Coalition Liberals were eventually adopted. Only 24 of these were in constituencies that had not been allocated to Coalition Liberal or National Democratic candidates in the 'coupon' election. Only seven of these 24 fought against sitting Conservatives. The bulk of the attack was directed at Labour. In addition to Scotland and the East End of London, the Coalition continued virtually undisturbed in such towns as Bristol and Newcastle. Some 121 Coalition Liberals (Churchill among them) escaped any Conservative opposition. Compared to the 144 Coalition Liberals, the Asquithians launched a determined challenge with 333 candidates. The Conservatives brought forward 482 candidates. Labour fielded 414, its largest contingent so far.

The outcome of the election was a triumph for Bonar Law, a major advance for Labour, a meagre return for Asquith and a total humiliation for the Lloyd George Liberals. (See Table 7.1.)

Table 7.1   1922 General Election Result

	Total Votes	% Share	Candidates	MPs Elected	Unopposed Returns
Conservative	5,502,298	38.5	482	344	42
Liberal	2,668,143	18.9	333	60	6
National Liberal	1,412,772	9.4	144	53	4
Labour	4,237,349	29.7	414	142	4
Others	571,480	3.5	68	16	1
	14,392,330	100.0	1,441	615	57

For the Asquithian Liberals, the results were a bitter disappointment. Admittedly, their numbers elected rose to 62, but this was only a minor success. Yet even this advance could hardly disguise several disturbing features. Fourteen of the seats won in 1918 had been lost, nine of them to Labour. The Liberals fared particularly badly in the mining areas. In Durham the three remaining Liberal constituencies were all lost. Other traditional Liberal mining strongholds lost included Peebles and South Midlothian (Sir Donald Maclean's constituency), Leigh, and North East Derbyshire.

On the other hand, the Independent Liberals managed to gain 43 seats. Of these, ten were won from Coalition Liberals, 32 from Conservatives and Independents, but only one from Labour. It was significant that the best results for the Asquithian Liberals were in the traditionally Liberal rural seats lost in the 1918 debacle.

However, the most disturbing feature of this partial revival, outside the occasional area such as rural Scotland or the West Country, was its lack of a secure regional base. Very many traditional Liberal seats, especially in the cities, had not been recovered, while several of the Liberal victories were in areas which had not returned Liberals for a generation. In Oxford, Frank Gray's success was the first Liberal victory since 1885. Likewise, the Liberal gain in Bootle was the first victory after forty years in the wilderness. In fact, one Liberal Federation Secretary noticed that party organisation bore little relation to success. In many cases, the worse the organisation, the better the party fared. The explanation seemed to lie in the fact that, in 1922, the Liberals gathered the protest votes at the shortcomings of the Coalition.

This was particularly true of the series of Liberal victories in rural seats which had rarely, if ever, returned Liberals before 1922. Typical of Liberal gains in these areas were the victories in Grantham, Horncastle, Holderness and Taunton.

A further disturbing feature for the Liberal Party was that its best results were, almost without exception, in straight fights against the Conservatives. In the 31 constituencies in which Independent Liberals enjoyed straight fights with Conservatives in 1918 and 1922, the Liberal share of the vote increased by over 10 per cent. These seats, however, were almost exclusively rural or residential. In the 54 constituencies in which the three major parties contested in 1918 and 1922, the Liberals increased their share of the vote by only 4.5 per cent from 22.7 per cent to 27.2 per cent. The Liberal recovery in industrial working-class seats was, in general, conspicuously absent. The occasional exception, such as Walsall, which Pat Collins won for the Liberals, only made the general pattern more obvious. In the rural seats, however, the presence of Labour candidates had less effect, and in such seats as Westbury and Chippenham the Liberals were still able to regain lost territory.

If the results of the 1922 election were disappointing for the Asquithians, they were utterly disastrous for the Coalition Liberals. Many of the leading Lloyd George supporters went down to defeat: Churchill was beaten at Dundee, Hamar Greenwood at Sunderland and Freddie Guest in East Dorset. Whereas, in 1918, 138 Coalition Liberals had been returned, only 60 survived the 1922 election. No fewer than 81 seats were lost, 21 of which had even lacked defenders. Whilst 57 seats were retained, only three new seats were won.

In the industrial areas the rout assumed the proportions of a massacre. In Sheffield, only the Park division survived as the lone outpost of Coalition Liberalism. Attercliffe was lost to Labour on a swing of 33.5 per cent; Hillsborough fell on a similar huge swing. South Wales was the scene of a similar debacle. Neath was lost on a swing of 24.3 per cent, while Labour also captured Aberdare, Llanelli, Merthyr, Aberavon and Swansea East, which the Coalition Liberals had narrowly retained in the by-election of July 1919. In Scotland, despite the continuation of local Conservative–National Liberal agreements, it was the same story of industrial Liberal seats swamped by a Labour tide. Eight of 12 seats in industrial Scotland were lost.

Only in its stronghold of rural North Wales was Coalition Liberalism able to survive unaided against Conservative and Labour attacks. The net result of 1922, as far as the Coalition Liberals were concerned, was a disaster.

Faced with the dramatic increase in Labour support, and with the Conservatives under Bonar Law secure with a comfortable overall majority, it is hardly surprising that the Liberal Party found little comfort in the verdict of November 1922. Over breakfast with C.P. Scott, the editor of the *Manchester Guardian*, Lloyd George asked him for his views on the result. Scott replied that the election constituted a worse disaster for the Liberal Party than 1918 because there was less excuse for it.

The return of Bonar Law to power, with its promise of a period of political tranquillity, seemed at least to offer the Liberals a breathing space to put their house in order. And the first prerequisite to this was the question of reunion. Throughout 1923, the Liberals spent much effort grappling with the problem of reunion. Unlike the other difficulties facing the party, it was a problem about which they might do something. However, the circumstances and conduct of the 1922 election had hardly given reunion a good start. With the notable exceptions of such areas as Manchester and Leeds, the two Liberal factions had spent the 1922 election fighting each other.

And, as Trevor Wilson wrote, for most Independent Liberals, including Asquith, the only satisfaction to be derived from the election results was to 'gloat over the corpses which have been left on the battlefield'.[8] After the election, memories of these bitter scenes presented a major obstacle to reunion. Yet, to members in both wings, it seemed a vital and pressing question. Many Coalition Liberals saw reunion as giving them a more definite place in politics, most particularly in the light of Labour's advance. Here, indeed, was the crunch. Lloyd George, more than Asquith, could see the realities of the political situation after Labour's advance in 1922. And yet, a lingering pride prevented submission, whilst Asquith seemed to want nothing less than just that.

This position, in spring 1923, continued unchanged as summer approached. At the same time, growing evidence of the desire for reconciliation in the constituencies became apparent. In two by-elections, in Anglesey and Ludlow, local reunion was achieved. But throughout the spring and early summer of 1923, National Liberal reconciliation initiatives were summarily brought to a halt. Thus, the Welsh National Liberals held a meeting in March to consider the reunion position and appointed nine delegates with full power to meet Independent Liberals in any conference. This was communicated to a meeting at Shrewsbury of the Welsh Liberal Federation. The response to this friendly gesture was not encouraging. The Federation passed the following resolution: 'That the consideration of the letter from the National Liberal Council be deferred for six months.' A further major speech by Lloyd George – on 28 April at Manchester – again produced only a frosty reception from Asquith. Supplied with an opportunity of accepting the hand of friendship, Asquith chose as an alternative, in a speech at Bournemouth, to catalogue some of the difficulties, stressing particularly that the Coalition Liberals had been voting with the Conservatives.

May produced no further real moves towards Liberal reunion, except in the constituencies, where the *Lloyd George Liberal Magazine* reported:

> The month has seen a considerable increase in the number of resolutions from rank-and-file organisations throughout the country advocating cooperation and consultation between the Party leaders as the first step towards complete reunion.[9]

It was against this background that the annual conference of the National Liberal Federation took place at Buxton. It was a moment of crucial importance for the success of Liberal reunion attempts. The concrete results of the conference in terms of Liberal reunion were virtually nil. It was true that the delegates put on record their satisfaction with the growing desire for party union. It was also the case that the friendly reception given to such National Liberals as Mond and McCurdy contrasted very favourably with the hostility shown at Leamington in 1920 to Hewart and Addison. Nevertheless, the conference rejected the crucial amendment to a pro-reunion resolution calling on the Independent Liberal leaders to discuss with the National Liberal leaders the best means of promoting party unity. The *Manchester Guardian*, in its comments on the Buxton proceedings, declared that the blunt truth revealed by the gathering was that the party was so dangerously preoccupied with its internal problem that it had little time for the external problems of policy, especially domestic policy. How, it asked, can Liberal leaders hope to rouse enthusiasm until they have themselves enough enthusiasm to endure one another for the good of the cause?

There is little doubt that Buxton was the moment of lost opportunity for Liberal reunion. Despite an insistent call from the constituencies for reunion, conference had turned an almost deaf ear. This was reflected in a growing number of associations such as Thornbury and Ashton-under-Lyne making their own local arrangements for reunion.

But with the exception of these few local arrangements, the continued party split led to an even further deterioration in party morale at constituency level. This loss of morale had both cause and effect in a depressing Liberal by-election record between 1922 and 1923. Although the party gained Willesden East and Tiverton, in general its vote had failed to make any marked improvement. The main significance of the by-elections was Labour's ability to consolidate and extend its 1922 advance in industrial areas, mainly at the expense of the Liberals, and Labour's slow but definite advance in rural areas, once again hitting hardest at the Liberals.[10]

At the same time that the moves towards reunion at local level were increasing, there is strong evidence to suggest that Asquith's intransigence in ever readmitting Lloyd George to real power within a reunited party was increasing. If this is correct, the sad paradox of Liberal history stands out: Asquith succeeded in keeping out Lloyd George until October 1926, but at a cost of seeing the party destroyed. Lloyd George became leader when only a rump was left for him to lead. And Simon – whom perhaps Asquith saw as heir apparent – repaid his former chief by leading a breakaway Liberal National Party after November 1930.

Meanwhile, to add to the multitude of political cross-currents at work in July 1923, Lloyd George was once again – having despaired of Liberal reunion – refusing to abandon his contacts with the Conservatives.

With the months of August and September relatively empty of political activity, the position regarding reunion remained unchanged. With the exception of local reunion in Bradford (largely caused by the raising of Tariff Reform by Baldwin), so the position rested when in September 1923 Lloyd George set off for what was to become a triumphant lecture tour of America. By the time he returned, Baldwin's unexpected announcement of his conversion to Protection had transformed the political climate.

8
Revival and Decline: 1923–1926

Baldwin's decision to call an immediate election over the issue of Protection transformed the position of the Liberal Party. At one stroke, the road to Liberal reunion lay open. Baldwin succeeded, where every Liberal had failed, in reuniting the two warring factions.

Although there had been rumours that Lloyd George was planning to abandon Free Trade, these doubts were removed when, on his return to Southampton from the United States, the former Prime Minister declared himself unreservedly against Baldwin's fiscal departure.

The main essentials of reunion were settled at a meeting on 13 November attended by Asquith, Lloyd George, Vivian Phillipps and Mond. It was agreed to fight the election as a united party, with a united Liberal Campaign Committee (chaired by Lord Beauchamp) and a single campaign fund. All candidates were to stand as 'Liberals', without any prefix or suffix.

The most interesting discussion centred on the Liberal campaign strategy. Free Trade presented no problems, for Lloyd George spoke as an unqualified Free Trader. Regarding unemployment, Lloyd George suggested the use of National Credit during depression, while the Asquithians proposed an extended Unemployment Insurance Scheme. On foreign policy, it was decided to launch a major attack on the government's handling of the Ruhr question and reparations. These lines of attack, on Free Trade, unemployment and foreign affairs, were to be expected. Nothing very radical or new was proposed. The meeting agreed that nothing corresponding to a 'Newcastle Programme' could or ought to be attempted, but that what was wanted was 'a limited number of bold but effective pronouncements'. A manifesto on these lines was drafted the same evening by Mond and Phillipps. This decision was of vital significance, for the whole Liberal campaign was subsequently to centre on a negative defence of Free Trade.

The ease with which reunion seemed to be accomplished, and a campaign policy agreed on, in fact disguised several factors. It certainly disguised the extent to which Lloyd George retained control not only over his money, but also over his Coalition Liberal organisation.

The financial arrangements soon caused considerable acrimony. At the 13 November meeting, Lloyd George had promised considerable financial support, although no record of the exact amount has survived. It was left to Herbert Gladstone to be responsible for collecting Lloyd George's contribution from Sir Alfred Cope. After more discussions, it was agreed that a contribution of £100,000 from the Lloyd George wing and £50,000 from the Independent Liberal headquarters would be sufficient. But actually getting the money out of Lloyd George proved a source of conflict.

The possibility of future conflict between Lloyd George and Asquith stemmed also from another source. In taking up the cause of Free Trade, and rejoining the Liberal ranks, Lloyd George had effectively become Asquith's second. As Beaverbrook expressed it, 'he really had a choice between death and surrender on fairly easy terms'.[1] The Free Trade Liberal Party was in Asquith's control, not Lloyd George's. Lloyd George's position after the election, when his National Liberal followers were decimated, only reinforced the realisation upon Lloyd George.

Meanwhile, Lloyd George had not entirely abandoned the old Coalition. At a meeting at Cherkley on 12 November, a somewhat unreal plot had been hatched to secure a Free Trade victory followed by a new Coalition, but the details were soon leaked to Baldwin. The plot subsequently collapsed.

Although rumoured in the press, Lloyd George's intrigues with his old Coalition partners did not mar the galvanising effect of Liberal reunion on constituency morale and activity. Hitherto dormant associations were brought by the onset of Free Trade and a reunited party into hurried activity. The net result was that the Liberals were able to field 457 candidates, compared to 536 Conservative and 427 Labour.

The ease with which Liberal reunion was achieved at this national level was not so easily repeated in the constituencies. Five years of division were not healed overnight. Indeed, in two constituencies (Camborne and Cardiganshire) rival Liberal candidates were adopted in 1923. In addition, in several constituencies, particularly in Highland Scotland, local faction continued with the Asquithian Liberals refusing active support to sitting National Liberals.

Despite the old battle-cry of Free Trade, even in the optimistic atmosphere of 1923, local associations in many industrial areas failed to generate sufficient energy to field a candidate. This was particularly true of such areas as Durham, South Wales and the Clyde. Even in 1923, local cooperation with the Conservatives was one factor at work, together with the difficulty of attracting good candidates and the problems of raising sufficient finance.

If the nominations provided evidence of Liberal decline, the campaign itself favoured the Liberals. For the Liberals were fighting on their home ground in defending Free Trade. The tone of the Liberal campaign was firmly set by Asquith. It was, essentially, the orthodox defence of Free Trade that had been debated twenty years before. Asquith set himself out to establish that Protection would raise food prices and that neither nationalisation nor the capital levy could be introduced without damaging the economic system. If the Liberals had a programme other than this, it was hardly spectacular. Speaking on 23 November, Asquith went on to outline some other Liberal aims: he called for a remodelling of the Insurance Act, courageous use of national credit, development of Imperial resources and the full operation of the Trade Facilities Act.

Nor, except for occasional remarks by Lloyd George, did the Liberal leadership think they needed anything more radical or constructive in terms of policy. As Cowling observes, although Lloyd George declared that Liberals would be as successful in the future in introducing major social reforms as they had been previously, the details of this future legislation were left to look after themselves.[2] The radicalism of April 1923 had vanished from Lloyd George's speeches. In the campaign, little distinguished Lloyd George, Asquith or Grey. The emphasis, again and again, was on the negative virtues of Free Trade.[3]

It was ironic that much of the Liberal success in 1923 was the result of the party fighting on an essentially conservative policy, with the party portraying itself as the party of common sense and established right.

Despite this negative campaign, the Liberals achieved a marked electoral revival in December 1923. The first results, from Free Trade Lancashire, seemed to confirm the worst fears of those Conservatives who had argued against Baldwin's electoral strategy.

The Liberals swept to victory in no less than five Manchester constituencies, in addition to taking both the Wavertree and West Derby divisions of Liverpool, constituencies with a consistent Conservative tradition since 1885. Even in such areas as Nottingham, where the Conservatives might have expected to benefit from high unemployment and severe foreign competition, the Protectionist platform made little impact. The final results are shown in Table 8.1.

Table 8.1

	Votes	%	Candidates	Members	Unopposed
Conservative	5,514,541	38.0	536	258	35
Liberal	4,301,481	29.7	457	158	11
Labour	4,439,780	30.7	427	191	3
Communist	39,448	0.2	4	–	–
Nationalist	97,993	0.4	4	3	1
Others	154,452	1.0	18	5	–
Total	14,547,695	100.0	1,446	615	50

The Liberals, although doing well, had not achieved an unqualified success. Although, on balance, they had gained 53 seats from the Conservatives, they had suffered a net loss of ten to Labour.

The party did particularly well in three areas. In the South West, the Liberals secured 12 gains. The South Midlands and northern Home Counties produced another six victories, while in Lincolnshire and East Anglia Liberals took a further six.

The party also gained a few semi-industrial county divisions such as Nuneaton, Bosworth and Cleveland, all with a strong Nonconformist vote. Much the most curious series of Liberal victories, however, were the large number of normally 'safe' Conservative seats which fell to the Liberals. Such constituencies as Basingstoke, Blackpool, Chelmsford, Chichester, Lonsdale and Shrewsbury, never previously Liberal, were captured.

At the other extreme, the most disappointing feature of the Liberal revival was the failure to make substantial inroads into the Labour vote. Indeed, in the majority of industrial areas with the partial exception of north-east England, the Liberals suffered a further loss of ground. Whereas the Liberals took 69 seats from the Conservatives, losing only 16 themselves, vis-à-vis Labour the party gained only 13 for the loss of 23.

In several industrial areas which the Liberals had long regarded as their own preserve, the results were further proof of the rapidly fading Liberal support amongst the working classes. In South Wales, the party lost further ground. But perhaps the most disheartening was the series of losses to Labour in such Midland seats as Northampton, Wellingborough, Derby and Leicester.

The result of the 1923 election left the Liberal Party holding the balance of power. Protection had been rejected with no uncertain voice. But what government should take the place of Baldwin? Should the Liberals put

MacDonald into office? Or should some other formula be found to avoid the experiment of a Labour Government?

The occasion found the party deeply divided. On the right, opposition to the policy of putting Labour into office was most strongly voiced by Churchill. He was supported by such right-wing Liberals as Freddie Guest, Sir Beddoe Rees, the Member for Bristol South, and Brigadier-General Spears.

The *Liberal Magazine*, however, together with the constituency and federation organisations supported the experiment. Fear of the renewal of any form of tacit or open Conservative alliance far outweighed the dangers that might result from a Labour Government.

It was against this background of a divided party that the Liberal leadership had to adopt its course of action.

When the Liberal leaders first met to discuss their future course of action, Asquith's own immediate idea, which received the support of Simon, was to turn the Conservatives out as soon as possible, then to do the same with Labour through a combination with the Conservatives.[4] Lloyd George strongly opposed this plan with the argument that any such minority Liberal Government so dependent on Conservative votes would be entirely without freedom of action.

However, the feeling of the meeting was against him: Lloyd George then proposed an adjournment. Asquith, always ready to adjourn anything, agreed. When the leaders met again, Asquith had changed his views: Asquith now wanted a policy of total independence. Lloyd George, who was clearly envisaging a period of cooperation with Labour, accepted this as a first step in the right direction.

Thus, at a crucial moment in the history of the party, the Liberal leaders had been divided. The net result of all this was that the Liberals voted Labour into office without ever having considered how they would fare if Labour refused to cooperate. In this vital respect, Asquith's policy was without reality from the start. The Liberal Party would *not* be able to judge Labour on its merits. Either the Liberals would have to support Labour measures or vote against. To vote against meant an election which the Liberals could not, for financial reasons, contemplate. It was to prove to be a policy without room to manoeuvre. But the decision had been made. On 18 December Asquith made it clear, in a speech to the Liberal Parliamentary Party, that the Liberals would not keep the Conservatives in office or join in any combination to keep Labour out. If a Labour Government were ever to be tried, Asquith declared, 'it could hardly be tried under safer conditions'. Asquith went on to add that, whoever might be in office, 'it is we, if we really understand our business, who really control the situation'.

The outcome was that when, on 21 January 1924, the Labour amendment to the Royal Address was put, it was carried by 328 votes to 256. Rumours of a large revolt by back-bench Liberals to maintain Baldwin in office failed to materialise. Only ten Liberals voted against the Labour amendment.

The following day, Baldwin tendered his resignation to the King. Shortly afterwards, following a meeting of the Privy Council, at which MacDonald was sworn a member, the King invited Ramsay MacDonald to form a government. The first Labour Government had arrived. With its advent, the Liberal Party was about to be launched on the disastrous course which culminated in the debacle of October 1924. The decision to install a Labour Government was both a vital and crucial decision for the Liberal Party. For such a decision to succeed, it was imperative for the Liberals, whilst the minority Labour Government remained in power, to achieve several targets. To begin with, strong leadership was essential. And this meant a complete healing of the Asquith–Lloyd George split, as opposed to the hurried coming-together that Baldwin's Tariff Election had brought about.

Secondly, it was imperative to use the coming months to develop constructive policy proposals – in social reform, industry, unemployment and foreign affairs – so that in any subsequent general election the Liberals could offer a distinctive, constructive and wide-ranging manifesto. Further, so that the party could fight on as broad a front as possible, derelict constituencies would have to be revived, candidates recruited and finance made available.

United and purposeful leadership was the prerequisite for new policies, revived organisation and sustained morale. It was essential if, in the changed order of British politics after the advent of Labour to office, the Liberals were to have a powerful and central position on the political stage. Although, nominally, the party was united, in reality it remained as divided as ever. The nearer one came to the centre of Liberal Power, the greater the divisions that were evident.

Nor, perhaps, was this so surprising. The reunion brought on by the Tariff Election had been both sudden and incomplete. During the election campaign, Lloyd George's Coalition Liberal headquarters were still operating, and were not finally disbanded until February 1924. Moreover, many Asquithians found it difficult to accept the return of the Prodigal Son with his hankerings after Coalitionism so recently buried. Indeed to a large extent, it was not so much personal animosity between Lloyd

George and Asquith (Lloyd George insisted he could get on well with 'the old man') which marred reunion, but the bitter distrust of Asquith's close colleagues such as Donald Maclean, Herbert Gladstone, and Vivian Phillipps – to say nothing of Margot.

However, the real cause of suspicion and distrust during 1924 centred much more on the realities of political power rather than on lingering personal animosities – although personalities exacerbated the problem. The root of the problem lay in the weakened position of Lloyd George and his supporters after the results of 1923 were known. During the campaign, Lloyd George had very much played 'second fiddle' to Asquith – not because he wanted to, but because there was no alternative. The results of 1923 had decimated the ranks of the former Coalition Liberals, leaving the balance of power within the new Liberal Party undeniably in Asquith's favour. Yet Lloyd George retained one asset of unrivalled value: his Fund. Virtually bankrupted by two successive general elections, the Independent Liberal organisation was desperate for funds. Without money, it simply could not wage a general election on a broad front. This fact Lloyd George knew only too well. It was the one card he had left to play.

However, more than simply an internal power game between Asquith and Lloyd George divided the two men in 1924. They were both divided (as was the party they led) on the tactics to be adopted towards Labour.

Asquith's position is easier to understand, because it remained more stable. Once Asquith had decided that Labour should be given its chance to govern, he seems to have hoped (with the condescension that so infuriated MacDonald) that before long it would make such a mess of affairs that MacDonald would resign, the King would send for Asquith and all would be right again with the world. In the meantime, the Liberals would support Labour, whilst repairing their own party machine.

Having decided on this general course, the early months of 1924 were characterised by a total lack of positive leadership by Asquith, whether in Parliament or the country. His attitude, once again, was that the best plan was to 'wait and see'. Before very long, his lack of leadership (made more noticeable by an illness in March) was producing widespread discontent within the Liberal ranks in the country.

Lloyd George, meanwhile, viewed the political scene very differently. In the very early days of December 1923 and January 1924 (if Lloyd George is to be believed, and if Scott's diary is a reliable testimony) Lloyd George hoped to see a period in which, in constructive partnership, the Labour Party, supported by the Liberals, would put a series of radical, reforming measures on the statute books. How long (given MacDonald's only too obviously hostile attitude) Lloyd George held to these views is unclear. By early February, however, other doubts had already begun to set in. The Abbey by-election (of March 1924) set Lloyd George's mind thinking in another direction: back to a revival of Coalition.

Thus, the summer of 1924 arrived with relations between the Liberal and Labour parties at an embittered level (see pp. 99) and with no sign of any coming together of Asquith and Lloyd George.

The consequences of this divided leadership in the party were made worse by the attitude of those below Asquith and Lloyd George who might, by positive and constructive leads, have helped fill the vacuum. None was to succeed. Churchill, defeated in West Leicester in December 1923, and bitterly hostile to the decision to install Labour, had already deserted the Liberals. By March, with the Abbey by-election in Westminster, the break was final. Guest was occupied in trying to organise a right-wing breakaway. Simon, who might have filled such a vacuum, was bent on a negative anti-Socialist campaign, whilst Maclean and Gladstone were too busy fighting Lloyd George.

This failure of leadership, together with bitter personal divisions in their ranks, tended to obscure a more fundamental weakness in the party: its whole fundamental philosophy.

Given the political situation after the 1923 general election, and the advent of a minority Labour Government, it was doubly important that the Liberal Party adopted a positive and constructive policy – and a distinctive one – that would set it aside from both Conservatives and Socialists in the eyes of the electorate. Without it, radical Liberals would increasingly feel that little separated them from moderate Labour, whilst the right-wing Liberals (to say nothing of those electors who had voted for Free Trade against Protection in 1923) would become increasingly tempted to rally to the Conservatives in the face of a Socialist (albeit moderate) Government.

The circumstances of the 1923 election – in particular the dominant role played by Free Trade in the campaign, had disguised the lack of distinctive policies held by the Liberals. Admittedly, Labour had attacked the Liberals on their lack of a social reform programme (and Conservatives had asked what Liberal policies would aid unemployment), but in general the campaign had been on favourable ground in 1923.

Now, all the factors in the equation had changed. The Conservatives – having buried Protection – were once again the party of the status quo. More than any other party, they could simply fight on a negative anti-Socialist policy. Labour had an equally straightforward task: Ramsay

MacDonald's dual aim was to show the respectability of his party and prove that it could govern.

For the Liberals, their first basic objective lay still in deciding where they stood in relation to the Labour Party. In addition, on the major topics of the day – on economic policy, social reform, on industry and nationalisation – Liberal policy was equally unclear or non-existent. This was particularly true of economic policy, although this is not to say that the Liberals lacked economic thinkers. Such figures as Ramsay Muir, Keynes and Beveridge all found a home in the Liberal ranks. But the fruition of their ideas did not come until later.

As the months of 1924 progressed, this double Liberal failing – of leadership and policy – was exposed in a variety of ways. It was seen in the chaotic indiscipline of the party in the lobbies at Westminster; it was to be seen also in the disintegrating morale and organisation of the party in the constituencies; and it was to be witnessed in the important series of by-elections that occurred during the first Labour Government.

The total lack of unity in the Liberal ranks at Westminster rapidly degenerated towards a situation of farce. One section of the parliamentary party would support the Government; another section, often including Asquith and Lloyd George, would abstain; yet another group would consistently vote with the Conservatives.

Thus, a Conservative motion protesting against the Labour decision to discontinue the Singapore naval base, was defeated by 287 votes to 211 on 25 March. In the division, 118 Liberals voted with Labour, nine more paired, nine voted for the Conservative amendment while the rest abstained. A similar three-way split, with both Asquith and Lloyd George abstaining, occurred on the second reading of the Eviction Bill early in April. In this division, Labour was defeated by 221 votes to 212.

Against this background, morale in the constituencies rapidly began to decline. This was doubly ironic, for in several areas, most especially in the regions of Liberal revival in 1923 such as the Home Counties, East Anglia and the agricultural Midlands, Liberal Party organisation responded well to the stimulus of 1923.[5]

However, as 1924 progressed, even in such former strongholds as Wales, Scotland and the industrial North, the Liberals made little or no attempt either to adopt candidates, distribute propaganda, or improve organisation. Thus, in South Wales, as late as September 1924, the Liberals were without a single prospective candidate in Cardiff, Swansea, Newport and Merthyr. In industrial Scotland, the position was even worse. On the eve of the 1924 election, only one prospective Liberal candidate was in the field in Glasgow compared to 13 Conservatives.

Meanwhile, to add to the difficulties of the hard-pressed Liberal Party was the attack by Labour in the constituencies on sitting Liberal MPs, whether radical or not. As early as April 1924, Vivian Phillipps was bitterly complaining that, despite Liberal help at Westminster, Labour's only response was to attack in the constituencies.

The net result of all these factors was a rapid disintegration of Liberal morale. Dreary reports came in of former Liberal candidates defecting to the Conservatives and of a general collapse of confidence.

Against this background, it was hardly surprising that the Liberals found themselves in a series of disastrous by-elections. Although only nine contested by-elections occurred during the lifetime of the first Labour Government, they provided clear evidence of the decline in Liberal fortunes. The Liberals not only lost their Oxford seat in June, but polled dismally in such constituencies as Kelvingrove and Westminster (Abbey).[6] The writing was already on the wall, and such Liberals as Lloyd George realised the party's plight. Indeed, in July, the rejection by Labour of any possibility of electoral reform decided Lloyd George that a showdown with MacDonald must now come. According to Scott, Lloyd George determined to force the issue over the question of unemployment. Lloyd George reasoned that, with Ramsay MacDonald personally closely involved at a delicate diplomatic juncture, he would not dare risk dissolution. However, Asquith and the other Liberal hierarchy refused to take the risk. The opportunity passed, with the Liberal Party more helpless than ever before.[7]

This disagreement in July between Asquith and Lloyd George was only one example of a far more fundamental difference between the two. The reunion in November 1923 had been, in many ways, a reunion in name only. Suspicion had remained, most particularly with such old Asquithians as Herbert Gladstone and Donald Maclean. Lloyd George, for his part, was determined to hold on to the one very tangible asset he possessed – the money in his Fund. This factor was crucial to Liberal fortunes, for with the Independent Liberals almost without resources after fighting two elections within two years the party was desperately short of finance. This factor, more than anything else, prevented the party rebuilding its organisation and adopting candidates. Throughout 1924, protracted negotiations took place to settle the financial question. But by the summer, despite repeated contacts, nothing had been achieved.[8]

By then, however, the political scene was also significantly changing, for an issue had arisen which was to end the life of the minority Labour Government: the question of relations with Soviet Russia. The issue of the Russian Treaty, however, was one on which Liberals again found themselves as divided as on most others – divisions reflected in the *Daily News* (sympathetic to MacDonald) and the *Daily Chronicle* (very much opposed to the Treaty, in line with Lloyd George's attitude). Lloyd George's antipathy to the treaty probably reflected the majority view of the party. Whilst a radical element, that included J.M. Kenworthy and J.M. Hogge, gave support to the treaty, most of the left-wing Liberals lined up with the right.[9]

The clamour against the treaty, led by Lloyd George, rapidly gained the support of Simon, Runciman, Grey, Mond, Maclean and C.F. Masterman. Possibly the Carmarthen by-election of 15 August also encouraged the Liberals to take a firmer line. On 3 September, the Liberal Party publication department produced a pamphlet entitled 'A Sham Treaty'. On 8 September, the *Daily Chronicle* followed up the attack with a series of articles entitled 'In Darkest Russia'.

Much, however, would depend in the last resort on Asquith's attitude. Asquith, who was ill at the time, gradually moved over towards the Lloyd George position. When Lloyd George saw Asquith early in September, he found him 'quite firm' in opposing the Treaty.[10] In a letter to *The Times* on 22 September, Asquith attacked the Russian Treaties as 'crude experiments in nursery diplomacy' and urged Parliament not to accept 'a loan of undefined amount, upon unspecified conditions'. However, at the same time, Asquith seemed to be urging the Liberals not to reject the Treaties totally but to amend them.

MacDonald, however, was determined to have no deal with the Liberals. At Derby, on 27 September, he left no doubt that he would fight an election rather than abandon his position. Four days later, as Parliament reassembled on 1 October, the Parliamentary Liberal Party supported a hard line. With only a handful of dissenters, the meeting passed a motion rejecting the idea of a guaranteed loan. It was notice on the Labour Government to quit.

Yet the Liberals were in an invidious position. If they stuck to their guns, a Labour defeat was inevitable. Yet was the issue of the Russian Treaty good ground on which to do battle? Kenworthy had warned the party meeting on 1 October that an election on this issue would be a disaster, a viewpoint shared by the *Manchester Guardian*.

The Russian Treaty had another tactical disadvantage for the Liberals. They occupied a dangerous middle ground; for whatever the party might think of a guaranteed loan, there was a considerable desire to improve relations with Russia.

The Liberals were, in fact, caught in their own trap. They could not compromise with Labour, because Labour would not compromise. They had to face an election, or abandon their posture that they were keeping Labour to a safe moderate course.

In fact, at this eleventh hour, the Liberal dilemma was unexpectedly resolved, for Labour chose to accept defeat, not on the issue of the Russian Treaties, but over the Campbell Case.

On 1 October, at the same meeting at which the Parliamentary Liberal Party decided to oppose the Russian Treaties, Asquith stated that his party would support a 'reasonable motion' on the Campbell affair. On 2 October, the Liberals put down an amendment to the Conservative motion of censure, calling for the establishment of a Select Committee to inquire into the matter. The fate of the Labour Government was effectively sealed when, at the end of the Campbell debate on 8 October, Baldwin announced that the Conservatives would vote for the Liberal amendment and not for their own motion. The Liberal amendment was subsequently carried by 364 votes to 199. Fourteen Liberals on the left wing of the party voted against the amendment proposed by their own party. They included Hogge, Kenworthy, Percy Harris and Jowitt.

After the defeat of the MacDonald Government on the Campbell Case, events moved swiftly. Parliament was dissolved on 9 October. The election itself was fixed for Wednesday 29 October. It was an horrific prospect for the Liberal Party, even though an event which they themselves had precipitated. For the advent of the general election in October 1924 found the Liberal Party totally and completely unprepared for the battle. At the dissolution, the party had only 280 candidates ready, whereas senior Liberals believed that 450 was the minimum necessary to wage an effective campaign.

The reason for this limited field of candidates was to be found in Lloyd George's unwillingness to provide money from his Fund. Eventually, with the election upon the party, Lloyd George agreed to contribute £50,000 – a hopelessly inadequate sum.

This financial handicap, however, was only one factor causing the massive reduction in Liberal candidates. In 1924, there was simply no will at constituency level to fight, even in constituencies where Liberals were within striking distance of victory.

Even more significant in reducing the numbers of Liberal candidates fielded was the arrangement of local anti-Socialist pacts by Liberals at constituency level. This, as much as any other factor, helped set the seal on the Liberal fate in the election.[11]

The overall result of Liberal lack of money, pacts with the Conservatives, a general disinclination to fight and problems in finding candidates was tremendous. The Liberals abandoned 136 seats fought in 1923 – no less than 96 in former three-cornered contests (55 in Conservative-held seats). At the close of nominations, whereas Labour fielded 514 candidates, an increase of 87 over December 1923, the Liberal total had slumped from 457 to 340.

The disastrous effect of fielding only 340 candidates was further compounded by an equally abysmal campaign. The Liberal election manifesto offered little new. Free Trade still figured prominently, whilst most other proposals could be found, in greater or lesser degree, in the Conservative and Labour manifestos. In the emotional and bitter campaign atmosphere of October 1924, the Liberals' lack of any real or distinctive Liberal policy was a calamity. Essentially, the 1924 election campaign was fought on three issues: Russia; the need for stable government; and the record of Labour in office, particularly in respect of housing and unemployment. All three were topics on which the Liberals had nothing to contribute. Or rather, the Liberals said nothing not being said already by Labour and Conservative. In the circumstances of 1924, Labour could thus launch a major attack on the Liberals – both for their lack of policy and their alliance with Conservatism.

Few Liberals had expected the party to fare well in the circumstances of October 1924. Few, however, envisaged quite the total annihilation that the party would suffer. The outcome of the election of October 1924 returned the Conservatives to power with 412 seats (46.8 per cent of the votes cast), Labour emerged with 151 seats (33.3 per cent of the total votes) and the Liberals with a mere 40 seats (17.8 per cent).

There were hardly any comforting factors for the party. Liberals lost no less than 105 seats to the Conservatives, who swept back to victory in the rural and middle-class constituencies lost in 1923. Virtually no area of the country escaped: in the English counties, the Liberals lost all but four of the 67 seats they were defending. In the South East, Greater London and East Anglia not a single seat the Liberals were defending was retained. In South Wales, the only seat to return a Liberal was in Swansea West. In Scotland, although the Highland Liberal strongholds remained faithful (perhaps because three of the five seats here were uncontested), outside this Celtic fringe not a single other county constituency returned a Liberal.

If the counties had deserted the Liberals, even worse was the almost total annihilation of the party in the boroughs. In the 139 constituencies in the 11 largest cities, the Liberals had elected only six members, while only Percy Harris, in South West Bethnal Green, had faced Conservative opposition. Throughout the country, only seven Liberals managed to secure election in three-cornered contests. Even these only survived by the narrowest of margins: Lambeth North had a majority of only 29 and

Bethnal Green South West a majority of 212. Only a single Liberal took over 50 per cent of the poll in a three-cornered contest.

Of the 40 Liberals who survived the massacre, only perhaps 15 could be said to have won their seats unaided by Conservative or Labour votes. Of these, seven were in Wales and four in Scotland. To those Liberals who had voted with Labour over the Campbell affair, there could seem little justice in politics, for only two survived the election.

The size of the Liberal debacle could not simply be measured in terms of seats lost. In many cases, sitting Liberal MPs found themselves suddenly at the foot of the poll. No less than 31 Liberal candidates defending Liberal-held seats finished third. They included such figures as W.R.M. Pringle (in Penistone) and Hogge in Edinburgh. In 26 seats the Liberal share of the vote fell by over 15 per cent. To make matters even worse, of the five unopposed Liberal seats in 1923 which were contested in 1924, only one was retained (at Wolverhampton East).

Hardly any Liberal leaders (except Lloyd George, Mond and Simon) escaped the massacre. Asquith lost his seat, and his fate was shared by Macnamara, W.R.M. Pringle, George Lambert (who had represented South Molton since 1891), Leif Jones, Geoffrey Howard and Isaac Foot.

In the wake of such an electoral disaster, the old historic Liberal party was finished. After the false dawn of 1923, the election of October 1924 had consigned the Liberal Party to virtual destruction.

What future was there for the Liberals? During the period from November 1924 to October 1926, the last phase when Asquith was leader of the party, the future looked bleak indeed. The old problems remained for the party – of finance, candidates, organisation and morale. For Asquith (now removed to the Upper House as Lord Oxford) the election results added a new problem. In 1923, the election returns had decimated the former Coalition Liberals and greatly increased the numbers of Asquith's followers. During 1924, the Parliamentary Liberal Party was overwhelmingly Asquithian. After October 1924, over half of the small band of Liberals were former Coalition Liberal MPs or candidates.

On 2 December Lloyd George secured his own election as Chairman of the Parliamentary Liberal Party, by 26 votes to seven, with seven abstentions. Meanwhile, a group of nine MPs who refused to acknowledge Lloyd George formed themselves into a 'Radical Group' under Runciman. Only weeks after a disastrous election, the Liberals were again an openly divided party. Not only was the party quite clearly deeply divided, it was more than apparent that, unless urgent action was taken, its grassroots organisation would simply collapse.

Hence, immediately after the election, Asquith's first act was to appoint Maclean as head of a committee to find out what was wrong with the Liberal Party – the first of many such inquests – and an attempt was made to put the finances of the party in order

It was not long before the attempt to restore the finances of the party (through the 'Million Fund' launched at a major Liberal Convention in January 1925) had also begun to collapse. By the end of 1925 the idea of restoring Liberal finances through an appeal to the ordinary supporter had foundered.[12]

At the same time, organisation was collapsing further as agents left and money was not forthcoming. As Lloyd George bitterly observed, whatever the decay of agriculture might have been, it was nothing to that which had fallen upon the Liberal organisations in a very large number of constituencies throughout the country.[13] Candidates were equally unobtainable.

Even in by-elections the tide went against the Liberals. In March 1926 the party lost a seat in the Combined English Universities to the Conservatives. The worst humiliation came on 29 November 1926 when Kenworthy, the Liberal MP for Hull Central, defected to Labour. In the ensuing by-election, Kenworthy was re-elected with 52.9 per cent of the poll, the Liberal taking a mere 9.5 per cent.

Meanwhile, relations between Asquith and Lloyd George deteriorated even further during 1925 and the first part of 1926. The perennial question of Lloyd George's contribution to the finances of the party continued to plague relations (most especially with the failure of the Million Fund). Lloyd George's radical plans for land and unemployment (see p. 106) further alienated Asquith – who was largely unconsulted about them. It only needed one more crisis to bring about the final rupture between Asquith and Lloyd George. It was to occur in May 1926 with the General Strike.

9
Lloyd George Again: 1926–1931

As with most other events, the advent of the General Strike exposed a further series of divisions in the Liberal ranks. Although there was much sympathy with the miners among many Liberals, the party recognised that the Strike was in effect directly challenging the Government. It was a challenge that few Liberals could support. The outstanding exception was Lloyd George.

The Liberal Shadow Cabinet made clear its position at the outset: all the resources of the Government should be used to achieve victory over the strike. As if to reinforce Liberal opinion that the strike must be crushed, Simon warned the trade union leaders that they stood liable at law to damages 'to the uttermost farthing' of their possessions – a highly dubious assertion. But whilst Simon was saying exactly the words that made music in Conservative ears, Lloyd George was adopting a more radical position.

He wrote to Sir Godfrey Collins (the Liberal Chief Whip) declining to attend the Liberal Shadow Cabinet meeting fixed for 10 May. Lloyd George declared that he would not join in denouncing the strike unless the Government's handling of the situation and its refusal to negotiate were also denounced. Although Asquith seemed at first to react calmly, on 20 May he took issue with Lloyd George, denouncing him roundly to the delight of his followers.

The uneasy shadow war between the two antagonists was over: their last battle was under way. But it was a battle in which Asquith was to emerge the loser. A most acrimonious exchange of letters and views took place. On 1 June, 12 Shadow Cabinet Liberals wrote to Asquith, supporting his stand against Lloyd George. Its bitter language marked a new degree of acrimony in a struggle never lacking in vitriol.

Though Lloyd George had secured his position as Chairman by 26 votes to seven, it was unclear that he would win so easily if a vote of confidence was required. But, having assured his right-wing supporters that he had no intention of allying with Labour, Lloyd George won by 20 votes to ten. At this moment, Asquith suffered a stroke on 12 June, keeping him out of politics for three months. Five days later, the annual meeting of the National Liberal Federation began at Weston-super-Mare. Though recriminations were kept out, and a virtually unanimous resolution of support for Asquith was carried, these events were only shadow politics. In October, Asquith resigned the Leadership. He died on 15 February 1928.

In the circumstances of October 1926, the Liberals had to look to Lloyd George. Without him, the party was both leaderless and penniless. Knowing the strength of his position, now Asquith was removed from politics, Lloyd George laid down his terms. His price was nothing less than full control of the party machine, together with the departure or retirement of those Asquithians he so disliked. Lloyd George's offer of massive financial aid to the party meant the end for Phillipps, Gladstone and Hudson.[1]

Lloyd George was intent on a new broom. In place of the departed Asquithians, a new appointment of great importance for the future history of the party was made. The new head of the party organisation was Sir Herbert Samuel. It was an inspired choice, for Samuel was one of the few Liberals acceptable to all sections of the party, since during the bitter internal quarrels in the party he had been High Commissioner in Palestine.

The choice of Samuel to head the party machine was the first step towards revival. But Lloyd George's greatest contribution was in the field of policy. During 1925, with Asquith still leader of the party, Lloyd George had poured money and resources into devising and producing new Liberal policies – even though few Liberals except Lloyd George and his associates took much part in their formulation.

The first of the new policies – the land scheme – had already been published in October 1925. It had been greeted with mixed feelings. The report of the 'Land Inquiry Committee', published in book form as *Land and the Nation*, but popularly known as the Green Book, aroused criticism, both of its contents and of the way in which it appeared.[2]

Further opposition, from candidates and Liberal Associations, flared when it was announced that Lloyd George had founded a new organisation, the Land and Nation League, to campaign for the implementation of the Green Book. Despite opposition to both his methods and his proposals, Lloyd George had carried on regardless. His next major contribution was in the field of unemployment, where a 'Liberal Industrial Inquiry' had been set up in 1925. A remarkable team of politicians and economists, including E.D. Simon, W.T. Layton, J.M. Keynes, Ramsay Muir, Herbert Samuel, Philip Kerr, Hubert Henderson and Lloyd George himself, had collaborated in this project. The fruit of their work was published as the first 'Yellow Book', *Britain's Industrial Future*, in February 1928. As Robert Skidelsky comments, the far-reaching proposals for government planning which it advocated were well in advance of anything else in existence at the time.[3]

Following the publication of the 'Yellow Book', a special committee headed by Lloyd George, Lord Lothian and Seebohm Rowntree was established to work out in detail the various schemes of national development. Its report, issued in March 1929 as *We Can Conquer Unemployment* provided the basis of the Liberal campaign in the 1929 general election.

The emergency programme outlined in *We Can Conquer Unemployment* gave priority to road-building. A programme of roads, costing £145 million and employing 350,000 men for two years was envisaged. Housing was also given particular attention. In all, the programme constituted one of the boldest and most imaginative schemes yet put forward.

These sweeping policy proposals demonstrated that, once again, the return of Lloyd George, with his energy and dynamism, had brought a new sense of purpose to the party. And indeed, within six months of his return it seemed that at long last a real recovery was at hand. On 28 March 1927 the Liberals gained Southwark North from Labour. A series of by-election victories followed: Bosworth was won on 31 May 1927, Lancaster fell on 9 February 1928 and St Ives a month later. On 20 March 1929 Eddisbury fell to the Liberals, and the following day Holland-with-Boston was also gained. All these gains were from Conservatives and, with the partial exception of Bosworth, were in rural, agricultural areas. Had the Liberals been able to follow up their initial victories in Southwark North and Bosworth with a gain in the Westbury by-election of June 1927 (which the Conservatives retained by a mere 149 votes), the revival might have gathered even further momentum.

As it was, in the spring of 1928 optimism ran very high. Lord Rothermere wrote to Lloyd George on 10 April 1928: 'You are back to where the Liberal Party was at the election of 1923. ...In my opinion, an election today would give you just about the same number of followers.' Rothermere went on: 'Continue as you are doing and I think you and I will agree... that there is almost a certainty that the Liberals will be the second party in the next House. This would give you the Premiership beyond any question.' While Rothermere's political judgement does not have to be taken too seriously, nonetheless the Liberals were doing undeniably well, as Table 9.1 indicates.[4]

Table 9.1

	No.	Average Con. %	Lab. %	Lib. %
May 1926–end 1927	10	37.9	33.6	28.5
Jan.–Dec. 1928	15	39.8	30.5	29.7
1929–Gen. Elec.	5	33.6	44.6	21.8

However, even at the height of Liberal success in 1928, Lloyd George himself realised that Liberal by-election victories would not necessarily mean gains at a general election. He wrote to Garvin of the *Observer* in October 1928: 'I have followed your analysis of the by-election figures. I am convinced that "the triangle" will enable Labour to sweep the industrial constituencies next time.' Lloyd George had written in similar vein to Philip Snowden: '...owing to the fact that Liberal and Labour candidates are fighting each other, there are 170 seats which will go to the Conservatives which in straight fights would have been either Labour or Liberal.' Lloyd George's judgement was nearer the mark.

Labour was, indeed, the Achilles heel of the Liberal Party. Although the Liberals succeeded in winning a series of rural seats from the Conservatives, Labour was continuing to be the main beneficiary of the Government's unpopularity – capturing no less than 12 Conservative-held seats between 1924 and 1929.

Despite the strength of Labour, however, the coming of the 1929 election found the Liberals more confident and in better shape than for very many years. Armed with Lloyd George's sweeping proposals on unemployment, and with party organisation, as a result of Samuel's work, in a healthier state than at any time since before 1914, the Liberals entered the 1929 election making their last great effort of the inter-war period for power. As Trevor Wilson has written of the Liberal appeal in 1929,

> ...It is unlikely that the British electorate has ever been paid the compliment of a more far-sighted and responsible party programme.[5]

Although the Liberals entered the 1929 election in confident mood, pouring out a mass of literature and propaganda, and although they fielded 513 candidates well supplied by the Lloyd George Fund, there were doubts on how well the party would really do. As Douglas has written,

there were strange signs of doubting, even in the moment of battle.[6]
With three-cornered contests in most constituencies, Liberals anxiously
awaited the result as the nation polled on 30 May 1929.

The outcome of the general election was to prove a bitter disappointment for the Liberal Party. It was, as the *Liberal Magazine* sadly
admitted, 'a lost battle in view of our hopes and aims'.[7] The result is
shown in Table 9.2.

Table 9.2

	Votes	%	Cands	MPs
Conservative	8,656,225	38.1	590	260
Liberal	5,308,738	23.6	513	59
Labour	8,370,417	37.1	569	287
Others	312,995	1.2	58	9
Total	22,648,375	100.0	1,730	615

Labour, for the first time in its history, had become the largest single
party, but still without an overall majority. The Liberals finished with
59 seats. Although they had polled 5,308,738 votes (23.6 per cent of the
total) they had won only 35 seats not captured in 1924 and lost 19. Of
these 19 losses, 17 were to Labour. These figures demonstrated only too
clearly Liberal inability to recapture industrial seats – indeed, the party
lost further ground to Labour in the North East, Yorkshire, Lancashire
and the East End of London.

Virtually all of the 35 Liberal victories came in rural areas, including
some such as Ashford, with no vestige of a Liberal tradition,[8] but mainly
in the traditional areas of Liberal support – rural Scotland and Wales
(where seven seats were captured), East Anglia (nine Liberal gains) and
Cornwall (five Liberal gains). Apart from these traditional areas, no other
part of the country returned a solid phalanx of Liberal MPs.

However, although 1929 was a battle lost in terms of seats won, in
terms of votes cast the Liberals had achieved a remarkable result. In the
513 seats contested by Liberals, the party obtained 28 per cent of the
votes cast. No less than 310 candidates (64 per cent of the total) polled
between 14 per cent and 34 per cent of the votes – clear evidence of a
more even spread of the Liberal vote throughout the country. In contrast,
only 15 Liberals obtained more than 50 per cent of the total votes cast
in their constituencies.

The best Liberal performance came, as we have seen, in the areas where
the party was traditionally strong. The Liberals fared worst in Glasgow

and Birmingham. Although not capturing any of Labour's strongholds in the mining areas, the Liberals polled well in the valleys of South Wales, coming second to Labour in Aberavon, Caerphilly, Gower, Neath, Ogmore and Pontypridd.

In the 103 constituencies which all three major parties contested in 1924 and 1929 the Liberal share of the poll increased from 24.8 per cent to 29.0 per cent. Yet, whichever way the Liberals argued, either in terms of seats or votes, they had lost the election. No change in the voting system would have given them a majority. They were now destined to the position of a third party, holding the uncomfortable middle ground in the politics of the second Labour Government. The high hopes engendered by the revival under Lloyd George had suffered a bitter disillusion.

The years between the formation of the second Labour Government in May 1929 and the general election of 1935 saw a transformation in British politics. The financial crash of 1931, the break-up of the Labour Government and the subsequent National Government all presented new problems and possibilities for the Liberals. During this period the Liberals experienced further dissension and serious decline, even though enjoying a taste of office that had not been theirs for a decade. By 1935, the Liberals had been reduced to the unimportant sidelines of British politics.

This disastrous period for the Liberals opened, as it had in January 1924, with the party once more supporting a minority Labour Government. Unlike 1924, however, Liberals did not need to give constant support to Labour in the division lobbies, since the government could survive even if Liberals abstained. This refinement, however, was of little consolation for the Liberals. They had fought for victory in 1929. The modest advance that had been achieved in fact only served to disguise a major disaster. The party had thrown everything into the battle. Its reserves of energy and purpose were gone. Leading Liberals were not long in recognising this. Hardly had the dust of the electoral battle settled before defections from the party began. William Jowitt (Liberal Member for Preston) accepted the post of Attorney-General in the Labour Government. Others, such as F.E. Guest, at last formally joined the Conservative Party.

For those who remained within the party, in Parliament and in the constituencies, the outlook was one of gloom. The most immediate problem facing the party organisation was finance. The 1927 agreement expired automatically three months after the election. Despite attempts by the Administrative Committee, Lloyd George obstinately refused to finance the party any longer. Eventually, under pressure, financial assistance continued until June 1930. Nothing was forthcoming after that date.

The consequence was not long delayed. Headquarters grants to the Federations ceased entirely. The Eastern Counties Federation reluctantly dismissed its last full-time officials. It was typical of other District Federations. Worse still, the party was forced to let by-elections go uncontested. In only a tiny number of the by-elections from 1929 to 1931 were Liberals brought forward. All fared disastrously. In the constituencies, candidates were simply not being adopted. Ramsay Muir estimated that at least £250,000 was required for improving organisation and supporting candidates.

Not surprisingly, Lloyd George's refusal to contribute further brought a renewal of bitter attacks. Old Asquithians, such as Vivian Phillipps, bitterly attacked the Fund as against the 'best traditions of our public life'. Less heated but quite definite attacks came from the *Manchester Guardian* and the *Daily News*.

It was against this background that the Parliamentary Liberal Party faced the position of once again holding the balance of power – a position with an unhappy precedent in 1924.

In 1929, the position was rather different. Baldwin had resigned straight after the election, so there was no question of the Liberals putting Labour into office. The first preoccupation of the Liberals, remembering their experience in 1924, was to present a united front. This feeling was strongly put forward at the first party meeting after the election in June 1929. Despite good intentions, this party unity lasted only a few months, destroyed by the basic and unanswered question – what should be the Liberal policy towards the Labour Government?

The publication of the Coal Bill in December 1929 brought this problem to a head. For whilst Liberals sympathised with many objectives of the Bill, in their view the many problems of the coal industry could be saved only by an imaginative policy imposed from above, including the amalgamation of pits into economic units. The Labour measure involved nothing so drastic. Liberals particularly objected to the Bill's proposed 'quota system' which would have tended to bolster inefficient pits. Despite attempts by William Graham, the President of the Board of Trade, to conciliate the Liberals, Lloyd George led the Liberal Party in voting against the second reading.

The result was the first of many Liberal splits. Two Liberals (Geoffrey Mander and Sir William Edge) voted with the Labour Government. Six others remained deliberately seated in the Commons. The outcome was a Labour majority of eight on 19 December. Two months later, in February 1930, on a crucial amendment to the Bill, four Liberals voted with the Government, whilst eight more abstained. On each occasion, three prominent Liberals helping to save the Coal Bill were Runciman, Maclean and Leif Jones, all on the 'right' of the party and Liberal Council members. As in 1924, an incipient 'three-way split' was developing in the Liberal ranks at Westminster. The Chief Whip, Sir Robert Hutchinson, subsequently tendered his resignation. Although this was refused, the damage had already been done. Meanwhile, the Labour Party's inactivity on the unemployment front was being attacked by the Liberals. At the annual conference of the party in October 1929, Samuel attacked Thomas for having failed to rise to the level of the task ahead of him. More rudely, referring to Thomas's six-week trip to Canada, Sir Charles Hobhouse gibed that the government was rapidly becoming a subsidiary of Cook's Tourist Agency. In March 1930, Lloyd George had been widely expected to launch a major attack on the Government's handling of the unemployment question. The Liberal fiasco on the Coal Bill, however, initiated a dramatic change of policy on the part of Lloyd George. From March 1930 onwards Lloyd George adopted the policy of granting the Government general Liberal support – in particular in the two important areas of agriculture and unemployment. But Lloyd George's policy of Liberal–Labour cooperation had already been overtaken by events beyond his control.

During 1930, the unemployment question took a critical turn for the worse. So serious, in fact, that on 18 June MacDonald declared that the unemployment issue required the assistance and cooperation of all the parties. Although the Conservatives refused any cooperation, Lloyd George pledged that the Liberals would give assistance. A friendly, if unproductive, series of discussions then took place between Lloyd George, Lord Lothian, Seebohm Rowntree and the Labour leaders. These friendly discussions turned, on 18 September, to the wider question of future relations between Liberal and Labour. Lloyd George, making no secret of the fact that he would prefer to see a period of cooperation with Labour, made it clear that in return for such support Liberals would need the promise of electoral reform.

Such a dialogue between Lloyd George and the Labour Government was taking the party towards trouble. The rifts within the Liberal ranks over the degree of cooperation that should be extended to Labour were already wide. In November 1930, they cracked.

The occasion was precipitated by the outcome of a vote on 3–4 November on a Conservative motion on the King's Speech. Despite the official Liberal instruction to abstain, five Liberals supported the Conservative amendment and four voted with the Labour Government. Among those voting with the Conservatives was the Liberal Chief Whip,

Sir Robert Hutchinson. He subsequently resigned, and was replaced by Sir Archibald Sinclair.

At the same time as Hutchinson resigned, a further calamity hit the party. Sir John Simon, who had warned Lloyd George late in October that he could not support Labour on a vote of confidence, made public his letter in the press. The Liberals were at war with one another once again. Simon, by declaring that he wished to ally with the Conservatives to bring down the Labour Government at the earliest opportunity, had effectively destroyed the unity and credibility of the party. As Roy Douglas has written: 'It was no longer a question of isolated rebels opposing Lloyd George on isolated measures; rather Simon had publicly declared war on Lloyd George's whole policy towards the Labour Government.'

Simon, whatever many Liberals thought of his action, was in many ways only telling the unpalatable truth: namely, that the Liberals were only maintaining a Labour Government for fear of the electoral consequences. Meanwhile, the fortunes of the Liberal Party went from bad to worse. In March 1931 Sir Archibald Sinclair (Hutchinson's successor as Chief Whip) resigned after a particularly hopeless example of Liberal cross-voting. The outcome of the crisis was a party meeting to lay down future policy. This meeting passed a weak resolution affirming the independence of the party, outlining the principles of Liberal policy and agreeing to support this or any government which would help put this policy into effect.

Even this tepid resolution failed to produce a united front. Only 33 voted for the motion, with 17 against. Of these, seven were Simonites, the rest, led by Ernest Brown, argued against the Liberals providing even 'general' support to the Labour Government.

The net result of this division and disunity, together with the growing support for Protection in the country, left the Liberal Party in a parlous condition in mid-1931. To add to its difficulties, the Liberal Press was becoming a rapidly depleted force. Two important dailies, the *Westminster Gazette* and the *Daily Chronicle* both passed out of existence.

On the electoral front, the Liberal by-election record proved equally dispiriting. In the first contests after the 1929 general election, the Liberal vote was uniformly so, with particularly poor results at Twickenham (August 1929) Nottingham Central (May 1930) and Bromley (September 1930). Although the party did well at Shipley (November 1930) and Whitechapel (December 1930), during 1931 the outlook grew bleaker. In every contested by-election (except for Scarborough, where no Labour candidate stood) the Liberal share of the poll had fallen, in many cases disastrously. Other seats simply went uncontested. To complete the misery being heaped on the party, Simon's breakaway came to a head when he, together with Ernest Brown and Hutchinson, resigned the Liberal whip on 26 June 1931, thus provoking a fresh crisis in the party. A month later, on 27 July, just before Parliament rose for the summer recess, another blow hit the party: Lloyd George became very seriously ill. The effective management of the party passed to Sir Herbert Samuel, the Deputy Leader of the Parliamentary Liberal Party. With Lloyd George out of action, the party split, taunts from the Conservatives, and persistent humiliation at the hands of Labour, the Liberal Party faced a bleak future when Parliament adjourned on 31 July 1931.

This situation was transformed in August 1931 when the Labour Government collapsed. On 23 August, MacDonald went to see the King. The King subsequently saw both Samuel, who supported the case for a National Government, and Baldwin, who also argued a similar case. On Monday 24 August, after the resignation of the Labour Cabinet, MacDonald became Prime Minister of a new National Government. Samuel, after consulting Lloyd George (who was still seriously ill) suggested various Liberal names to serve in the new Government. In the event, the new Cabinet included four Labour Ministers, four Conservative and two Liberal. Sir Herbert Samuel became Home Secretary; and the Marquis of Reading Foreign Secretary. Other senior Liberals to take office included Sir Donald Maclean (President of the Board of Education), Sir Archibald Sinclair (Secretary of State for Scotland) and the Marquis of Crewe (Secretary for War).

Not surprisingly, a meeting of Liberal MPs, peers and candidates gave warm support to the decision to enter the National Government. The decision was similarly widely approved at constituency level, with the Liberals showing a rare degree of unanimity.

The reason was clear to see. MacDonald, though splitting his own party, offered a way of salvation for the Liberals. The hard-pressed party had been offered an alternative to the election they so feared which gave them the chance to cooperate with a government and, indeed, to take office in it.

It was only later that the trap into which the Liberals had fallen was revealed. The Conservatives had welcomed the National Government in that it meant the end of a Labour government, but they were also determined to have an election. Pressure to this end mounted during September, despite dogged Liberal resistance.

On 23 September, a meeting of Liberal MPs instructed Samuel to convey to MacDonald their determined opposition to a general election. The Liberals, however, had no effective way of preventing an election. MacDonald, with only the support of a tiny breakaway Labour group, himself could provide no barrier to add to the Liberal argument. The Simonites, secure in the knowledge that they would not face Conservative opposition, were not slow to discomfort Samuel by agreeing with the Conservative clamour for an election.

On 4 October, Samuel saw Lloyd George, who argued vehemently against an early election. On the evening of 5 October, despite the opposition of Samuel and Reading, the Cabinet decided on an appeal to the country. On 6 October, MacDonald formally saw the King. Polling day was fixed for 27 October.

Despite their opposition to an election, neither Samuel nor Reading resigned from the Government. Meanwhile Lloyd George fumed at the decision that had been taken; and two of his family resigned junior posts in the Government. The Liberal decision to fight the election as part of the Coalition did not only alienate Lloyd George. The Conservatives were far from pleased fighting alongside a party they were hoping to discredit. Not surprisingly, Liberal–Conservative relations became considerably strained during the campaign.

The Liberals, in fact, entered the 1931 election in a hopeless position. With Lloyd George hostile to the election, no funds were forthcoming from his Fund. In consequence, only a mere 112 candidates were fielded by the Samuelites, leaving many of the promising seats fought in 1929 uncontested. Money, however, was not the only factor. Few Liberals in 1931 evinced much fighting spirit. The will to win had vanished. For, in everything but name, the Liberals fought the election as prisoners of a Conservative-dominated Coalition.

The Liberals thus entered the 1931 election with few illusions on the likely result. As Ramsay Muir admitted, the dice were loaded against the party. On every side, the prospects for the party were bleak. The Liberals had simply no independent policy to put forward – except support for National candidates who were in most cases Protectionist. Meanwhile, the fact that the Liberals supported the National Government, and were represented in it, did not stop Conservatives attacking sitting Liberals. Although Samuel himself was supported by Baldwin, no less than five Liberal Ministers were opposed by Conservatives, whereas all 30 Conservative Ministers were unopposed by Liberals. No less than 81 clashes took place between Samuelite Liberals and Conservatives.

By way of contrast, the Simon Liberals enjoyed a much happier position. Not only, by and large, were their constituencies more safely Liberal, but by agreeing to support the Government's tariff proposals, they enjoyed far more Conservative goodwill. No less than 35 of the 54 Conservative candidates withdrawn in 1931 were to support Liberal Nationals (as the Simonite Liberals became known). Only one solitary straight fight occurred between a Conservative and a Liberal National, whereas 26 occurred between Conservatives and Samuelite Liberals, and only four constituencies saw a clash of Simonite and Conservative candidates.[9] Thus although the Simonite Liberals fielded only 41 candidates, their electoral prospects were immeasurably brighter. With Lloyd George opposed to Samuel's policy, and encouraging Liberals to vote Labour in the absence of Liberal candidates, the hapless Liberal Party entered the election attempting to travel in three directions simultaneously. The Simonites had adopted a semi-Conservative position, the Samuelite official party adopted a non-Conservative, anti-Labour stance and finally there was Lloyd George's attempt to revive a Liberal–Labour alliance.

In the circumstances of 1931, a victory for the National Government was almost inevitable. The Conservatives were returned with no less than 473 seats, Labour secured only 52 while the Liberals returned 72. Of these 72 Liberals, 35 were Liberal Nationals, 33 were followers of Samuel and there were the four Independent Liberals, all members of Lloyd George's family group.

On the surface, the Liberals had increased their representation by 13. This, however, was an increase in numbers without real substance. Its seats gained were won from Labour in the absence of Conservatives, whereas in 1929 its seats had been won by its own merit. Only ten of the 72 elected Liberals had been faced with Conservative opponents, six of these in Wales or Scotland. The Liberals held 46 of the seats won in 1929, losing 13 (all to Conservatives) and taking 26 – again all from Labour. Thus in Durham, Liberals captured such normally solid Labour seats as Consett and Bishop Auckland in the absence of Conservative candidates. Although Samuel retained his seat at Darwen with a 4,000 majority, Donald Maclean only narrowly held North Cornwall. Two Liberal Ministers, Milner Gray in Mid-Bedfordshire and E.D. Simon in Penryn, were both defeated.

It was in terms of votes cast, however, that the Liberal reverse was most noticeable. Compared to 1929, the combined Liberal vote had fallen by over 3 million, the Labour vote by only 1¾ million. From virtually every side, the Liberals had lost ground. In the 51 seats contested in 1929 and 1931 by all three parties, the Liberal vote slumped. Only where no Conservative candidate was in the field were Liberals able to benefit from the swing to the National Government. Once again, as the party looked at the debris of the 1931 battle, the old truth again became apparent. Without Lloyd George, the Liberal Party did indeed seem doomed.

10
Dissension and Decline: 1931–1945

The outcome of the 1931 general election was a disaster for the party. The reconstruction of the Cabinet which followed the election reflected the greatly diminished importance of the Liberals in the new Parliament. Both Reading and Crewe retired from the Government; no Liberals replaced them, thus reducing the Liberals to an even smaller voice in the Cabinet. The Liberal Nationals, in contrast, were well rewarded. Simon was offered the Foreign Secretaryship, whilst Runciman became President of the Board of Trade.

The 1931 election had not merely been a severe defeat in electoral terms. The outcome left the party totally lacking in any sense of direction or purpose. This was particularly noticeable over the key question of the party's participation in the National Government.

As 1932 progressed, Liberal discontent at the National Government mounted. In March 1932, the National Government's decision to introduce the Import Duties Bill provoked a rebellion by the Samuelite Liberals. Although the Free Trade Cabinet Ministers were persuaded not to resign (through the agreement to differ), some 31 Liberals voted against the Bill's Second Reading. The growing hostility of both backbenchers and constituency opinion to the National Government was much in evidence at the annual conference of the party at Clacton in April 1932. At local level, this increasing hostility was soon evident in by-elections in such seats as Henley and North Cornwall, where Liberals waged virtually open war on Government candidates.

Meanwhile, as the National Government continued, the gulf between the Liberals and Liberal Nationals widened. In July 1932, the Liberal Nationals had set up a 'Liberal National Council'. The new organisation, with Hutchinson as chairman of its Executive Committee, set about coordinating Liberal National relations with the Conservatives and acted as a general propaganda and fund-raising machine.

This growing separation of Liberals and Liberal Nationals was brought to a head by the Ottawa Imperial Economic Conference. The agreements reached at Ottawa culminated in the resignation on 28 September of Samuel and the other Liberal Ministers (with the exception of Runciman) from the Government.

Samuel, although resigning from the Government, attempted a peculiar compromise. The Liberals took up seats on the Government back-benches, as critics but not as outright opponents of the Government. Although Samuel's curious compromise was approved by the Liberal Council and the National Liberal Federation, it was to prove an unworkable formula.

Samuel's decision to leave the National Government marked yet another divide with the Liberal Nationals. By October 1932, the gap between the two wings was virtually unbridgeable. Simon and the Liberal Nationals tightened their links with the Conservatives, whilst Samuel was left to work out what the role of the Liberals should be on the Government back-benches.

Both in Parliament and in the constituencies, Liberal difficulties mounted throughout 1933. In Parliament Liberal back-bench opposition to National Government measures increased. In March, Liberals opposed the Agricultural Marketing Bill, in May Liberals voted against the Rent Restrictions Bill, and in June the Government's proposals for a World Economic Conference were denounced. By July, the Liberal position on the Government back-benches was becoming ludicrous. Within the party, it was clear to such figures as Sir Archibald Sinclair that the party would have to move into outright opposition. Sinclair, in fact, echoed the voice of the party at the grassroots. In May 1933, the party's annual assembly carried a motion calling for a move into opposition. A similar motion was passed at the Scottish Liberal Federation's annual meeting. Both assemblies carried a variety of motions strongly critical of the Government's unemployment and fiscal policies.

There was, perhaps, an unspoken reason why the party needed to move into opposition. The very identity of the party, and its morale, was visibly disintegrating. The party was virtually bankrupt; its by-election record was hardly encouraging; constituency organisation was in chaos. On 18 October, Samuel returned to England from an overseas visit. After sounding out the party, Samuel at last decided to bring the party into opposition. On 13 November, Samuel finally crossed the floor.

Even this decision, however, prompted further defection. Four of the 33 Liberals who had previously supported Samuel refused to follow him.[1] To offset this, Samuel's decision was warmly welcomed by the National Liberal Federation and all the area organisations.

The move into opposition, however, made little effective change in the fortunes of the party. Indeed, with the completion of Samuel's move to the opposition benches, as Liberals took stock of their position, the outlook looked dismal beyond measure. By 1933 the Liberals seemed really to have come to the point of no return. The party went on because it could go nowhere else.

The electorate seemed to share this view. In a disastrous by-election at Manchester Rusholme on 21 November the party polled a mere 9 per cent, compared to 33 per cent in 1931. A by-election at Harborough on 29 November confirmed that Liberal fortunes were fast declining. At the same time, the death in October of Lord Cowdray removed one of the party's chief benefactors.

Despite the move into opposition, the party found itself still unable to offer a very clear alternative to the National Government or Labour opposition. Vis-à-vis Labour, Liberals found themselves in particular difficulties, for although the party was opposed to nationalisation, on such issues as disarmament, support for the League of Nations, Free Trade, opposition to the cuts in unemployment pay and in plans for housing and social reform, Liberal policy was almost identical with Labour's.

Equally, vis-à-vis the National Government, Liberals found themselves as much at a loss to put forward a distinctly separate image. Over India, Liberals were in agreement; tariffs were proclaimed as a temporary expedient only; Baldwin claimed to support the League of Nations; and cuts in unemployment pay were restored in the Budget of 1934. On many major issues, the National Government occupied the middle ground in British politics towards which Samuel aspired, and try as he might he could not dislodge it.

Thus the Liberal move into opposition, far from restoring the fortunes of the party, only served to make them worse. The by-elections of 1934 were even more disastrous than in 1933. On 8 February, the Liberals polled a mere 7 per cent at Cambridge, a seat where they had picked up 25 per cent of the votes in 1931. Only five of the 12 by-elections between April and December 1934 were fought by the party, with disastrous results in Weston-super-Mare, Rushcliffe and North Lambeth.

Against such a background, a distinct air of defeatism pervaded the party. Both the *News Chronicle* and the Liberal and Radical Candidates Association supported a revival of 'Lib–Labism'. Some Liberals abandoned the party altogether – the most important defector being H.L. Nathan, Liberal MP for Bethnal Green North East, who joined Labour in July 1934. Lower down the scale, the number of prospective candidates deserting the party increased. All these defections, and rumours of defections, did nothing to increase Samuel's stature in the party.

It was hardly surprising that, once again, many Liberals turned their thoughts towards their one-time leader Lloyd George. In February 1934, the North Wales Liberal Federation called on Lloyd George to lead a great revival campaign throughout the country. In May, the National League of Young Liberals added their voice to the call. But Samuel was not willing to approach Lloyd George, whilst Lloyd George himself was still determined to pursue his own highly individualistic path, intervening in several by-elections not contested by Liberals to support Labour candidates, as at Swindon (in support of Christopher Addison) and Putney (in support of Edith Summerskill).

Consequently, the Liberal Party entered 1935 still lacking firm leadership or any stiffening of morale. Even more than hitherto, lack of finance and lack of enthusiasm in the constituencies resulted in by-elections being left uncontested. No by-election in 1935 was fought until May, when in a disastrous contest at Edinburgh West the party's share of the vote slumped. The previous month, to add to Samuel's problems, control of the Scottish Liberal Federation was temporarily lost to the Liberal Nationals. Whilst the Samuel Liberals were suffering these additional setbacks, and whilst the party drifted aimlessly on, Lloyd George returned to the political limelight.

On 17 January 1935, in a much-publicised speech at Bangor, Lloyd George launched his 'New Deal' campaign. The campaign, aimed at uniting under one banner all those opposed to the National Government, was essentially designed to ensure that as many 'progressive' MPs as possible were returned at the next election. Lloyd George's 'New Deal', however, did nothing to restore the Liberals. The coming of the 1935 general election found the Liberal Party disheartened, disorganised and in disarray.

Hopelessly short of finance, the Liberals fielded only 159 candidates, 41 more than in 1931 but 354 fewer than in 1929. With Liberal advocacy of Free Trade appearing almost unrealistic in the midst of world recession, and with the Abyssinia crisis forcing Liberals both to condemn and support the National Government simultaneously, the campaign hardly augured well for the Liberals. Gloomy predictions of a Liberal disaster by such figures as Ramsay Muir proved to be only too accurate.

The outcome of the election was yet another disaster for the Liberals; the party could win only half the seats won in the debacle of 1924. With a mere 21 seats, the Liberals had been reduced to almost total impotence.

No significant area returned any number of Liberals: a few agricultural seats, such as the party's victory in Cumberland North, together with the isolated urban strongholds such as East Wolverhampton and East Birkenhead, were all that the party had left. The Liberals also lost their best men: Herbert Samuel was out at Darwen, Isaac Foot lost Bodmin and Walter Rea was ousted at Dewsbury. Only six Liberals returned had been opposed by both Labour and National Government candidates – three of these in rural Wales. The party's share of the national vote had fallen to a mere 6.4 per cent, even lower than the 7.2 per cent achieved in 1931. On average, each candidate obtained only 13 per cent of the votes cast. Even worse, many of the party's best seats went uncontested in 1935 because of the collapse of local organisation. In the 30 seats contested by all three major parties in 1931 and 1935, the Liberal share of the vote fell by 4 per cent. Whether in terms of votes or seats, whichever way Liberals attempted to analyse the results, there was only gloom to be seen.

On the surface, the Liberal Nationals, with 33 members, seemed to have done well. But their seeming strength was illusory; all were dependent on Conservative votes in their constituencies – indeed, no Liberal National was opposed by a Conservative. Curiously only in Denbigh and Oldham were Liberal Nationals opposed even by Liberals.

One consequence of the election, following the defeat of Sir Herbert Samuel by 1,157 votes in a contest in Darwen, was the election of a new leader. On Lloyd George's suggestion (the results of 1935 had partly healed the breach with the Lloyd George family group), Sir Archibald Sinclair, MP for Caithness and Sutherland, and Liberal Chief Whip in 1930–1, was elected. Sinclair appointed Percy Harris (MP for Bethnal Green South West and the only Liberal to be returned in London) as Chief Whip.

The results of the 1935 election were additional proof, not only of the fading popular support for the Liberals, but of the almost total decay into which constituency organisation had fallen. Between 1931 and 1935 such Liberal Associations as had survived until then began to fall apart. The few organisations still active had either defected to the Liberal Nationals or were in a state of suspended animation, waiting for a lead that never came.

The disastrous results of 1935 were followed almost immediately by a by-election humiliation in Ross and Cromarty. In a Highland seat with a strong Liberal tradition, the party could only poll 4 per cent of the votes cast.

These shattering election results had a curious sequel. They revealed not only that the party was in complete decline but that it might disappear altogether. Even the blindest of Liberals could see the peril facing the party – a peril made even more imminent now that the Liberal Nationals were Conservatives in everything but name.

Thus the sequel of the 1935 election was the appointment of the Liberal Reorganisation Commission (under Lord Meston) to reconsider the whole structure of party organisation. Its task was nothing less than to consider how to rebuild the party, and how to reshape the confused and uncoordinated bodies that dated back to before 1914 – the National Liberal Federation, the Liberal Central Association and the variety of other autonomous bodies.

The proposals of the Meston Report were discussed at a party convention in London in June 1936. The essential central feature of this Report was the creation of the Liberal Party Organisation in place of the old National Liberal Federation. But the change was one of name rather than structure. Although aiming to provide a single policymaking body for the party, this new body left effective authority still in fact divided between the Annual Assembly, the party council, the executive and the leader. One longer-term effect of the Meston Report was to give considerably extra power to the Parliamentary Party and the Whips. The most immediately obvious weak feature of the report was its failure to pay much attention to the constituencies – the weakest part of the party. Meston's report had concentrated on rebuilding the party from the top, not from the foundation.

The essential fact of the Liberal Party in the late 1930s was that it lacked any very definite image. Sinclair, undoubtedly, saw his party as the non-Socialist alternative to Baldwin and Chamberlain. It was hardly realistic. Others, such as the Duke of Montrose, a recent convert from the Conservatives, saw the Liberals as the 'Centre Party'. Finally, the young radicals, rather foreshadowing developments thirty years later, wanted Liberalism to pursue a course away from the sterility and conservatism (as they saw it) of both the major parties. It was against this background that the idea of a 'United Front' gained much attention.

This idea was not absolutely rejected by the Liberals, although a fairly firm dismissal of the proposal was given by the Executive Committee of the Liberal Party in February 1937. The reasons for this rejection were set out in a letter from Milner Gray, the chairman of the Executive, to Aldous Huxley. Gray emphasised that, if the Labour Party was willing to cooperate on an agreed programme of reform, and if proportional representation could be introduced, then it would be possible for the two parties to fight on a united front at the polls and subsequently to cooperate in Parliament.

In fact, this possibility was never really on. As Lord Lothian remarked in April 1937, for the Liberals cooperation with Labour was never possible as long as Labour retained nationalisation at the forefront of its programme. Even had this barrier been overcome, it was clear that the great majority of the Labour Party were against any such 'United Front' proposal. The Labour annual conference at Edinburgh in 1936 had rejected the 'Popular Front' idea. By the end of 1937 the proposal had completely faded.

Relations with Labour were one problem for Liberals. Equally, the party's position vis-à-vis the Liberal Nationals was still in the balance. On both sides, hopes of a reconciliation still remained – during 1937 prolonged discussions between the two sides took place. But the issue of Free Trade remained a crucial stumbling-block. In January 1938 the talks finally broke down.

Despite the recommendations of the Meston Report, there was no obvious sign of a noticeable Liberal recovery, either in by-elections or in municipal elections. In the first 12 by-elections following the party's disaster in Ross and Cromarty, no Liberal candidates appeared. But from mid-1937 the by-election scene appeared a little more cheerful; Liberals did well, although not well enough for victory, in St Ives (30 June 1937) and in Dorset North (13 July 1937). During 1938, however, only two candidates came forward in 18 by-elections. Meanwhile Liberals suffered two further defections to the Liberal Nationals. In municipal elections, the two trends which had dominated municipal Liberal politics in the decade from 1918 to 1929 continued after 1930: a slow but persistent fall in the number of candidates brought forward, and an equally uninterrupted and persistent net loss of seats each November.

The percentage of Liberal candidates, which had stood at 18 per cent in 1922, had fallen to 12½ per cent by 1929. By 1931, the total had fallen below 10 per cent, by 1935 it was down to 7.9 per cent and by 1938 to a mere 5.6 per cent. The reduction in the number of Liberal municipal candidates, in itself a symptom of the malaise afflicting the party, was mirrored in the net loss of seats suffered each November. In every year (apart from the anti-Labour landslide of 1931) Liberals suffered a net loss of seats. Perhaps a better indication than this was to be found in the *share* of seats won by Liberals each November. The percentage of council seats won by Liberals fell from 14 per cent in 1931 to 10 per cent in 1935 and a mere 7.2 per cent by 1938.

These overall figures of gains and losses to a certain extent disguised a significant change in the *type* of seats won by Liberals during the 1930s. During this period Liberals lost steadily and persistently to Labour in a variety of Midland and Northern industrial districts, whilst themselves picking up isolated gains from the Conservatives in a few seaside and middle-class resorts.

Throughout the 1930s, the temptation of hard-pressed Liberal councillors to join forces with the Conservatives in an anti-Socialist 'municipal alliance' continued to increase. Each November, it was possible to detect another borough where the anti-Socialist forces had joined ranks. Thus, in 1932, it was the turn of Plymouth; in 1934 of Doncaster and Ipswich.

In the late 1920s, these anti-Socialist pacts had often provoked division and dissent within the Liberal ranks, especially from the more radical Young Liberals. During the 1930s, few such revolts occurred. Indeed, one of the most consistent features of municipal Liberalism in the 1930s was the absolute lack of any attempt to provide an independent Liberal challenge.

The domestic problems of the Liberal Party, however, were increasingly overshadowed by the growing threat of war. The Munich settlement itself provoked a division in the parliamentary party – 14 Liberals voting with Labour, four with the Government. Similar cleavages developed with the introduction of conscription in 1939, six Liberals supporting the measure, seven voting against. With the outbreak of war, however, the party lined up unanimously in support of the war. No senior Liberal spoke out against the declaration of hostilities.

With the outbreak of war against Nazi Germany in September 1939, it was agreed to suspend party electoral activity. Accordingly, the Whips of the three parties signed an agreement under which the general election (due in 1940) would be suspended for the duration of hostilities, the three parties would cease from political activities and that, when by-elections occurred, the party which had last gained the vacant seat would be allowed an unopposed return.

Whilst, quite obviously, wartime conditions demanded some form of electoral truce, nonetheless the actual signing of this agreement came as a surprise to the Liberal Party, whose Council had met only in June 1939 to make plans for a possible autumn general election. In fact, the electoral truce occasioned not only surprise but considerable resentment. This was perhaps natural in the Liberal ranks, for the party stood to lose more than Conservative or Labour from an indefinite cessation of political activity.

Although no important Liberal voice was raised against the declaration of war, many Liberals shared a total lack of confidence in Neville Chamberlain as war leader. In his last memorable speech to Parliament, in May 1940, when Norway had fallen, Lloyd George urged Chamberlain to make his own sacrifice to the war effort by laying down the seals of office. Other Liberals, most particularly Clement Davies, urged the removal of Chamberlain and his replacement by Churchill.

Chamberlain in fact resigned on 10 May 1940. The same day, Churchill formed a Government. The Liberals, like Labour, agreed to serve. And, although no Liberal was included in the five-man 'Inner War Cabinet', Sir Archibald Sinclair was appointed Secretary of State for Air. Other Liberals accepted less senior positions.

With Sinclair fully occupied at the Air Ministry, the task of marshalling the Parliamentary Liberal Party devolved upon Percy Harris. Before long, the task had become a most difficult one as the party at the grassroots became increasingly restive over the electoral truce. This discontent found focus with the birth in 1941 of the Liberal Action Group.

The originators of the Liberal Action Group, later known as Radical Action, included Lancelot Spicer (Chairman of the Group), Honor Balfour and Everett Jones. The group rapidly grew in size and influence. By February 1943 it was claimed that over 23 prospective candidates and as many members of the Council belonged to it. By the autumn of 1944, its supporters included five MPs and 34 prospective candidates.

Although not committed particularly to any distinctive 'line', most members of the group opposed the Parliamentary truce. As protests and complaints on the truce mounted, the Party Council was faced (on 17 June 1942) with a resolution urging the party to reconsider its position over the matter. This motion was withdrawn when a compromise was reached that it would be presented to the Leader, but nonetheless a variety of Independent Liberals began contesting by-elections.

The first such by-election occurred in Chippenham in August 1943. Dr Donald Johnson, a prominent member of the Council of the Liberal Party, resigned his position to contest the division as an Independent Liberal. The result was highly significant. In a safe, rural Conservative seat, which had been won with a majority of 5,421 in 1935, the Conservative scraped home with a tiny majority of only 195.

Further embarrassment for the Liberal Party came when, in November 1943, a prominent member of the Liberal Action Group, Miss Honor Balfour, similarly resigned her offices in the party to fight the Darwen by-election. Admittedly, the constituency had returned Herbert Samuel as a Liberal until 1935, but nonetheless Honor Balfour's performance in coming within 70 votes of victory, despite a letter from Archibald Sinclair supporting the official government candidate, was impressive.

The advent of 1944 only saw the split and discomfiture within the Liberal ranks widen. In February, Honor Balfour wrote a spirited article in *Liberal Forward* entitled 'I Challenge the Electoral Truce'. Shortly afterwards, the chairman of the Women's Liberal Federation resigned her offices to contest the by-election in Bury St Edmunds. Her candidature was endorsed by the Radical Action Group and the result was again close.

At the same time that Radical Action was embarrassing the party, further defections occurred. Sir Richard Acland, the Liberal MP for Barnstaple, formed an organisation known as Forward March which later became Common Wealth. Acland resigned from the party in September 1942.

These defections from the Liberal ranks were partly compensated for by very clear signs of disintegration within the Liberal National ranks. When Churchill had formed his coalition in May 1940, with Sir John Simon taking a peerage to become Lord Chancellor, the Liberal Nationals were henceforth led by Ernest Brown. His leadership was hardly a happy time. In February 1942, three MPs resigned from the party – Edgar Granville eventually joined Labour in 1945 and Hore-Belisha the Conservatives.

During the war an abortive attempt was made to fuse the Liberals and Liberal Nationals. This stemmed from an offer by Ernest Brown for discussions in July 1943 which Sinclair clearly welcomed. The stumbling block, however, was that Brown wanted the National Government to continue after the war. Both to Sinclair and to grassroots Liberal opinion, such an attitude was impossible. The talks finally collapsed in November 1944. To compensate for these problems, the war saw one major recruit to the party – Sir William Beveridge. He was subsequently to play a prominent part in the 1945 election campaign.

In May 1945, with victory over Germany achieved, the Labour Party withdrew from the Churchill Government. In the subsequent 'Caretaker' government which preceded the general election, the Liberals did not continue in office.[2]

Thus, after the six-year electoral truce, party politics resumed in earnest in the summer of 1945. However, the Liberal Party machine was totally unprepared for an election. Despite this unpreparedness, and despite its parliamentary strength of only 18, the party had certain grounds for optimism. They rightly believed that the electorate would reject the Conservatives, despite the prestige of Churchill; more mistakenly, the Liberals believed the country would reject Socialism, and turn instead to the Liberal social reform programme.

In this respect, the party placed great hopes on Beveridge. Beveridge himself had become a Liberal Party member in July 1944; and in October 1944 he had succeeded George Gray as Liberal MP for Berwick-upon-Tweed. For the 1945 election, Beveridge provided the Liberal Party with his report, *Full Employment in a Free Society*. It was the most important policy contribution the Liberals had offered since Lloyd George's 'We Can Conquer Unemployment' in the 1929 election.

Beveridge was the party's greatest hope, but far from their only one. The leader of the party, Archibald Sinclair, had an impressive record as head of the wartime Air Ministry. Lady Violet Bonham-Carter was a forceful platform campaigner. In addition, the Liberal ranks were fairly united – in itself an achievement. Moreover, there was some evidence that the party was appealing to a younger generation – 87 per cent of the Liberal candidates in 1945 were fighting their first Parliamentary election.

Any hopes that the Liberals would field over 500 candidates for the general election were rapidly doused when the election was called for July. Only 307 Liberal candidates were nominated – an insufficient total, even if all had been elected, for the party to have formed a government.

For the election, the Liberals put forward a radical manifesto that was propounded with great energy by Beveridge, the campaign chairman. These efforts, however, brought the party an almost nil return when the votes were counted. The election proved yet another disaster for the Liberals. The Conservatives, together with their National Liberal allies, polled 9,988,000 votes. Labour swept to power with nearly 12 million, whilst the Liberals could manage only 2,252,430, a mere 9 per cent of the total votes cast.

The Liberal Party in Westminster was decimated. Its total fell from 18 to 12. All the party leadership suffered defeat. Sinclair was out by 62 votes in Caithness and Sutherland; the Chief Whip, Sir Percy Harris, was defeated in Bethnal Green South West; Beveridge himself failed at Berwick-upon-Tweed – one of seven sitting Liberals to lose their seats.

Of the 12 Liberals who survived, one, Gwilym Lloyd George, ought really to be classed as a Conservative. He never attended meetings of the Liberal Parliamentary Party; he had remained a member of Churchill's caretaker Government after the Liberal Party had withdrawn, and his candidature in Pembrokeshire had the full support of the Conservatives. Only two Liberals could really be said to possess safe seats, Clement Davies in Montgomeryshire and Roderick Bowen in Cardiganshire.

Apart from the 12 elected Liberals, only 11 other candidates had come within striking distance of victory. In percentage terms, Rasmussen has calculated that only 8.8 per cent of Liberals secured second place, whilst 84.9 per cent came third.[3]

There were other equally dismal features in 1945. Liberal-held seats at the dissolution (such as Bristol North) were not even contested; the average percentage vote achieved by each Liberal candidate fell to 18 per cent. After the disasters and dissensions of the inter-war years, the post-war period had brought the party to its lowest-ever level. It was, perhaps, a fitting comment on the fate of the party that the most traditionally Liberal of all seats – Lloyd George's old constituency of Caernarvon Boroughs – should desert to the Conservatives.[4]

It was against this dismal background that the leadership of the party fell to Clement Davies. He was expected to be only a caretaker leader, but he lasted until 1956 – mainly because no preferred successor (such as Frank Byers) could secure a seat. Already suffering from alcoholism, and recently bereaved, Clement Davies at least struggled to keep the depleted party alive.

11
A Party in the Wilderness: 1945–1956

In the general election of 1945, the Parliamentary Liberal Party had come near to extinction. In the years that followed, the party came very close to disappearing altogether. In the municipal elections, the story was the same. By 1938, except in an occasional stronghold in Yorkshire and Lancashire, the party had almost ceased to be represented on many borough councils. The municipal elections of November 1945, with their sweeping Labour gains, finally ended what remained of the old Liberal Party. A mere 92 Liberals (4.2 per cent), from a tiny field of 360 candidates, were successful, compared to 1,372 Labour and 384 Conservatives. Labour's tally of gains amounted to a massive 972 seats.

Such sweeping gains removed the last Liberal councillors in a variety of centres. In Wolverhampton, the elections left the town without a single Liberal councillor. In Birmingham the last three Liberals were swept away, in most cases in total humiliation. In Leeds, only a solitary Liberal was left on a council of 104.

The provincial boroughs where Liberals now retained a separate and strong identity had virtually all vanished. In none of the 80 largest county boroughs were Liberals in overall control. Only in Huddersfield did the Liberals just remain the largest single party. They were not even the second largest except in three towns – Burnley, Halifax and Keighley.

Elsewhere, Liberals had temporarily survived either by amalgamation with the Conservatives (as in the 'Citizens' Party' in Bristol, or the 'Progressives' in Sheffield) or by fighting as 'non-party' independents. In parliamentary by-elections, the party suffered the same fate. In the 52 by-elections during the Labour Government, Liberals fought only 14. Indeed, only in contests in the City of London and Bermondsey Rotherhithe could they obtain over 20 per cent of the votes polled. Elsewhere, they forfeited nine deposits from 14 candidates.[1]

With the party in such dire straits, only one course was open to it; a complete reconstruction and reconsideration of the whole organisation and machinery of the party. This the Liberals lost no time in doing. An eight-man Committee on Party Reconstruction was appointed, whose report duly appeared as *Coats off for the Future*. This was submitted to the Liberal Party annual assembly in the spring of 1946. At the same time, the party began turning its attention towards the problem of finance.

Throughout the inter-war period, the party had relied for financial help on the Lloyd George Fund, on rich candidates, and on such wealthy supporters as Lord Cowdray. By 1945, these sources of revenue were increasingly insufficient. The Lloyd George Fund was no longer there: radical candidates who could also pay their election bills had become increasingly rare. And yet the party had relied heavily on such candidates in 1945. The defeated Liberal Chief Whip wrote after the 1945 election:

...to have found the number of candidates we did was no mean achievement. We had no large Headquarters fund to finance candidates and they had to depend, first on contributions out of their own pockets and secondly on monies raised locally.[2]

Such dependence on candidates who were financially well-off was hardly healthy. Hence, at the end of 1945, a committee was set up to examine the financial question.

The result was the launching of a 'Foundation Fund' in May 1946, designed to raise £125,000 over a five-year period. It started well, and after eight months of operation pledges of over £58,000 had been received. The annual official report to the assembly of March 1949 was able to state that the party's accounts were in the black.

Likewise, the organisation of the party in the constituencies improved. By 1947, according to Philip Fothergill, the chairman of the party executive, over 500 active local associations existed, compared to 200 only eight months earlier.

Although the financial position was improving, and to a certain extent morale was reviving, the recruitment of suitable prospective candidates remained a major problem. It was a problem partly of the Liberals' own making, for the party had no organised, systematic policy to recruit candidates. Chronic lack of funds left this matter largely in the hands of the secretary of the Liberal Central Association with the result that, in practice, much of the responsibility for securing candidates rested with the local associations.

To some extent, a corollary of the difficulty of attracting candidates was a fall in candidate standards. In 1946, the party established a five-man Prospective Candidates Committee whose main function came to be the quality of adopted candidates, but in the rush to adopt candidates in 1950, this standard was virtually abandoned as 'vetting' of candidates lapsed. The result was a flood of inexperienced candidates who seriously weakened the party's image.

An even more fundamental problem than finance or candidates also faced the Liberals after 1945: to what degree, if any, should the party assist or cooperate with either the Conservatives or the Liberal National group which had severed itself from the main body in 1931?

Attempts had been made during the war, as we have seen, and had failed, to restore unity between the Liberal Party and the Liberal National Party. After 1945, the latter (which changed its name to National Liberal Party in 1948) moved closer into the Conservative ranks. In May 1947, an agreement was arrived at between Lord Woolton, the chairman of the Conservative Party, and Lord Teviot of the National Liberals. This provided for the establishment of joint Conservative–Liberal Associations in those constituencies where both parties were already in existence. In constituencies where only one of the parties was organised, it was agreed to offer membership to all those who supported joint action against the Socialists, and to rename the Association accordingly.

The Woolton–Teviot agreement found a quick response in the independent Liberal ranks, who called on their members to stand firm against this insidious Conservative overture. At the time, however, there was speculation whether the Liberal Party, as well as the National Liberal Party, might succumb to the Conservative embrace. In November 1946, the Liberal headquarters issued a statement denying rumours of a Liberal–Conservative pact.

Such statements eventually ended these rumours; but much valuable time for reconstruction was lost by these debates within the party on relations with the Conservatives and National Liberals. The vital consequence was that, with the advent of the 1950 general election, the revitalisation of the party had still a long way to go.

Whether the Liberal leadership really expected that 1950 would see the long-awaited revival is open to doubt. True, the party fielded 475 candidates, but at the same time the party insured itself with Lloyds for all deposits lost after the first 50 up to 250. It was a wise move, for the result of the 1950 election was an unrelieved debacle. The loss of 319 deposits literally reduced the party to a music-hall joke.

The Liberals had, it is true, increased their vote to 2,621,487 – but with 169 more candidates than in 1945 this was hardly an achievement. Turnout, in any case, rose from 72.7 to 84.0 per cent, so the Liberal percentage of the total vote had merely remained stable at 9.1 per cent. The results of the 1950 election are shown in Table 11.1.

Table 11.1

	Votes	%	MPs
Conservative	12,490,507	43.4	299
Labour	13,267,466	46.1	315
Liberal	2,621,487	9.1	9
Communist	91,812	0.3	–
Others	301,043	1.1	2
Total	28,772,315	100.0	625

Nor had any particular region showed any major Liberal revival. The Liberal vote was in fact fairly evenly distributed throughout Britain. In only three areas – the South West, North East Scotland and rural North Wales – did the party obtain more than 20 per cent of the vote. In the whole country, only in three urban constituencies, all of them geographically dispersed, were Liberals able to achieve 20 per cent. By 1950, the party had been reduced almost without exception to the agricultural backwaters – though even here, in such areas as Gloucestershire and Southern Scotland, Labour had become the alternative to the Conservatives. Nor did the middle-class constituencies – the backbone of the Liberal revival after 1962 – offer any signs of encouragement.

Yet, if the party thought the position could hardly be worse after 1950, it was mistaken. To recover from the disaster of 1950, the Liberal Party desperately needed time to rebuild. Such a period of recuperation was not allowed the party. The second Attlee administration, weakened by death and dissension, ended with the calling of an election. Parliament was dissolved on 5 October 1951, and polling day fixed for 25 October 1951. A combination of factors left the Liberals able to field only 109 candidates. Morale was low, funds scarce, but above all candidates were virtually unobtainable. Even experienced Liberal candidates held back. These factors, together with the patent disunity of the parliamentary party in the lobbies in the 1950–1 period, ensured that 1951 was to be another disastrous election.

It proved to be more than this. It marked the nadir of the electoral fortunes of the party. Table 11.2 shows the full results of the 1951 election. The total Liberal vote had fallen to 743,512, a mere 2.6 per cent of the total poll. Although six MPs were returned, 66 of the 109 candidates forfeited their deposits. In all, 92 of the 109 had suffered either massive defeat or total rout; only eight came near to joining the six elected members.

Table 11.2

	Votes	%	MPs
Conservative	13,718,199	48.0	321
Labour	13,935,917	48.7	295
Liberal	743,512	2.6	6
Others	198,966	0.7	3
Total	28,596,594	100.0	625

The party lost four seats, including Anglesey, which Lady Megan Lloyd George had represented. Only one seat was gained, Bolton West. This, though ostensibly a gain, was really the result of a local Conservative–Liberal pact. No Conservative opposed the Liberal, Arthur Holt, in Bolton West, while the Liberals gave the Conservatives a free run in Bolton East. In fact, with the solitary exception of Jo Grimond in Orkney and Shetland, no Liberal member was returned in the face of Conservative opposition.

The party thus faced the first peacetime Churchill Government with a parliamentary force of six, a demoralised party in the constituencies, and with no conceivable prospect in the near future of revival.

It was in this position that, immediately after 1951, Churchill offered Clement Davies, the Liberal leader, the tempting proposition of a position in the new Government and a Conservative–Liberal coalition in the Commons. Since the Conservatives had a perfectly workable majority of 17, the offer was presumably one of genuine goodwill to the Liberals.

Whatever the motives, Churchill and Davies met at Chartwell on 28 October 1951. Davies then consulted leading Liberals before making public his refusal to join the Conservative Administration. The Liberals had decided to soldier on alone.

It was a brave decision in the face of mounting evidence of the party's lack of morale. In by-elections, the record of the party was abysmal, whilst in municipal elections, the Liberals fared equally disastrously. Only 2.2 per cent of the borough councillors elected in 1950 were Liberals; by 1955 this total had fallen even further (to 1.5 per cent) as Table 11.3 shows. No significant council remained in Liberal control during this period, whilst such major cities as Liverpool and Birmingham, later to see a municipal Liberal revival, had no Liberal representation.

Table 11.3

	Con. and Con.-Supported Ind.	Ind. without Con. Support	Labour	Liberal	Total
1950	1,610	510	1,132	72	3,324
1951	1,893	548	883	79	3,403
1952	1,138	448	1,718	53	3,397
1953	1,571	447	1,448	60	3,526
1954	1,498	511	1,438	74	3,521
1955	1,604	514	1,470	56	3,644

However, in all this darkness there appeared one beacon. In a by-election in Inverness in December 1954 a Liberal who had not even contested the seat in 1951 took 36 per cent of the poll, sweeping Labour into third place. Admittedly, turnout was very low, but the by-election heralded, a decade in advance, the breakthrough the Scottish Liberals were to make in the Highlands in 1964 and 1966.

It was against this background that the Liberals faced the 1955 general election. The outcome was once again depressing. Of the 110 candidates fielded by the party (one more than in 1951) no fewer than 60 lost their deposit. The total poll of the party was a mere 722,402 – even less than 1951, although turnout was down. Many of the Liberal campaigns were efforts wasted – only 32 of the 110 candidates had professional agents. The party failed to gain any seats although it retained all six it was defending – itself a remarkable feat. Overall, the party had marginally improved its position – the average share of the vote for each candidate rose from 14.7 per cent to 15.1 per cent.

Although 1955 was the first election since 1929 in which the party had made any improvement on its previous election performance, the ground for optimism was hardly very great. As in 1950, it was the agricultural seats which held out most hope. Sixteen of the 18 seats in which Liberals won more than 20 per cent of the poll were primarily rural, whilst the other two constituencies (Bolton West and Huddersfield West) were both the subject of local Conservative–Liberal pacts.

Despite these minor improvements, the 1955 election had again demonstrated two major shortcomings in the party. First, leadership at the top was lacking: Clement Davies, though much respected, had no longer the force necessary to revitalise the party. Secondly, the party lacked real political direction or discretion – thus, for example, Lord Moynihan and Lord Salter were urging Liberals to vote Conservative where no Liberal was standing, at the same time as Lady Megan Lloyd George was urging them to vote Labour. In 1955, the party still had not decided which road it was to travel.

However, immediately the election was over the first move taken by the party was the establishment of a committee to lay plans for the next general election. Under Sir Andrew McFadyean, the committee included such future Liberal notables as Jeremy Thorpe, then prospective candidate for North Devon, John Baker, Edwin Malindine and Roy Douglas, then chairman of the National League of Young Liberals.

The establishment of this committee was important as a psychological reassurance that the party, though as much in the wilderness as ever, did still mean business. A second lift in morale came with the Torquay by-election of 15 December 1955, when the party took 23.8 per cent of the poll, compared to 14.2 per cent in the general election. In February 1956, the Hereford by-election provided further ground for optimism. Frank Owen, the Liberal, forced Labour into third place, taking 36.4 per cent of the poll.

At the same time as the party was slowly lifting itself from the electoral trough of 1951 and 1955, there were further defections, the most notable being Dingle Foot, formerly Liberal MP for Dundee, who joined the Labour Party. Contrariwise, the party lost Lord Moynihan and Edward Martell to the Right.

Though these defections, particularly in the case of Dingle Foot, were serious, in the end they benefited the party. It was an inevitable part of the process of transition.

But transition to what? This was unclear so long as Clement Davies remained leader. Despite many hints that Davies ought to make way for a younger man, the old leader at first displayed no sign of departure. But a change was not to be long delayed. Clement Davies resigned the Liberal leadership on 29 September 1956, choosing the Folkestone Assembly to make the announcement.

12
The Sound of Gunfire: 1956–1967

Clement Davies was succeeded as leader of the party by Jo Grimond. The day before the announcement of Clement Davies' retirement, Grimond had addressed the assembly with a powerful speech which left little doubt that the challenge of the Liberal leadership would fall in his direction. It was a challenge which Grimond took up with vigour and enthusiasm. And his leadership was to have a lasting impact, not only on the Liberal Party, but on the course of British politics.

Grimond rapidly proved to be the most attractive and popular leader the party had secured in its recent history. At a comparatively youthful 43, with an excellent academic and war background, Grimond soon showed that he was also a forceful and attractive speaker. His personal popularity was evident in his constituency of Orkney and Shetland, which he had won in 1950 and converted into a Liberal stronghold.

Under Grimond's leadership, the party enjoyed a revival that had seemed impossible in the dark days of 1951. But the first years of Grimond's leadership proved far from easy. An immediate test of Grimond's skill arose over the Suez crisis. The Liberals, like the Conservative and Labour parties, split over the issue. With only a small Parliamentary force, this Liberal division was more obvious. On 30 October 1956, three Liberals, Davies, Arthur Holt and Donald Wade, voted in support of the Conservative Government's ultimatum to Egypt. Then, only two days later, the Liberals present in Parliament voted for a Labour motion deploring the Egyptian action.

On the one side were those Liberals, such as Holt, supported by others such as Howard Fry, Peter Cadbury and John MacCallum Scott, who gave support to the Conservative line. At the other extreme were the radicals, totally opposed to military action by the British Government.

This initial division was remedied on 2 November 1956, when the Liberal Party organisation issued a forthright condemnation of the

Conservative Suez policy. Four days later, the Liberal parliamentary party endorsed this policy. This Liberal condemnation was, to a degree, a dangerous policy. In the 1955 election, all the Liberals except Grimond had been elected without Conservative opposition. What would happen if, by attacking so vigorously over Suez, the Liberals forfeited this Conservative restraint?

This problem was soon answered with the occasion of a by-election in Carmarthen, the seat formerly held by Sir Rhys Hopkin Morris for the Liberals. In the event, the Liberals defended the seat with a pro-Suez candidate who was without a Conservative opponent. These tactics failed to help the Liberals. In the by-election held in February 1957, Labour took the seat from the Liberals. To add the final touch of humiliation, the victorious Labour candidate was none other than Lady Megan Lloyd George. With the loss of Carmarthen, Liberal representation in the Commons was down to a mere five, the lowest-ever total in the long and uninterrupted decline of the party. It was an inauspicious opening for Jo Grimond's tenure of the leadership.

Yet there was consolation for the Liberals. Carmarthen was not typical of the general trend of by-election results as 1957 progressed. Rather, the main feature was the growing disenchantment with the Conservative Government. It was evidenced mainly in a series of marked swings to Labour in successive by-elections. But it was noticeable also in a variety of good by-election results for Liberals. The party began to achieve some impressive results during 1957, taking over 20 per cent of the vote at Edinburgh South (20 May 1957) and over 36 per cent of the vote in North Dorset (27 June). Further impressive results followed at Gloucester (12 September) and Ipswich (24 October).

The Liberals began 1958 in even happier fashion with a remarkable by-election result at Rochdale. For the by-election, in a seat which had seen a straight fight in 1955, the Liberals chose Ludovic Kennedy, a well-known television personality, as their candidate. His spirited and energetic campaign produced a Conservative humiliation and a near-triumph for the Liberals. Labour won the seat with 22,138 votes (44.7 per cent); the Liberals finished in second place, only 4,500 votes short of victory, with 35.5 per cent of the poll; the Conservatives managed a mere 19.8 per cent.

Two weeks later the Liberals achieved the by-election breakthrough that had eluded them for a generation, when they won Torrington from the Conservatives. Without detracting from Mark Bonham-Carter's individual triumph, the by-election was not quite the dawn of the promised era that many Liberals imagined. The seat had been held by George Lambert, sitting as a Conservative and National Liberal. No independent Liberal had fought in 1955, and clearly much of the traditional Liberal vote in this constituency had either abstained (turnout rose by 11.4 per cent to 80.6 per cent in the by-election) or found a temporary home in the Conservative ranks. As it was, the Liberals gained Torrington by the narrow margin of 658 votes – only to lose the seat again in 1959.

Torrington failed to inspire any similar Liberal breakthrough, although the party polled some impressive performances in a variety of residential and agricultural seats: 24.5 per cent at Weston-super-Mare and 27.5 per cent in Argyll (both on 12 June 1958), 24.3 per cent in East Aberdeenshire (20 November 1958), 24.2 per cent at Southend West (29 January 1959) and 25.7 per cent in Galloway (9 April 1959).

The revival represented by Torrington was noticeable in other ways. The number of affiliated constituencies, which had risen to over 330 in both 1956 and 1957 rose to over 360 in 1958. Even the perennial financial problem facing the party eased. The party gained control of Blackpool council, but narrowly avoided a disastrous party conference. The success at Torrington, and other by-election results, had acted as a much-needed tonic to the party.

When Harold Macmillan called an election for October 1959, the Liberals were able to field 216 candidates. The result was a modest but important improvement in the Liberal position (see Table 12.1). Although the party had returned only six members, failing to hold Torrington or regain Carmarthen, the Liberals had polled 1,640,761 votes, over twice their percentage share in 1955. Only 56 of the 215 candidates had forfeited their deposits, whilst the average vote in contested seats rose from 15.1 per cent in 1955 to 16.9 per cent in 1959.[1]

Table 12.1

	Votes	%	Seats
Conservative	13,750,935	49.4	365
Labour	12,216,166	43.8	253
Liberal	1,640,761	5.9	6
Others	254,846	0.9	1
Total	27,862,708	100.0	630

However, there were many unhappy features about the Liberal results. Although Jeremy Thorpe gained the rural North Devon constituency, there had been no other breakthrough. Indeed, the party fared worst where its electoral prospects were strongest. The Liberal vote fell in eight of the 13 seats in which the party had received over 30 per cent of the votes in 1955. Significantly for the future, by and large the party was unable to hold its position in the seats in which it had done well in by-elections.

Despite these qualifications, however, the Liberals could comfort themselves with the fact that, at a time when the Labour Party had suffered its third consecutive electoral defeat, the party was making discernible, if slow progress. When the Conservatives captured the highly marginal Brighouse and Spenborough constituency from Labour in March 1960, it began to seem that the Labour Party would soon tear itself to pieces.

But before Liberals could benefit from this Labour split, they had to overcome internal problems of their own. A bitter row developed over the role the Liberal Campaign Committee (established with Frank Byers as chairman to organise the 1959 campaign) should play in the running of the party once the election was out of the way. The Campaign Committee rapidly assumed powers which it had never been expected to exercise. The affair concluded with the resignation of H.P.F. Harris, the General Director of the party. The editor of *Liberal News*, Reginald Smith, resigned in protest at the treatment Harris had received. Byers had triumphed; but the consequences of the bitter argument lingered.

The second problem to arise dated from the dark days the party had faced in 1951. In that year, the Bolton Liberals had created a local arrangement with the Conservatives, in which the latter were not opposed by Liberals in East Bolton, whilst Arthur Holt was returned as a Liberal MP in West Bolton with Conservative support. The net result had been to deny both seats to Labour. In 1960, a by-election vacancy arose in Conservative-held East Bolton. What policy should Liberals adopt?

It was arguable that, if the Liberals allowed the by-election to go uncontested in an industrial Northern constituency with a Liberal tradition, the Liberal claim to be the alternative to Labour would be very open to ridicule. For whatever reasons, the decision was made to contest. In the event, a leading Liberal figure, Frank Byers, was adopted. He finished in third place, polling 10,173 votes and 24.8 per cent of the poll. It was a highly creditable result, and it proved to be a harbinger of the beginnings of a Liberal awakening.

The first real indication – in parliamentary terms – of the Liberal revival came with the by-election in April 1961 at Paisley (Asquith's old constituency). A spirited campaign by John Bannerman brought the Liberals within 2,000 votes of victory.

In the space of the next ten months, the Liberals managed to secure second place in eight by-elections in constituencies in which the party had been third in 1959. Similarly, in the municipal elections, the party improved its base in May 1960 (130 Liberals elected) and in May 1961 (196 Liberals elected). By the autumn of 1961, the increase in Liberal support had gathered momentum, and by the spring of 1962 a Liberal tide was undoubtedly flowing.

The climax of the Liberal revival came in March 1962. On 14 March, a Liberal candidate came within 973 votes of victory in the rock-solid Conservative seaside resort of Blackpool North. The following day, when polling took place in Orpington, a middle-class Kent commuter suburb, a Conservative majority of 14,760 was overturned into a Liberal majority of 7,855. The Conservative share of the poll had fallen by 22 per cent to give Eric Lubbock a resounding victory. There was little doubt that Orpington had proved to be the most sensational by-election since East Fulham in October 1933.

For the Liberals, after a generation in the wilderness, the promised land seemed at last to have arrived. Indeed, for a fleeting moment, the *Daily Mail* National Opinion Poll (published on 28 March 1962) showed the Liberals to be the most popular party in the country (the figures were: Liberals 30 per cent, Labour 29.9 per cent, Conservatives 29.2 per cent). Meanwhile, on the same day as Orpington, the Liberals forced the Conservatives into third place at Middlesbrough East. Other by-elections, though not repeating the Orpington victory, indicated the force behind the Liberal revival. The party took 27 per cent of the poll in Stockton-on-Tees (April 1962), 25 per cent in Derby North (also in April), whilst in the Montgomeryshire by-election following the death of Clement Davies this Liberal stronghold was easily retained. In West Derbyshire, the party missed victory by a mere 1,220 votes, whilst on 12 July in North East Leicester the excellent Liberal vote, coupled with a humiliating Tory performance, prompted Macmillan's drastic Cabinet reshuffle. It was this event which brought about Thorpe's scathing remark against Macmillan: 'greater love hath no man than this, that he lays down his friends for his life'.

In addition to these by-elections, the most impressive evidence of the Liberal advance was to be seen in the May 1962 municipal elections. The size of the Liberal advance could not be disguised. In such safe home counties territory as Aldershot, Finchley, Kingston and Maidenhead, the Conservatives lost every seat they were defending. In a variety of seaside and spa towns (such as Southend, Blackpool and Harrogate) the Liberals made equally impressive gains.

Outside this type of middle-class and suburban area, however, Liberal progress was markedly less. Thus in the Midlands and North (except for such towns as Leicester and Bolton) their gains were very much smaller.

However, much the most disquieting aspect of the Liberal upsurge was that virtually no gains had been made at the expense of Labour. Even in the commuter suburbs, the Liberals secured very few seats in the Labour-controlled boroughs – none at all in Acton, Watford or Mitcham. The Labour strongholds emerged unscathed from the Liberal attack.

The result of these election triumphs was predictable. The party achieved a publicity it had not known for a generation. Even the finances improved and the party treasurer, Colonel Gardner-Thorpe, was able to raise the target for income for 1962 from £100,000 to £150,000. New recruits such as Sir Frank Medlicott (former National Liberal MP for Norfolk Central) joined the party. But this Indian Summer was soon to be over.

It was evident by the autumn of 1962 that the Liberal tide had begun to recede. By October those intending to vote Liberal had dropped below 20 per cent in the opinion polls; thereafter, the decline in support was steady and uninterrupted.

Although the May 1963 local elections rather disguised the fact (since the Liberals were contesting seats last fought in 1960), Liberal support in the boroughs was ebbing fast. Further evidence of the rapid Liberal decline came from the by-elections. At Luton (November 1963) the Liberal failed to save his deposit. The following month (in Sudbury and Woodbridge) the party actually polled a worse percentage than at the preceding general election.

The polarisation towards the two main parties continued during 1964 – as the date of the general election approached. In May, in the last three by-elections fought by Liberals under the Conservative Government, the results proved depressing. By June 1964, support for the Liberals in the National Opinion Poll was down to 9 per cent. Meanwhile, Labour's lead over the Conservatives in the Gallup Poll fell from 8 per cent on 3 July to 6 per cent on 7 August and to 5 per cent on 13 September.

Before the election campaign proper was under way, Grimond delivered a keynote speech (on 20 June 1964) on the theme 'Charter for New Men'. It was a major appeal for a classless, dynamic society, emphasising greater promotion opportunities for the young technologists and executives, a reduction of the burden of income tax on earned incomes and a ceiling on mortgage rates. This appeal provided the basis of the 1964 Liberal manifesto, *Think for Yourself, Vote Liberal.*

Although sadly short of money, the party fought a vigorous and enthusiastic campaign in October 1964. With 365 candidates in the field (an increase of 149 over 1959) the party was challenging on a wide front. Grimond's successful television appearances further encouraged Liberal optimism. And yet, when the results came in, the Liberals had little tangible comfort. The outcome of the 1964 election was a bitter disappointment (see Table 12.2).

Table 12.2

	Votes	%	Seats
Conservative	12,002,906	43.4	303
Labour	12,205,779	44.1	318
Liberal	3,101,103	11.2	9
Others	367,094	1.3	–
Total	27,676,882	100.0	630

The Liberals had gained only four seats: Bodmin in Cornwall, and Inverness, Caithness and Sutherland, and Ross and Cromarty in Scotland. They lost Bolton West and Huddersfield West, where Conservatives fielded candidates for the first time since 1950.

At least, the Liberals had the consolation in 1964 that all their nine MPs had been elected in three-cornered fights, whilst the marginal victory won in North Devon by Jeremy Thorpe in 1959 was now secure with a 5,136 majority.

The real Liberal success in 1964, however, was not in seats won but in votes polled. The party, with 365 candidates in the field, polled 3,101,103 votes and forfeited only 53 deposits. The Liberal share of the poll was 11.2 per cent compared to 5.9 per cent in 1959. In the seats contested by Liberals, each candidate polled on average 18.4 per cent and in the seats contested in both 1959 and 1964 this percentage rose to 20.6 per cent. Whilst the seats won had been in the 'Celtic fringe' the party polled well in many parts of Britain. In the South East area, in addition to Orpington, which was retained with a reduced majority in the face of a massive Conservative challenge, the Liberals took over 25 per cent of the poll in a variety of Home Counties seats. Similarly, in the North West, the party polled well in such Manchester commuter suburbs as Cheadle (which recorded the highest Liberal vote in the country). In all, there were 68 seats in which the percentage gap between the Liberals and the winning party was less than 25 per cent. However, the irony of the 1964 election was that, in the best performance by the party since 1929, the Liberals returned only nine MPs – all of whom, with the solitary exception of Eric Lubbock, were elected in the 'Celtic fringe'.

As in 1959, however, the real significance of the election lay not in how well the Liberals had done, but in the cardinal fact that, by however small a margin, Labour had narrowly snatched victory from the Conservatives. Nor could the size of the Labour victory have been more harmful to the Liberals – because, whilst the party never actually held the balance of power, it had come as near as made no difference. In the tightrope parliamentary situation between the general elections of 1964 and 1966 very few things went right for the Liberals. Almost the only exception was the victory of David Steel in the Roxburgh by-election of March 1965. Even this victory, however, though giving a boost in morale to committed Liberals, had little wider impact. Except in the earlier by-election in East Grinstead (February 1965), where the party pushed up its percentage of the poll to 31.5 per cent, the by-elections told a depressing story. In three-cornered contests in the seven other by-elections fought by Liberals up to the summer of 1965, the percentages were: Leyton, 13.9; Nuneaton, 16.2; Altrincham and Sale, 19.4; Salisbury, 12.9; Saffron Walden, 11.9; Birmingham Hall Green, 16.4; and Hove, 16.7.

Behind these uninspiring by-election results lay more fundamental troubles. The narrow Labour victory in 1964 had effectively destroyed the cherished Liberal hope of replacing Labour as the alternative to the Conservatives. The Liberal Party, after 1964, had lost both its sense of purpose and its sense of direction. The Liberal dilemma took a new twist when Grimond gave an interview to the *Guardian* in which he quite clearly indicated that he would be prepared to contemplate coming to terms with Labour if the parties could agree on long-term policies and aims. Whatever Grimond intended to produce by these remarks, he must have been considerably pained by the instant hostility aroused in the party. The idea was shelved, but the future role the party should play remained as undecided as ever. Such divisions within the Liberal hierarchy did nothing to improve the image of the party.

The by-elections in Erith and Crayford and the Cities of London and Westminster in November 1965, in which the Liberal polled 7.2 per cent and 6.3 per cent of the poll respectively, were further evidence of the slump in Liberal fortunes. In both seats, the result was a worse performance than even the 1950 general election.

This pattern of a 'squeeze' on Liberals in third place was repeated in the crucial Hull North by-election in January 1966. The Liberals could poll only 6.3 per cent in the by-election, compared with 15.9 per cent in the preceding general election. As one correspondent wrote, the party had been ground to fine powder beneath the upper and nether millstones of government and alternative government.

The result in Hull North, with its tonic for Labour morale of a 4.5 per cent swing in their favour, was widely interpreted to herald an early election. The speculation was soon proved correct.

Facing a second election within two years was not a happy prospect for the Liberal Party. By late February, the Liberals had only 251 prospective candidates ready – significantly, 175 of these in Conservative-held seats and only 72 attacking Labour constituencies.

Not only was the party relatively short of candidates. It entered the election against a triple disadvantage: there was a clear 'squeeze' on the party in every constituency in which it was not the 'alternative' party; the 1964–6 Parliament had ensured a quite distinct loss of identity for the party, which was almost inevitable in the tightrope parliamentary situation after October 1964 – only in the debate on steel nationalisation had the Liberals really made a distinctive, constructive contribution. Finally, and linked to these factors, was the definite loss of unity at the top that had accompanied the decline in fortunes – in particular, criticism of Grimond's leadership had mounted after an episode in which he had openly discussed his future as leader.

It was against this background that the party entered the 1966 election. The party manifesto, *For all the People*, emphasised the moderating role which, it claimed, the Liberals had played; and committed the party to major defence cuts, entry into Europe and a new approach to industrial relations.

When nominations closed, the party fielded 311 candidates, 54 fewer than in 1964. This reduction, however, disguised the fact that the party entered the fray in 33 constituencies which had not been contested in 1964, but withdrew from 87 seats fought at the previous election. The 1964 and 1966 election results are compared in Table 12.3.

Table 12.3

| | 1964 | | | 1966 | |
	Vote	*Seats*		*Vote*	*Seats*
Labour	12,205,779	318	Labour	13,064,951	363
Conservative	12,002,906	303	Conservative	11,418,433	253
Liberal	3,101,103	9	Liberal	2,327,533	12
Others	347,094	-	Others	452,689	2
Total	26,676,882	630	Total	27,263,606	630

Although, with a reduced field of candidates, the Liberal vote had fallen by more than 750,000, the party had emerged with its representation increased to 12. On the 'Celtic fringe' the party lost two seats (Cardiganshire, unsuccessfully defended by Roderic Bowen, and Caithness and Sutherland, involving the defeat of George Mackie) but gained North Cornwall and West Aberdeenshire. The most encouraging gains were Cheadle, a Manchester residential commuter seat, won by Michael Winstanley, and Colne Valley, won by Richard Wainwright.

It was ironic, however, that the election which produced the largest Liberal contingent for over twenty years also marked the end of the road for 'Orpington-style' Liberalism. Whichever way the position of the party was reviewed, the underlying fact was that the hopes of the Orpington era had been finally shattered.

This was particularly true of the seats in which the Liberals had been the major challengers in 1964. Then, the party had finished second in 55 constituencies: by 1966, this total had fallen to 29.

Even these 29 seats (largely confined to safe Conservative suburban or remote agricultural seats and equally safe Labour-held industrial backwaters) were hardly promising territory. In only eight constituencies throughout Britain were the Liberals within 5,000 votes of victory. There were other equally depressing aspects of the election for the Liberals. Whilst the party had won Colne Valley (by virtually eliminating the Conservative vote), in the former Liberal strongholds of Bolton and Huddersfield the party's vote had rarely been weaker. John Vincent was to write of the results in *New Society*:

> Even where you would have expected results there are none. In every seat round Orpington (Chislehurst, Bromley, Dartford, Sevenoaks, Reigate), the Liberals ran third, behind Labour, in 1966. There is no general 'Orpington syndrome' in suburban areas. Drawing-room constituencies like Wokingham, Poujadist landlady seats like Southend, Brighton, Blackpool, Bournemouth and Southport, areas of intense local activity like Finchley and Maidenhead, all failed to return a Liberal in second place.[2]

To this extent, the hopes engendered by Orpington were indeed dead. The Liberals had proved they had considerable support as the middle-class, suburban alternative in Tory-held seats. But they had totally failed in the assault on Labour's natural areas of strength. The 1966 election marked the end of the road in another sense also. For it was followed, not very long afterwards, by the resignation of Jo Grimond as Leader of the party.

Although Grimond stated that his resignation was timed to give the new leader time to prepare for the next battle, in terms of 'real politic' the resignation seemed to confirm the failure of the dreams of the radical alternative. At least, so it appeared to contemporary opinion. Writing in *New Society* on the leadership change, John Vincent declared:

> ...It alters nothing. It introduces no new factor. It stresses, if it needed stressing, that the hopes of the Grimond era are as dead as the liberal conservatism of the Macmillan era.

And Vincent concluded:

> For ten years it has lived in a dream that was never probable and is now probably impossible.

13

The Thorpe Leadership: 1967–1976

Jo Grimond was succeeded as Leader of the party by Jeremy Thorpe. Although Thorpe was probably the best known of the Liberal MPs, he was by no means the obvious successor. When the Parliamentary Liberal Party first voted on the leadership, Jeremy Thorpe received six votes, whilst his two rivals, Emlyn Hooson and Eric Lubbock, each received three. Both Hooson and Lubbock then withdrew from the election, leaving Thorpe to be elected unanimously. Born in 1929, Thorpe was 38 when elected leader of the party. Educated at Eton and Oxford, he had subsequently made a distinguished legal career. He had first been elected for North Devon in 1959 (which he had won by a mere 362 votes) but had since held the seat continuously. He was a brilliant speaker, with a gift for mimicry which led some critics to see him as essentially a political lightweight, and his experience in Liberal politics had included the Treasurership of the party since 1965.

Thorpe became leader at a difficult and frustrating period for Liberals. The election of 31 March 1966 had returned Wilson to power with a massive majority. For the first time in British history, an outgoing Labour Government had been returned to power with an increased majority. Within a very short period, however, public opinion shifted violently against the government. In a variety of by-elections, Labour fared disastrously. Normally safe Labour seats fell to Conservative candidates, whilst in Scotland the Nationalists also gathered a large protest vote. But the Liberals made almost no electoral impact. The early years of Thorpe's leadership thus proved an unhappy time for the party. Morale in the constituencies was low. There was a sharp decline in the number of really active associations. The numbers of delegates at the Party Assembly went down from 1,400 at Brighton in September 1966 to 900 at Brighton three years later. By April 1970, the party had only 17 constituencies with full-time agents. The performance of the party in by-elections was equally unencouraging. In 12 of the 28 seats contested the party lost its deposit.

Faced with a swing to the Right at by-elections, and with Parliament preoccupied with the economic crisis, Liberals found it increasingly difficult to identify the party on many issues or to present a clear image to the electorate – a problem compounded by the recurrence of the party's perennial financial problems. Ironically, the issues on which the party was most active (such as its vigorous opposition to the Immigration Bill) were hardly issues likely to win the middle-class seats in which Liberals were in second place.

Among Thorpe's many difficulties within the party, the growing radical militancy of the Young Liberals was perhaps the most pronounced. The leftward trend in the Young Liberals had, by the time Thorpe became leader, already gone a very long way. By 1966, the radical Young Liberals were demanding the withdrawal of all American troops from Vietnam; workers' control of nationalised industries; non-alignment in the Cold War; Britain's withdrawal from NATO; opposition to the wage freeze; unconditional support for the 1965 seamen's strike; majority rule for Rhodesia; massive reductions in armaments; and entry into a Europe that would include the Communist bloc states of Eastern Europe.

These policies, adopted at the 1966 Young Liberal conference at Colwyn Bay, seemed to older Liberals more representative of the Young Socialists (or indeed Maoists) than of the party of the middle-class suburbs. Not surprisingly, when the Young Liberals attempted to convert the party's annual conference at Brighton in 1966 to the new ideology, bitter clashes developed.

Young Liberals attacked the party leadership for being overcautious, for being too worried about defending their constituencies rather than launching a crusade in the country. The party establishment attacked the Young Liberals as Marxists and disruptive militants. From 1966 onwards, the Young Liberals and the party hierarchy grew increasingly further apart. Virtual civil war in the party occurred in 1970 when Louis Eaks (the chairman of the Young Liberals) seemed to be claiming responsibility for the sabotage of county cricket grounds that had been done by those hoping to stop the South African cricket tour. Thorpe, with the support of his Parliamentary colleagues, denounced these tactics as 'hooliganism'.

On 25 January 1970 the National League of Young Liberals disclaimed responsibility for the cricket 'sabotage' and reaffirmed their belief in non-violent opposition to the tour. They nevertheless carried a vote of confidence in Eaks, who promptly proceeded to provoke a new storm by attacking Israel, declaring that Zionist apartheid was no more acceptable than South African apartheid. Renewed demands for his dismissal and even expulsion from the party followed.

On 31 January the Party's national executive hit back officially. A vote of censure was passed by a large majority which 'requested' the Young Liberals to dismiss Eaks. This only drew a rebuke from the Young Liberal wing for 'interfering' and it soon became obvious that many Young Liberals were rallying behind their leader. To some extent the tension eased when, at the Skegness Young Liberal conference in March 1970, Eaks was succeeded as chairman by Tony Greaves, albeit by the narrow margin of 222 votes to 199.

Greaves's victory was symbolic of another development within the party during these years that was to see its fulfilment after 1970: the rise of 'community politics'. The roots of this new 'community politics' lay in student and radical disillusion with the Labour Government after 1964. Experience in direct action campaigns and demonstrations convinced many young activists – particularly in the YLs – that the only way to secure effective change was at a grassroots, community level. In particular, this idea had been developed since 1968 by two radical Young Liberals, Gordon Lishman (the vice-chairman of the Young Liberals) and L. Freedman (then chairman of the Liberal Students). The background model for 'community politics' was neither particularly Liberal nor indeed British.

The most direct model was the kind of community work project organised by the civil rights movement in America. This was mirrored in Britain by grassroots activists like George Clark, who left the Campaign for Nuclear Disarmament to live and work in Notting Hill.

The technique of 'community politics' was soon perfected by Liberals. Ordinary people in a given area would be encouraged to fight for local improvements. Such groups were not Liberal, but their success in local battles with the town hall tended naturally to breed support for the Liberals who encouraged and guided them. From then onwards, using local newsletters and every form of propaganda, Liberals rapidly built up a strong council base. Thus, after 1966, Liberals succeeded in building up local election successes in Liverpool, parts of Leeds but most of all in Birmingham, where Wallace Lawler had proved himself a highly successful exponent of these tactics.

The luck of a by-election in the Ladywood division of Birmingham, almost at the heart of the Lawler empire, provided a critical test for the new 'community polities'. Ladywood hardly seemed likely Liberal territory. It was a rock-solid Labour stronghold, with much slum housing; it was also the most depopulated constituency in Britain, in a city that had not sent a Liberal to Westminster since 1886. Yet the outcome was a triumph for Wallace Lawler. On 26 June 1969, he gained the seat from Labour with a comfortable majority.

The Ladywood result was a spectacular success, not merely for Wallace Lawler but for the 'community politics' Liberalism which he represented. Yet as the realists in the party knew, Ladywood was not representative of the party nationally. Other by-elections showed disappointing Liberal results, whilst the party's financial problems together with the Young Liberal rebellion left the party with poor press publicity.

Meanwhile, the party devoted itself at the 1969 annual conference to the discussion (in private session) of a new constitution prepared by a Constitutional Committee under the chairmanship of Baroness Seear.

The new constitution authorised the Liberal MPs to elect the party leader (as they had in effect done in the past), but only after the Chief Whip had called a meeting of a new national committee of the party to sound opinion. A controversial plan to switch the authority of the annual assembly to a series of quarterly conferences, which would clearly be dominated not by delegates but by candidates and MPs, was defeated. The policy resolutions accepted by the Assembly included proposals for a 15-year education plan, a £50 million community works scheme, a Bill of Rights, a floating rate of exchange and widespread co-partnership in industry.

These somewhat grandiose and ambitious plans contrasted rather starkly with the electoral prospects of the party. When an election was called for 18 June 1970, the party was hardly optimistic: the last by-elections had been very bad for the party: the 1970 municipal elections produced the worst results for a decade. Nor was the party particularly well prepared, with only 282 prospective candidates when the dissolution was announced.

However, large donations during the campaign (amounting to nearly £200,000) eased the party's financial position, whilst the number of candidates in the field rose to 332. The candidates, in fact, provide an interesting comment on the types of person the Liberals were attracting. Over 56 per cent of the candidates were fighting their first election. Only 23 were women. Over 55 per cent of the candidates had been to university, nearly one in four to Oxbridge. Even more overwhelming was the preponderance of middle-class candidates – the Liberal tally included 37 lecturers, 55 company directors, 32 solicitors and barristers, 57 business executives and consultants and a strong contingent of journalists, writers and white-collar workers. In marked contrast, only five manual workers were in the lists of Liberal candidates.

Although the Liberals had entered the election without any great hopes, the actual result was worse than any Liberal had supposed. The party secured 2,117,638 votes, compared to 2,327,533 in 1966. Its share of the total vote fell from 8.5 per cent to 7.5 per cent. No fewer than 182 of the 332 Liberal candidates forfeited their deposits. Even worse, Liberals lost no fewer than seven seats – Ladywood and the Colne Valley to Labour; Orpington, Cheadle, Bodmin, West Aberdeenshire and Ross and Cromarty to the Conservatives. Thorpe retained North Devon by a mere 369 votes; David Steel was in at Roxburgh by only 550.

Even more disastrous than the seats lost by the Liberals was the fact that only in a few seats was the party able to poll over 20 per cent of the vote.

Not only had the number of seats in which the Liberal challenge had brought the party near to victory declined alarmingly, but the party was back to its position of really only putting up a challenge in very safe Tory-held seats. With six MPs, and not a really safe seat amongst them, the party had come full circle to its parliamentary representation of 1959.

The June 1970 election seemed to set the seal on the revival that had followed in the wake of Orpington. Indeed, it had seemed to mark the end of the road for Nationalists as well as Liberals. On separate occasions, each of the three smaller parties had seemed set to achieve a major political breakthrough – the Liberals at Orpington in March 1962, Plaid Cymru with the triumph of Gwynfor Evans at Carmarthen in July 1966, and the Scottish National Party when it swept to victory in the hitherto Socialist citadel of Hamilton in November 1967. The results of the 1970 election hardly seemed to indicate that the forthcoming Parliament would be one where both Liberals and Nationalists would secure their greatest triumphs so far. But so it proved to be. After 18 June 1970, public disillusion with the Conservative Government and Labour Opposition reached new heights.

In the immediate wake of June 1970, however, very little went right for the Liberals. The Liberal by-election record produced some of the most depressing results the party had ever suffered, and Jeremy Thorpe suffered a personal tragedy with the death of his wife in a car accident.

It was at this nadir of the party's fortunes that the first signs of the new 'community politics' became evident. At the 1970 party conference, at which most delegates were sunk in gloom at the party's prospects, conference accepted a radical Young Liberal resolution which proposed that the party should start campaigning and working on a community level.

These new advocates of 'community politics' had often little time for Jeremy Thorpe or other party leaders. Peter Hain, the former Young

Liberal Chairman, stated: 'The party leadership does not understand what community politics is all about, and if they did they wouldn't like it.' The new radicals constituted almost a separate entity within the party. The 'Radical Bulletin' group (as they called themselves) held their own seminars, published their own journal and helped secure election to key posts in the party. The group was to produce the famous Liberal names of the 1972–3 revival; thus David Austick, the by-election victor at Ripon, was a founder member; Graham Tope, the victor of Sutton, was equally prominent.

In a variety of cities, the new radicals began work; but above all Cyril Carr and Trevor Jones ('Jones the Vote') in Liverpool were the pioneers.

In the 1971 local elections, the first gains became apparent. Significantly, the Scarborough Assembly in 1971 was notable for the deep hostility between the mass of the party and the new radicals. But the radicals went on undismayed, making spectacular progress in local elections in Liverpool, a city in which in May 1968 Liberals had only one councillor, compared to 79 Conservatives and 34 Labour. By 1973, Liberals had become the largest single party. All this in a town where the Liberals had not won a Parliamentary seat since the Free Trade election of December 1923.

By autumn 1972, 'community politics' was to score its second major victory. At the Margate Assembly, Trevor Jones, the radicals' new standard-bearer, was elected President of the Party, defeating the leadership's candidate. Meanwhile, the advocates of 'community politics' moved from purely municipal successes to by-election triumphs.

The first breakthrough for Liberals came with a by-election in Rochdale (one of the very few constituencies in the country where Liberals were the main challengers to Labour). Cyril Smith won a decisive (if no doubt partly personal) victory, taking the seat with a 5,093 majority on 26 October 1972.

Critics of the Liberal revival were able to dismiss Rochdale relatively easily. The sensational result in the Sutton and Cheam by-election of 7 December 1972 could not be dismissed so easily. In a rock-solid true blue Conservative commuter suburb, an able and youthful Liberal candidate, preaching (and indeed practising) the gospel of community politics, swept to a landslide victory.

The understandable Liberal euphoria at overturning a Conservative majority of 7,417 on a greater turnover of votes than even Orpington had witnessed was soon sharply lessened by the result of the Uxbridge by-election which (on the same day as Sutton in a constituency not so very far distant) produced a Liberal lost deposit.

Meanwhile, partly as a result of a growing shift to the Left in the Labour Party, coupled with poor by-election performances by Labour, the winter of 1972 began to produce much comment on the possible desire of the voters for a 'Centre Party' and a realignment of British politics.

It was against this background that three by-elections were held on 1 March 1973 – at Lincoln, Chester-le-Street, and Dundee. The results were sensational: at Lincoln, the outcome was a victory for Dick Taverne with a majority of 13,191, a result which was widely interpreted as evidence of a growing desire for a 'Centre Party'. Meanwhile the very strong Liberal poll in Chester-le-Street, part of the Labour stronghold of the industrial North East (an area of virtual Labour one-party rule for a generation), also seemed to support this argument, whilst in Dundee East the Nationalist challenge brought the party to within 1,141 votes of victory. Dundee, coming after very strong Nationalist votes in Merthyr Tydfil (13 April 1972) and in Stirling and Falkirk Burghs (16 September 1971) provided yet more evidence that party loyalties were more than ever in flux and that a political realignment was a distinct possibility.

After the by-election sensations of March, the Liberals continued to attract attention with an assault on the Labour city-centre stronghold of Manchester Exchange. Michael Steed, the Liberal candidate, took 36 per cent of the vote leaving the Conservative with a humiliating 7.1 per cent.

Meanwhile, the 1973 round of local elections provided the Liberals with plenty of jubilation. In addition to a striking breakthrough in Liverpool the party not only swept to outright control in Eastbourne but became the largest party in five other authorities. In a further 20 councils Liberals succeeded in becoming either the main opposition group or the second largest party. Among the district councils where Liberals were now the largest party were Maidstone, Newbury, Pendle (Lancs.) and two authorities in Sussex.

Perhaps even more pleasing to the party was the toehold Liberals were able to establish in such hitherto barren areas as Bristol (where the party won a ward that had not returned a Liberal since before the war), Stoke and Harlow (an authority where Liberals now provided the only opposition to a solid Labour phalanx). The string of Liberal successes in local elections in 1973 (culminating on 7 June when 36 per cent of all Liberal candidates were elected) was not, however, quite as impressive in many of the larger industrial areas where Labour's strength was concentrated.

In the elections to the GLC and the new metropolitan and county councils, Liberals won only 178 of the 2,514 seats at stake. Even these 178 seats were heavily concentrated. Liberals won only six seats out of

308 in the metropolitan areas of South Yorkshire, Tyne and Wear and the West Midlands. Outside Merseyside (where Liberals picked up 19 of 99 seats at stake), the Liberals polled well, albeit unevenly, in Greater Manchester (13 out of 106) and West Yorkshire (11 out of 88). Even these figures disguised the extent to which many industrial towns, especially in South Yorkshire and the West Midlands, were still utterly barren Liberal territory.

These qualifications about the Liberal municipal revival, however, tended to be overlooked as, in parliamentary by-elections, the Liberal upsurge reached its climax. On 26 July polling took place in two of the safest Conservative strongholds in the country – Ripon and the Isle of Ely. At Ripon David Austick, the Liberal candidate, fought a community politics campaign centred on suburban Lower Wharfedale (three fifths of the constituency), where he had won a metropolitan county seat. All the tactics of a Liberal 'community politics' campaign were once again to be seen, with *Focus* newsletters (airing local grievances) using the techniques of tabloid journalism to sound out local grievances.

Austick achieved a remarkable victory, taking the seat with 43 per cent of the vote and a 946 majority. Meanwhile, an equally sensational victory was achieved by Clement Freud in the Isle of Ely. Freud won by 1,470 votes, taking 38.3 per cent of the poll. It was the first occasion in living memory that the Liberals had won two by-elections on the same day. Two further by-elections completed the triumph of the Liberal and Nationalist bandwagon: Berwick-upon-Tweed fell to Alan Beith and the Scottish Nationalists won Glasgow Govan.

Even when every excuse was made to try to explain the Liberal success, its dimensions could not be played down altogether. It was a revival greater in degree and scale than anything seen for a generation. During this period of revival, the main lines of Liberal policy remained largely unchanged, although there was a more marked emphasis on the need to redistribute wealth and tackle inflation. At the 1973 Liberal Assembly, motions were passed calling for a guaranteed minimum wage, higher pensions and a tax credit system. Motions calling for major industrial reform, including worker directors, also received much attention.

Against this background of by-election triumph, striking successes in local government elections and a revitalised radical policy, Liberals were understandably buoyant. As the winter of 1973 approached, Liberal support in the opinion polls was now at a high level and gathering increasing momentum.

How far this Liberal bandwagon might have continued to progress has to be conjecture. For, faced with an intractable miners' strike, and with the country in the throes of a three-day week, Heath chose to call an election to seek a renewed mandate for his government. Polling day was fixed for 28 February. It provided the Liberals with an opportunity that few had expected to come so soon to appeal to the electorate. Never before had the Liberals faced an election when riding so high in the opinion polls. Never had the opportunity to transform a by-election revival into a general election breakthrough seemed so possible. An immediate consequence of this Liberal optimism was to be seen in the nominations. When nominations closed, the Liberals had fielded 517 candidates, the highest total the party had ever fielded (exceeding the 513 brought forward in 1929 and the 475 who contested the 1950 election). The Liberal standard-bearers in the February 1974 election provided interesting evidence on the type of person attracted to the 'New Liberalism'. The Liberal candidates were overwhelmingly middle-class, predominantly young with a pronounced radical slant. The professions accounted for no less than 279 candidates, mainly teachers, academics, lawyers, journalists and white-collar workers. The average age of the Liberal candidates was only 37. There were again very few women candidates and almost no manual workers.[1]

With the largest ever Liberal contingent, with Plaid Cymru fighting every seat in Wales, and with SNP candidates fighting all but one of the seats in Scotland (Jo Grimond's in Orkney and Shetland), no one could deny that the British electorate had their opportunity to vote for a third force.

The main lines of the Liberal manifesto followed the resolutions adopted at the 1973 annual conference. The party manifesto laid much emphasis on a permanent prices and incomes policy backed by penalties on those whose actions caused inflation. Among other proposals put forward by the party were: a statutory minimum earnings level; profit-sharing in industry; a credit income tax to replace means tests and existing allowances; pensions of two-thirds of average industrial earnings for married couples; a Bill of Rights, the replacement of the Housing Finance Act and a permanent Royal Commission to advise Parliament on energy policy.

For Liberals, armed with a wide-ranging policy programme having a strong radical flavour, as well as with a massive force of candidates, the outcome of the election was doubly disappointing. Having entered the contest with their highest hopes for a generation, they came out of the battle with a staggering 6 million votes, but a mere 14 seats. The only Liberal gains were Cardiganshire and Colne Valley (from Labour), Bodmin and the Isle of Wight from the Conservatives and the new seat of Hazel

Grove, won by the former Liberal MP for Cheadle, Michael Winstanley. Perhaps the greatest individual triumph was the victory of Stephen Ross in the Isle of Wight, where he increased the Liberal share of the poll from 22.2 per cent to 50.2 per cent. The Liberal leaders also achieved outstanding personal results – thus Jeremy Thorpe obtained an 11,072 majority, David Steel was in by 9,017 votes, John Pardoe by 8,729 and Clement Freud by 8,347 in the Isle of Ely.

However, the greatest Liberal achievement in February 1974 was not in seats won, or even in the remarkable personal triumphs of leading Liberals, but in votes polled. Seats like Petersfield, Wrexham, Shrewsbury, Devizes, Taunton, Burnley and Chorley saw a near trebling of the vote, while in others – such as Bedford and Hereford – the vote was more than trebled. But in only a few of these seats was the Liberal total good enough to run the winners close – mostly in Conservative-held seats. In only 14 Conservative-held seats were Liberals within 4,000 votes of victory, whilst the Labour citadels had hardly suffered at all from the Liberal advance.

Lack of seats won in 1974, and lack of inroads into Labour strongholds (such as the North East, where Liberals had entertained high hopes), were only two out of many disappointments for the Liberals. Even the Liberal share of the vote was only 19 per cent, not the 22.3 per cent predicted by the polls, nor the 25–30 per cent they needed for their 'take-off'. The greatest Liberal disappointment was in those seats in which the party had polled well in 1970 and might have seemed in sight of victory in 1974. In a long list of these seats which they hoped to win, they seemed to run up against a ceiling which kept the prize from them; places like Eastbourne, St Ives, Dorset North, Liverpool Wavertree, Southport and Oswestry.

The Liberals also suffered a different disappointment in that they had hoped to gain seats not only in areas of past strength but also in the territory where they had recently had such local government successes. But in London they lost Sutton and failed to take Richmond from the Conservatives or Enfield from Labour. In Liverpool, the magic of 'Jones the Vote' worked so ineffectually that they were nowhere near success in Edge Hill and not even second in Trevor Jones's own constituency of Toxteth. In areas outside Liverpool where Liberals had built up a local power base, such as Nelson and Colne (Liberals nearly gained control of Pendle District Council in 1973), local government success again failed to transform itself into seats at Westminster.

Despite these disappointments, however, in certain areas of the country – especially in the South East, the Home Counties and the West Country – Liberals had made amazing progress. The peak of the Liberal revival came in the fenland seats around the Isle of Ely by-election breakthrough.

Elsewhere the Liberal impact varied, not only by region, but by the type of seat contested. In Conservative marginals, where the pressure to vote for one of the big two parties was strongest, the Liberals were getting about 21 per cent of the vote. In Conservative strongholds, where Labour had no chance of winning, the Liberal vote was on average 31 per cent. In many of the Conservative 'strongholds' the Labour vote almost collapsed and the Liberals – strengthened by these extra votes – surged ahead, as happened in Berwick, the Isle of Ely and the Isle of Wight. In each case former Labour votes helped to win them for the Liberals.

Overall, however, the 'squeezing' of Labour votes in safe Conservative seats could not disguise the essential fact that the Liberals had failed to make their expected breakthrough. What, then, had really gone wrong for the Liberals?

Their failure was centred round two factors: the Liberals did not poll quite as well as they (and many others) had expected in the final days of the campaign: and they underestimated the extent to which the electoral system discriminated against them.

The election results confirmed that the composition of the Parliamentary Liberal Party would stay markedly to the right of the Liberal activists in the country – particularly of Trevor Jones and the Young Liberal radicals. However, although the party might be to the right in terms of internal Liberal politics, there was little possibility that the offer made by Heath for Thorpe to support a Conservative administration would ever succeed. Heath's attempt to thwart a Labour Government duly failed.[2] However, the brief but stormy furore in the Liberal ranks when the proposal was made had only served to emphasise that the party could easily indulge in fratricidal warfare if talk of coalition was not handled very carefully.

As it was, Thorpe faced a difficult task after the February election. With a minority Labour Government, and with a general election widely forecast for the autumn, it was essential to keep the Liberal Party in top gear and in the public view. Although Liberal support in the opinion polls held relatively steady during 1974, the absence of by-election contests prevented the Liberals from getting any renewed momentum going.

As substitutes for by-election victories, the Liberals found two alternative weapons: the launching of a coalition campaign and the defection of Christopher Mayhew from Labour. The Liberal 'coalition campaign' was launched in a party political broadcast on 25 June by David Steel, the party's Chief Whip. The broadcast, with its appeal for a 'Government of National Unity', stated that Liberals would be 'ready and willing to participate in such a government if at the next election you give us the power to do so'. In an ITV interview the same evening

Thorpe stated that such a Government of National Unity 'reflects the views of millions of people'.

Thorpe may have been right. But within the Liberal Party the coalition plan was not received with total approval. Ruth Addison, the Young Liberal chairman, attacked the scheme as ludicrous. Radical candidates, who needed Labour votes to win Tory-held county seats, were equally sceptical. The fact that any Government of National Unity would almost certainly not include any significant part of the Labour Party also tended to diminish the whole political realism of the scheme.

In July, however, Liberal attempts to foster a realignment in politics achieved a marked step forward with the defection of Christopher Mayhew, a former Labour Minister and MP for Woolwich East, to the Liberal ranks. His defection increased the number of Liberal MPs from 14 to 15 and was accompanied by very wide press coverage. But those who expected further defections from sitting Labour members were to be disappointed. Meanwhile, the Liberals began frenetic activity to revitalise derelict constituency associations so that the party could fight virtually every constituency in the coming election. By the late summer of 1974, both Liberals and Nationalists were prepared for the largest-ever assault on the two-party system. When nominations duly closed for polling day, no less than 619 Liberal candidates had come forward, a rise of 102 on the February total – and an all-time record for the party. Every seat in England and Wales (except for Lincoln) was contested by a Liberal. In Scotland only Argyll, Glasgow Provan and Fife Central were not.

The Liberal election manifesto (*Why Britain Needs Liberal Government*) pledged the party to break the two-party system, to break what Thorpe attacked as the party of management alternating with the party of trade unionism. The twin pillars of the Liberal manifesto were social reform, together with the introduction of a statutory prices and incomes policy. Among the social reform proposals advocated were reform of family welfare provisions, higher pensions, the introduction of flexible mortgage schemes and a complete overhaul of the social security system. Other proposals included self-government for Scotland and Wales, greater autonomy in the regions, reform of the voting system, teachers' salaries to be paid by the Exchequer, the introduction of worker-participation in management, reform of company law and a major attack on monopolies.

To some extent, however, Liberal policy mattered less than the overriding question of which party Liberals would support in the event of a deadlock election. Labour's repudiation of any 'Government of National Unity' effectively meant that, if Liberals entered a Coalition, it would be a Conservative-dominated Government. For Liberals seeking

Labour votes to unseat Tories in rural-suburban seats, this was hardly a good vote-winning line. In the event, despite widespread predictions that Labour would win with a fairly massive majority, the result proved to be yet another cliff-hanger. As more and more Conservative-held marginal seats stubbornly defied the swing to Labour, computer forecasts of Labour's eventual overall majority came lower and lower. In the event, Labour won 319 seats, the Conservatives 277, Liberals 13, the Scottish National Party 11 and the Welsh Nationalists 3.

Once again, Liberal dreams had been rudely shattered. The party had entered the October election with their largest-ever field of candidates and with high hopes that the 6 million votes secured in February would prove a springboard for parliamentary success. They came out of the battle with fewer votes, a reduction in seats and with morale having suffered a severe setback.

The Liberals managed only a solitary gain in October 1974, at Truro, where David Penhaligon, an able Liberal who had been widely tipped to secure the seat, was in by 464 votes. Meanwhile two seats went down to the Conservatives, Hazel Grove and Bodmin, lost by Michael Winstanley and Paul Tyler. Not one of the many hoped-for Liberal gains materialised. Bath defied Christopher Mayhew's assault, whilst Leominster, Newbury, Skipton and Hereford all survived a strong Liberal attack.

Meanwhile the total Liberal vote had fallen from the 6,063,470 (19.3 per cent) cast in February to 5,346,800 (18.3 per cent) in October. This decrease tended to disguise the fact that, with 102 more candidates than in February, their vote in most constituencies had fallen quite considerably. In 93 per cent of constituencies contested by Liberals on both occasions, the Liberal share of the vote declined. Nor did the Liberal leaders fare as well as they had in February. With the exception of Richard Wainright in Colne Valley and Jo Grimond in Orkney and Shetland, all the sitting Liberals had their majority cut – by 6 per cent in the case of Jeremy Thorpe and 11.5 per cent for Cyril Smith at Rochdale. As a result only four Liberals possessed majorities over their nearest rivals of more than 10 per cent.

As a result of the October election, the areas of relative Liberal strength and weakness also saw some changes. The South West (and most particularly Devon and Cornwall) remained the best area for the Liberals, followed by the suburban metropolitan areas, whilst East Anglia lost much of the February upsurge.

The change in areas of traditional Liberal strength can perhaps best be seen in comparison with the 1970 results (Table 13.1). In 1970, Liberals were strongest in Devon and Cornwall; their two next best areas were both their traditional Celtic fringe strongholds, rural Wales and rural Scotland. By 1974, whilst Liberal strength in the South West had firmed greatly, and Liberal strength in the Home Counties had doubled or even more than doubled, rural Scotland has hardly changed in percentage terms. To this extent, the SNP upsurge had achieved what could well be the end of Liberalism as the dominant party of the Celtic fringe.

Table 13.1

	% 1970	% October 1974
Devon and Cornwall	20.6	31.5
Rural Wales	15.0	20.5
Rural Scotland	13.1	13.7
South-East (Outer)	12.7	23.3
Outer Metropolitan Area	11.0	23.2
South-West (exc. Devon and Cornwall)	11.0	25.3

Meanwhile, the areas of greatest Liberal weakness had seen less change. Industrial Scotland remained barren Liberal territory (and rural Scotland was now nearly as bad), whilst the West Midland conurbation and South Yorkshire remained equally desolate. Merseyside, once the great hope of the 'New Liberalism', slipped back in October 1974 to become one of the party's weakest areas.

Although the increased number of Liberal candidates produced more lost deposits than in February (some 125 deposits were lost), on average the party polled a respectable 15 per cent in seats not fought in February (indeed, in Houghton le Spring Liberals took second place with 21 per cent of the vote in a seat not fought since 1929). The worst Liberal area remained Glasgow and industrial West Scotland, where in such Glasgow seats as Govan, Cathcart and Shettleston Liberals polled under 3 per cent of the votes cast. In those seats in which Liberals intervened it seems that Liberals took a bigger share of votes from the Conservatives in Labour seats, and from Labour in Conservative seats. It is also interesting that the fall in turnout was considerably less in seats where Liberals 'intervened', indicating that there are clearly many voters who will deliberately abstain in the absence of a Liberal candidate. Although, in seats fought in both elections, the Liberal vote dropped, only in ten seats was this percentage fall greater than 6 per cent. The worst collapse of Liberal support, ironically, was at Eastbourne (13.2 per cent), the one local council with an overall Liberal majority. Of the other drops of over 10 per cent, two were in Liverpool and one was at Nelson and Colne (part of Pendle, where the Liberals were the largest party on the council). In Liverpool, despite a local power base, there were lost deposits in six out of eight seats; the average Liberal vote, at 12.7 per cent was lower than in any other English or Welsh city.

Outside these areas in which Liberals had entertained high hopes, the Liberal decline tended to be most marked in the key marginal seats, where the Liberal vote had been effectively squeezed.

One of the greatest single disappointments for the Liberals in October 1974 was the almost complete absence of 'tactical voting', whereby supporters of a party in a hopeless position would vote Liberal to unseat the sitting Conservative or Labour Member. In such seats as Bath, Chippenham, Hereford and Newbury Liberals had entertained high hopes that the Labour vote would go over to their camp. As the first results came in on election night it became clear that this was not happening. In one or two seats (such as Truro) a very limited amount of tactical voting occurred (and in Colne Valley and Cardiganshire Tories seem to have voted Liberal to keep Labour out) but such examples were rare in the extreme. The number of Labour lost deposits dropped from 28 in February to only 13 in October, thus reflecting the rise in the Labour vote even in the most hopeless of constituencies. Indeed, far from losing votes to the Liberals in strong Liberal areas, Labour appear to have recaptured votes lost in February. The election of October 1974 had thus seemed to set the seal on the high hopes of the 1973 revival. The party, despite its ability to poll a very large number of votes, had seemed to have come full circle to the situation of 1966. But there were some optimistic features of the results. In 27 seats, the party still managed to increase its share of the vote. The Liberals still remained in second place in some 102 constituencies, 92 of these held by Conservatives and ten by Labour.

The disappointing outcome of October 1974 was continued in a series of relatively poor by-election results. With Thorpe having already led the party for seven years, speculation began to mount over whether he would lead the party into the next election. Very shortly the leadership issue was to be at the forefront of Liberal politics. A luckless association with a collapsed secondary bank (London and County Securities) did nothing to help Thorpe, but it was the Scott affair that precipitated his downfall. Scott, a former male model, alleged that Thorpe had had a homosexual relationship with him. Thorpe denied the allegation, but the affair refused to die. Indeed, the allegations grew ever more lurid. Events moved swiftly. On 4 March the Liberals narrowly lost their deposit in a by-election in Coventry North West. On 8 March Pardoe made it clear that he was a contender for the Leadership. Cyril Smith rather less clearly, seemed to be about to resign.[3] At the same time the party had published its proposed new scheme for electing its future leaders, a plan based on a complex system involving the establishment of an electoral college based on constituency associations. On 11 March polling took place in the Wirral and Carshalton by-elections. In the Wirral the party fared disastrously, losing its deposit for the first time since 1950. Steel urged that the leadership issue be settled. Thorpe countered by offering to fight a leadership election when the new procedures had been agreed. He again categorically denied the Scott allegations. It seemed the crisis was over. In May however more rumours over the Scott affair surfaced. The local election results were dismal. Against this background Thorpe took his decision to resign the Liberal leadership. On 10 May, in a letter to the acting Chief Whip, David Steel, Thorpe resigned his position as leader which he had held since January 1967. In the unseemliest possible way the Thorpe era had come to an end.

Thorpe's unhappy exit left the party in a turmoil. With its proposed new electoral college not yet approved by the party, the Liberals in fact devised a welcome escape from their dilemma. Almost unanimously the Liberal Parliamentary Party invited Jo Grimond to return as Leader on an interregnum basis. On 12 May Grimond accepted this invitation. Shortly afterwards, at a specially called Assembly, the party accepted the new proposals for electing its Leader. The new system required a vote by all constituency party members for the leadership candidate. Each candidate, in order to be validly nominated, had to be backed by one quarter of the Liberal MPs. This was a pioneering democratic initiative in the constitution of a British political party. Paradoxically, in the political realities of 1976, it limited the actual number of contestants to two – John Pardoe and David Steel. Both men were different in style rather than content. Pardoe was pugnacious and ebullient; Steel, more orthodox, less flamboyant but by far the more skilful campaigner. After a not terribly dignified contest, on 7 July Steel was declared victorious by 12,541 votes to 7,032.

14
Pacts and Alliances: 1976–1983

The election of David Steel in July 1976 brought to an end the unhappy final saga of the Thorpe era. But it did not change the fundamental problems facing the party, in particular its strategy to avoid being relegated again to the sidelines of British politics. When Steel made his first conference speech as party leader he effectively also launched his own beliefs in Liberal strategy – namely the politics of cooperation. Not that, in many ways the leadership battle had been one of strategies; rather it was one of style marked as the *Annual Register* noted, by unedifying personal exchanges. The victor, Steel, had been the youngest MP in the House when returned for Roxburgh, Selkirk and Peebles in the 1965 by-election. By profession a journalist and broadcaster, in political terms he was firmly in the left of centre Grimond mould. He was equally convinced that the Liberal Party could only lever its way to power by working with politicians of other parties in order to achieve a breakthrough on to the political stage. In fact David Steel's enthusiasm to take the Liberal Party into a cooperation strategy with other politicians was to be tested at an earlier moment than could have been expected. By early 1977 the Callaghan Administration was in dire straits. On 23 March an opposition motion of no-confidence was due for debate. Weakened both by by-election losses (Workington and Walsall had been lost to the Conservatives in November 1976) and by defections (two Labour MPs had formed the breakaway Scottish Labour Party) Callaghan's position was perilous. Defeat was possible, even probable, with an immediate general election to follow. In these circumstances Callaghan looked urgently to negotiations with the Liberals. On the Liberal side the climate was favourable. Few Liberals wanted an early election with Margaret Thatcher returning on a landslide to Westminster. Hence within the party there was a natural anti-Conservative element that welcomed the discussions that led to the Steel–Callaghan deal – the 'Lib–Lab Pact' as it became dubbed.

On 23 March, the day of the crucial debate, a joint statement by Callaghan and Steel outlined the agreement they had reached. A joint consultative committee was established (chaired by Michael Foot) to examine governmental policies prior to their presentation to Parliament; there were to be regular meetings between Callaghan and Steel and between the Chancellor and the Liberals' chief economic spokesman. The Cabinet agreed to introduce a Bill for direct elections to the European Parliament, and to 'take account' of Liberal desires for these elections to be conducted on a proportional representation system. The Government also agreed to proceed toward devolution in consultation with the Liberals and to provide time for the Housing (Homeless Persons) Bill which the Liberals strongly favoured. It was announced also that the pact was to last until the end of the current parliamentary session. Margaret Thatcher denounced the agreement as 'shabby, devious manipulations', but Labour was saved. The Government won the no-confidence debate by 322 votes to 288. Although David Steel claimed the pact had 'stopped socialism', it was less obvious what benefits grassroots Liberals had gained from the pact.

Indeed, Liberal criticism of the pact was vocal. Liberal activists had wanted tangible gains – in, for example, electoral reform – whereas Steel himself seemed more interested in the *concept* of an agreement. These criticisms, led by such figures as Cyril Smith, centred on the argument that, for having saved the life of the Government, more favourable terms could have been obtained. These criticisms mounted, and the pact almost succumbed to an early death over the direct elections to the European Parliament due to be held for the first time in June 1979. By an Act of the Community each member state was to be allowed to adopt its own electoral system and procedures for these elections. At the conclusion of the Lib–Lab Pact in March 1977, the Steel–Callaghan talks had included undertakings on this subject. Callaghan committed his Government to introduce the necessary legislation for the elections to be held (it was official Labour Party policy to oppose direct elections and many Labour anti-Europeans wished to boycott them). The European Assembly Elections Bill was duly published on 24 June and included in its provisions a regional list system of proportional representation. Although the Bill passed its second reading on 7 July by 394 votes to 147, no fewer than 126 Labour MPs, including six Cabinet Ministers and 26 junior ministers voted against direct elections.

It was against this background that, on 28 July 1977, the pact was renewed for the coming session, with the Liberals insisting that the Government adhere rigidly to its pay policy objectives. The ever vocal

Cyril Smith opposed the renewal of the pact.[1] Jo Grimond, the party's elder statesman, warned that continued collaboration would make it more difficult to present a separate identity to the electors. The party assembly supported Steel (despite the Association of Liberal Councillors' warning that the party was bleeding to death), but on condition that the Cabinet and a majority of Labour MPs vote for proportional representation in elections to Europe. This was naive politics. The vote on the second reading had already demonstrated the extent of anti-Europe hostility in Labour ranks. The crunch came in November 1977. Only 147 out of 308 Labour MPs voted for the Bill with its provisions for a regional list system of proportional representation. Electoral reform for the European elections was lost. Many Liberals felt bitter and cheated. A special party conference was called for January to discuss the future of the pact. In the event, despite a sizeable and vocal minority against continuing the arrangement, at the special Assembly held on 21 January 1978, the Lib–Lab Pact was endorsed by 1,727 votes to 520, a majority of 1,207. In electoral terms, critics of the pact continued to point to a sharp and continuing decline in the party's fortunes in both local elections and parliamentary by-elections. In the ten by-elections between the formation of the pact and its termination, the Liberal share of the vote dropped by an average 9.5 per cent.[2] Liberals reckoned that the 1977 county council elections were the worst results for the party in the ten years from 1972 to 1981, while in the Birmingham Ladywood and Stechford by-elections the party finished a disastrous fourth place behind the National Front. As David Steel was later to remark, it was the failure and unpopularity of the Labour Government that had rubbed off on the Liberals. Indeed Labour lost such hitherto impregnable strongholds as Stechford and Ashfield in the aftermath of the pact. This unpopularity of Labour intensified when Callaghan, to the amazement of most political commentators, continued to soldier on until 1979. The 'winter of discontent' played into the hands of the Conservative Party. Eventually the whole lamentable Labour Government collapsed when the referenda on devolution in Scotland and Wales (held on 1 March 1979) proved an embarrassing fiasco. Faced with an opposition vote of no-confidence, with the Liberal pact having ended and the Nationalists embittered and furious, this time Labour had no means of escape. On 28 March 1979, for the first time since 1924, the Government fell in a vote in the House of Commons. In these circumstances, the Liberals therefore entered the 1979 election very much on the defensive. The Conservatives could attack the Liberals for propping up an increasingly unpopular Labour Administration, whilst the Liberals could see little evidence in by-elections or opinion polls of any electoral upsurge in their favour. Indeed, only in two by-elections between October 1974 and 1979 had the Liberals achieved good results. Both were in extremely unrepresentative seats. The first was at Newcastle Central on 4 November 1976; the second, on the very eve of the general election was at Liverpool Edge Hill on 29 March 1979. In the first, the Liberals achieved a remarkably good result in a city centre working-class area of Newcastle. The Liberal candidate, a local councillor and active community politics advocate, transferred a lost deposit to a good second place with 29 per cent of the vote. In Liverpool Edge Hill the outcome was even more dramatic. An able Liberal candidate, David Alton, scored a sensational victory, raising the Liberal vote from 27 per cent to a commanding 64 per cent with Labour collapsing from 52 per cent to 24 per cent and the Conservative losing his deposit. Although both results demonstrated the efficacy of community politics in inner city areas, neither had any very wider significance. Otherwise, the Liberal by-election record presaged the set-back that was to occur in May 1979.

The Liberal manifesto, like that of the Conservatives, had been geared for a 1978 election. Indeed, as early as March 1978 the Liberals had decided on the four main issues on which it proposed to campaign: political reform, industrial and economic reform, tax reform and ecological issues. Among specific political reform proposals in the manifesto (entitled *The Real Fight is for Britain*) were electoral reform, a Freedom of Information Bill, a new Second Chamber to replace the House of Lords, a Bill of Rights and devolution for the English regions as well as for Scotland and Wales. Among the party's other proposals were energy conservation (the ecology movement was catching public attention at this time), a switch from direct to indirect taxation, encouragement of employee share ownership, the abolition of the domestic rating system and a permanent statutory prices and incomes policy.

The campaign itself (despite the fillip of the Edge Hill by-election triumph) was a difficult one. The Conservatives started very much as favourites with Labour an easy target and the Lib–Lab pact an equally easy weapon with which to fight the Liberals. Steel conducted a skilful campaign and the fact that the Liberals did not suffer even more serious reverses owed much to his leadership.

In the event the Liberals returned 11 MPs, compared to the 14 with which they entered the election. The three Liberal losses were Emlyn Hooson in Montgomeryshire (a seat previously held by Liberals at every election that century), Jeremy Thorpe in North Devon and John Pardoe in North Cornwall. The outcome is shown in Table 14.1.

Table 14.1

Party	Votes	%	MPs
Conservative	13,697,923	43.9	339
Labour	11,523,218	37.0	269
Liberal	4,313,804	13.8	11
Nationalists	636,890	2.0	4
Others	1,060,613	3.3	12

Although the Liberal share of the vote had fallen from 18.3 per cent to 13.8 per cent, with the loss of a million votes, there were some encouraging features. Indeed, in 62 constituencies the Liberals increased their vote, mainly in seats where they were already strong and credible contenders. But overall the set-back was clear. In the 531 constituencies comparable to 1974 in England and Wales, the Liberal vote fell by 5.1 per cent. The fall was fairly even, with local factors accounting for deviations from this pattern. Thus the adverse publicity surrounding Jeremy Thorpe (and also another former Liberal, Peter Bessell) probably accounted for the disaster in the Liberal heartland of Devon and Cornwall. In five contiguous seats in this area the Liberal vote plummeted 9.4 per cent. The two best areas for the Liberals were in Liverpool (where David Alton held the Edge Hill constituency gained in the by-election) and the Anglo-Scottish border country (the strongholds of David Steel in Roxburgh and Alan Beith, the Chief Whip, in adjacent Berwick).

The convincing victory of Margaret Thatcher in the 1979 election seemed to point to an end to the volatile and uncertain politics of the 1974 to 1979 period. In fact, precisely the opposite was to happen. With Labour's internal feuds reaching a new level of bitterness, an upheaval was about to happen in British politics. In November 1979 Roy Jenkins, in his Dimbleby Lecture, called for a realignment in British political life. In effect it was the signal to launch the Social Democratic Party. Jenkins had previously cultivated the ground assiduously before making such a move. In fact, the antecedents of what was to become the Social Democratic Party stretched back many years. Thus, back in March 1973 Dick Taverne had forced a by-election (and been successfully returned) in his Lincoln constituency as a Democratic Labour supporter in protest at the growing activities of the Left in the party. The Liberals had welcomed Christopher Mayhew, the Labour MP for Woolwich East, as a defector to their ranks in July 1974. But these had been isolated examples. The 1979 Labour defeat opened the floodgate as more and more of Labour's Right found conference decisions on such issues as unilateral nuclear disarmament and withdrawal from the EEC impossible to tolerate. The Special Labour Conference at Wembley in January 1981 (which reaffirmed the decision to establish an electoral college for future leaders, with a strong weighting towards the trade unions) marked the breaking-point. The four leaders of the new movement (Shirley Williams, David Owen, William Rodgers and Jenkins himself – popularly known as the 'Gang of Four') moved swiftly. A week after the Wembley conference the Gang of Four published the Limehouse Declaration, announcing the establishment of a Council for Social Democracy. Initially this was not a separate party, simply a pressure group round which potential support would gather. On 2 March, however, 12 Labour MPs (including David Owen and William Rodgers) resigned the party whip and announced that they would not seek re-election as Labour MPs. On 26 March 1981 the new Social Democratic Party was formally launched, consisting initially of 14 MPs (13 Labour and a lone Conservative, Brocklebank-Fowler, MP for Norfolk North West). A new Party had been launched in British politics, aided by the largest defection of Labour MPs since the days of MacDonald in the 1930s. But it was not only a new party. One of the SDP's first decisions was to start to negotiate an electoral arrangement with the Liberals. A new Alliance had been born, the product of the lengthy series of negotiations between David Steel and Roy Jenkins.

In the opinion polls the Alliance got off to a heady start. This was a welcome turnaround for the Liberals. Indeed, the first test for the Liberals after the 1979 elections had come with the first direct elections to the EEC. Held in June 1979 the elections engendered a turnout of only 32 per cent in Great Britain. The result was a disaster for the Liberals in terms of representation. The results for Great Britain are set out in Table 14.2.

Table 14.2

Party	Seats won	Votes	%
Conservative	60	6,509,000	51
Labour	17	4,253,000	33
Liberal	–	1,691,000	13
SNP	1	219,000	2
Plaid Cymru	–	83,000	1
Others	–	88,000	1

With 1,691,000 votes, 13 per cent of those cast, the Liberals had emerged without a single representative in the European Parliament. Only in the north of Scotland had the Liberals even come within striking distance of victory.[3] Nor had the by-elections prior to the birth of the Alliance brought any great encouragement. The local elections of May 1981, in the wake of the advent of the SDP, brought the Liberals a welcome net gain of 250 seats. Although a few individuals fought under the SDP banner, the party had declared that it would not fight as a national party. On 16 June the SDP and Liberals issued an important policy statement, *A Fresh Start for Britain*. There were no surprises in its main proposals. These included parliamentary reform and proportional representation, a Freedom of Information Act, devolution, industrial partnership, support for NATO and continued EEC membership. These proposals formed the core of the party's 1983 manifesto policies. Critics noted it was less precise over economic matters (such as incomes policy) and defence issues (especially the nuclear deterrent).

Although the SDP was riding high in the opinion polls, it had yet to fight its first real electoral battle. This came on 16 July 1981 with the Warrington by-election. Warrington was a safe industrial Labour seat in Cheshire. Although a Liberal candidate was already in the field, it was widely expected that a leading SDP figure would seek to fight the seat. After a nasty dose of the dithers, Shirley Williams declined. Roy Jenkins took on the challenge. In a seat in which the Liberals had polled less than 3,000 votes in 1979, Jenkins achieved a major moral victory. The outcome was Labour (14,280), SDP (12,521) and Conservative (2,102). Although it was the first election battle Jenkins had ever lost, he described it as 'by far the greatest victory in which I have participated'.

Prior to the autumn party assemblies the SDP continued to strengthen its organisation. The Llandudno Liberal conference marked an important stage forward. The previously unratified alliance with the SDP was over-whelmingly supported at the conference, only 112 out of 1,600 delegates voting against. The Liberal conference also voted in favour of a statutory incomes policy, but defied the leadership by voting for unilateral British nuclear disarmament. The following month the SDP held its first ever conference, beginning on 10 October in Perth before moving on to Bradford and London. The Alliance with the Liberals was endorsed by enthusiastic acclamation. Meanwhile, the SDP (their ranks now swollen to 21 by further defecting Labour MPs) faced the problem of the by-election in Croydon North West. The Conservative-held suburban marginal seat had fallen vacant in July. This time, backed by David Steel, Shirley Williams eagerly indicated that she would run. The local Liberals, equally eagerly, insisted on readopting their own candidate. Since the Alliance involved Liberals and Social Democrats alternating in fighting by-elections, the Liberals got their way. On 22 October William Pitt, the Liberal candidate, swept to a remarkable victory, with 13,800 votes compared to 10,546 for the Conservatives and 8,967 for Labour. Although the seat was near to Sutton (won in a famous 1973 by-election) it was the first time ever in modern times that Liberals had won a Tory–Labour marginal.

If Croydon North West was a remarkable victory, the Crosby by-election produced a political sensation. Crosby, a middle-class Merseyside constituency, had been a rock safe seat for the Conservatives since its creation. In May 1979 the Conservative majority had exceeded 18,000. It was a daunting majority which, when the local Liberals withdrew in her favour, Shirley Williams decided to tackle.

The result was a dramatic triumph for Shirley Williams, who captured the seat with 28,118 votes compared to the 22,829 of the Conservative. A left-wing Labour candidate lost his deposit. Thus Shirley Williams became the first elected SDP MP, having captured one of the safest Conservative seats anywhere in the country. This trio of Liberal–SDP by-election votes was mirrored in local authority by-elections. Of 214 contests from July to December 1981 the Alliance made 100 gains. Meanwhile, on 13 October, the Alliance leaders announced their electoral pact for the next general election. Each party would field candidates in half the constituencies. The arrangements concerning the allocation of individual seats would be worked out at regional level.

With Shirley Williams returned to Westminster, only Roy Jenkins of the 'Gang of Four' was without a seat. The by-election at Glasgow Hillhead provided the opportunity. On 25 March 1982 Jenkins won a remarkable victory, taking the seat with 10,106 votes to 8,068 Conservative and 7,846 Labour.

The capture of Hillhead, however, was the prelude to a dramatic change in the political mood of Britain. On 2 March 1982 Argentina invaded the Falkland Islands. Thatcher reacted by sending a naval task force to retake the islands. The British public responded with a wave of patriotic enthusiasm. A month after the recapture of Port Stanley, the opinion polls gave the Conservatives 46 per cent, with the Alliance third with 24 per cent. In March the Alliance and Labour had shared first place with 33 per cent. The 'Falklands factor' had arrived. Its effect was to be seen in the first *national* test of public support for the Alliance which came with the May 1982 local elections. In the wake of the victorious Falklands task force, the results showed a 9 per cent swing from Labour to Conservative since the previous year. For the Alliance a close analysis revealed some very worrying factors. Overall, the Alliance polled an average 28 per cent of votes cast (almost exactly in line with the opinion polls), but the number of seats won came nowhere near to this level of support. The

SDP actually lost more seats than it gained (mainly the result of defecting Labour councillors being soundly defeated). And, as *The Economist* noted,[4] the different performance of the two Alliance partners was dramatic: the Liberals won nearly five times as many seats as the SDP. The significance of individual results was also very noticeable. In Mitcham and Morden (where a parliamentary by-election was to be held on 3 June) the Alliance vote was only 20.1 per cent, a poor third. And in Croydon North West, scene of the by-election victory, the Alliance vote was only half of the Conservatives. The lesson for a general election was clear. Without an increased level of support the Alliance would garner a huge tally of votes, but win only a handful of seats.

The parliamentary by-elections after the May elections repeated this pattern. The Alliance lost Mitcham and Morden on 3 June 1982, came a deposit-losing fourth in Coatbridge and, even with Dick Taverne as candidate, came nowhere near to winning Peckham. The only further by-election victory of the Alliance came in the exceptional circumstances of the Bermondsey contest. Here, a left-wing Labour candidate, Peter Tatchell, was opposed by a rebel Labour candidate who was supported by the former Labour MP. The by-election was one of the dirtiest in recent history. The Liberal, Simon Hughes, fought an excellent campaign, capturing the docklands seat with 58 per cent of the vote.

Bermondsey was an exceptional contest. All the opinion polls showed a commanding Conservative lead. By May 1983 the pressure was on the Conservatives to take advantage of this and call an early election. On 9 May it was announced that polling would take place on 9 June. The time had come to see if the Alliance could indeed break the mould. Despite some rival Alliance candidates (notably in Liverpool Broadgreen and Hackney South and Shoreditch) the Alliance campaign went well. The Alliance manifesto (the first to be published) offered a firm commitment to a programme of economic expansion aimed at reducing unemployment by 1 million within two years. Among the other proposals were the imposition of compulsory secret ballots for union elections, reform of the social security system, an incomes policy, continued membership of the Common Market and multilateral disarmament. The Alliance also called for proportional representation and for devolution of power to Scotland, Wales and the regions. With their opinion-poll support increasing, Alliance hopes ran high as the campaign closed. The result, in terms of seats, came as a bitter disappointment (see Table 14.3).

Only 23 Alliance MPs had been elected. Although the Liberals had gained five seats, most were in their traditional areas of strength. The gains were Yeovil, Montgomery, Gordon, the new constituency of Roxburgh and Berwickshire and Leeds West – the only Liberal gain from Labour in the election. Although the Liberals retained their by-election gains in Southwark and Bermondsey, the Croydon North West seat was lost.

Table 14.3

	Votes	%	MPs
Conservative	13,010,782	42.4	397
Labour	8,456,504	27.6	209
Liberal/SDP Alliance	7,781,764	25.4	23
Nationalists	457,284	1.5	4
Others	962,940	3.1	17

For the SDP the outcome was a disaster. Only five of their sitting MPs escaped defeat. Two of the Gang of Four (Shirley Williams and William Rodgers) were among the casualties. Not a single seat was gained from Labour, the solitary SDP gain being in the Ross, Cromarty and Skye constituency – an area of traditional Liberal strength in any case.

One consolation for the Alliance was the strength and evenness of the Alliance vote. As the polls had forecast, support was highest in the shire counties of the South and Midlands (28.6 per cent), followed by the Northern shires (24.9 per cent) but weakest in the metropolitan areas (23.8 per cent). The figures for Scotland (24.5 per cent) and Wales (23.3 per cent) are less comparable because of the presence of Nationalist candidates. Very significantly only 11 Alliance candidates forfeited their deposit, compared to 119 Labour.

This geographical spread of support was mirrored in the appeal of the Alliance to different sections of the population. According to a MORI poll in the *New Statesman* (17 June 1983) Alliance support was high in class ABC1 (upper and middle) at 28 per cent, the same figure in C2 (skilled working class) but less in DE (semi- and unskilled working class) at 24 per cent. According to MORI, 29 per cent of trade unionists voted for the Alliance. Among age groups of the electorate, support was 22 per cent (18–24 band), 29 per cent (25–34 band), 27 per cent (35–54 band) and 24 per cent (55 and over). Approximately the same proportion of men (25 per cent) and women (27 per cent) voted for the Alliance.

As a result of the 1983 election, the areas of best Alliance support showed some interesting differences compared to the historic Liberal heartlands (see p. 156 for 1974 comparisons). Table 14.4 demonstrates how Liberals (with six of the seven seats at stake) had captured the two extremities of Scotland: the border area in the South and the Highlands and Islands of the far north. It also shows the relative decline of Devon – the Alliance polled a greater percentage of votes in Northumberland and Somerset than in Devon.

Table 14.4   Areas of Highest Alliance Votes: June 1983

Area		Alliance %	Seats	Alliance Seats
1	Scottish Borders	54.2	2	2
2	Isle of Wight	51.0	1	1
3	Highlands and Islands	40.8	5	4
	Cornwall	40.8	5	1
5	Somerset	37.0	5	1
6	Northumberland	36.3	4	1
7	Devon	35.4	11	1

The tragedy for the Alliance in 1983 was not in votes cast but seats won. With 23 per cent of the vote in 1929, Liberals had won 59 seats; with 29 per cent of the votes cast in 1923, 158 seats. In 1983 the Alliance had a mere 23. In a sense, the electoral system had treated the Alliance cruelly. Thus, there were three seats in which the Liberals were within 500 votes of victory (Richmond and Barnes, Chelmsford and Edinburgh West) while the SDP were within 1,000 votes of victory in Islington South and Erith and Crayford. In all, there were 27 constituencies in which a 5 per cent swing from the eventual winning party would have given the Alliance victory and thus 50 seats in Parliament. Significantly, however, of the 27 Alliance 'near misses' in 1983, 22 were in seats won by Conservatives, while seven were in seats defended unsuccessfully by sitting SDP members. The Alliance was thus very far from threatening anything but an isolated handful of Labour-held industrial constituencies. Moreover, the Alliance knew that some of its own seats had been won with fragile majorities. Three of the 23 Alliance seats had majorities under 1,000 (Stockton South, Montgomery and Gordon).

In terms of seats won, the 1983 election was a bitter disappointment. Its real significance, and the real achievement of the Alliance in June 1983, was in terms of votes cast. The 25.4 per cent polled exceeded with ease the 19.3 per cent achieved by the Liberals alone in February 1974 and even exceeded the 23.6 per cent achieved in the Lloyd George revival of 1929. It was the best result since the 1923 'Free Trade' election, when Liberals had polled 29.7 per cent of votes cast.

The massive vote for the Alliance in 1983 proved beyond doubt that, after a generation in the political wilderness, the Liberal Party was very firmly back in the mainstream of British politics. It remained to be seen whether the support attracted in 1983 could be translated into a force powerful enough to break the mould of British political life.

15
A Tale of Two Leaders: 1983–1987

In the wake of the 1983 election, a swift change occurred in the leadership of the SDP wing of the Alliance. Roy Jenkins, the elder statesman and founding father of the Social Democrats, resigned as leader. Given the depleted ranks of the SDP in Parliament, the departure of Roy Jenkins effectively opened the way for David Owen to become leader. Able and ambitious, he had long been seen as the heir apparent by many Social Democrats and he was duly elected unopposed.

Born in 1938, Owen had achieved a meteoric rise in politics. Elected in 1966 as Labour MP for Plymouth Sutton (until 1974, after which he represented Devonport), he had risen to become Foreign Secretary under Callaghan in 1977 at the tender age of 39. He thus became the youngest Foreign Secretary since Anthony Eden in 1935. In 1981 he formed one of the Gang of Four which had launched the Limehouse Declaration and established the SDP. He had since been the Deputy Leader. He clearly had skill, ability and most certainly ambition. His charm and good looks endowed him with a certain charismatic appeal. On the other hand, especially among Liberals, his style was seen as frequently dogmatic and authoritarian. Nor were his radical credentials always clear. Whilst he was clearly anti-Socialist, he was less clearly or fervently anti-Conservative. Cynics also wondered how pro-Liberal he was.

Although some of these doubts were only to surface in future years, even from the earliest days the relationship of Steel and Owen was to have its problems. As *The Economist* later observed:

> Dr. Owen's reluctance to play the role of Mr. Steel's deputy is not simply a matter of pride. Unlike Mr. Steel, Dr. Owen has been in government (he ended up as foreign secretary in the Callaghan administration). And the two men have never been close friends. The separateness also reflects his instinct that the SDP, founded in 1981 by four former

Labour ministers, is a different kind of party from the Liberals. As for Mr. Steel, his early links with the SDP's founders had been mainly with Mr. Roy Jenkins, the amiable elder statesman who by the early 1980's was looking forward more to his next lunch than to his next post in government. Dr. Owen's appetite was – and is – unmistakably for power.

And *The Economist* concluded:

...the differences between the two leaders are more obvious than their similarities. They are, in fact, differences of temperament. Dr. Owen is bossy, impatient and arrogant – characteristics that the Liberals hate and some Social Democrats rather admire.[1]

At the same time that Owen became Leader of the SDP, the Labour Party also faced a leadership battle that brought a youthful Neil Kinnock to the forefront. With Labour revitalised, the Conservatives entrenched with a massive majority, observers eagerly awaited the outcome of by-elections as a test of public opinion in the new political situation.

The first opportunity for the Alliance after the 1983 general election to test its strength in a parliamentary by-election had come when William Whitelaw, the Deputy Leader of the Conservative Party, was elevated to the House of Lords. His sprawling constituency of Penrith and the Borders (in area the largest in England) was traditionally a very safe Conservative seat. It had returned Whitelaw with a 15,421 majority in June 1983. It was the type of constituency, however, with a 'soft' Labour vote, in which the Alliance could mount a strong campaign. The outcome was that, on a swing of 14.8 per cent from the Conservatives, the Alliance missed victory by only 552 votes. It was an outcome, with the Alliance frustratingly within range of victory, that mirrored so many of the results in the general election that had just been fought.

No further by-election opportunity occurred for the Alliance until the Chesterfield contest of 1 March 1984. Most of the media interest centred in this by-election on the attempted return to Westminster of Tony Benn (who had been defeated in his Bristol East constituency in June 1983). Chesterfield was a safe industrial Derbyshire constituency for Labour. Although the Alliance was easily able to push the Conservatives into a relatively poor third place, Labour held the seat with a 6,000 majority. On a swing from Labour to the Alliance of 8.5 per cent the Liberal share of the vote had increased by 15 per cent. It was an encouraging result.

A trio of by-elections occurred in May 1984. One of these (Cynon Valley in South Wales) was a rock-solid Labour stronghold in which the Alliance, although taking second place, made no impact. Labour held the seat with a 12,800 majority over the SDP Alliance, with the Conservatives forced into a lowly fourth place behind the Plaid Cymru candidate.

The two other by-elections were in the normally safe Conservative-held seats of Stafford and South West Surrey. In 1983 Stafford had produced a 14,277 Conservative majority with an even safer 14,351 majority in South West Surrey. This latter seat in particular was the type of constituency in which Labour had little chance of victory. As the campaign progressed, the Alliance began to squeeze the Labour vote. In Stafford, the SDP finished with 14,700 votes, less than 4,000 behind the Conservative and over 2,000 ahead of Labour. In Surrey South West, the Liberals with 18,900 votes were only 2,500 votes short of victory. Labour finished in a humiliating third place. This evidence of a strong Liberal revival was partly confirmed in the 1984 local election results. Together, they gave encouragement to the Alliance as it faced the most major test of national opinion since the 1983 election – the second direct elections to the European Parliament in June 1984. In the first direct elections in 1979 (see p. 168), the Alliance had been bitterly disappointed. In the huge Euro-constituencies, fought on the same electoral system as Westminster, the party had failed to win a single seat. Hopes were higher in 1984, but they were to be similarly dashed. Apathy was again the most obvious feature of the election. However, an analysis of the votes cast in the Euro-elections does reveal considerable evidence of the areas of Alliance strength.

The 12 best results for the Alliance in the June 1984 European elections are set out in Table 15.1. In only these 12 constituencies had the Alliance polled over 25 per cent of the votes cast. And in only a mere three seats, all in the west of England, had the Alliance secured over 30 per cent of the vote. Except for Merseyside West (a Labour seat) and the Highlands and Islands (won by the Scottish Nationalists), all were Conservative seats. And all (except North Wales and the Scottish Highlands) were in England south of a line drawn from the Bristol Channel to the Wash.

If the Euro-elections seemed to reinforce the political 'mould' in Britain, a series of by-elections soon destroyed this complacency. On 14 June, the same day as the European elections, polling took place in the Portsmouth South by-election. Whereas the nationwide European elections had produced bitter disappointment for the Alliance, the Portsmouth by-election produced a sensational victory.

The seat, which had returned Conservatives at every election since 1918, was the sort of middle-class constituency which the Conservatives regarded as their own. But, on a low 54 per cent turnout, Michael

Hancock, a local SDP city and county councillor, scraped through to victory, with 15,358 votes to the Conservatives' 14,017, to give the SDP their first victory since the general election. It was an excellent Alliance result in a town with no recent Liberal traditions.

Table 15.1

Constituency	Alliance %	Winning Party	% Maj.
Cornwall & Plymouth	33.3	Con.	9.2
Wiltshire	33.1	Con.	14.4
Somerset & Dorset West	30.2	Con.	20.7
Merseyside West	29.9	Lab.	12.4
Wight & East Hampshire	28.8	Con.	28.8
Highlands & Islands	28.1	SNP	13.8
Surrey West	27.0	Con.	32.2
Devon	26.6	Con.	28.1
Sussex West	26.3	Con.	32.4
Wales North	26.0	Con.	5.6
Cotswolds	25.8	Con.	27.7
Oxfordshire & Buckinghamshire	25.3	Con.	27.5

The momentum of this dramatic victory was difficult to sustain, for no further by-elections occurred until the contest in the safe North London Conservative seat of Enfield Southgate, a vacancy caused by the death in the IRA Brighton bomb blast of Sir Anthony Berry. Although not producing a sensation, once again the Liberal vote soared to leave the party in a very good second place, only 4,711 votes behind the Conservatives. However, the dearth of by-election vacancies continued.

During the whole of 1985, only two by-election vacancies occurred to test Alliance popularity: the contests of July in Brecon and Radnor in mid-Wales and the Tyne Bridge by-election in December in the safe Labour territory of north-east England. The Brecon contest took place against the background of the May 1985 municipal elections. Here the Alliance had done well, with its successes, if not dramatic, at least leading to many more 'hung' councils.

The dramatic victory for which the Alliance had been searching came in Brecon. In a vast, mainly rural mid-Welsh constituency, the Liberals secured victory by a narrow margin of 559 votes over Labour in a seat which, in the 1983 general election, had returned a Conservative with an 8,784 majority. But, as with Portsmouth South, no chance came to maintain any momentum. Labour safely retained Tyne Bridge, the Alliance coming second but nowhere near to challenging. For their next opportunity, the Alliance had to wait until the contest in Fulham on 10 April 1986.

Fulham posed particular difficulties for the Alliance. The seat, traditionally Labour, had been won by the Conservatives in 1983. It was thus a marginal seat in a part of London where local Liberalism had few firm roots. Furthermore Labour chose as its candidate an impeccable moderate. The outcome was a Labour victory with its percentage share of the poll up over 10 per cent. The Alliance vote remained virtually stationary.

Fulham had never looked promising Alliance territory. But the next two contests, on 8 May 1986, fell vacant in the sort of Conservative-held rural seat in which Alliance revivals had previously occurred. Of the two contests, in West Derbyshire and Ryedale, West Derbyshire seemed the better opportunity. Although the Conservatives had won by 15,000 votes in 1983, the Liberals had been a comfortable second with 14,370 votes and 27 per cent of the vote. It was a springboard for a knife-edge result, with the Liberals failing by a mere 100 votes to win the constituency which embraced much of Derbyshire's Peak District.

Ryedale, a vast rural constituency stretching from York across the moors to the coast, was the sort of Conservative fiefdom in which weighing the votes was usually the only form of political excitement. In 1983, with a majority of over 16,000, the Conservatives had secured 59.2 per cent of the vote, the Liberals a creditable 30 per cent. With Labour nowhere in the race, the Alliance produced a political sensation as memorable as Orpington or Crosby. The 16,000 Conservative majority was overturned to give the Alliance victory by 5,000 votes. The Alliance vote was up 19.8 per cent, the Conservative vote down 17.9 per cent.[2]

The two by-elections were held the same day as the municipal elections which also showed some Liberal successes, particularly the capture of Adur in Sussex and Tower Hamlets in London's East End. No other by-elections occurred until the vacancy in Newcastle under Lyme, a safe Staffordshire Labour seat, which polled on 17 July 1986. The strength of the Alliance upsurge was again apparent when the Alliance stormed from third place to within 799 votes of unseating Labour.

Against this background of quite remarkable by-election results in summer 1986, the Liberals approached their Eastbourne Assembly in good heart. The Conservative Government was highly unpopular and clearly accident-prone. Labour had problems of its own. The sun was shining for the Alliance.

At Eastbourne, disaster struck. The occasion, in an otherwise constructive conference, came with the debate over defence policy. The Liberal defence debate was opened by the party's defence spokesman, Jim Wallace, who argued convincingly for the leadership line and attempted to reassure delegates who feared the creation of a third nuclear superpower in Europe. A similar line was taken by Malcolm Bruce who, in his summing-up speech, again argued for an expansion of the European option. But the advocates of the amendment were perhaps nearer the pulse of the delegates. The mood was in part summed up by Michael Meadowcroft:

> We have accepted the implications of coalition politics and joint policy-making. But a Liberal Assembly must make Liberal policy. It must be rooted in our Liberal values, and it must be intellectually sustainable.

Meadowcroft concluded:

> ...we must stick to a strong, non-nuclear defence option which was in tune with Liberal policy, in tune with the wishes of a majority of voters, and would help strengthen the hand of Liberal leaders as they negotiated on policy for an Alliance Government.[3]

Even more persuasive was a speech by Bermondsey MP Simon Hughes which brought him a standing ovation. Simon Hughes concluded:

> We must never replace the independent British deterrent, and a European alternative is not acceptable... our children must have the hope of a non-nuclear world to inherit.

Thus, by the narrowest of margins – 652 votes to 625 – delegates voted for an amendment, opposed by most of the parliamentary party, which provided that any closer cooperation between Britain and its West European partners should *not* include a nuclear defence capacity. It was not the result the leadership wanted, and it had disastrous consequences. In the opinion poll ratings, Gallup recorded Alliance support at its lowest level for two years. The press had a field day. The tone of the right-wing press was reflected in the comment of the *Daily Telegraph* that 23 September was 'likely to be found engraved on the heart of Mr. Steel'.[4]

Urgent measures were thus needed to heal the rift in Alliance defence policy and limit the damage already being done amongst the electorate. On 19 October, David Steel hosted key figures in the defence tangle at his Ettrick Bridge home. Present were Des Wilson, the party President, Simon Hughes, a prominent defence rebel and Jim Wallace, the party's defence spokesman.

On 22 October the Liberals moved to heal their split with the Social Democrats over defence. The Liberal MPs agreed unanimously to back a new policy commitment to maintain and, if necessary, modernise a minimum nuclear deterrent. Thus the policy, drawn up by Steel and his senior colleagues, effectively overturned the Eastbourne debacle. Although it brought the party virtually into line with the SDP, Owen's 'Eurobomb' idea was downgraded. It now remained for the party rank and file to endorse the policy statement of the parliamentary party. Meeting in Bristol, the Liberal Party Council in December agreed a detailed accord with the SDP over defence. The Liberal MPs, Simon Hughes and Michael Meadowcroft, who were among those who voted against Steel in his defeat at the Eastbourne party assembly, were at the council which supported the new formula. A resolution from Liberal unilateralists which sought the calling of a special Liberal Assembly to endorse the new policy was withdrawn. The details of the accord were essentially those agreed on 22 October, with some elaboration. The three key items of the new policy were: to maintain (with whatever necessary modernisation) a minimum nuclear deterrent until it could be negotiated away as part of global arms reductions; to freeze Britain's nuclear capacity in any modernisation at a level no greater than that of the Polaris system; and finally, to give much higher priority to the disarmament negotiations. Other main features of the accord were: the scrapping of the Trident ballistic missile system, but retention of the existing Polaris as a 'minimum nuclear deterrent'; the withdrawal from President Reagan's 'Star Wars' policy; the removal of 'battlefield' nuclear weapons 150 kilometres either side of the Russian border; and the strengthening of conventional forces.

Meanwhile, after the disastrous events of Eastbourne, another tragedy was to strike the beleaguered Liberals. On 22 December 1986, there occurred the untimely death in a road accident of 42-year-old David Penhaligon, the Liberal MP for Truro. His death came as a grievous blow to the Liberal Party. Apart from being one of the most able and likeable of Liberal MPs, he had played a crucial role in the development of the alliance with the Social Democrats and was one of the party's foremost strategists and campaigners. Indeed, it was this role behind the scenes that was even more important than his official party title as spokesman on economic affairs. His death created a by-election in the Cornish constituency of Truro which he had first gained from the Conservatives in 1974. Whilst few expected anything but a comfortable victory in Truro, the events of 22 December, coming on top of the defence debacle of 23 September, had together made it a bleak end to 1986 for the Alliance.

These events made all the more necessary a 're-launch' of the Alliance at the beginning of 1987. This was to take place in January 1987 with a major rally to launch the joint Alliance policy document 'Partnership for Progress'. The rally, the biggest joint event the two parties had ever staged, undoubtedly helped rejuvenate party fortunes. What was needed, however, was a sensational election triumph. This came, in the most unexpected form, with the death of the sitting Labour MP for Greenwich.

At first sight, a contest in Greenwich hardly seemed likely territory for an Alliance by-election victory. In the general election of 1983, Labour had narrowly held the seat with a majority of 1,211 over the Conservatives. The Alliance had trailed in third place. But these figures in themselves disguised the fact that Greenwich should have been safe Labour ground. Labour had previously held the seat with very comfortable majorities at every election since 1945. It was thus a safe Labour seat where local Labour Party activists regarded the narrow majority in the 1983 election as a freak aberration. Indeed, a Thames riverside constituency was exactly the sort of heartland that Labour needed to claim as its own. The death of Guy Barnett, a much respected moderate member of the Labour Party, put the loyalty of Greenwich to the test.

Behind the statistics, several factors arose to cause Greenwich to occupy the centre of the political stage. First, Labour selected as its candidate Deirdre Wood, a left-winger whose views were rapidly portrayed as extremist by the press. The Conservatives chose a relatively unseasoned youngster with little political experience. By way of contrast, with Rosie Barnes the Alliance had a personable and engaging candidate.

As the campaign developed, and as the Conservatives began to trail consistently in third place in the opinion polls, the Alliance bandwagon began to roll. The outcome of the by-election, on 26 February 1987, was a sensation. Rosie Barnes swept to victory, polling 18,287 votes, a majority of over 6,600 over Labour's 11,676 votes, with the Conservatives polling a meagre 3,852. Not only was it the first ever by-election success by the SDP in a Labour-held seat (all previous victories had been in Conservative-held seats), but it was the *scale* of the victory that sent shock waves around the political world.

The Alliance had polled 52.9 per cent of the vote (up 27.8 per cent), Labour fell by 4.4 per cent and the Conservative vote fell to less than a third of its 1983 figure (down 23.6 per cent). Overall, the swing from Labour to the SDP was 16.2 per cent and from Conservative to SDP 25.7 per cent.

Given that this was the worst by-election performance by the Conservatives at the hands of the Alliance since Sutton and Cheam in 1972, much attention focused in the press on the significance of the 'tactical voting' that had clearly occurred, with Conservatives voting Alliance to keep out a left-wing Labour candidate. Certainly, the Greenwich contest, with its highly personalised attacks on Labour's hard-left candidate had been among the dirtiest campaigns in recent times. But the outcome at last enabled the Alliance to break out of the electoral trough in which it had found itself since the disastrous defence debate at the 1986 party conference. Even the *Daily Telegraph* editorial declared that 'the outcome of the Greenwich by-election is a triumph for the Alliance'.[5] Equally significant, however, was the impact of Greenwich on Labour's morale.

Confirmation of the slump of the Labour vote after Greenwich was also to be seen in the by-election for the European Parliament in the West Midlands constituency. Whereas the media had given saturation coverage to Greenwich, the Euro by-election was relatively ignored. Although Labour narrowly retained the seat over the Conservatives, Labour's support crumbled from 50.7 per cent to 39.1 per cent. The Alliance share of the vote more than doubled, from 12.1 per cent in June 1984 to 24.4 per cent in the by-election. Given the difficulties of campaigning in such a large constituency, and given that the West Midlands was hardly a notable area of Liberal strength, it was a good Alliance result.

The West Midlands by-election, however, attracted almost no press coverage. In contrast, much more media attention centred on the by-election held on 12 March 1987 at Liberal-held Truro. Here was just the opportunity for the Alliance to maintain its momentum. And so it proved. The Truro contest proved to be a triumph for the Liberals. The party swept to their biggest-ever post-war by-election victory when 24-year-old Matthew Taylor, a former research assistant to David Penhaligon, held the seat with a 14,617 majority to become the youngest MP in the House of Commons. The majority comfortably exceeded the previous best Liberal post-war majority – the 11,072 secured by former leader Jeremy Thorpe in the February 1974 general election. The Liberal vote at Truro had increased by over 4,000 compared to the 1983 general election. Whilst personal loyalty to the memory of David Penhaligon, together with the marked Cornish loyalty of many voters, meant that Truro was not necessarily a good guide to the true political pulse of the country, nonetheless, the upsurge in Alliance support after the Greenwich and Truro victories was swiftly reflected in the opinion polls. On 26 March 1987, *Today* carried a Marplan poll showing the Alliance level with Labour on 31 points each, five points behind the Conservatives. The following day, the Gallup poll, conducted for the *Daily Telegraph* was even more sensational. It showed the Conservatives in the lead (with

37.5 per cent) but with the Alliance now on 31.5 per cent compared to Labour's 29.5 per cent. On the sixth anniversary of the founding of the SDP, it could hardly have been a more fitting birthday tonic. For the first time since Kinnock had become Labour's leader three years earlier, the Alliance had moved into a highly significant challenging position to the Conservatives. Suddenly not only the timing but even the outcome of the next election seemed to be thrown wide open. The fact that the Alliance upsurge was continuing, despite (some even said because of) bitter attacks by such leading Conservatives as Norman Tebbitt, sent shivers down the spine of those back-bench Conservatives whose majorities now looked highly vulnerable.

Away from the by-elections and opinion polls, however, observers sensed that the longer-term political outlook was rather different. Nationally, the tide seemed to be flowing very much towards the Conservatives. Labour was clearly in disarray (with further damaging internal rows over 'black sections' and the dismissal of a prospective parliamentary candidate in Nottingham). The economy was improving, with unemployment at last falling, interest rates coming down and a budget lowering income tax. Margaret Thatcher made a highly publicised, high-profile visit to Moscow, in which Mikhail Gorbachev was portrayed as some sort of long-lost brother.

In the opinion polls, the Conservatives now maintained a steady and commanding lead. In the City, stock markets rose as the anticipation of a Conservative election victory mounted. Before deciding on the timing of an election, however, the Conservatives waited, as they had in 1983, on the outcome of the 7 May municipal elections. These thus presented the Alliance with their last opportunity for a breakthrough prior to an election.

With a very large field of candidates, and with a net gain of some 50 seats in local by-elections since 1986, the Alliance entered the elections in hopeful, indeed buoyant, mood. But, although the Alliance achieved its announced target of 400 net gains, it did not achieve the sort of dramatic breakthrough that it was seeking as a launch pad for a general election campaign.

The major prize which the Alliance had sought to capture – Liverpool – reverted to Labour control. Other hoped-for prizes, such as Hastings and Cheltenham, proved obstinately loyal to the Conservatives. The Alliance had to be content with the capture of a handful of relatively medium-sized councils – Pendle, South Somerset, West Lindsey and, perhaps most remarkable, Blyth Valley (an Alliance gain that ended 65 years of unbroken Labour rule). There were also disturbing aspects of the results, with the voting in such areas as Leeds and Stockton pointing to possible Alliance losses at a general election.

After analysing the municipal election results, the Conservatives had few hesitations in calling a snap poll. At the same time, the Alliance had every reason to have high expectations of a good result in the election of 11 June. The Alliance could look back over the 1983–7 period with considerable satisfaction at its by-election record (see Table 15.2).

Table 15.2   The Alliance By-Election Record: 1983–7

Date	Constituency	Con. % Change	Lab. % Change	Lib./SDP % Change	Result
28.7.83	Penrith and the Borders	−12.8	−5.9	+16.7	Con. hold
1.3.84	Chesterfield	−17.3	−1.6	+15.2	Lab. hold
3.5.84	Surrey South West	−10.4	−1.5	+11.3	Con. hold
3.5.84	Stafford	−10.8	+3.7	+7.1	Con. hold
3.5.84	Cynon Valley	−6.8	+2.8	−0.7	Lab. hold
14.6.84	Portsmouth South	−15.7	+3.9	+12.2	SDP gain
13.12.84	Southgate	−8.5	−5.9	+12.2	Con. hold
4.7.85	Brecon and Radnor	−20.5	+9.3	+11.4	Lib. gain
6.12.85	Tyne Bridge	−14.2	+1.3	+11.4	Lab. hold
10.4.86	Fulham	−11.3	+10.4	+0.6	Lab. gain
8.5.86	Ryedale	−17.9	−1.9	+19.8	Lib. gain
8.5.86	Derbyshire West	−16.3	+2.7	+12.3	Con. hold
17.7.86	Newcastle-under-Lyme	−17.4	−1.2	+17.7	Lab. hold
13.11.86	Knowsley North	−13.8	−8.2	+19.8	Lab. hold
26.2.87	Greenwich	−23.6	−4.4	+27.8	SDP gain
12.3.87	Truro	−6.5	+2.6	+3.1	Lib. hold

In terms of policy and programme also, the Alliance was ready. The Alliance manifesto (described as a 'programme for government') was published on 18 May, under the title *Britain United* and with the subtitle, *The time has come*. In their joint foreword Steel and Owen declared that 'the task of drawing Britain together again can only be achieved through political, economic and social reform on a scale not contemplated in our country for over 40 years'. If the Alliance held the balance of power, the two leaders promised to judge issues on their merits, 'curbing the Tories' divisive policies and stopping the destructive antics of the Labour left'. As the foreword declared, 'the two-party, two-class pantomime would finally be over'. Specific proposals in the Alliance manifesto included a 'Great Reform Charter', aimed at strengthening democracy both locally and nationally. Electoral reform was again emphasised, along with repeal of Section 2 of the Official Secrets Act. A Freedom of Information Act would be introduced, while the Alliance reaffirmed its commitment to devolve power to Scotland and Wales. The Alliance also proposed fixed-term parliaments, removing the right of the prime minister to determine general election dates, and the possibility of 18-year-olds becoming MPs. Other proposals included major legislation in the area of equal opportunities for women and strengthening individual rights by enacting the European Convention on Human Rights into British Law.

Despite the publicity and hopes achieved by the launch of the Alliance manifesto, the campaign never fulfilled the hopes of Liberals and Social Democrats. The Conservatives never really looked like losing, while Labour never really looked like disintegrating. The two-headed leadership of the Alliance never looked comfortable. Yet few leading Alliance supporters realised how disappointing the outcome of the election would be.

The tally of 22 Alliance seats won was a bitter disappointment (see Table 15.3). After all their high hopes, the Alliance gained precisely three seats, all won by Liberals. The three gains were the Lancashire coastal resort of Southport and two rural Scottish constituencies (Fife North

Table 15.3   Seats Won by Liberal/SDP Alliance: June 1987

The 22 Alliance Seats (in order of majorities secured)

Constituency	Majority	Party Second
Brecon and Radnor	56	Con.
Argyll and Bute*	1394	Con.
Fife North-East*	1447	Con.
Southport*	1849	Con.
Woolwich	1937	Lab.
Greenwich	2141	Lab.
Liverpool Mossley Hill	2226	Lab.
Montgomery	2558	Con.
Rochdale	2779	Lab.
Southwark and Bermondsey	2779	Lab.
Orkney and Shetland	3922	Con.
Roxburgh and Berwickshire	4008	Con.
Ceredigion and Pembroke North	4700	Con.
Truro	4753	Con.
Inverness, Nairn and Lochaber	5431	Lab.
Yeovil	5700	Con.
Tweedale, Ettrick and Lauderdale	5942	Con.
Plymouth Devonport	6470	Con.
Caithness and Sutherland	8494	Con.
Berwick-upon-Tweed	9503	Con.
Gordon	9519	Con.
Ross, Cromarty and Skye	11319	Con.

* Alliance gain in 1987 Election

East and Argyll and Bute). The SDP failed to gain a single seat. To set against the three Alliance gains, a whole string of constituencies was lost. The Liberals saw the Conservatives regain Ryedale (won in the May 1986 by-election) together with Cambridgeshire North East, the Isle of Wight and Colne Valley, whilst Leeds West was lost to Labour. Equally bad were the losses suffered by the Social Democrats. Glasgow Hillhead, the constituency of Roy Jenkins, was lost to Labour. Stockton South and Portsmouth South were won by the Conservatives. Table 15.4 lists the 20 seats in which the Alliance came closest to victory.

Table 15.4   Alliance Marginals after June 1987

Constituency	Majority	Winning Party
Portsmouth South*	205	Con.
Stockton South*	774	Con.
Islington South	805	Lab.
Blyth Valley	853	Lab.
Edinburgh West	1234	Con.
Bath	1412	Con.
Hereford	1413	Con.
Cambridgeshire North-East*	1428	Con.
Colne Valley*	1677	Con.
Richmond and Barnes	1766	Con.
Hazel Grove	1840	Con.
Kincardine and Deeside	2063	Con.
Conwy	3024	Con.
Plymouth Drake	3125	Con.
Glasgow Hillhead*	3251	Lab.
Sheffield Hillsborough	3286	Lab.
Plymouth Sutton	4013	Con.
Devon North	4469	Con.
Bow and Poplar	4631	Lab.
Leyton	4641	Lab.

* Seat lost in June 1987

Although, in general, the Alliance vote had remained remarkably stable, in no way had there been a breakthrough.[6] The party was no nearer winning anything but the isolated Labour stronghold. Of its 20 most winnable seats after June 1987, all but six were Conservative-held rural or suburban seats. Some 13 of the 22 Alliance seats were in rural Wales or Scotland. Three more were in the West Country. The electoral geography of June 1987 had changed relatively little vis-à-vis the old Alliance areas of support. In this sense, June 1987 was the end of a chapter. The era of two leaders and two wings of the Alliance was now to be challenged by Steel's pre-emptive call for unity.

16
Merger Most Foul: 1987–1988

The electoral disappointments of June 1987 were rapidly followed by moves initiated by David Steel on behalf of the Liberals to secure an early and full Liberal–SDP merger. His call, almost before the dust of the election battle had settled, was for 'democratic fusion'. It met a widely differing response from within the ranks of the SDP.

The leading supporters of a merger from the SDP ranks were three of the original Gang of Four – Roy Jenkins, Bill Rodgers and Shirley Williams. Among the five-strong SDP parliamentary band, however, only Charles Kennedy (in Ross, Cromarty and Skye) initially supported the merger. But outside Parliament the great weight of SDP senior figures campaigned for a merger. Their ranks were joined by Alex McGivan, the SDP National Organiser, who resigned in order to campaign freely for a merger.

In many parts of the country, SDP members had already voted with their feet by merging at constituency level with the local constituency Liberal Association. The *Liberal News* reported 'grassroots mergers' in such constituencies as Cambridge, Saffron Walden, Bexhill and Vauxhall, whilst its own readership poll found 91 per cent of Liberals favouring a merger.[1]

In contrast to those earnestly favouring merger, Steel's call met with an intensely hostile reaction from those, led by Owen, who bitterly opposed fusion. Owen and his supporters interpreted 'democratic fusion' as an unwelcome attempt to bounce them into merger. The issue, however, was to be resolved by a ballot of the entire SDP membership. On 29 June, after much internal wrangling, the SDP National Committee agreed upon the wording of the proposed ballot. The membership was balloted on whether members (i) wanted the national committee to negotiate a closer constitutional framework for the Alliance, short of a merger, which preserved the identity of the SDP or (ii) wanted it to negotiate a merger of the SDP and the Liberal Party into one party.

From the outset, David Owen and his supporters prepared to fight a fierce campaign within the ranks of the Social Democrats to prevent a merger with the Liberals. Owen promptly made it clear that, whatever actions might be taken by other members of the SDP's founding Gang of Four, he would not be influenced by them. Owen's allies on the SDP National Committee also made it clear that they were determined to preserve the separate identity of their party. They made the point that on numerous issues, such as defence, terrorism, the miners' strike and the market economy, they regarded the Liberals as both weak and unreliable.

Thus the SDP split into two clearly defined camps. The pro-merger campaign was led on the SDP side by Shirley Williams (the Party President), supported by two other members of the original Gang of Four – Roy Jenkins and Bill Rodgers (all of whom had been out of Parliament since the 1987 general election). Senior SDP figures who supported the merger were quick to suggest that, if Owen succeeded in blocking a merger, the party would disintegrate, for neither Jenkins, Williams nor Rodgers would remain in an SDP which remained on its own. Opposing the merger Owen's closest supporters included Cartwright (MP for Woolwich) and Rosie Barnes (newly-elected MP in adjacent Greenwich). If fewer in number than the pro-merger camp, they had considerable support from the financial backers of the SDP and the very considerable personal asset of Owen himself.

On the whole, however, the ballot debate was both unedifying and vindictive, characterised by personal attacks and little constructive argument. These personal attacks included a particularly strong attack on Owen by Gwynoro Jones, the SDP Chairman in Wales, who accused him of 'failing miserably as a leader' and having shown 'lack of judgement and vision'.

The result of the ballot of the SDP's 58,509 members was announced on 6 August. The result was a comfortable, rather than a runaway, victory for merger. The pro-merger vote totalled 25,897 (57.4 per cent), the anti-merger vote 19,228 (42.6 per cent). With a turnout of 45,125 votes (77.7 per cent),[2] the majority for merger was 6,669. Nonetheless, the 42 per cent preferring the alternative option of a constitutional framework for the Alliance 'short of merger' which would preserve the identity of the SDP was substantial. Thus the majority for merger was just enough for David Steel and the pro-merger faction of the SDP to voice confidence that the new party could be up and running by early 1988.

The outcome of the ballot, however, was dwarfed in the newspaper headlines by the rapid and dramatic resignation of David Owen, 'sad and distressed' by his party's vote. Owen's resignation statements brought into the open his bitterness and dissatisfaction with events since the election. Owen made it clear that Steel's decision to force the issue and pace for merger had been 'a folly and great tragedy'. Thus Owen's resignation on 6 August left the SDP leaderless and with a crucial party conference only weeks away.

The resignation of Owen and the SDP split had, in the words of Roy Jenkins, taken 'the gilt off the gingerbread of this result'. Nonetheless, the road to merger now lay ahead. But more immediately, the SDP had to find itself a new leader.

At first, it seemed that Charles Kennedy, the only SDP MP to have declared himself in favour of merger, might become the new leader. On 15 August, however, he announced that he was standing aside in order to nominate Robert Maclennan, the MP for Caithness and Sutherland. There was also speculation that Owen's close ally, John Cartwright, would also be nominated. However, at the vital meeting of the SDP MPs on 27 August, Maclennan's was the only nomination to go forward and he duly became leader. At 51, Maclennan had first been elected in 1966 as a Labour MP for Caithness. However, in January 1981 he had been one of the earliest supporters of the Council for Social Democracy. His constituency of Caithness and Sutherland had remained fiercely loyal to him.

Maclennan became leader on 29 August. The following day the SDP annual conference opened at Portsmouth. On 31 August, the Portsmouth conference passed its historic vote. The motion proposed by Shirley Williams, and an amendment proposed by Charles Kennedy were carried overwhelmingly. The Kennedy amendment specifically proposed:

(i) that the objective of the negotiations shall be to create a new party incorporating the SDP and the Liberal Party; (ii) that there shall be one democratically elected leader; (iii) that there shall be a common set of principles and a single democratically elected policy-making machinery; (iv) that there shall be a constitution for this party based upon one member one vote and a national membership list. This council further requests the national committee to set up a negotiating team that represents the views of the members as expressed in the ballot, and requests the national committee to put the negotiated terms before the CSD and before the members in a second membership ballot.[3]

It was a historic conference. Certainly, it seemed to mark a final parting of the ways for Owen. The split in the Social Democratic Party became irrevocable when David Owen rejected an impassioned appeal by Shirley

Williams, the SDP President, not to lead a breakaway faction into the political wilderness. Owen was given a standing ovation at the SDP annual conference in Portsmouth by his supporters, many of whom wanted him to stay as their leader.

However, outside the highly charged atmosphere of Portsmouth, it seemed to many that Owen, like such famous names before him as Randolph Churchill and Oswald Mosley, was walking into the wilderness. Owen's dream of a fourth party hardly seemed credible when the 1987 election had demonstrated all the difficulties facing even a third party. In the press, the alternative proposed by Owen received short shrift. Peter Jenkins wrote in the *Independent*:

> The alternative which Dr Owen is pressing upon the party conference today is a fraudulent prospectus. There is no room for a fourth party in the British two-party system. There is not enough room for a third party. An Owen party consisting of himself and two MPs can have no electoral future whatsoever. The Owenite claim to be the exponents of a 'new politics' is nonsense. There is no possibility of practising 'multi-party politics' under the British system.[4]

Thus, if Portsmouth marked the end of the road for Owen, it was the beginning for Maclennan. His advent to the leadership had been scornfully greeted in the press. 'The ideal leader for a party whose time has gone', quipped the *Sunday Telegraph*.[5] At Portsmouth, however, Maclennan consolidated his position as leader with a powerful speech laying down tough conditions for a union of the two parties.

After the SDP conference at Portsmouth, the Liberal Party met for its annual conference at Harrogate on 14 September. The crucial and historic debate on merger took place on 17 September. After a lengthy debate, delegates cheered enthusiastically as the resolution to begin merger talks was passed by 998 votes to 21, a majority of 977 with just nine abstentions. The successful motion declared its resolve 'to set its hand, together with the SDP, to the creation of a new political party as the successor to the Liberal Party and the SDP'.

The new party, the motion declared, must be open, democratic and participatory, with a statement of principles and the following key constitutional features:

(i)   one member one vote;
(ii) national membership lists based on a locally administered membership scheme;

(iii)   a leader elected by all members;
(iv)   a federal structure with a UK federal level of institutions distinct from the institutions of the parties in the nations and regions of Britain;
(v)   representative assemblies which would be the sovereign part of a democratic and accountable process of policy formation, which would determine policy at the appropriate tier of the federal party and which should have sole powers to amend the constitution;
(vi)   a constituency basis of association; and
(vii) the right of members having a common interest to organise in autonomous groups, with defined procedures for recognition and representation within the party.

The motion then set out procedures for consultation, including the establishment of a team to participate with the SDP in the process leading to the founding of the new political party.[6] Eventually there would be a special Liberal Party assembly and thereafter a final ballot of all members. The Liberal negotiating team was chosen on 18 September, the SDP team on 21 September and preliminary talks between the two sides began on 29 September.[7]

The Harrogate conference was a triumph for Steel. It gave a massive and historic vote in favour of merger. It was an overwhelming mandate from the Liberal Assembly to negotiate a merger with the SDP, although it was qualified by a powerful warning not to compromise on traditional Liberal values.

Thus, during late autumn, the Liberal and SDP negotiating teams began the lengthy process of merger discussions. Meanwhile, the Owenite separatists had also been active. A 'Campaign for Social Democracy' was established in mid-September with Owen at its head and Cartwright as chairman of its executive committee. This was widely regarded as the first step in Owen's declared aim of establishing a fourth party.

As the Liberal–SDP negotiations wore on, it became clear that progress would be neither swift nor easy. And so it proved. Frustration of some SDP activists was reflected by the resignation of John Grant from the SDP negotiating team. It was clear that, on the Liberal side, such negotiators as leading Liberal activist Tony Greaves and Young Liberal Chair Rachel Pitchford, harboured doubts that the new constitutional proposals were too centralised, too elitist and lacked accountability.

On 18 December, the draft constitution for the new party was published jointly by David Steel and Robert Maclennan. The constitution began with a preamble which included a commitment that Britain should play a full and constructive role in NATO, itself an item of controversy for the many Liberals who believed that this should be regarded as a current policy rather than an enduring statement of values.

Other proposals included the party name ('The New Liberal and Social Democratic Party') which, it was suggested, 'may be known as The Alliance'. The object of the new party would be to act as successor to the Liberal Party and the Social Democratic Party. A federal structure was proposed for England, Scotland, Wales and possibly Ireland. A complicated formula for membership was proposed that was essentially a compromise between Liberal localism and the centralism of the SDP. The controversial section on policy-making was contained in Articles 5 to 7. The federal party conference would be the sovereign representative body of the party, but procedures would limit what conference could decide. In all, it was a controversial constitution.

The new constitution was enthusiastically described by David Steel as 'the most democratic and decent' offered by any of the British political parties, putting the greatest control in the hands of its members.

On the whole, the judgement of the *Guardian* was fair. The *Guardian* summarised the proposed constitution thus:

> ...on balance, the new order represents a sizeable shift towards the sort of political realism which most voters seem to respect.
>
> The new federal conference, the constitution ordains, will be supreme, speaking in the end with greater effective authority than a Liberal Assembly (which its leaders were at liberty to ignore if they wished) ever did. Unlike the old Liberal assemblies, which had no set composition, opening their doors to those with the will and the means to attend, the new-style conference will be strictly representative, with delegates chosen by constituency parties to represent them over a two-year period. And the familiar, impetuous pattern of Liberal policy-making, where something which on Monday was no more than a gleam in the eyes of a few enthusiasts who chose to turn up at a Liberal 'commission' became by the end of the week a consensual and cherished Assembly commitment – that, absolutely rightly, has gone. The new party has picked up the SDP system of policy-making by slow, deliberate stages: green paper first, white paper next, and enshrinement in policy only after protracted thrashing-out. But there are Liberal successes, and SDP concessions, here too: most of all, perhaps, in the commitment to decentralisation both at federal and constituency levels. And the Liberals' old insistence on a prominent

role for councillors is perpetuated here alongside the SDP's stress on special treatment for women.[8]

And the *Guardian* concluded:

> There is bound to be nostalgia, in this new professional world, for those old free-wheeling improvisatory Liberal Party occasions when almost anything might happen. Some may find it all a little earnest and drab. Few will put their names to the lot of it without reservations. The Alliance's negotiators look, even so, to have done a solid, sensible job. The necessary planks are in place. There's a platform to mount and to begin, after too long a silence, addressing the world from again.

These sentiments, however, were not shared by Liberal critics of the draft constitution. This grassroots opposition by such people as Tony Greaves and Young Liberal leaders found its strongest outlet at the Liberal Party Council's December meeting in Northampton. In the event, the Northampton Council Meeting delivered a severe rebuff both to Steel himself and the merger proposals. It passed amendments condemning the choice of Alliance as the short title by which the new party would be known; the inclusion of support for NATO in the constitutional preamble; and several detailed aspects of the proposed constitution including arrangements for constituency representation at the new party's conferences and procedures for ballots on policy issues.

Mr Steel opened the proceedings in Northampton by warning that 'any stridency, any over-heated language, any attempt to blow up matters of detail into exaggerated issues of principle will backfire on each and everyone of us, and fatally damage the prospects for our new party of Liberals and Social Democrats'. If the Liberals and Social Democrats fell out over a name, the voters would not understand. Despite Steel's warning, delegates overwhelmingly rejected the proposed short title of the 'Alliance'. The name 'Liberal Democrats', proposed by the Association of Liberal Councillors' President Miss Maggie Clay, was the only one to get substantial support in a straw poll of alternatives, which included the Social Liberal Party and the Democrats. Delegates also agreed by 106 votes to 76 to call for the deletion of the section on playing a full and constructive role in NATO.

It became clear, in the wake of Northampton, that a marked split was developing within the party. Steel made it clear that he was not willing to renegotiate the merger terms with the SDP. Opposing him, such activists as Michael Meadowcroft made it equally clear that they would never join the new party if their demands over NATO and the name of the new party were not heeded. Although the Liberal Party Council's role was advisory rather than mandatory, its vote to remove the reference to NATO in the constitution by 106 votes to 76, and its overwhelming vote to carry a motion rejecting the use of 'Alliance' as the short title of the new party, were clear evidence of the grassroots feeling in the party.

Against this background, Steel's extraordinary behaviour in agreeing the *policy* proposals of the new party with Maclennan in January 1988 becomes even more astonishing. For these events came close to reducing the centre stage of British politics to a pantomime farce.

The merger deal agreed by Steel and Maclennan was eventually concluded at 4 a.m. on the morning of 13 January. In the long night of negotiations, the fury of the Liberal negotiating team erupted. The first to walk out was Michael Meadowcroft (over the NATO issue); he was followed by Tony Greaves, Rachel Pitchford and Andy Millson (at odds over the name of the party). Thus, by early morning, half of the eight-strong negotiating team had resigned. This was as nothing to the fury that followed when details of the Steel–Maclennan 'mini-manifesto' emerged. This proposed, amongst other things, to extend VAT to food, children's clothes, fuel and newspapers, to phase out tax relief on mortgages, to end universal child benefit and to pledge firm support for the Trident nuclear missile. Such policy declarations produced astonishment and incredulity. Des Wilson, the former party President, sent an open letter to Steel describing the policy declaration as 'barely literate' and 'politically inept'; Alex Carlile called the ideas 'loopy'. The Liberal ranks were in angry rebellion.

By the afternoon of 13 January, the situation was grim. The merger hopes seemed wrecked, the Liberal MPs were united in revolt and Steel's leadership of the party was in jeopardy. Isolated, weary and dejected, Steel had no alternative but to retreat. An emergency meeting of the Liberal National Executive was called for that evening. At this meeting, Steel accepted that the policy document which he had signed earlier that day was not acceptable to the party and would not be part of any merger package put to rank and file Liberals at the Blackpool Assembly. The Liberal National Executive then agreed by 19 votes to 11 that the merger negotiations should continue as long as the controversial policy declaration was abandoned.[9] The executive called for the two parties to unite on the basis of the Alliance's general election manifesto, *Britain United*. To rescue the merger negotiations, a new negotiating team had to be established as a matter of the greatest urgency. With the Blackpool Assembly only ten days away, this task was assigned, on the Liberal side, to Des Wilson (the former party President), Jim Wallace (the Liberal Chief Whip) and Alan Leaman (the Vice-Chairman of the Party's Policy Committee). The SDP team was made up of Edmund Dell (a party trustee), together with Tom McNally and David Marquand (both former Labour MPs). These two teams were rapidly locked in urgent last-ditch attempts to save the merger from total collapse.

Certainly the events of 13 January had been chaotic and bewildering. Fiasco, as the *Guardian* editorial proclaimed, was too mild a word.[10] The whole sorry mess was well summarised by the *Observer*:

> If the Liberals and the Social Democrats do finally reach the altar, it will be despite – rather than because of – the efforts of the two men who originally appointed themselves the marriage-brokers. Neither Mr David Steel nor Mr Robert Maclennan can escape responsibility for having done their unconscious best to inhibit the banns over the past few days. Even in retrospect, their joint performance over the so-called 'leaders' document' seems so bizarre as to be almost unbelievable.[11]

On 18 January, after such a shambles, the ability of the new six-man negotiating team to resurrect a credible deal was all the more remarkable. When the revised deal was proclaimed the relief was all too evident. Gone were the controversial proposals of 'voices and choices'. The new policy document threw overboard the radical innovations of the previous week. Proposals to extend VAT were shelved, there was no firm commitment to retaining Trident and the policy was markedly equivocal on the future of civil nuclear power. It represented a considerable climb-down by Maclennan, who had been pressing for a firm policy stance by the new party on issues like nuclear defence.

The anti-merger camp in the SDP accused him of having 'caved in' on key policy commitments which he had earlier said were central to the new party. But the new statement received enthusiastic approval from other leading Social Democrats desperate to prevent the merger negotiations foundering over Mr Maclennan's insistence on firm policy commitments.

After a day of frenzied activity and soundings in both parties, Maclennan finally gave the document his backing at a meeting of the full negotiating teams at the SDP headquarters. It was later that night that Maclennan made his eleventh-hour visit to see David Owen.

Maclennan's decision to make his sudden, highly publicised Limehouse visit to attempt a reconciliation with Owen may have been laudable. But it achieved nothing, except to dent Maclennan's prospects of leading a united party. Owen angrily accused him of indulging in a public relations stunt and made it clear he would have absolutely nothing to do with merger. Owen was later to declare that 'the farcical fracas of the past fortnight has made the centre of British politics a music-hall joke'.

Meanwhile, Liberal opponents of the merger (who proclaimed themselves the 'Grand Coalition') continued to insist that behind this new merger agreement lay a 'hidden agenda' that would surface once merger had taken place. The 'Grand Coalition' insisted they had the support of more than the third of delegates required to block merger at the forthcoming assembly.

Thus after Steel's disastrous miscalculations earlier in January, all attention switched to the special Liberal Assembly held at Blackpool on 23 January. Its outcome was not merely an overwhelming victory for those advocating merger but a personal triumph for David Steel after his earlier humiliations. The size of the merger vote surprised even the most convinced pro-merger supporters. The key vote was won by 2,099 votes to 385 with 23 abstentions.[12] Beyond this, the Blackpool conference approved a series of measures providing for the constitutional machinery to set up the new party bodies, determine a vesting date and transfer the assets of the Liberal Party.[13]

A resolution to review the inclusion of NATO in the preamble to the constitution at the first conference of the new party was carried by a show of hands. Thus, the fiasco of the merger negotiations two weeks earlier was forgotten as Liberals rallied to their leader's call for the setting up of a new, truly effective Centre-Left party 'able to challenge the Tories at the next election'. Despite fervent speeches by anti-mergerites, warning that the new party would be dominated by the SDP, Steel easily gained the two-thirds majority constitutionally required for the winding up of the Liberal Party.

In fact, Steel's victory at Blackpool owed much to the extraordinary levels of political organisation which his camp had engineered. Jim Wallace, the Liberal Chief Whip, was the architect of this, determined that the platform should not suffer the type of humiliation that had happened at Eastbourne in 1986. These efforts succeeded. As Meadowcroft afterwards declared, 'there was a tremendous amount of heavying from the top'. Other Liberals were less restrained: 'We were playing on a Pakistani pitch', complained one anti-merger activist; the decision was 'rammed through' protested Hannan Rose of *Radical Quarterly*.[14] Of the Liberals who had resisted merger, most vowed to continue the battle for their radical principles *within* the new party. Some, however, bade farewell to the party.

Inevitably, also, in the wake of the crises of the previous weeks, the Blackpool Assembly witnessed much speculation over the leadership issue. Three names received particular mention: Paddy Ashdown, the MP for Yeovil; Alan Beith, Deputy Leader of the party and MP for Berwick-upon-Tweed; and, as something of an outsider, Malcolm Bruce, MP for Gordon. After Steel's triumph in Blackpool, however, he made it clear that he had not yet ruled himself out as a potential leader of the new party – a view not shared by those Liberal activists leaving Blackpool determined that Steel should never have such a role.

A week after the Liberal conference at Blackpool, the SDP met to decide on merger at Sheffield on 30 January. The debate was bitter and emotional, but the outcome was decisive. The Council for Social Democracy voted 273 for union to 28 against, with 49 abstentions. In fact, the result had never been in doubt, for Owen's supporters were determined to show their strength by abstaining or not participating, rather than blocking the merger. The outcome of the vote was greeted by the mergerites as an overwhelming endorsement. The Owenites, however, claimed that, since only 57 per cent of the 480 eligible to vote at Sheffield had actually supported merger and that the great bulk of those who abstained or did not vote were Owenite, they had won the moral victory.

Whatever the interpretation of the events at Sheffield, it was a sad day for the SDP. The debate was marred by personal attacks on Owen, the slow hand-clapping of Jenkins' speech and protracted and unseemly procedural wrangling. But the consequences of the Sheffield vote were only too clear. After just under seven years, the separate existence of the old SDP was over. A new party, the Social and Liberal Democrats, would now be established in March, subject only to the final ballots of party members still to be held.[15] There was no doubt that Sheffield was not only a significant and historic conference but a political turning-point. As the *Guardian* commented:

> Yet no serious observer of British politics should mistake the achievement of which the SDP's Sheffield vote marks the latest stage. Three weeks ago that prize of uncertain worth was put at real hazard by the combined recklessness and carelessness of the Liberal and SDP leaders in their now discarded policy declaration. It was the darkest hour for the third party so far. But at this crucial time its members and above all its supporters have held their nerve.

The *Guardian* continued:

> Sheffield's historical significance was that it marked the end of the limited but nevertheless extremely influential realignment of British

politics which began with the driving out by the left of a group of Social Democrats from the Labour Party in 1981. What has happened in these last seven years has never been as decisive or as apocalyptic as some participants and acolytes have wanted to believe. On the contrary, it has been messy and contradictory and it is still self-evidently uncompleted. It has failed to replace the Labour Party while ensuring that Labour has no serious prospect of governing. To say the least of it, that is a mixed achievement.

And the *Guardian* concluded with a bitter attack on Owen:

Yet on an altogether less historic level, Sheffield also marked the moment at which the waters of political self-delusion closed finally over the head of Dr David Owen. During the last eight months Dr Owen has behaved with indefensible condescension and contempt towards the party he once led, the allies with whom he so recently fought and the cause to which he seemed so dedicated. He has erected largely imaginary barriers on policy and he has disregarded the basic principles of the one member one vote democracy which has always been central to the SDP's identity. Dr Owen's behaviour at Sheffield, where he acted at all times like the leader of a party within a party (which is what he is), made Militant look like democratic loyalists.

By February, the realignment of the Centre-Left in British politics was taking shape. After the ferment and near disasters of the previous weeks, the birth of the Social and Liberal Democratic Party was at hand.

The last stage in the merger journey of the Liberals and SDP was the ballot of members, the results of which were declared on 2 March 1988. For the Liberals, of the party's 101,084 members some 52,867 voted (52.3 per cent). Of the votes cast, 87.9 per cent (46,376) were for merger with 12.1 per cent (6,365) against.[16] Thus, in all, 54 per cent of the party membership either did not vote, voted against merger, or abstained. For the merger camp, this was at best a half-hearted Liberal vote. Even worse was the SDP result. On a fractionally higher turnout of 55.5 per cent, some 65.3 per cent voted for merger while 34.7 per cent voted against. The details were that 28,908 out of 52,086 cast their votes with 18,722 for merger, 9,929 against.[17] In total, 64 per cent of SDP members did not vote, voted against merger or abstained.

Despite these inauspicious results, Liberal and SDP leaders put a brave face on the lacklustre ballot. Steel declared himself 'very heartened' and for Shirley Williams the vote was a 'ringing confirmation' of the support for merger. Not surprisingly, Owen, who declared that the merger vote had been 'a fiasco', declared that his position had been considerably strengthened by the ballot outcome. In reality, there was a far more important consequence of these unenthusiastic merger votes. As the *Independent* commented, with two competing parties on the centre stage of British politics, the day seemed yet more distant that would see the formation of an effective opposition to the Thatcher era.[18]

That, however, was forgotten when, on the morning of 3 March 1988, the new Social and Liberal Democratic Party was formally launched with David Steel and Robert Maclennan as joint interim leaders. With its new logo of a gold diamond with black border, the party was launched with 19 MPs, a claim of 3,500 councillors and a declared membership base of 100,000.

17
A New Agenda: 1988–1992

From the formation of the new party in March 1988 until the election of Paddy Ashdown in July, the Democrats made a somewhat faltering start. Although Steel and Maclennan were joint interim leaders, once Steel declared he would not run for the leadership, the Democrats were in a state of limbo. Neither were the early omens for the party very promising. Support fell rapidly in the opinion polls – membership was reported to have reached only 80,000 – while among the public at large there was obvious confusion over the continuing existence of the Owenites. Not surprisingly, the Democrats lost seats in the May elections, although there was comfort of a sort in the virtual annihilation of the Owenites from all but a handful of councils. Meanwhile, faced with a rival SDP candidate, the Liberals registered a disastrous performance in the first by-election of the new Parliament, at Kensington on 14 July 1988. The SLD, in a poor third place, could poll only 10.7 per cent of the vote.

Curiously, the press concentrated more on Kensington than on the Democratic leadership election where, as had been predicted, there was a straight fight between Paddy Ashdown and Alan Beith. Although in many ways Beith represented the more traditional 'safe' Liberal image and Ashdown a more adventurous, dynamic future, in fact the leadership debate was far more about styles than policies. Throughout the arduous eight-week campaign, Paddy Ashdown had remained the favourite to win the leadership. When the result was announced on 28 July, these predictions were comfortably fulfilled. Of the 80,104 ballot papers issued, 57,603 valid votes were cast for the leadership election (a turnout of 71.9 per cent). Paddy Ashdown received 41,401 votes (71.9 per cent of votes cast); Alan Beith, 16,202 (28.1 per cent). It was, as Ashdown declared, a very clear mandate for him to take up the reins of the new party. In the contest for the presidency of the party, Ian Wrigglesworth, with 28,638 votes and 50.2 per cent of the vote, easily defeated Des Wilson with

21,906 votes (38.4 per cent). Gwynoro Jones trailed in third place with 6,479 votes.

Paddy Ashdown's victory marked not only the dawn of a new era but also the passing of the older generation. Roy Jenkins, duly ennobled, was now Chancellor of Oxford University; Shirley Williams was about to take a professorship at Harvard; Bill Rodgers had effectively left politics. Among the former Liberal ranks, the Steel era had equally finally come to an end. A new leader with a new agenda had entered the Centre-Left stage of British politics.

The new leader was a relative newcomer to party politics. Paddy Ashdown had been born in India in 1941, but was brought up in Northern Ireland. Baptised Jeremy John Durham Ashdown, he had been known as Paddy since his time at Bedford School. His early career, from 1959 to 1972, had been with the Royal Marines. An able linguist (he spoke fluent Mandarin Chinese and Malay) he served in the diplomatic service from 1972 to 1976 (being based largely in Geneva). He was first elected to Parliament for Yeovil in 1983, capturing a hitherto safe Conservative seat. Aged 47 when elected Leader, his previous party portfolios had been as Liberal spokesman on Trade and industry (from 1983) and as Alliance voice on Education from 1987.

A daunting array of tasks faced Ashdown after the divisions and debacles of the preceding months. Ashdown faced major problems of party morale, low membership and financial problems – as well as the continuing existence of the Social Democratic Party under Owen. This SDP had been relaunched in March 1988 under the leadership of David Owen and the presidency of John Cartwright.

Paddy Ashdown's first challenge – and his first opportunity to shape the party in his own image – came with the initial annual conference of the SLDP in September 1988. Ashdown announced his allocation of the key portfolios – including foreign affairs to David Steel and the important Treasury and Economy post to Alan Beith. Home affairs went to Robert Maclennan. The conference formally adopted the short title Democrats (although it was to reverse this decision a year later, settling on Liberal Democrats after much debate and wrangling). Paddy Ashdown's first major conference speech set out the policy priorities he was to develop over the coming years – with emphasis on fair voting, Scottish and Welsh parliaments, industrial democracy, freedom of information, high-quality education, proper housing and an effective health service.

During 1989 the problems of the SLDP failed to go away. On the electoral front, the party's showing in the opinion polls plummeted. In the May 1989 local elections, the Democrats gained only 83 seats, losing 190; the second conference of the SLDP, held in Bournemouth in March, was overshadowed by the question of rival SDP candidates contesting by-elections, and the direct elections to Europe in June were an unmitigated disaster. The most galling problem was that of SDP candidatures in by-elections. Table 17.1 shows how Liberal Democrats fared in these contests between July 1988 and March 1990.

Table 17.1

Date of By-election	Constituency	Lib. Dem. %	SDP %
14 July 1988	Kensington	10.8	5.0
15 Dec. 1988	Epping Forest	26.0	12.2
23 Feb. 1989	Pontypridd	3.9	3.1
23 Feb. 1989	Richmond (Yorks)	22.1	32.2
4 May 1989	Vale of Glamorgan	4.2	2.3
15 June 1989	Glasgow Central	1.5	1.0
22 March 1990	Mid-Staffordshire	11.2	2.5

The outcome of these competing candidatures was obvious. In weak seats (such as Kensington or Pontypridd), the erstwhile Alliance vote disintegrated even further. In good seats (such as Epping Forest but, most of all, Richmond) rival candidates enabled the Conservatives to hang on by a thread. If such by-elections were demoralising, even worse were the European elections.

The third direct elections for Europe, held in June 1989, provided a nationwide test of electoral support for the newly-founded Liberal Democrats. The outcome was a shattering humiliation. The result was as shown in Table 17.2.

Table 17.2

Party	Seats Won	Votes	% Votes
Labour	45	6,153,604	40.2
Conservative	32	5,224,037	34.2
SLDP	0	986,292	6.4
Greens	0	2,292,705	15.0
Others	1 (SNP)	521,748	3.5

On a turnout of only 35.9 per cent, the Liberals had polled a mere 6.4 per cent of the vote. Once again, they failed to elect a single MEP. To compound the party's misery, Labour was resurgent on 40 per cent of the vote and, even more alarmingly for the SLDP, the Greens had come from nowhere to sweep into third place nationally. Moreover, the Greens had done best in the south of England and those middle-class constituencies in which Liberals had formerly prospered. Greens came second to the Conservatives in six seats (Devon, Dorset East and Hampshire West, Somerset and Dorset West, the Cotswolds, Surrey West and Sussex West). Moreover, in all 78 constituencies in Great Britain (with the solitary exception of Cornwall and Plymouth) the Greens polled more votes than their SLDP or SDP rivals. This was all the more remarkable given that the Alliance had come second in 14 seats in 1984. Now the Liberal Democrats had suffered the indignity of losing 34 deposits (their rivals, the SDP, went one better, and lost their deposit in all 16 seats they contested). The Greens, in contrast, saved their deposit in every seat. It was hardly surprising that Paddy Ashdown had to call for calm in the wake of the worst election performance by a third party since the 1950s. This humiliation was reflected in a continuing membership and financial crisis. By September, membership was around 82,000 – down 10,000 over 12 months. There were doubts that the party could retain its Cowley Street headquarters in Westminster for much longer. And the continued wrangling over the party's short name resurfaced. The one small comfort for Paddy Ashdown was that the continuing SDP was visibly disintegrating.

The tide at last turned for the Liberal Democrats during 1990. Both in opinion polls and by-elections, the upsurge in Green support receded as quickly as it had arisen. By September 1990, the Greens were registering 4 per cent in the polls, compared to the Liberal Democrats' 10 per cent. Liberal Democrat morale was further boosted by the final demise of David Owen's 'continuing SDP'. The 'independent fourth force' that Owen had relaunched on 9 March 1988 had rapidly become a political laughing-stock. The municipal elections of May 1989 had been disastrous. On 25 September 1989, Rosie Barnes (one of Owen's closest supporters) had conceded that the party would concentrate on only ten targeted seats at the next election. But the crowning humiliation came with the Bootle by-election of 24 May 1990, when Jack Holmes polled 155 votes for the SDP, making the 418 secured by Screaming Lord Sutch seem positively respectable.

After Bootle, Owen and his two fellow MPs called an emergency meeting of the SDP's 25-strong National Committee. With support in the opinion polls at a derisory 1 per cent, with membership down to 6,000 and financial reserves exhausted, it was agreed that the game was over. Owen defiantly stated that he would never rejoin the Labour Party (he had not been asked to), but the SDP which had begun amid a blaze of publicity and high hopes back in 1981 was now finally dead. The final epitaph was written in the April 1992 election. Owen did not stand in Plymouth (he announced his retirement from politics in September 1991), while Rosie Barnes and John Cartwright were defeated by Labour in Greenwich and Woolwich (despite being given a clear run by Liberal Democrats).

Hence the Liberal Democrats, buoyed by an upturn in their fortunes, approached the 1990 party conference in better heart. As Michael White wrote in the *Guardian*:

> The overwhelming mood of 1,600 or so Liberal Democrat activists heading for the Blackpool conference this weekend will be one of relief. The worst is over, and they can now make light of the nightmare they privately feared in Brighton a year ago that Labour's renaissance, their own post-Alliance feuds and the Green surge threatened them with annihilation.
>
> Instead, the party machine is solvent, the leadership cheerful and the grassroots have held on in the town halls. The party has even agreed on a name.[1]

The September 1990 Blackpool party conference marked an important step in the evolution of party policy. Ashdown made clear his desire not to lose the opportunity of getting rid of Margaret Thatcher at the next election if the opportunity arose. His vision of the Liberal Democrat future was one of a radical, reforming party. Ashdown's keynote speech repeated the party commitment in four key areas: investment in education; protection for the environment; a full, enthusiastic role in a new 'Europe of the Regions'; and democratic constitutional reforms including proportional representation, home rule for Scotland and Wales and the transformation of the House of Lords into a Senate.

The Liberal Democrats would thus be a party which supported both social justice and the enterprise culture, wholeheartedly committed to Europe and ready to innovate with such ideas as the pollution added tax (PAT) and ready to risk electoral unpopularity by raising basic rate tax to fund education.

In a sense, the new emblem the party had adopted (the bird of freedom) was apt. The party had at last broken free of the traumas of the merger era. Local election support was consistent at 18 per cent. Membership was reported to have held steady at 80,000, while even the party's accumulated debts had fallen to £200,000 from £500,000 a year earlier.

All that was needed now was a by-election victory to galvanise the party. The opportunity came in the unlikely constituency of Eastbourne – a seat better known for the age-profile of its largely retired population than its radicalism (it had been a Conservative stronghold since 1906). The by-election was caused by the assassination of the sitting Conservative Ian Gow by the IRA. Gow, who had held the seat for 16 years, was a close confidant of Margaret Thatcher and it was widely assumed a sympathy vote would keep the seat safely Conservative – even though the Liberals had a strong local base in the constituency. However, David Bellotti, a 47-year-old East Sussex Liberal Democrat councillor, swept to victory by 4,550 votes on a swing from the Conservatives of 20.1 per cent. After the Liberal Democrat humiliation in the European elections, it was a result which galvanised the party. At last it seemed Paddy Ashdown had exorcised the ghost of the disastrous merger and that the Liberal bandwagon was rolling again. In 1991, the success of Eastbourne was repeated at Ribble Valley and at Kincardine.

The Ribble Valley by-election, caused by the elevation of Home Secretary David Waddington to the Lords, took place in the fourteenth safest Conservative seat in the country (they had taken over 60 per cent of the vote in 1987, a majority of 39 per cent over the Liberal challenger). It was, however, a by-election dominated by the issue of the poll tax – a particularly emotive issue in this part of Lancashire. The constituency, which stretched from the Pennine Hills to the suburbs of Preston, contained a multitude of small terraced houses whose owners faced the prospect of a poll-tax bill of over £400 compared to rates of around £180. The Liberal Democrats easily captured the seat with a majority of 4,601, on the highest swing (24.8 per cent) recorded in a by-election since Bermondsey in February 1983.

Fortune continued to favour the Liberal Democrats with a by-election in Kincardine and Deeside, a Conservative-held marginal where the Liberal Democrats had one of their most winnable prospects north of the border. Local issues also aided them. The opting-out of the local Foresthill hospital, and the threat to the Gordon Highlanders as a result of the defence cuts, were all issues the Liberal Democrats could exploit. With the Conservatives in Scotland very much on the defensive (Thatcherism had been an object of great hostility), the Liberal Democrats easily captured Kincardine and Deeside on a swing of 11.4 per cent, briefly reducing the Conservatives to the third largest party in Scotland (in terms of representation at Westminster). The very obvious tactical voting in Kincardine (i.e. voting to unseat a sitting Conservative) led to much speculation that such tactical voting at the coming general election might well virtually eliminate the Conservatives in Scotland. As it was, with 22 MPs now at Westminster, the Liberal Democrats were now the largest third party Britain had seen since 1935.

An even broader electoral success came with the municipal elections of May 1991. The Liberal Democrats, defending seats gained by the Alliance in 1987, expected losses. Instead, they enjoyed a night that was little short of a triumph. In terms of party gains and losses, the Liberal Democrats gained 750 seats for the loss of 230, a net gain of 520. The 1991 local elections transformed the political map of local party control in Britain, with the Conservatives routed and with Liberal Democrats taking such prizes as Cheltenham. Alongside this progress in local elections, both the party ratings in the polls, and public approval of Ashdown continued to improve (see Table 17.3).

Table 17.3   Liberal Democrat Progress, August 1990–August 1991

Month	% Support in Polls	% Approval Ashdown
1990		
August	8	31
September	11	35
October	13	40
November	11	44
December	9	44
1991		
January	9	44
February	9	48
March	16	55
April	14	53
May	17	58
June	16	58
July	15	58
August	15	56

Meanwhile, party policy had continued to evolve, particularly at the March 1991 Nottingham conference which approved the new policy document, *Shaping Tomorrow, Starting Today: Liberal Democrat priorities for the year 2000*. Although the architect of the document was Lord Holme, the core of the policy programme reflected Paddy Ashdown's priorities – in particular, electoral reform, a flourishing enterprise economy, toughened anti-monopoly measures, road pricing as part of an environmental programme and an enthusiastic commitment to European union. By the end of 1991, with the party machine honed up for the approaching general election, Liberal Democrats were rapidly gaining in confidence.

These pre-election hopes received a potentially catastrophic setback early in February 1992 when the press revealed that Paddy Ashdown had once had a brief affair, five years earlier, with his secretary, Patricia Howard. The so-called 'Ashdown scandal' in fact backfired completely. Paddy Ashdown was already, by a very large margin, the party's leading asset. Following these press revelations (and Ashdown's calm, dignified handling of them) his personal ratings soared in the polls. Only 5 per cent of those asked indicated that Ashdown should have resigned and most expressed more distaste of the press coverage than of his activities.

After this brief interlude, most press attention duly reverted to the attitude the Liberal leader would adopt towards any deal or coalition with Labour or Conservative. Ashdown made clear he would require the introduction of proportional representation, an agreed programme covering four years in power and ministerial posts for himself and senior colleagues. However, what was left unanswered was the vital question of what he would do if either John Major or Neil Kinnock rejected his demands and defied him to vote down a Queen's Speech.

When the election was called for 9 April, the party was well prepared. Des Wilson, as campaign director, was ready for the off, whilst the 15,000-word manifesto, *Changing Britain for Good*, set out the party pledges to reform the voting system, give home rule to Scotland, introduce a £6 billion recovery package and (this was a bold move) commit the party to raise basic rate income tax by one penny to finance education.

When nominations closed, the electorate had a choice of 2,948 candidates (compared to 2,325 in 1987 and 2,600 in 1983). There were no straight fights between two candidates. Labour fought 634 seats, the Conservatives 645 (a higher total than Labour because they contested 11 of the 17 seats in Northern Ireland) while the Liberal Democrats contested 632 (all the seats on mainland Britain except for Greenwich and Woolwich, where Rosie Barnes and John Cartwright were not opposed). The Greens fielded 254 candidates, nearly twice the 1987 figure.

The commitment to raise taxes, as well as increased questioning on the position Liberal Democrats would take in the event of a hung parliament, dominated media treatment of the Liberal Democrats. However, the Liberal Democrats in general, and Paddy Ashdown in particular, fought a well-organised and (or so it seemed at the time) highly effective campaign. As the *Guardian* commented:

> But in fact, so far, Mr Ashdown is the only real winner of this campaign. Labour, in broad terms, has merely defended the vote it seemed to have when the election was called. The movement and the arguments and

the actual switches in allegiance have all come from Liberal Democrat advance. They are the movers and shakers. And Mr Ashdown himself has indefatigably carried so much of the fight on his own shoulders.[2]

The *Guardian* editorial continued:

> Today's Liberal Democrats are not the Liberals of old. They now possess – the only boon from the severed Alliance – a structure of serious decision-making. They are a proper party. And this, for 1992, has produced a proper manifesto. Like all such documents, of course, it has its left-over sections and dodgy figurings: and the unreality of a leap straight into Downing Street naturally produces matching unreality in the promising game. But, for emphasis and for symbolism, it's the best show in town.

As the campaign progressed, and the polls seemed to indicate the prospect of a hung parliament, the Liberal Democrats were increasingly questioned on their role in such a situation. Paddy Ashdown reiterated that only a formal pact with a commitment to electoral reform would satisfy his party. Whether this prospect of a 'hung parliament' helped persuade would-be Liberals to return to the Conservative fold was much discussed in the wake of the election.

After such a well-run, acclaimed campaign, the outcome of the 1992 election was a bitter disappointment. The full result was as shown in Table 17.4.

Table 17.4

	Votes	Seats	% Vote
Conservative	14,092,891	336	41.9
Labour	11,559,735	271	34.4
Liberal Democrats	5,999,384	20	17.8
Nationalists	783,991	7	2.3
Others	1,176,692	17	3.5

Nationally, the party had polled nearly 6 million votes, taking 17.8 per cent of the vote (down 4.8 per cent from the 22.6 per cent achieved by the Alliance in 1987). Considering the dark days of 1988 and 1989, this was a reasonable achievement. Nationally, the swing from Liberal Democrat to Conservative was 2.09 per cent, from Liberal Democrat to Labour a rather more marked 4.15 per cent (reflecting, no doubt, the collapse of the old SDP vote in constituencies such as Stevenage or Norfolk North West which had no Liberal tradition).

The greatest disappointment, however, was in terms of seats gained and lost. The final tally of 20 reflected four gains and six losses. The gains, all in England and largely in the South West, included Bath (the sensation of the election, where Tory party chairman Chris Patten was defeated) and Cheltenham (where the local Conservatives had not been totally united over the selection of a black candidate). The remaining two gains were in that most traditional of Liberal areas, Devon and Cornwall, where Liberal Democrats won North Devon (once Jeremy Thorpe's seat) and North Cornwall (regained by Paul Tyler). The losses, however, included all three seats won in the by-elections of 1987 to 1992 (Eastbourne, Ribble Valley and Kincardine) together with Southport, Brecon and Radnor and Ceredigion. The loss of these last two (both in Wales) reduced Liberal representation in Wales to the solitary seat of Montgomery. Perhaps most galling was the total failure to exploit tactical voting and gain such seats as Hazel Grove, Portsmouth South or Richmond in which Liberals were within close range of victory. In fact, Liberals slipped back from second place in many seats – finishing second in 154 seats, third in 389 and a lowly fourth place in 68. Only three of the 20 Liberal Democrat MPs had won a majority of votes cast in their constituency, while the Liberal Democrat dream of replacing Labour as the main challenger in Conservative-held seats had not been realised. An examination of the Liberal Democrat vote by region provides some remarkable results (see Table 17.5).

Table 17.5   Liberal Democrat Performance by Region

Region	Votes	% Vote	Seats Won
London	542,733	15.1	1
South East	1,507,299	23.4	0
South West	916,905	31.4	6
East Anglia	242,886	19.5	0
East Midlands	376,603	15.3	0
West Midlands	466,048	15.0	0
Wales	217,457	12.4	1
North West	582,177	15.8	2
Yorkshire & Humberside	481,246	16.8	0
North	281,236	15.6	1
Scotland	383,856	13.1	9

By far the strongest Liberal Democrat support was in the South West (31.4 per cent), followed by the South East (23.4 per cent). No other area exceeded 20 per cent, although East Anglia with 19.5 per cent was near. By contrast, the two areas which had once been Liberal strongholds (Wales, 12.4 per cent and Scotland 13.1 per cent) had now fallen to bottom place, although, of course, the rural Scotland of the Highlands and Borders still retained areas of impregnable Liberal strength.

One small feature of the results provided Liberals with some grounds for consolation. All 254 Green candidates lost their deposit (the best single result in percentage terms was 3.75 per cent in Islington North). Their overall share of the vote (1.3 per cent) was but a shadow of the 15 per cent achieved in the 1989 European elections.

Apart from the unevenness of Liberal Democrat support, a further disturbing feature of the results was the precarious nature of many of the seats won. The 20 seats are set out in Table 17.6 (in order of marginality). These figures reveal only too well how unsafe many Liberal Democrat seats appeared to be. On a swing of only 5 per cent away from the Liberals, the party would be left with a mere nine seats. Of the 20 seats, 12 had majorities under 5,000, and of these six were held by less than 2,000 votes.

Table 17.6   Liberal Democrat Seats after April 1992

Seat	Majority	% Majority
Gordon	274	0.5
Inverness, Nairn & Lochaber	458	0.9
Devon North	794	1.4
Cheltenham	1,668	2.6
Cornwall North	1,921	3.1
Rochdale	1,839	3.5
Liverpool Mossley Hill	2,606	6.3
Argyll & Bute	2,622	7.2
Bath	3,768	7.2
Fife North East	3,308	7.9
Tweeddale, Ettrick & Lauderdale	2,520	8.2
Berwick-upon-Tweed	5,043	11.6
Truro	7,570	12.2
Roxburgh & Berwickshire	4,257	12.6
Yeovil	8,833	14.8
Montgomery	5,209	15.8
Ross, Cromarty & Skye	7,630	18.6
Caithness & Sutherland	5,365	24.1
Orkney & Shetland	5,033	24.4
Bermondsey & Southwark	9,845	26.1

The geographical distribution of Liberal seats was also significant. No less than nine were in Scotland, five in the West Country. Wales, once a stronghold of the party, now boasted only one Liberal Democrat. Moreover, the party remained as far as ever from making a breakthrough except in a handful of Conservative-held seats, mainly in the West Country. Of the 17 seats in which Liberals had less than a 5,000 majority to overturn, 16 were Conservative held. Seven were in seats formerly held by the party, but recently lost.

On a broader canvas, as Table 17.7 shows, the Liberal Democrats had won only three seats with a majority of votes cast, had finished in third place in 389 seats and had had to amass an average 299,922 votes to win a seat.

Table 17.7   Liberal Democrats April 1992

First place	20
Second place	154
Third place	389
Fourth place	68
Lost deposits	11
Majority of votes cast	3
Votes per seat	299,922

Thus, in electoral terms, the 1992 election was hardly the breakthrough that had been hoped for. The inquest on the poor Liberal Democrat performance naturally placed the blame on the last-minute defection of many supporters into the Conservative ranks on 'scare stories' that a vote for the Liberal Democrats would put Neil Kinnock into Downing Street. Yet, though talk of a 'hung parliament' and the prospect of a minority Labour Government probably hurt the party, its support of 18 per cent in the polls would have given it 108 seats in Parliament under proportional representation. It was still a major improvement on the 6 per cent opinion poll support of three years earlier (and party membership had reportedly passed the 100,000 benchmark during the campaign). On a different level the election confirmed Paddy Ashdown's predominance in the party as it prepared to face a fourth consecutive Conservative administration.

18
Voting for Change: 1992–1997

The five years from 1992 to 1997 constituted a period of both change and consolidation for the Liberal Democrats. There was obvious consolidation at the grassroots in terms of a huge growth in elected Liberal Democrat councillors in the boroughs and shires (such that by 1994 the party had overtaken the Conservatives nationwide in its tally of councillors elected). There was consolidation also in its ability to continue its tradition of by-election successes. From 1992 to 1997 the party was to win Conservative seats such as Newbury, Christchurch and Eastleigh in the south and Littleborough and Saddleworth in the north. In the 1994 European elections it achieved its first-ever breakthrough, winning two seats. At Westminster it attracted two Conservative defectors to its ranks (Emma Nicholson in late December 1995 and, in the following year but to a lesser fanfare of trumpets, Peter Thurnham).

The climax of these five years came in May 1997 when, in the general election which ended 18 years of Conservative rule, the party returned no less than 46 MPs. This was not only by far the best result in the post-war period but its highest number of elected MPs since the great revival of Lloyd George back in 1929.

But these achievements were always in the shadow of the changes taking place in the Labour Party, where the untimely death of John Smith brought a new leader in Tony Blair. Under Blair, the party cast off almost as much of its previous clothing as could be done without a prosecution for indecency. 'New Labour' became a centrist party, its antennae eager to shift to perceived changes in the public mood even if these took the party ever more towards the right. With the Conservatives under John Major enmeshed in a web of problems from sleaze to Europe, and with Labour riding high in the opinion polls, it became increasingly difficult for the Liberal Democrats to occupy a distinctive niche in the political spectrum. Indeed, the Liberal Democrats' first problem after the 1992 election was to a certain extent one of morale.

The disappointment – even demoralisation – of the party's performance in 1992 was well summed up by Patrick Wintour. Writing in the *Guardian Political Almanac* he declared of the general election:

> Paddy Ashdown's party saw its vote drop nationwide by 4.8 per cent overall on its 1987 performance. The decline was registered in every single region. It was the second election in a row in which the party's overall vote had fallen, leaving the party with only 20 seats. Ashdown's carefully prepared war games in the event of a hung parliament, including the demand for four seats at the Cabinet table proved to be nothing more than that – games. Every by-election gain trumpeted in the previous parliament – from Eastbourne to Ribble Valley – had been lost.[1]

It was little surprise that the election had left Paddy Ashdown disheartened and indeed exhausted. And other problems stared Ashdown in the face. Labour, even though beaten for a fourth consecutive time, hardly seemed on the point of despair. No realignment, or a gathering together of radical forces, seemed likely. Speaking at Chard on 9 May Ashdown tried to set out an agenda for realignment, but his attempt met with little response from Labour and many in his own party were deeply suspicious of any talk of deals with Labour. And in any case so long as Labour refused to contemplate proportional representation, no real dialogue could take place.

Paddy Ashdown also faced the need not to reopen old Liberal divisions. The 1992 election had also demonstrated a continuing appeal for candidates fielded by the relaunched 'old' Liberal Party. Having been formed on 11 March 1989, it fielded some 70 candidates in 1992. Its leading figure was former Leeds West MP Michael Meadowcroft. In 1992, the party polled 2.5 per cent or over in nine seats, with Meadowcroft himself polling 8.3 per cent. The fortunes of the 'continuing' Liberal Party are discussed in more detail in Appendix VI.

In the wake of the 1992 election, Paddy Ashdown had become increasingly immersed into the seemingly interminable problem of Bosnia. As Patrick Wintour remarked, 'Ashdown seemed to have more to say on Bosnia than on any domestic subject, but he said it well.' Ashdown also devoted himself early in 1993 to living and working with ordinary people, spending two to three days a week over a six-month period listening to their views. If people were disenchanted with politicians, some of this rubbed off on to Paddy Ashdown. He became something of an anti-politician's politician. His reputation among his critics for sanctimoniousness at Westminster was now coupled with a certain populism of the Ross Perot variety. It perhaps reached a climax in his July 1993 address to the pressure group Charter 88 in which he declared in favour of regular policy referendums, floated the idea of unelected Cabinet members and put forward the idea of hypothecation (earmarking revenue from taxes to specific welfare services).

As Paddy Ashdown's political odyssey took place, the electoral scene, which had been so unpromising a year earlier had considerably brightened for the Liberal Democrats by spring 1993. The cause of the transformation was the collapse of the Major Government's popularity – buffeted by economic recession, divisions over Maastricht and a seemingly uncanny ability to slip on political banana skins of any shape or size.

The Conservative collapse, well monitored in the opinion polls, was at last reflected in by-elections. On 14 April 1993, the writ was moved for the Newbury by-election – creating the first by-election of the Parliament after a year when for the first time since 1900 no by-election had taken place. From the start, Newbury looked a good Liberal Democrat prospect. The party had a strong local government base (it controlled Newbury District Council) and in the 1992 election had polled nearly 25,000 votes. Labour's cause was always hopeless. It had only 150 local members, had only elected one local councillor in a decade and did not even possess a permanent headquarters. The Conservatives were defending a 12,357 majority. But times had changed since the 1980s when the constituency was known as 'Thatchertown'. The constituency, stretching from Hungerford to the outskirts of Reading, had suffered badly from falling property prices. It was dubbed the 'negative equity' capital of the South. Many small businesses were also suffering in the recession. In all it was fertile territory to build on an already strongly entrenched Liberal vote in Newbury, Hungerford and Thatcham. In the event, the Liberal Democrats took Newbury with a 28.4 per cent swing with a 22,055 majority. It was the most successful victory yet in the five-year history of the party. It was paralleled in the local elections elsewhere in the country, where the Liberal Democrats scored 400 gains to leave them with control or influence in a swathe of councils.

Even the most optimistic Liberal Democrats were daunted, however, when a subsequent by-election occurred in Christchurch – a true-blue East Dorset constituency – where Conservative votes were more normally weighed rather than counted (it was the eighteenth safest Conservative seat in the whole country). The Christchurch by-election of 29 July 1993 thus appeared an almost impossible Liberal task. With 63.5 per cent of the vote, a mountainous majority of over 20,000 and very little local

Liberal Democrat strength (only one local councillor in Verwood), the Tories seemed entrenched. But, fortified by Newbury and with the MORI poll of 28 May showing Liberal Democrat support of 24 per cent (up 50 per cent in a year) the tide was flowing strongly in their favour.

Several factors aided the Liberals. The government's 'double whammy' of falling interest rates and the extension of VAT on domestic fuel was disastrous in a constituency where 34 per cent of the voters were over 60 (the highest proportion anywhere in England). The constituency also had the highest proportion of detached houses anywhere in the country (but local property prices had fallen 40 per cent in four years). Unemployment had also trebled in the previous three years. Aided by a strong Liberal Democrat candidate in Diana Maddock (Liberal Democrat leader on Southampton City Council), the outcome was a sensation – victory by 16,427 votes on the highest swing in post-war politics (35.4 per cent). The Liberals had achieved victory with 62.5 per cent of the vote, the Conservatives polling 31.5 per cent and Labour a minuscule 2.7 per cent. The victory, a 'Conservative Culloden' ranked as the most sensational of all post-1945 Liberal Democrat victories over Conservatives (see Table 18.1). It was the largest majority to be overturned since 1945.

Table 18.1   Ten Biggest Swings from Conservative to Liberals/Liberal Democrats since 1945

Constituency	Party	Year	% Swing
Christchurch	Lib Dem	1993	35.4
Torrington	Lib	1958	32.9
Sutton and Cheam	Lib	1972	32.6
Isle of Ely	Lib	1973	31.6
Newbury	Lib Dem	1993	28.4
Orpington	Lib	1962	26.8
Crosby	SDP/All	1981	25.5
Ripon	Lib	1973	25.3
Ribble Valley	Lib Dem	1991	24.8
Croydon NW	Lib/All	1981	24.2

If the by-election triumphs of Newbury and Christchurch had captured the headlines, in many ways the *real* change in British politics had been in the local elections (held the same day as Newbury). Even before the May 1993 county elections, the Liberal Democrats had made impressive gains over the years in a variety of local councils. With over 3,000 local councillors, the Liberal Democrats had been successful in establishing an apparently permanent power base in local government in both rural and urban areas. SLD councillors had gained control of areas as diverse as Stockport, Hereford, Plymouth and even Blyth Valley in the north-east Labour heartland. The elections of May 1993 transformed the electoral map of the shire counties. Prior to May 1993, Liberal Democrats controlled only one county council (the Isle of Wight), although the party held the balance of power in 12 of the 45 English and Welsh counties.

The results in May 1993 were a nightmare for the Conservatives. Although Labour gained only one council (Northamptonshire) and the Liberals won outright control of only Cornwall and Somerset, the Conservative power base was obliterated. The litany of Tory losses to No Overall Control included almost every county in the Home Counties and South East. Such counties, hitherto the stern unbending heartland of Conservative loyalty, included Surrey (after 103 years), Kent, both East and West Sussex, Hertfordshire, Essex (home of Essex man and woman), to say nothing of the rest of East Anglia. Only Buckinghamshire survived as the lone county in Tory control. The disaster extended westwards to include Dorset and Devon.

It was the end of an era in British local government. If, at Westminster, parliamentary politics remained a two-party monopoly, the May 1993 elections ended the era of two-party politics across the length and breadth of the shire counties of England.

However, it was not simply the voting which altered the local political structure of Britain. A new era of enforced political cooperation had begun. Whatever the politicians continued to say at Westminster, at local level Lib–Lab cooperation had, of necessity, become a reality in many areas.[2] Although, in some urban areas such as in industrial Lancashire or the inner London boroughs, hostility between Liberal Democrats and Labour remained as intense and bitter as ever.

At county council level different local arrangements emerged. Lib–Lab pacts were established in Essex, Hereford and Worcester, Lincolnshire, Shropshire and Suffolk. In Berkshire there was a Lib–Lab–Independent pact. In Cambridgeshire, Labour and Liberal Democrats agreed a policy statement and Labour had all the committee chairs. In Cheshire, there was a three-party deal with a Liberal Democrat chair. In Leicestershire, where Labour was the largest party, there was a Liberal Democrat chair with a three-party rotation of committee chairs. All these arrangements gave Liberal Democrats valuable experience of political cooperation and responsibility in the arena of local government.

Meanwhile, the Liberal local election successes and by-election breakthrough were reflected in the opinion poll ratings. On 9 July, the *Daily Telegraph* Gallup Poll put the party in second place for the first time since 1985 with 26.5 per cent, two points ahead of the Conservatives. In *The Times* MORI gave the Liberals 45 per cent of the vote in the South West, opening up the prospect of capturing a swathe of Conservative seats in Dorset, Somerset, Devon and Cornwall. Not surprisingly, the party met for its autumn conference in confident mood.

Certainly, the background to the 1993 party conference, as *The Times* found, was highly encouraging:

> The government is unpopular, the Opposition is in disarray, and the Liberal Democrats are making sensational gains in by-elections and riding high in the opinion polls. It must be time to predict that the third party will break the mould at the next general election. But, as Liberal Democrats begin their party conference in Torquay, they may well recall that they have been here before.
>
> So there are reasons for Liberal Democrats to be less than triumphalist this week. Yet behind the ephemeral support in the opinion polls – hovering around 25 per cent at the moment – lies a slightly more concrete expression of voters' views. At local government by-elections, the centre party has been doing far better than either big party, picking up seats from Conservatives in the shires and from Labour in inner cities. Since January it has gained three times more seats from the Tories than Labour has.[3]

The 1993 party conference turned out to be a relatively ordered affair, although partly overshadowed in the media by accusations of racism within the Liberal Democrat controlled Tower Hamlets council.[4]

The Torquay conference developed several important policy proposals. On constitutional reform the conference approved a party document which proposed the introduction of state funding of political parties, fixed-term parliaments, a Bill of Rights and the abolition of the royal prerogative. On Europe the party urged the United Kingdom to take the lead in seeking a timetable for a single European currency and called for the creation of an autonomous European central bank. The Liberal Democrat green paper on the environment, *Tax Pollution, not People* was also approved (it included proposals for the introduction of an EU tax on energy use and carbon dioxide emissions – but pledged help for the poor and pensioners to compensate for increased fuel costs).

On 20 September the Torquay conference took the major step of adopting its new policy document, *Facing up to the Future*. Among the key planks of the Liberal Democrat proposals were decentralisation of government, the adoption of proportional representation for all elections, and a move away from taxing income and towards taxing pollution and the use of finite resources. A novel proposal was that the key economic indicator of success, Gross Domestic Product (GDP), should be redefined to include indicators of pollution and depletion of natural resources.

In all, the Liberal leadership could be well satisfied with the achievements of 1993 – in parliamentary by-elections, local election success and development of party policy. It was unfortunate that the bitter wrangling over the activities of the party in Tower Hamlets (a big row over a small council) dominated the media as the year ended.

The Tower Hamlets episode which came to a head in December 1993, was one of those events which was almost inevitable with the proliferation of success in community politics. Inevitably, campaigns on popular issues at local level could easily degenerate into populist politics. And populist politics, in an area of ethnic problems such as the East End of London, could easily descend into allegations of racism.

The Liberals had built up their first successes back in the early 1980s. Control of the council had been secured in 1986, winning control from a decrepit Labour regime through a vigorous campaign of FOCUS leaflets. Once in power the party had decentralised services to seven 'neighbourhoods' in the borough and had championed the grievances of existing residents by taking a strict line on homeless families with their 'sons and daughters' scheme.

In a borough with a numerous Bangladeshi community, a local by-election in Millwall in September 1993 was to produce Liberal Democrat campaign literature which, it seemed to many, clearly pandered to racist sentiments. The victory of the British National Party candidate, Derek Beackon, focused national attention on Tower Hamlets. A subsequent inquiry into local party tactics by the Liberal Democrat peer Lord Lester and a scathing report, led three Liberal councillors to resign. One, indicted of pandering to racism, was a Jew married to a black woman. This, in turn, caused some to believe Ashdown's launching of an inquiry was over-handed. The whole unsavoury episode reached its climax when Labour swept to victory in the 1994 local elections.

As the Conservative Government plumbed new depths of unpopularity in the opinion polls (and the succession of banana skins on which the government slipped grew ever longer), the Liberal Democrats approached the May 1994 elections in confident mood. Nor were they to be disappointed. It was a historic night where Liberal Democrat euphoria could be excused. Never in living memory had the party forced the Conservatives into a humiliating third place in a poll held in the length and breadth of England (and to fourth place north of the border). Never before had Liberals triumphed in so many councils in such diverse areas. And rarely had Liberals secured such a springboard for future advances against a seemingly demoralised, discredited and divided Conservative Government.

A closer analysis of the Liberal performance in May 1994 shows considerable evidence of the nationwide support of the party (albeit before the death of John Smith and the advent of Tony Blair added a major new element into the political equation). Voting took place in May 1994 for 198 councils. The Liberal Democrats increased the number of councils they controlled from nine to 19.[5] To put this into perspective, Labour controlled councils rose from 89 to 93, while those under Tory rule fell from 33 to 15. In terms of seats, Liberal Democrats captured 388 (bringing their total up to 1,098), Labour increased its tally by 88 to 2,769, and the Conservatives lost 429 (down to 888).

Significantly, the Liberal Democrats out-performed, albeit by a whisker, the Liberal–SDP alliance at the peak of its support in the mid-1980s. Liberal Democrat gains were mainly at the expense of the Tories but, importantly, the Liberals also infringed on traditional Labour inner city territory. In Islington, for example, Labour retained control but the Liberals captured eight seats from the ruling party. Lambeth remained under no overall control, but the Liberals took 20 seats (14 from Labour and six from the Conservatives). In neighbouring Southwark – which included the comfortably Liberal Democrat Bermondsey parliamentary constituency – the Liberals gained five seats, three from the Tories and two from Independents.[6]

Outside these inner city areas, the real triumph for the Liberal Democrats was against Conservatives. In a virtual triumphal progress Liberal Democrats took Bath with a gain of 12 seats. The Liberal Democrats took Worthing from the Conservatives, capturing five of their seats. In Eastbourne they consolidated their control by seizing two Tory seats. In Eastleigh – where a parliamentary by-election was pending – the Liberals took control by ousting two Conservatives.

Nationwide, the Liberal Democrats had thus forced an unpopular Conservative Party into third place, but not the Labour Party into second place. Where the Liberals performed well against Labour it was where Labour was in power, a protest vote, or where Labour was clearly not in the contest against the Conservatives.

A month later, however, the focus had shifted from Liberal Democrat strengths and weakness at local level to the contests for the European elections. The difficulties facing the Liberals were to be all too obviously displayed in the June 1994 European elections. Once again, the size of the Euro-constituencies was a potential obstacle to the Liberals, making it more difficult to claim they were the obvious alternative to the Conservatives. Moreover, after the debacle of the 1989 European elections, in which the Greens had forced the Liberal Democrats into a humiliating fourth place (see p. 203) there was also a certain nervous apprehension.

However, before the voting took place for Europe, a dramatic and landmark tragedy changed the face of the left of centre of politics in Britain. The Labour leader, John Smith, died suddenly of a heart attack on the morning of 12 May 1994. The repercussions of John Smith's untimely death, and the subsequent advent of Tony Blair, were to be enormous. For the moment, however, it was the European elections which required immediate attention. The outcome is shown in Table 18.2.

Table 18.2 June 1994 European Elections

Party	Votes	1994 % of Poll	Seats
Labour	6,753,863	44.24	62
Conservative	4,248,531	27.83	18
Lib Dem	2,552,730	16.72	2
Scot Nat	487,239	3.19	2
Green	494,561	3.24	–
Plaid Cymru	162,478	1.06	–
SDP	–	–	–
Others	568,151	3.72	–
Total	15,267,550	100	84

Compared to 1989, the party had limited cause for celebration. It had won its first-ever seats, taking the seats of Somerset and Devon North (won by Graham Watson with 43.6 per cent of the vote and a 22,500 majority) and the Cornwall and Plymouth West seat, taken with a majority over 29,000. It had polled 16.7 per cent of the vote, restoring its third place. The Greens (who had polled 14.9 per cent in 1989) had been obliterated. But beyond this, the party had failed to go. The Conservatives had been routed, but the real victors were the Labour Party. Labour had secured 62 seats to the 18 of the Conservatives. Outside the south-west corner of England, a new revitalised Labour Party was on the march. These were dangerous omens for the Liberal Democrats.

For although the party won comfortably in Cornwall and Plymouth West, and also in Somerset and Devon North, the outcome was generally one of frustration. The Liberal Democrats narrowly failed to capture Devon and Plymouth East by 700 votes (a result muddied by the presence of a Literal Democrat candidate who polled 10,203 votes). The Liberal Democrats unsuccessfully contested the legality of this election in the courts. Elsewhere in the South West, as Table 18.3 shows, Liberal Democrats narrowly missed taking such seats as Dorset and Devon East, and Wight and Hampshire South.

Table 18.3   Areas of Liberal Democrat Strength: June 1994 European Elections

Lib Dem Seats	% Vote	Majority	Runner Up	% Majority
Cornwall and Plymouth West	41.8	29,498	Con	13.5
Somerset and Devon North	43.6	22,509	Con	9.3
Lib Dem near misses			*winner*	*% majority*
Devon and Plymouth East	31.4	700	Con	0.3
Dorset and Devon East	36.2	2,264	Con	1.0
Wight and Hampshire South	32.1	5,101	Con	2.8
Itchen, Test and Avon	32.4	6,903	Con	3.0
Sussex East and Kent South	35.8	6,212	Con	2.3
Hampshire North and Oxford	31.3	9,194	Con	4.5
Wiltshire North and Bath	30.6	8,787	Con	4.3
South Downs West	32.7	21,067	Con	10.9
Surrey	29.2	27,018	Con	14.5
Sheffield	19.3	50,288	Lab	39.0

However, apart from the ten 'near misses' listed above, nowhere else had the party come second. Moreover, apart from Labour-held Sheffield where the party was a very poor second, all the best results were in the South West or in Surrey and Sussex – the traditional Conservative heartlands of the South. There was much that was disturbing in the results. Labour showed a remarkable resurgence in areas where Liberal Democrats might have expected to be the main challengers (Sussex South and Crawley). Some areas, such as Scotland were little short of a disaster. If the Greens were shattered (their best vote was 4.2 per cent in the Cotswolds) and if the 17 'old' Liberals had made little impact (Meadowcroft himself only polled 4.2 per cent), the Liberals had missed out on the real prize – a breakthrough outside the West Country.

The Liberals did, however, have one consolation prize on 9 June 1994. Polling was also taking place in the third Conservative seat to fall vacant since the 1992 general election. This was the Hampshire constituency of Eastleigh,[7] where the Conservatives had secured a 17,702 majority over the Liberal Democrats in 1992. The by-election was caused by the death (having apparently strangled himself in a sexual ritual) of 46-year-old Stephen Milligan, one of the new intake of 1992.

Eastleigh, with the fourth largest number of voters in the country, was a good prospect for the Liberals. The Liberal Democrats required only a modest swing to take the seat (far less than they had achieved at Newbury and Christchurch in 1993). They also had a strong presence on Eastleigh council (with 18 councillors, compared to 20 Conservatives and only two Labour). But the Labour vote in Eastleigh (20.7 per cent in the 1992 general election) prompted the party to make a major effort. It was a diverse constituency. Eastleigh itself was partly a Victorian redbrick railway town where railway privatisation was none too popular in the British Rail maintenance depot. The constituency wound round the north-east side of Southampton. According to the *Daily Telegraph*, it was '...the quintessential, lower middle-class, upwardly mobile England that fell in love with Mrs Thatcher and the values she espoused in the 1980s'.

Certainly by June 1994 any ardour for Thatcherism had cooled. The Liberal Democrat, David Chidgey, took the seat with a 9,239 majority over Labour, the Conservatives pushed into third place.

A major development in 1994 was the announced retirement of Sir David Steel. It was a departure that marked the end of a significant and substantial chapter in modern Liberal Party history. As the *Guardian* noted, it would mean that after the election due by 1997

... all of the key figures in the history of the SDP–Liberal alliance would have moved onwards and upwards but now irrevocably out of the parliamentary frontline.[8]

Taking stock of the position of the Liberal Democrats the *Guardian* continued:

The foreseeable future of the Liberal Democrats is by no means glum or lacking in possibilities. But it is a very different future from the one glimpsed a dozen years ago, when Warrington, Crosby and Hillhead seemed to imply that anything was possible and when the alliance came within a whisker of exceeding Labour's share of the vote in the 1983 general election. Today the party's future has to be seen more modestly. David Steel exhorted them to prepare for government. Paddy Ashdown's best hope is to exhort them to prepare for influence.

As if to signal the changes in the personnel of British politics, Paddy Ashdown announced a reshuffling of his parliamentary team on 19 July 1994. Alan Beith, who remained as Deputy Leader, moved from the Treasury to take charge of Home Affairs. He was replaced as Treasury spokesman by Malcolm Bruce (moving up from Trade and Industry). Replacing Sir David Steel at foreign affairs and defence was Menzies Campbell. Among other changes Simon Hughes took over a new post as community and urban affairs team leader, combined with education. Matthew Taylor headed the environment team, Charles Kennedy, Europe and Alex Carlile, the party leader in Wales, led on health and welfare.

An increasingly urgent need for the new team was to concentrate on policy. As the *Guardian* had observed at the time of Steel's announced retirement:

> At the moment most voters only know three things about Lib-Dem policy, if they know anything; they know that the Lib-Dems stand for proportional representation, for green policies and for spending more on education. Self-evidently that is not enough. Most people would be stretched to say what the Lib-Dem education policy contains beyond more money up front. And even an expert would have difficulty outlining the party's distinctive economic stance. Clearly the prospective reshuffle of the party's Westminster portfolios – with a new economics spokesman at its centre – will be important in heralding the new start.[9]

Against this background, the Liberal Democrats very much needed a good autumn party conference. But the conference, held at Brighton from 18 to 22 September, was hardly a happy one (at least for the party leadership and the party image in the country at large). In part, the Liberal Democrats were trying to adjust to the changed circumstances in the Labour Party with a youthful and telegenic leader in Tony Blair (who had been elected on 21 July) and a soaring rating in the opinion polls. With the earlier call (back on 3 August) by three of the four founder members of the SDP for the Liberal Democrats to establish closer links with Labour, there was much press speculation on how the parties of the left would develop. Could the Liberals maintain a policy of 'equidistance' from Conservative and Labour given the ever-deeper unpopularity and revulsion of many at the Major Government with its sleaze and arrogance? But what would be the relationship of Liberal Democrats with any future Blair-led government? Was 'New Labour' going to marginalise the Liberals? And what of those Liberals whose main target in local elections (as in Northern areas such as Rochdale or Sheffield) was Labour itself? And what, also, were Tony Blair's credentials as a radical? Was he pale pink, even light blue, or indeed an almost invisible blur?

The Brighton conference activists responded by giving the party leadership a rough ride – 'Paddy's Raspberry Rebels' as they were dubbed – not least on the issue of the decriminalisation of cannabis.[10] Although all 23 Lib Dem MPs voted against, the conference voted by 426 votes to 375 to decriminalise pot (that is to end prosecutions for the use and possession of cannabis) – amid much media excitement. Divisions also surfaced on the subject of a minimum wage (the platform lost the vote here). Even the monarchy did not escape a vote – although a call for a referendum on the future of the monarchy was heavily defeated. However, a strong anti-royalist element endorsed a motion calling for a radical trimming of the £7.9 million Civil List and the 'redefining of the roles of members of the Royal Family apart from the Monarch'.

In the wake of this Brighton rebellion, Paddy Ashdown's personal rating in the polls fell to its lowest level since the end of 1990. The Liberal Democrat rating had now fallen by 25 per cent since the death of John Smith in mid-May. After Brighton, the happily rebellious delegates went away to their constituencies. The issues of relations with Labour, and the 'Blair factor', would not vanish so easily.

The Liberals thus entered 1995 with a three-fold challenge. They had somehow to differentiate themselves more sharply from Labour and also avoid the squeeze in the polls and in elections removed from their local power bases, while at the same time keeping alive hope of joining the Labour opposition in government.

To a large extent, future problems with Labour could be temporarily forgotten as the continuing electoral trough of the Conservatives provided another bumper crop of municipal election victories in May 1995.

The Liberal Democrats could savour a net gain of 420 seats, plus control of 18 of the new unitary councils. At 23 per cent their share of the vote was slightly down, but it was sufficiently concentrated to ensure substantial net gains in areas such as Torbay, Chichester, Sheffield Hallam and the Isle of Wight. Liberal strength in the South West was rippling over into formerly Tory areas of Wiltshire, Sussex and Hampshire.[11] A less noticed feature of the Liberal Democrat advance was its progress in some metropolitan areas to become the main challenger to Labour. Liberal strength in some of the Labour dominated metropolitan district councils is set out in Table 18.4. Whilst these developments at local level were of obvious importance, very significant changes were taking place nationally.

Table 18.4   Liberal Democrat Strength in the Metropolitan District Councils
(as at end May 1995)

Gateshead	Lab 50	Lib Dem 13	Con 1
Liverpool	Lab 49	Lib Dem 43	Con 2
Manchester	Lab 82	Lib Dem 14	Con 3
Newcastle-on-Tyne	Lab 62	Lib Dem 13	Con 2
Oldham	Lab 30	Lib Dem 23	Con 5
Rochdale	Lab 26	Lib Dem 22	Con 11
St Helens	Lab 40	Lib Dem 10	Con 3
Sheffield	Lab 58	Lib Dem 25	Con 4
South Tyneside	Lab 53	Lib Dem 6	Other 1
Stockport	Lab 23	Lib Dem 27	Con 10
Wigan	Lab 67	Lib Dem 3	Con 1

A key development on this front came in late May 1995 when, amidst immediate signs of tension amongst some sections of the party, Paddy Ashdown signalled his intention to move away from the party's long-established policy of equidistance (or neutrality) between Conservative and Labour.[12] Effectively, Ashdown was repositioning the political stance of the Liberal Democrats by ruling out any post-election deal or support for the Conservatives. Given the right-wing nature of the long period of Conservative hegemony after 1979, and given the myriad failings and weaknesses of the Major administration since 1990, such a move by Ashdown was not only sound tactically but probably long overdue. But it was criticised by those who had spent much of their time in politics attacking Labour as their main enemy. As the *Independent* observed, Liz Lynne, the Liberal Democrat MP for Rochdale, had made a career out of fighting Labour, whilst the former MP Sir Cyril Smith attacked Ashdown's decision as idiotic.[13] Liberal activists preparing to fight the pending by-election on the doorsteps of Littleborough and Saddleworth (part of this constituency was in Rochdale) were also upset.[14] Apart from those Liberal Democrats, mainly in the Northern cities, who were worried by Ashdown's move, others saw in his move the dangers of too close a fraternisation with Labour. Their worries were not dispelled by Lord Rodgers (one of the original SDP 'Gang of Four') urging a two-term parliamentary pact with Labour.

However, the abandonment of equidistance by Ashdown seemed a long way removed from the real world when it came to fighting the impending Littleborough and Saddleworth by-election.

The Littleborough and Saddleworth contest of 27 July 1995 provided the Liberal Democrats with an excellent opportunity. They had polled 35.9 per cent in 1992, only 8.3 per cent behind the Conservatives, with

Labour third. In this Pennine constituency, the Liberal Democrats had a commanding presence in local elections (with 46 per cent of the vote in May 1995 compared to 32 per cent for Labour and 21 per cent for the Tories). Moreover the local council comprised 19 Liberals, four Tories and one Labour. This seat on the edge of the Pennines boasted a long local Nonconformist tradition and it was one of the few seats where Liberal Democrats had advanced at the expense of Labour in 1992. From the start Liberals were favourites to win, although it held problems for the Liberals: with Tony Blair's 'New Labour' riding high in the opinion polls, Labour was always a real threat. After John Major's re-election as party leader, the Conservatives were also fighting a spirited contest. Locally, Liberals and Labour were fighting a bitter campaign (the 'mother of all by-elections' as the *Guardian* noted) and doubts about Paddy Ashdown's continuing leadership would be certain to surface if the Liberals failed to hold off the Labour challenge. Ashdown was criticised for devoting a great deal of time to the crisis in Bosnia, in which he was passionately interested, and had also been bitterly attacked locally by some in the party for ending 'equidistance'.

The Littleborough contest was perhaps most memorable for the bitterness of the fight between Labour and Liberal Democrats. It was, perhaps, the dirtiest and most bruising local contest between them since the days of Bermondsey. It was part of the broader canvas of Liberal–Labour hostility in the North West. Both parties had long fought each other tenaciously in such areas as Liverpool, Oldham, Pendle and Rochdale. Despite a hard-fought Labour campaign (organised by their Hartlepool MP and 'spin-doctor' Peter Mandelson) the Liberals held on to their early momentum, duly capturing the seat on a swing of 11.6 per cent with a majority of 1,993 votes for Chris Davies. However, several features of the Liberal victory were disquieting; the party's share of the vote was only up 2.6 per cent (from 35.9 per cent in 1992 to 38.5 per cent in 1995). In many ways Labour, who moved up to second place with a swing from Conservative to Labour of 17.3 per cent, could be most pleased with the result. The Conservatives, polling only 23.6 per cent of the vote, had little cause for comfort, notching up their sixth by-election defeat of the parliament. Not since 1989 had the Conservatives successfully defended a by-election vacancy.

It was against this background that, on 13 September 1995, Paddy Ashdown launched the new party policy statement, the *Liberal Democrat Guarantee* (according to *The Times* with much similarity of language and presentation to the right-wing *Contract with America*, launched earlier by US Republican politician Newt Gingrich[15]). This was rather unfair. Its three main policy strategies covered education, constitutional reform and an environmentally-friendly economic policy. On education, the statement reiterated earlier-announced plans for nurseries for all under fives as part of the party's £2 billion commitment to educational improvement.

These three main policy areas had not only been mapped out by Liberal Democrat policy strategists to separate the party from both Conservative and Labour, but also as the areas on which Liberals would put pressure on a future Labour government to take action. Indeed, it was clearly vital for the Liberals to be seen to have a separate identity from the new Blairite Labour Party.

The *Guardian* well summarised the position in which the Liberal Democrats found themselves as they approached their September 1995 conference in Glasgow:

> Mr Ashdown and his party come to Glasgow after one of the toughest years of the seemingly endless post-war march towards the sound of political gunfire. The special problems which have faced them over the past twelve months could be summarised in two words: Tony Blair.[16]

But, as the *Guardian* admitted of the Liberal Democrats:

> ...Yet they have actually done quite well in the current scheme of things. Mr Blair may have surged ahead, but Mr Ashdown is still in there with a defined political project, a relatively united party, and some strong electoral successes to report. The local elections saw the Liberal Democrats rise to second place. They now have more than 5,000 councillors, an entire generation of party activists with experience – and perhaps judgement – which their predecessors never possessed.

Hence, the Glasgow conference was overshadowed by attempts to carve out a separate, distinctive identity for themselves. Certainly, Paddy Ashdown (by now in his seventh year as leader, the longest serving of the party leaders) did not shy away from bold plans on tax (a 50 per cent tax on those earning £100,000 per annum) but in general the conference agenda had been carefully and ruthlessly excised of any over-radical motions.[17] At the same time the party was marking its modestly radical credentials with plans for higher taxes, new curbs on private motoring and public control of the railways. And Ashdown had won overwhelming conference support for the abandonment of the policy of equidistance (although Tony Blair's talk of closer cooperation with Liberal Democrats and his remark that Labour was 'social democrat' did not make

Ashdown's task easier as Liberal Democrat activists reacted with anger). They reacted, declared *The Economist*, 'like a spinster propositioned by a handsome bachelor'.[18]

In general, however, conference had passed more easily than a year earlier. And the party's radical credentials were reinforced in the 'alternative Queen's Speech' put forward by the Liberals in November 1995.

Its centrepiece was a commitment to modernise the constitution. A Great Reform Bill would provide the most radical programme for reform this country had ever seen, declared Ashdown. As well as separate assemblies for Scotland and Wales, and an elected second chamber, Ashdown called for an elected strategic authority for London and wider use of advisory referendums, a fairer voting system for national, local and European elections and more openness in the way decisions were taken in Europe. The Liberal Democrats, he promised, would reduce taxation on jobs and wealth and place it on pollution and waste, and Railtrack would be brought back under public control.

At the same time, with a general election now becoming closer, Ashdown announced another reshuffle of his party team. Alan Beith was given a wider brief to embrace overall responsibility for their manifesto and a strategic oversight of the party's parliamentary teams. Alex Carlile took over part of home affairs (including justice and immigration). Simon Hughes moved from education to health, Don Foster was promoted to head education, housing and local government. David Chidgey (fresh from the Eastleigh by-election victory) became transport spokesperson.

Despite these initiatives, with Labour so dominant in the opinion polls, it was difficult for the Liberal Democrats to keep in the political limelight. They were very much in need of a big uplift. The defection of Emma Nicholson, on 29 December 1995, provided just such a welcome boost. The well-orchestrated defection of the high profile Conservative MP for Devon West and Torridge since 1987 was not only a personal coup for Paddy Ashdown but a particularly welcome boost for the party in the South West. Emma Nicholson had first been approached by the party's general election coordinator, Lord Holme, in mid-December, after casual conversations with Nick Harvey, Liberal Democrat MP for Devon North, in which she had expressed growing dissatisfaction with the government. A meeting with Paddy Ashdown followed on 23 December and, after time for reflection, the defection was duly announced.

Although Alan Howarth, the Conservative MP for Stratford had switched to Labour in October (much to the private fury of the Liberal Democrats) Emma Nicholson was the first sitting Conservative MP to switch to the Liberals in modern times. A former Conservative Party vice-chairperson, with a long commitment to liberal causes, she was a spectacular convert.[19] It provided the party with a welcome springboard for the May elections and raised the party's strength to 25, its highest yet.

The impact of Emma Nicholson's defection was partly limited by the leak of the party's internal document *Towards 1996* with its somewhat brutally frank assessment of the strengths and weaknesses of the party.[20] It suggested that voters would see the party as naive, over-federalist on Europe, too committed to higher taxes and that Paddy Ashdown cared more about Bosnia than any other issue. Although some of the right-wing press gave much coverage to the leaked document, the episode soon passed.

Certainly, the party was not harmed in the May 1996 municipal elections, which produced another eye-catching set of Liberal gains. The party won 636 seats (a net gain of 143), to take control of 23 councils (a net gain of five). These gains included Hastings, Royal Tunbridge Wells, Woking and Wokingham.

Typical of the councils to fall into Liberal Democrat control in May 1996 was the hitherto Conservative bastion of Royal Tunbridge Wells, the Kent town which had for long been a byword for staunch right-wing respectability. The Conservatives had held the town for 130 years until 1995, when the Liberal Democrats became the largest party with 22 seats (to the 18 of the Conservatives). In 1996 the Liberal Democrats took overall control with 27 seats to the Conservatives' 14. Back in 1976 there had been 38 Tories with just ten opposition councillors. 'Disgusted' of Tunbridge had clearly had enough.

As always, however, Liberal Democrat local election success was in the shadow of the coming general election, and the continuing question of relations with Labour. Prior to the September 1996 Brighton party conference, Lord Jenkins had suggested that Liberal Democrat supporters should consider voting Labour in order to defeat Conservatives in the forthcoming election. Jenkins stressed that there was now much common ground between 'New Labour' and the Liberal Democrats. *The Times'* editorial was, as always, eager to exploit the question:

> The future relationship between a Labour government and the Liberal Democrats is a love that dares not speak its name. Tony Blair, in public at least, affects to believe that a Labour majority will make any pact unnecessary. The Lib Dem leadership is still coyly pretending to have reservations that it does not really possess. But the flirtation was clearly evident in Paddy Ashdown's speech yesterday, even if, for the sake of political propriety, it was disguised.[21]

But, as *The Times* went on to point out:

> ...the closer that the two parties' policies become, the more absurd it seems for them to be fighting each other. Now that Labour has embraced constitutional reform, the old flagship of the centre party, there is little that differentiates the two... If Labour were to introduce a more proportional voting system after the next election the certainties of British politics would become more fluid. This is the future of which both party leaders must dream, but of which neither yet dares to speak.

Unwanted (at least from Ashdown's point of view) discussion of Lib–Lab cooperation, pacts and mergers preoccupied the press during the Brighton conference.

Alex Carlile, the retiring MP for Montgomery, seemed to see a future when Liberal Democrats and Labour would be merged; Lord Rodgers called on Liberal Democrats to vote tactically to oust the Tories; Robert Maclennan urged cross-party consensus on electoral reform. Paddy Ashdown, in turn, emphasised that equidistance in no way meant cosying up to Labour. His strong attack on aspects of the operations of the European Union partly deflected the press. Overall, the party emerged in reasonably good heart from Brighton. Its morale was soon to be bolstered when a final defection to the Liberal Democrat ranks came in October 1996. Peter Thurnham, MP for the highly-marginal Bolton North East, finally deserted the Conservatives. Thurnham had resigned the Conservative whip in February, to become an Independent Conservative. His final break came over lack of leadership and continued sleaze in the Conservative Party, although cynics emphasised that he had failed to secure a safe Conservative seat at the next election. (Thurnham countered by saying he had been offered a knighthood not to defect.) Whatever the real facts, this latest recruit did nothing to stop the steady erosion of Liberal Democrat support in the opinion polls that had been a feature of 1996.

Meanwhile, confirmation of possible future cooperation with a Labour government came on 29 October 1996 with the announcement that the Liberal Democrats and Labour would hold joint talks on introducing sweeping constitutional reforms in the next parliament. A cross-party committee would prepare plans for House of Lords reform, proportional representation, devolution and a Freedom of Information Act. The new committee was the outcome of long discussions between Robert Maclennan (as the Liberal Democrat constitutional affairs spokesman) and Robin Cook, Labour's Shadow Foreign Secretary. Both emphasised that the talks were not part of a wider policy of cooperation, or any sort of pre-election pact, but such statements failed to stop Stephen Dorrell, the Conservative Health Secretary (and an expert on constitutional matters) declaring that 'The Lib–Lab Pact which laid Britain low in the 1970s is back.'[22]

Such was hardly the case. But some senior Liberal Democrats, opposed to any form of courtship with Tony Blair, continued to warn that such a policy would cost votes.[23]

Meanwhile the last parliamentary by-election of the parliament (at Wirral South on 27 February) had found the Liberals in a doubly difficult position. The party had come a poor third in 1992. Known to some as 'Surrey on the Mersey' the 15-mile stretch of land between Liverpool and North Wales was just the type of seat in which New Labour hoped to do well to establish their middle-class credentials.[24] The Liberals had local problems (the party was on its third parliamentary candidate in the constituency in less than three months) and Labour duly swept to victory.

Hence, the approach of the general election found the Liberal Democrats in a seemingly difficult position. Support, as measured in at least one opinion poll, had slipped to around 10 per cent as New Labour retained an enormous lead over the Conservatives. Faced also with a six-week election campaign (easily the longest campaign for over half a century) the headquarters resources of the party would be sorely stretched. The Liberal Democrat Campaign team was centred round Lord Holme, with Tim Clement-Jones overseeing constituency campaigning and Dick Newby, the former SDP national secretary, in charge of the media operation. Much of the manifesto and policy work was under Neil Stockley (head of policy) and William Wallace. The emphasis of the Liberal Democrat campaign at the grassroots was on the traditional doorstep approach (whereas both Conservative and Labour were relying to a greater extent on telephone canvassing).

As in 1992, the party fought on the broadest possible front. With the exception of the Speaker's seat all constituencies were contested (except for the special case of Tatton where Liberals and Labour combined to field Martin Bell as an Independent 'anti-sleaze' candidate). An analysis of the candidates fielded by the Liberal Democrats produces a useful insight into the party. Women accounted for 22.2 per cent of candidates (24.8 per cent in the Labour ranks, a mere 10.8 per cent in the Conservative). Over 22 per cent of Liberal Democrats had been to public school, over 12 per cent to Oxbridge. With an average age of 46, a total of 44.9 per cent had experience as a local councillor in town halls. Of the 639 candidates, no less than 115 were teachers or lecturers.

The Liberal Democrat manifesto, *Make a Difference*, was launched on 3 April. It was the most radical of the party manifestos. It set out a 'fully-costed programme' with education as its centrepiece, coupled with a pledge to put one penny on basic rate tax to fund its education proposals. These included a large boost to spending, especially on school books, equipment and computers. Other headline-catching proposals included £565 million to cut hospital waiting lists, an extra 3,000 police on the beat, environmental priorities of clean air and pure water as well as a cut in carbon dioxide emissions, and a common age of consent which would include gays. The Conservatives attacked the Liberal proposals as a 'menu of tax and spend' that was effectively a 'Lib–Lab manifesto'.

During the campaign, the Liberals adopted a pincer-like policy. They continued to hammer out the key themes of their manifesto, their 'distinctive message' while clearly concentrating effort and resources into the 50 target seats they believed could be won. Hence the Liberal Democrats concentrated on health, education and crime. Other less vote-winning issues (such as constitutional reform) took a back seat. As the campaign developed, commentators noted that the Liberal message was getting across. After the election, William Wallace wrote:

> The Liberal Democrat campaign won widespread popular respect and recognition, both for its leader and for the arguments it advanced. Paddy Ashdown emerged not only as the most experienced leader but as the only one prepared to talk about specific policies and commitments, with a coherent and cohesive party behind him. Concentration of limited resources on target seats paid off extraordinarily well, and has given Paddy Ashdown a body of new MPs who will provide invaluable expertise in local government, economics, law and education.[25]

Certainly, the outcome of the election was a triumph (see Table 18.5). Not since 1929 had the Liberals elected so many MPs as they did in the May 1997 election. The 46 MPs returned constituted a breakthrough on a scale few had expected. Although the share of the vote won by the Liberals was fractionally down compared to 1992, the effects of the concentration of the Liberal vote saw an upsurge in the number of elected MPs. Almost all the seats they hoped to gain were won (and quite a lot more besides). Ten Liberals were elected in Scotland (but only two in Wales), whilst a whole swathe of territory in south-west England was now Liberal Democrat (most particularly in Cornwall, Devon and Somerset). The Liberal Democrats also seized tracts of south-west London, capturing

Richmond Park, Twickenham, Sutton and Cheam, Kingston and Surbiton, as well as Carshalton and Wallington.

Table 18.5

	Votes	Seats	% Votes
Labour	13,517,911	419	43.2
Conservative	9,600,940	165	30.7
Liberal Democrats	5,243,440	46	16.8
Nationalists	783,290	10	2.5
Others	2,142,621	19	6.8

Paddy Ashdown had prophesied a day of destiny. It became a night of delirious excitement for the Liberal Democrats as the voters, having seemingly discovered the power of tactical voting, went on to send more Liberals to Westminster than since the days of Lloyd George. The Sheffield Hallam seat fell on a swing of 18 per cent. The Liberals took Harrogate and Knaresborough on a swing of 15 per cent (thereby denying Norman Lamont the safe seat for which he had come in search). A 10.3 per cent swing secured Oxford West and Abingdon. Some of the Liberal gains had been in areas of traditional Liberal strength and frequent 'near misses' in general elections (such as Hereford or Hazel Grove) or seats where Liberals inherited past by-election success (such as Portsmouth South). But the capture of seats such as Winchester or Northavon at a general election was a real breakthrough. Liberals did particularly well in several seaside towns (taking Southport, Weston-super-Mare and Torbay and narrowly missing Southend West). Only one seat was lost to the Conservatives (the sensational Christchurch by-election seat went back to its traditional allegiance).

However, in the industrial and inner city constituencies, the election produced a very different outcome. The party lost Rochdale (where Liz Lynne was defeated by Labour by 4,545 votes) and also its by-election gain of Oldham East and Saddleworth (the former Littleborough and Saddleworth seat). Although Simon Hughes was returned in Southwark North and Bermondsey, there was a 4.3 per cent swing to Labour and his majority was down to 3,387. No Liberal was returned in Liverpool (where the retirement of David Alton and boundary redistribution had worked against the Liberals), nor did strong Liberal challenges in hopeful Labour-held seats such as Birmingham Yardley or Chesterfield come anywhere near success.

In the euphoria of the 1997 election, these disappointments could be forgotten in the celebration of victories in hitherto Conservative citadels. Perhaps the most remarkable feature of the Liberal Democrat gains was not just the capture of these seats, but the swing achieved to make victory possible (Table 18.6). One result of the swing to the Liberal Democrats was to turn existing Liberal seats into what now appeared almost impregnable strongholds. Table 18.7 sets this out.

Table 18.6   The 12 Largest Swings to Liberal Democrats (seats gained from Conservatives, May 1997)

	%
Sheffield Hallam	18.53
Harrogate and Knaresborough	15.75
Kingston and Surbiton	13.60
Sutton and Cheam	12.94
Hazel Grove	12.82
Cornwall South East	12.06
Edinburgh West	11.77
Carshalton and Wallington	11.76
Oxford West and Abingdon	10.34
Northavon	9.89
Richmond Park	9.69
Hereford	9.15

Table 18.7   The Ten Safest Liberal Seats (after May 1997 election)

Constituency	% Majority	2nd Place
Orkney and Shetland	33.72	Lab
Fife North East	24.75	Con
Hazel Grove	23.94	Con
Cornwall North	23.78	Con
Roxburgh and Berwickshire	22.63	Con
Truro and St Austell	22.03	Con
Yeovil	21.10	Con
Montgomeryshire	19.74	Con
Berwick-upon-Tweed	19.24	Con
Sheffield Hallam	18.19	Con

The list of safe seats only partly corresponded to regional strength in terms of votes cast in May 1997. Liberal Democrats had polled best in the South West (31 per cent of the vote) followed, albeit some way behind, by south-east England (21 per cent) and East Anglia (18 per cent). The party's worst performance in England was in the East Midlands (13 per cent), where no seats were won.

If, to a certain extent, luck had helped the Liberal Democrats to victory in four seats by a winning majority of under 150 (Winchester, two votes; Torbay, 12 votes; Kingston and Surbiton, 56 votes and Somerton and Frome, 130 votes), the Liberals could point to another 15 seats where they had come within 3,000 votes of unseating the Conservatives (see Table 18.8). This list makes for interesting analysis: all were normally Conservative seats. Of the 15, eight were concentrated in the South West, five more were in the South. In terms of geographical location and type of constituency, the seats *nearly* won mirrored very closely the seats *actually* won.

Table 18.8   The 15 Liberal Near-Misses

Constituency	Majority	% Maj	Held by
Teignbridge	281	0.4	Con
Wells	528	0.9	Con
Mid-Dorset and Poole North	681	1.4	Con
Totnes	877	1.6	Con
Norfolk North	1,293	2.2	Con
Conwy	1,596	3.8	Lab (Con until '97)
Tiverton and Honiton	1,653	2.8	Con
Bridgwater	1,796	3.3	Con
Dorset West	1,840	3.4	Con
Eastbourne	1,994	3.8	Con
Christchurch	2,165	3.8	Con
Southend West	2,615	5.7	Con
Surrey South West	2,694	4.8	Con
Dorset North	2,746	5.2	Con
Orpington	2,952	4.9	Con

Although 'tactical voting' was assumed to be a major factor at work, this explanation needs to be treated with some caution. If tactical voting means the *collapse* of the Labour vote in favour of a strongly placed Liberal Democrat in order to get a sitting Conservative out, this was often simply not true in 1997. Frequently, even where Liberals took a seat, the Labour vote actually *increased* (such was the strength of the anti-Conservative mood in the country). Indeed, in some seats in which Liberal Democrats might have expected tactical voting to help their cause, the party fell right back as Labour surged forward. Good examples in this category include seats such as Crosby, Hove, St Albans, Hastings and Rye, and Conwy (in three of these seats Labour came from third place to win).

Other factors must be called into play to account for some Liberal gains. Redistribution, and the redrawing of constituency boundaries played a part (as in Lewes which lost the Conservative area of the Peacehaven coast or Colchester which lost its Tory rural voters); strength of local party organisation and an established council base were clearly important; local personality factors still played a part (the attempt by the Tories to foist Lamont on Harrogate must surely have played its part in the 15 per cent swing to the Liberal Democrats); and, not least, the effect of intervention by the anti-Europe Referendum Party and UK Independence Party may have cost the Conservatives up to ten seats. For whatever reasons, Liberal Democrats could rejoice in their strongest presence in parliament in living memory. Thirty years earlier Jo Grimond had urged his troops to advance toward the sound of gunfire. This time the Liberals had returned as conquering heroes.

19
Living with Labour: 1997–2001

The period from 1997 to the general election of June 2001 can be divided into two halves. First, there was the last period of Paddy Ashdown's leadership, ending when he formally resigned as Liberal Democrat leader in summer 1999; second, there was the period since the advent of Charles Kennedy, from his victory in the August 1999 ballot to the 7 June 2001 election. Within this broad division, and throughout this period, one issue overshadowed the party: its relations with the 'New Labour' government of Tony Blair. This period also saw Liberal Democrats facing new electoral battlegrounds (in addition to the 1999 European elections, parliamentary by-elections and annual municipal contests) in terms of the Scottish Parliament, Welsh Assembly and Greater London Authority elections.

In the immediate aftermath of the 1997 general election, the Liberal Democrats had the opportunity to take stock of their position. On the surface they had emerged from the 1997 contest in fine shape. After a well-fought campaign they had secured their largest parliamentary force since 1929. At long last, concentrated Liberal voting had produced victories and the party now had well-established bridgeheads not only in the West Country but elsewhere in former Conservative strongholds. With 46 MPs, one result of the election success was that Ashdown could appoint the first full team of parliamentary spokespersons in fifty years. Although most senior appointments remained unchanged there was some shuffling of posts. Paul Tyler became Chief Whip in place of Archie Kirkwood (who was not seeking re-election to the post), Charles Kennedy moved to Tyler's former post at Agriculture and Rural Affairs, while Menzies Campbell took over Europe from Kennedy and Archie Kirkwood took on social security.

Despite the parliamentary breakthrough in 1997, there were some worrying features of their electoral success. Many seats had been won with tiny majorities, often aided by the presence of anti-Europe candidates who had siphoned votes away from the Conservatives. The election had left the party with 11 seats which would be vulnerable to a small swing of 2.5 per cent to the Conservatives at the next election.

In a sense, the marginality of Liberal seats was a *tactical* problem that would not have to be faced until a general election several years hence. Much more immediately problematic was the *strategy* question facing the party. Had 1997 finally marked the end of the Liberal attempt to replace Labour as the radical party of the centre-left? Or, perversely, had the very size of New Labour's victory (and its centre or even centre-right stance) opened up a possible new role for the Liberals on the radical left flank? And what attitude would Labour, now that it was ensconced in power, adopt towards the Liberals? Would the parties' common views on certain key issues (such as constitutional reform) lead to constructive cooperation?

In the immediate wake of the election, there were encouraging signs. By the end of July 1997 Liberal Democrats had the comforting prospect of fighting the June 1999 European elections under a form of proportional representation. Meanwhile, the proposals put forward in Labour's devolution White Paper on the creation of a Scottish Assembly envisaged that 56 of the 129 members would be elected on a proportional basis from party lists under the additional member system. But the jewel in the crown had come on 22 July when Tony Blair had invited Paddy Ashdown and senior Liberal Democrats to join a Cabinet Committee on constitutional affairs. It was, declared the *Daily Telegraph*, a 'historic step towards a Lib–Lab Pact' and the 'first formal step towards a potential alliance aimed at keeping the Tories out of power for a generation'.[1] This was a somewhat exaggerated claim, but the Blair initiative certainly gave Liberal Democrats a formal representation at the centre of government which even the Lib–Lab Pact of 1977 had not given them. Initially, the new committee would discuss constitutional reform, but its remit could move on to Northern Ireland and Europe.[2] For the Liberal Democrats, its most urgent task would be to discuss the composition of a new commission on electoral reform to make recommendations on proportional representation in readiness for a referendum on the issue within the lifetime of the existing parliament.

The first party conference since the general election took place at Eastbourne in September 1997. And, not surprisingly, relations with Labour (and especially 'Paddy's Pact') dominated the proceedings after the setting up of the Cabinet Committee. In the press, Conrad Russell led the attack on any form of coalition with Labour, under the headline

'A Lib–Lab pact would be a disaster'.[3] From the start, Ashdown needed to calm a conference which some portrayed as potentially mutinous over his policy to Labour. Certainly, as Charles Kennedy said, there was 'a current of apprehension'. Ashdown stuck to his policy of preparing the party for eventual power-sharing, declaring that he believed in the politics of solutions not the politics of tribalism.[4]

Among other developments at Eastbourne, the party president Robert Maclennan revealed that the Liberal Democrats would declare donations of over £5,000 to the party from the beginning of 1998. Despite criticisms that Ashdown was doing too little to increase the number of women Liberal Democrat MPs (and accusations that his circle of advisers was a 'woman-free' zone), attempts to give women 50 per cent of the places on every short list for parliamentary candidates failed to gain the necessary two-thirds majority. On a separate issue Ashdown faced embarrassment when the party voted for the establishment of a Royal Commission on Euthanasia.

The misgivings of those in the party who feared Ashdown's long-term agenda vis-à-vis Labour were well-founded. Only a month after the Eastbourne conference a secret meeting took place at Downing Street. At stake was the future not only of 'The Project' with New Labour but the future of the party itself. It was only two years later that details of the discussions between Ashdown, Blair and Jenkins (and particularly of the dinner at Downing Street on 21 October 1997) were eventually leaked.[5] Apparently Tony Blair had offered to replace two members of his Cabinet with the Liberal Democrat MPs Alan Beith and Menzies Campbell, thus forming a coalition even though Labour had won a landslide victory only six months earlier. Blair, who had kept his own Cabinet in the dark about his plans, eventually backed away from the deal because of fears of a Cabinet split.[6]

This offer would have been the natural fulfilment of 'The Project', the bringing together of Labour and the Liberal Democrats. It was close to the hearts of two of Blair's closest advisers – Cabinet Minister Peter Mandelson and Roger Liddle (a Downing Street policy aide and former SDP member). Their book, *The Blair Revolution* (1996) had talked of the need for a New Labour government to have the broadest possible political base. The theme had been taken up by another pro-Blairite with Philip Gould's *The Unfinished Revolution* which argued that a progressive alliance of centre-left parties would end the disunity which had seen the Conservatives in power so long. Whatever the merits or otherwise of 'The Project', the discussions on 21 October 1997 were clearly premature. The timing was not right. For the moment, at least, it was a project too far. However, the establishment of the Jenkins Commission on Electoral Reform in December 1997 was one major objective achieved by the Liberal Democrats.

In one more particular aspect, however, it did work. Blair promised Ashdown help in winning the forthcoming by-election in Winchester. The Winchester contest, on 20 November 1997, was the most unusual by-election of recent times (as well as being the first significant contest for the Liberal Democrats since the election). The Winchester seat had been won by the Liberal Democrat Mark Oaten in the general election with a majority of just two votes. The defeated Conservative candidate, Gerry Malone, a former health minister, successfully sought the annulment of the result (causing the first re-run by-election in such circumstances since 1910).[7] The outcome, a 20 per cent swing to the Liberal Democrats resulting in a 21,556 majority, was a powerful fillip for Ashdown against those critical of his links with Labour. Winchester now had the largest majority of any Liberal Democrat seat. Labour polled a minuscule 944 votes. On the same day as Winchester, polling took place in Beckenham. On a low turnout, the Liberal Democrats remained in third place with 18.4 per cent of the vote.[8]

Despite cooperation at Winchester and the establishment of the Jenkins Commission at Westminster, Liberal Democrats continued their attack on aspects of Labour policy (as Ashdown had warned that his party would at the 21 October Downing Street dinner). And, indeed, there was much to attack as Labour showed itself to be instinctively conservative on many issues and pusillanimous on a swathe of others. Thus Liberal Democrats would attack Labour from radical, civil liberties or redistributionist positions on such issues as investment in schools and the health service, cuts in single parent benefits, backsliding on environmental and civil liberty issues and so on.

The spring 1998 party conference, held at Southport, repeated many of the debates over links with New Labour (Ashdown's secret dinner at Downing Street was, of course, not known to his critics). With many safeguards, conference agreed to sanction closer links such as acceptance of Cabinet seats, if backed by three quarters of both the party's executive and parliamentary party.[9]

Given the dearth of by-elections since May 1997, and given Labour's seemingly immovable lead in the opinion polls, the local elections of 7 May 1998 provided the first real nationwide test since the general election of the political mood of the country. Given also that the seats being defended were last fought in 1994 (a year of very low Conservative fortunes), Liberals were fending off any Conservative revival. At the same time Liberal Democrats were hoping to make gains from Labour with Liverpool, Sheffield and Stockport among their hopefuls.[10] And they had cause to celebrate against Labour. As William Rees-Mogg wrote in *The Times*, the Liberal Democrats had now achieved substantial advances in the Labour strongholds of the North (as well as Liverpool, in which Liberal Democrats now had a majority, they had a strong presence in Manchester, Newcastle, Gateshead and Oldham).[11] Although the Liberal Democrats had suffered modest losses of seats to the Tories, the results in traditional Labour areas were impressive (the 27 per cent turnout in these local elections was the lowest since records began in 1947).

The following month, collaboration at national level with the Blair administration took a major step forward. On 11 June 1998, Tony Blair and Paddy Ashdown committed themselves to long-term cooperation in their attempts to dismantle and modernise the British constitution. In their joint declaration (a document mainly drafted on the Liberal Democrat side by Robert Maclennan and Lord Holme) the two leaders set out four guiding principles for reform: putting power 'closer to the people'; strengthening citizens' rights; making Government more open and accountable; and making public institutions more representative.

The development of Liberal Democrat policy advanced when, prior to the 1998 party conference, the early autumn saw the publication of *Moving Ahead*, a 113-page mid-term manifesto. Ashdown declared the proposals to be the most radical recasting of the party's agenda for a decade. Less kindly *The Times* editorial saw it as an offering of 'a few small nuggets packaged carefully in woolly thought'.[12] Among its proposals, to be debated at the forthcoming Brighton party conference, were compulsory second pensions, plans for neighbourhood trusts to run schools, measures to take low income earners out of tax and a constitution for the European Union.

The Liberal Democrats who gathered at Brighton would thus face a crowded agenda. The conference would be a pivotal one, for the time had now come to adjudicate on their relationship with Labour. And it was clear that, from such figures as Earl Russell and Des Wilson, there would be harsh criticism. More generally, conference made clear that Ashdown would face problems if he sought closer involvement with Labour before PR had been agreed for general elections (not that this was to deter Ashdown when the special Cabinet committee's agenda would be extended, in November, to cover areas such as welfare reform, education, health policy and preparation for the single European currency). The party conference, criticising those who were too timid in pushing for wealth redistribution, voted in favour of taxing child benefit for the better off, 50 per cent taxation on incomes over £100,000 and a full minimum wage at 16 rather than 21. But although Brighton was an important conference, delegates were only too aware that their debates would be overshadowed by the eagerly-awaited report of the Jenkins Commission on Electoral Reform established back in December 1997.

The Jenkins Commission report, finally published on 29 October 1998, proposed an alternative vote top-up system (known as AV Top-Up) intended to ensure fairer representation. Each elector would have two votes, one going to the constituency candidate and the other to top-up candidates. A constituency candidate winning half the vote would take the seat, but if no candidate reached 50 per cent the votes won by the least popular candidate would be redistributed until a victor emerged. The second vote would be used to give unrepresented parties in a county or city a top-up member. The House of Commons – which would be reduced from 659 members to a maximum of 560 – would consist of 80–85 per cent constituency members and 15–20 per cent top-up members.

Reaction to the Jenkins Report varied. The electoral reform lobby naturally welcomed it, but with varying degrees of warmth. Paddy Ashdown hailed the report as 'a historic step forward' which offered British voters a chance 'to break out of the prison of the first-past-the-post system'.[13] Although the Jenkins proposals were not the Liberal Democrats' preferred option, the party had little alternative but to make the best of what was being offered. Ashdown, sensitive to the tactical dilemmas facing Blair, was able to take comfort that a referendum was still on offer from the Labour leader. Presumably, a referendum delayed was better than one lost.

A further important stage in Ashdown's cooperation with Blair (as mentioned earlier) came in November with the extension of the remit of the Cabinet committee. Their intention, they said, was to end 'the destructive tribalism' of British politics. The inference drawn by many Labour and Liberal MPs – to whom the announcement came as a surprise – was that a coalition or even merger was being contemplated. The deputy Labour leader, John Prescott, was reportedly furious at Blair's failure to consult him. Tony Blair made his ambitions more explicit in a speech on 15 December. Labour was to become – like the Gladstonian Liberals – a 'broad coalition of those who believe in progress and justice'. It was all heady stuff. Certainly the November announcement had caused many commentators to suggest that the threshold of pluralist politics had been crossed. And Ashdown himself knew there would be a hostile response from within elements of his own party.

At the meeting of the party's Federal Executive Committee on 16 November 1998, Ashdown had to face some vociferous criticism. Although the Executive voted 14 to four in favour of extending the joint Labour–Liberal Democrat Cabinet committee, it was clear many in his party were unhappy. Ashdown was forced to agree to seek the permission of his MPs before agreeing to discuss an issue at the Cabinet committee. Further evidence of party unease was the humiliating two to one defeat suffered by Paddy Ashdown at the hands of his parliamentary colleagues on the issue of support for the Queen's Speech. Admitting there was a plot to depose him, he hinted at a ballot to test support for his cooperation with Labour. But on 20 January 1999 Ashdown stunned his party by announcing his intention to stand down as leader following the spring local and European Parliamentary elections.

It was a political bombshell which rocked his party.[14] In his surprise announcement, Ashdown declared that he would leave the leadership of the Liberal Democrats in the summer (after the elections in May for the Scottish Parliament and Welsh Assembly, and after the June European elections). Why had Ashdown resigned? Although he denied it, increasing strains over his policy of 'constructive opposition' to Labour were at least in part the reason for the sudden announcement of his resignation as leader.[15] Later in 1999 Ashdown was to disclose that he had resigned because of the failure of the secret deal with Blair to give him a Cabinet post.[16]

Between the March 1999 Edinburgh spring conference (at which Paddy Ashdown made his last address as party leader) and the 11 June date when he would officially step down, the party faced a series of crucial electoral tests: the elections for the Scottish Parliament and Welsh Assembly, the European elections and the annual municipal elections. In the local elections, voting was taking place in all but one of the 238 shire district councils, all 36 metropolitan districts, and 35 of the 46 English unitary authorities. All 32 councils in Scotland and all 22 in Wales were also included in 'Super Thursday'. The outcome for the Liberal Democrats was a mixed bag. In Sheffield, Liberals took their most sought after crown, ousting Labour who had held the city since 1929.[17] The party also gained Stockport and consolidated its hold in Liverpool. But the party lost control of Eastbourne, Taunton Deane, Cheltenham, North Dorset and North Wiltshire. The overall pattern was one of growing strength in hitherto safe Labour areas. This pattern of Liberal Democrat inroads into safe Labour areas could be seen in such towns as Leicester, where the party was now victorious in once rock-solid council estate wards such as Saffron, North Braunstone and Mowmacre.[18] The overall result of such

Liberal Democrat victories was that, whereas the party had a net loss of 313 seats to the Conservatives in the South, they had a net gain of 140 from Labour in the North. Their projected national share of the vote – at 27 per cent – was equal to their previous best.

At the same time, voting was taking place for the new Scottish Parliament and Welsh Assembly. In Scotland, the contest was mainly fought between the Labour Party and the pro-independence SNP. The Liberal Democrats faced a hard fight, with the Conservatives determined to stage a recovery. Under the electoral system, 73 of the total of 129 members were elected from first-past-the-post constituencies with 56 selected from party lists in eight super constituencies. The overall result is shown in Table 19.1.

Table 19.1   Scottish Parliament, May 1999

Party	Seats	% Votes (1st Vote)	% Votes (2nd Vote)
Labour	56	38.8	33.8
SNP	35	28.7	27.0
Conservative	18	15.6	15.4
Lib. Dem.	17	14.2	12.5
Others	3	2.7	11.3

The outcome left Labour with 56 seats, just short of an overall majority. With 35 seats, the SNP had done well, if not as well as they had hoped. The irony was that the Liberal Democrats (17 seats) were pipped into fourth place by the Conservatives (with 18). But because the Conservatives had ruled out any deals, the Liberal Democrats under Jim Wallace were left holding the balance of power.

The Scottish Parliament elections had returned 12 Liberal Democrats on the first-past-the-post system. These seats, which provide a good picture of Liberal Democrat strength in Scotland are listed in Table 19.2. Outside these seats, Liberal Democrats only secured second place in Greenock and Inverclyde. It was a patchy performance, with Liberal Democrats frequently in fourth place.

In Wales, elections were held for the 60 members of the new Assembly under a similar electoral system to that in Scotland, with 40 elected first-past-the-post and 20 additional members from five super constituencies. The final outcome is listed in Table 19.3.

As in Scotland, no party won an overall majority. Plaid Cymru, which recorded its best result in its 74-year history, scored spectacular success in Labour's heartlands in the South Wales valleys.[19] The Liberal

Democrats' best result was in Cardiff Central (which had returned Labour to Westminster in 1997). Apart from two victories in mid-Wales (Brecon and Radnor, and Montgomeryshire), the party could only manage one solitary second place (in the safe Labour Wrexham seat). See Table 19.4.

Table 19.2   Scottish Parliament: Liberal Democrat MPs elected (first-past-the-post) (12)

Constituency	Majority	Party in Second Place
Aberdeen South	1,760	Lab
Aberdeenshire West & Kincardine	2,289	Con
Argyll and Bute	2,057	SNP
Caithness, Sutherland and Easter Ross	4,391	Lab
Edinburgh West	4,583	Con
Fife North East	5,064	Con
Gordon	4,195	SNP
Orkney	4,619	Con
Ross, Skye and Inverness West	1,539	Lab
Roxburgh and Berwickshire	3,585	Con
Shetland	3,194	Lab
Tweeddale, Ettrick and Lauderdale	4,478	SNP

Table 19.3   The Welsh Assembly Election, May 1999

Party	Seats	% Votes (1st Vote)	% Votes (2nd Vote)
Labour	28	37.6	35.4
Plaid Cymru	17	28.4	30.5
Conservative	9	15.9	16.5
Lib. Dems.	6	13.4	12.6
Others	-	4.7	5.0

Table 19.4   Welsh Assembly Election: 'Liberal Democrat MPs elected (first-past-the-post) (3)

Constituency	Majority	Second Place
Brecon and Radnorshire	5,852	Con
Cardiff Central	3,168	Lab
Montgomeryshire	5,504	Con

The outcome of the Scottish and Welsh elections (particularly at first in Scotland) meant that coalition politics was back on the agenda. While it was to come in 2000 in Wales, it came immediately in Scotland. A coalition in Scotland had been a strong possibility since a meeting of top Liberal Democrats with Labour back in 1995.[20] Private negotiations between Jim Wallace and Donald Dewar (who became First Minister in the Scottish Parliament) apparently took place during the campaign. The major policy difference between the two parties centred around higher education funding.[21] Only certain concessions by Labour (ranging from proportional representation in Scottish local elections to a permanent freeze on tolls for the Skye Bridge) eventually salvaged a deal.[22] On 13 May, the 16 Liberal Democrat MSPs finally voted through a document drawn up by Labour and Liberal Democrat negotiators following a meeting lasting five hours.

Although the Liberal Democrats had been forced to back down on their pledge to abolish tuition fees, Jim Wallace secured the overwhelming endorsement of his MSPs (despite earlier predictions of a widespread revolt). Coalition politics was born, with Jim Wallace becoming Deputy First Minister.

No sooner were the May contests concluded than electioneering was underway for the June European elections. On 17 May, the Liberal Democrat manifesto *Ambitious for Britain* was launched. Its key manifesto pledges included:

- Completion of the European single market
- Holding a referendum at the earliest opportunity on joining the single currency
- Expansion of the EU to include countries from Central and Eastern Europe
- Pushing for an EU-wide clampdown on cross-border pollution and international crime
- Establishing a European constitution to make it more 'open, democratic and accountable'
- Replacing the common agricultural policy with a new subsidy targeted to economic, social and environmental goals.

After 'Super Thursday' in May, there was thus a further test of the electoral temperature with the fifth direct elections to the European Parliament in June. This time elections were held under a new voting system on the basis of regional lists (11 regions replaced the 84 single-member constituencies in mainland Britain, each region returning between four and 11 MEPs). Northern Ireland continued to elect its three MEPs by the single transferable vote system. On a low turnout, the result marked New Labour's worst electoral performance yet. The UK

Independence Party and the Greens both secured the election of MEPs for the first time. See Table 19.5.

Table 19.5

Party	% Vote*	Seats*
Conservative	35.8	36
Labour	28.0	29
Liberal Democrat	12.7	10
UK Independence	7.0	3
Green	6.3	2
Nationalists	4.5	4
Others	5.7	–

* Note: Excluding Northern Ireland. Source: *The Economist*, 19 June 1999.

These were bad results, particularly for New Labour, but also for the Liberal Democrats with only 12.7 per cent of the vote. There was a certain paradox. Many of the pro-European Liberal Democrats' best areas (such as the South West) were in areas of growing Euroscepticism (as with the fishing community of the Cornish ports). Partly, also, turnout at a meagre 23 per cent could be blamed. There were thus some bizarre consequences of voting reform. No longer were the Liberal Democrats the only home for protest votes. Other parties (notably the United Kingdom Independence Party) were able to secure not only votes but seats.

An analysis of the European voting showed that the Liberal Democrat vote (at 13 per cent) was down by 2 per cent on its general election performance. Although, as a pro-European party, they tended to fare badly in European elections, there were more worrying features of the result. Most alarming of all was their poor performance in their best areas, even allowing for a very low turnout.[23] In particular, their strength in the South West was seemingly weakening. See Table 19.6.

On 10 June 1999, the same day as the European elections, voting took place in a parliamentary by-election in the very safe Labour seat of Leeds Central (in 1997 the Labour majority was 20.68 per cent). In the worst turnout of modern times (less than 20 per cent), the Liberal Democrats moved into a strong second place, cutting Labour's majority to 2,293 and forcing the Conservatives into a somewhat humiliating third place.[24] It was further evidence of the Liberal Democrat challenge in Labour's Northern heartlands.

With the end of the campaign for the European elections and Ashdown's valedictory press conference, the period from 11 June (the date when the leadership became vacant) until 9 August (when the victor would be declared) was occupied by the battle for the Liberal Democrat leadership. Officially, no public campaigning was to be done before 11 June (although a great deal had been happening unofficially).

Table 19.6 European Parliament Elections, 10 June 1999
Regions with Highest Liberal Democrat Support (% Vote)

South West	16.45
South East	15.31
Yorkshire and the Humber	14.40
North East	13.50
East Midlands	12.77
Eastern	11.95
North West	11.74
London	11.66
West Midlands	11.28
Scotland	9.81
Wales	8.19

Source: *The Economist*, 19 June 1999.

The leadership contest itself had attracted a wide field of candidates. From the start, Simon Hughes (the MP for Southwark and Bermondsey) had seemed the strongest (and perhaps most serious) challenger. Since his by-election victory in Bermondsey in 1983 (when he defeated Peter Tatchell) he had become very much the left-wing conscience of the party and strongly supported environmental causes and animal rights issues. He was, declared the *Observer*, pro-gay, pro-cuddly animal and generally pro-kindness (adding, less charitably, that pigs might fly and Simon Hughes might say something interesting). Many saw Charles Kennedy as the main rival to Hughes.

There were many other contenders. Among early runners were Nick Harvey (MP for North Devon since 1992 and also an arch Eurosceptic), Jacquie Ballard (a tough grassroots campaigner, MP for Taunton since 1997 and the only woman candidate), Malcolm Bruce (MP for Gordon and the party's Treasury spokesman) and also David Rendel and Don Foster. An early withdrawal from the race (which probably helped the Kennedy camp) was that of Menzies Campbell on 27 May. Despite this withdrawal, there were still more contenders than the party had MPs back in the 1950s. The seven hopefuls were rapidly, if unkindly, christened the seven dwarves by a sceptical press.

The candidates divided broadly into those who were against Ashdown's efforts to take the Liberal Democrats closer to Labour (Ballard, Hughes and

Rendel) and those broadly (in varying degrees) supportive of Ashdown's actions (Kennedy himself, Foster and Campbell). From the start, Kennedy's campaign was efficient and professional, headed by Matthew Taylor (the MP for Truro). This was a good tactical move. Kennedy's Scottish support needed the backing of someone with key influence in south-west England. Kennedy's campaign also received the support of Don Foster who soon stood down to back him. Kennedy's policy statements during his leadership campaign emphasised the importance he would give to three themes: social justice, the environment and Europe. Kennedy was particularly emphatic on social justice, declaring:

> I want to see the Liberal Democrats arguing the case of the poor, the powerless and the dispossessed. Labour is no longer driven by a passion to fight poverty and inequality in Britain. I am, and so is our party.[25]

If little of what Kennedy offered was new, it was well-presented. *The Times* spoke of his 'smart suit, packaged policies and luminous leaflets'.[26] Certainly, Kennedy soon had an almost unassailable line-up of supporters. There was not only Shirley Williams, Menzies Campbell and Don Foster, but also the Chief Whip, Paul Tyler, the Campaigns' Chairman, Nick Harvey and the former Chief Whip (and now Social Security spokesperson) Archie Kirkwood.

With a clear majority of his parliamentary colleagues behind him, the election took on the air of a coronation. In the event, Kennedy had to fight hard for the orb and sceptre. But the campaign overall attracted little media attention. Even to some Liberal Democrats the debate seemed more about personal ambition than political reality. Certainly, most candidates seemed to be more concerned with the delicacies of how to live with Labour than any great statements of policy. Attitudes towards Labour shaped the contest from the start. Was a particular candidate left of centre, centre-left, moderate or radical? It was hard to be sure (and probably, for many, it mattered little). On 9 August 1999, on a turnout of 61.6 per cent with 51,006 votes cast out of an 82,827-strong electorate, Charles Kennedy was declared, on the fourth and final ballot, to be the winner of the Liberal Democrat leadership election, becoming only the second elected leader in the party's history. Aged 39, and first elected SDP MP for Ross, Skye and Inverness West in 1983, he had served as President of the Party from 1990 to 1994. He represented a new generation of Liberal leadership. Elected only on the fourth round of counting with 56.6 per cent of the vote, and often seen as the likely winner of a leadership election, his margin of victory was nonetheless neither massive nor utterly convincing. His final tally (28,425 votes to 21,833 for Hughes) was achieved after the elimination of Rendel, Ballard and Bruce and the subsequent distribution of their votes. The votes cast in detail (by round) are listed in Table 19.7.

Table 19.7

	1st	2nd	3rd	4th
Kennedy	22,724	+895 = 23,619	+1,545 = 25,164	+3,261 = 28,425
Hughes	16,233	+1,145 = 17,378	+1,982 = 19,360	+2,473 = 21,833
Bruce	4,643	+598 = 5,241	+827 = 6,068	– –
Ballard	3,978	+627 = 4,605	– –	– –
Rendel	3,428	– –	– –	– –

The election of Charles Kennedy focused much attention on the man himself. Born at Fort William in the Scottish Highlands, the son of a crofter, Kennedy as we have seen, had entered parliament as an SDP MP in the 1983 general election (at 23, the youngest person elected to Westminster in the twentieth century). It was an unexpected victory at Ross, Cromarty and Skye (where he had come from fourth place to topple the Conservatives). From the start Kennedy's image at Westminster was as a popular and jovial lightweight who was too keen on the good life and who shone on TV quiz shows, but did not take politics too seriously.[27] He was dubbed 'Inaction Man' for his perceived laziness. All this was a major misjudgement of a man with political grit and a firm grasp of detail.[28]

Now, however, that Kennedy was leader, a new era in his political career had begun. No longer was he a man with a great future behind him. He had now to deliver the goods. In his victory speech, apart from pledging to continue political cooperation with Labour, Kennedy vowed to forge a 'strong, independent, progressive' party. But how easy would this be? The achievements of the Ashdown years, in terms of MPs at Westminster and strength in the council chambers of the land, would not easily be surpassed. Rather, the Liberal Democrats might find themselves on the defensive from any revival in Conservative fortunes (especially in the southern half of England). All this, however, was for the future. Kennedy's immediate priority was the forthcoming party conference (held at Harrogate from 19 to 23 September). It did not prove to be the easiest of conferences. It was supportive of the new leader rather than ecstatic. The press made much of a remark by Simon Hughes that the new leader had initiated few policy ideas. Polly Toynbee, in the *Guardian*, remarked none too helpfully that the Liberal Democrats had a future – by meeting their destiny and merging with Labour.[29] Observers noted that party activists were still willing to defy the leadership on radical issues, such as wealth redistribution and the paying of benefits to students. It was against this background that Kennedy proposed that members of the party's federal executive and federal policy committee should be elected by all 90,000 party members, not just by the conference delegates – a move likely to weaken the radical element.

In his keynote speech, Kennedy affirmed continued political cooperation with Labour and argued powerfully for social justice and environmental issues, strongly supported a more powerful EU and rejected the demands of more radical delegates to move to the left of Labour with radical redistributionalist policies. But, although Kennedy had quickly dismissed the idea of a big spending party outflanking Labour from the left, it was less clear how much real content there was in Kennedy's speech. Certainly, the *Guardian* was dismissive, calling it 'a thin bowl of porridge' and declaring 'Mr Kennedy still has too little to say' and continued 'waspish carping at political rivals filled the place left absent by any attempt at an inspirational political vision'.[30] The difficulties facing the party were highlighted when, on the same day as Kennedy's first speech to the party conference as leader, polling took place in by-elections in Wigan and Hamilton South. Both produced appalling results. In Hamilton South the party came in sixth with a paltry 634 votes (3.3 per cent). In Wigan, an old industrial constituency where the Liberal Democrats could have expected to oust the Conservatives from second place, the party came a poor third with 13.3 per cent. It was an inauspicious start.

After the party conference attention focused on the team Kennedy would assemble to lead the Liberal Democrats into the next election. Two of the three key portfolios settled themselves. Menzies Campbell remained with Foreign Affairs, Simon Hughes at Home Affairs and for economic affairs, Matthew Taylor was given the portfolio. The chief Liberal Democrat spokespersons in Kennedy's team (excluding Kennedy himself and Alan Beith, the Deputy Leader) are listed in Table 19.8. To advise on policy, Kennedy was relying on Richard Grayson, a 30-year old former Oxford don, and currently the Director of the Centre for Reform, as the brains behind his ideas and speeches.

The problems facing the Liberal Democrats, and in particular the new problems of coalition politics were emphasised in December 1999 with the row in Scotland over student fees which threatened to break up the Lib Dem–Labour coalition. The row was eventually defused (neither party would benefit from the collapse of the coalition). The start of the new year at Westminster saw the Liberal Democrat–Labour partnership kept alive in a variety of ways. Despite reports that Labour would ditch a commitment to a referendum on proportional representation, a key meeting with Kennedy's advisers was held in the Cotswolds in January. *The Times* reported that Kennedy was willing to strike a deal over voting reform. If Labour proposed an alternative vote (AV) system for Westminster elections, Kennedy would begin a party-wide consultation on the issue. Although the AV system would be divisive, some believed it to be the best available compromise.[31] At the same time, it seemed the policy of constructive opposition to Labour would take on a more aggressive stance to distance Liberal Democrats from the 'nanny-state tendencies' of the government.[32]

Table 19.8

Agriculture, Rural Affairs and Fisheries	Colin Breed
Constitution, Culture and Sport	Robert Maclennan
Economy	Matthew Taylor
Education and Employment	Phil Willis
Environment, Transport, the Regions and Social Justice	Don Foster
Foreign Affairs and Defence	Menzies Campbell
Health	Nick Harvey
Home Affairs	Simon Hughes
Scotland	Jim Wallace
Social Security	Steve Webb
Trade and Industry	Vincent Cable
Wales	Richard Livsey
(Chief Whip and Shadow Leader of the House	Paul Tyler)

On 4 February, the Liberal Democrat partnership with Labour at Westminster was revitalised with the publication of a joint document setting out a common negotiating position for the next stage of European integration – the first time that the two parties had produced a joint declaration before important EU negotiations. Meanwhile the Plymouth spring party conference signified a change of direction from the Ashdown era with Kennedy raising the profile of environmental issues in the party's priorities. But, aside from relations with Labour and policy developments, the most urgent need as the new year progressed was for a by-election victory to galvanise the party. The opportunity eventually came with the death of the Conservative MP for the Hampshire constituency of Romsey.

Romsey, with an 8,585 Conservative majority, was among the top 50 safest Tory seats in the country. Armed with 46 per cent of the vote in the 1997 election (to the 29 per cent of the Lib Dems) the Conservatives might feel secure. But commentators warned of the 'M3 factor' – the string of recent Liberal by-election triumphs in this geographical corridor of middle England (Newbury, Christchurch, Eastleigh and, most recently, Winchester). Romsey, the first important by-election test of Kennedy's leadership, adjoined both Winchester and Eastleigh. Sandra Gidley, the Liberal Democrat candidate, a pharmacy manager for Tesco, campaigned hard on health, education and her local credentials (the Conservatives had chosen an Eton-educated farmer from outside the constituency). The outcome, on 4 May 2000, was a resounding victory for Sandra Gidley with a 3,311 majority on a swing of 12.5 per cent from the Conservatives. On a relatively low turnout of 55.4 per cent, the Labour vote had been squeezed to a derisory 3.8 per cent (down from 18.6 per cent). In terms of votes, Labour had collapsed from 10,000 to 1,500.

The Liberal Democrats had clearly benefited from tactical voting, a local candidate and a massed assault on the seat. For only the second time since 1945 had the Conservatives while in opposition lost a seat to the Liberals (the previous occasion being the victory of a youthful David Steel in Roxburgh, Selkirk and Peebles back in 1965). The number of Liberal Democrat MPs had now risen to 47 – a record since the days of Lloyd George. The result provided Charles Kennedy with a welcome leadership boost after growing murmurs within the party about his relatively low-key style. The local elections, held the same day as Romsey, provided a more complex picture. The general trend was Liberal Democrat losses to the Conservatives in the south (quite spectacular losses in Torbay and Eastbourne) counter-balanced by gains from Labour, mainly in the north of England. Here Liberal Democrats took control of Oldham. In London, Susan Kramer (the Lib Dem mayoral candidate) came fourth. No directly-elected seats were secured by the party in the new GLA assembly (although they gained four members under the top-up system). Overall, in the May 2000 local elections, Conservatives took 1,345 seats (a net gain of 593), Labour took 1,114 (a net loss of 568) and Liberals 718 (an almost insignificant net loss of 21 considering they were defending the gains of 1996). In terms of a projected national vote, the local elections were one of the best years for the party. Certainly, as a result of Liberal Democrat inroads into Labour territory, the composition of many Northern councils showed marked advances by the party (see Table 19.9).

The relative success of the Liberal Democrats against Labour in deprived urban areas was also reflected in the parliamentary by-election of 22 June 2000 in Tottenham. On a 12 per cent swing from Labour, the Liberal Democrats took second place (albeit on a very low turnout). Given that, in an earlier local council by-election, Liberal Democrats had taken control of Islington council for the first time in December 1999, it seemed even Labour strongholds in London could be attacked.

Table 19.9 Liberal Democrat Metropolitan Council Strength: Northern England, May 2000

	Lab	*Lib Dem*	*Con*	*Other*
Liverpool	21	69	–	9
Newcastle	62	16	–	–
Oldham	25	31	2	2
Sheffield	37	49	1	–
Gateshead	47	18	–	1
Leeds	61	19	16	3
Manchester	78	21	–	–
St. Helens	35	15	4	–

Despite these electoral successes, a year after Kennedy's election as leader there were still nagging criticisms of his impact. Writing in the *Independent*, Alan Leaman noted that Kennedy was not appearing enough in the media and was failing to make news.[33] More fundamentally, doubts were again raised about his political depth, his need to establish a clear identity and positive purpose. And the party remained unable to break out in the opinion polls or council by-elections.[34] A leaked memo purporting to carry details of the party's election manifesto did not help.

It was against a background of a nation nearly paralysed by mass protests concerning rising fuel prices that the Liberal Democrats met for their Bournemouth conference in September 2000. With Labour's popularity plummeting in the opinion polls, and with the Liberal Democrats gaining from an upsurge, spirits were high. This was particularly so among more radical members. The conference (the last autumn gathering before the general election) passed motions supporting a new 50 per cent top rate of tax, a change in the law to give legal recognition to homosexual relationships and a call for the Queen to be removed as Supreme Governor (Head) of the Church of England. Conference also called for reform of the 1701 Act of Settlement to allow the heir to the throne to marry a Catholic. The party leadership was able to defeat a radical motion on pensions. Meanwhile, the party's pre-election manifesto, *Freedom in a Liberal Society* was overwhelmingly endorsed. If Kennedy's closing speech was hardly impressive ('vacuous' declared *The Times* on 20 September), the Liberal Democrat leader had not had too bad a conference. This was more than could be said for its by-election record. Nothing but poor results followed from the clutch of by-elections on 23 November 2000. At Preston, where the Liberal Democrat Bill Chadwick had twice before fought the seat and was well known as council leader, the party polled 16.2 per cent. This was hardly an upsurge in a Northern industrial seat. At West Bromwich West and Glasgow Anniesland, held the same day, the party finished a poor third and an even worse fourth (with 8.1 per cent of the vote at Anniesland). Worse still was the final by-election result of the parliament, at Falkirk West on 21 December, when the Liberals finished fifth with a meagre 3.2 per cent of the vote.

As 2001 opened, the political landscape failed to look any more promising. Publicity was hard to come by (the party's spring conference passed almost unnoticed). Such publicity as there was was not always welcome, as Kennedy had to dismiss any notions of a leadership challenge.[35] The press also continued to speculate in March on possible deals with Labour.[36] The abrupt resignation of Peter Mandelson had not helped the party's cause either. Meanwhile the outbreak of a severe foot and mouth epidemic caused the postponement of the general election (and also the council elections) from 3 May to 7 June.

The advent of the election found the party facing potentially serious problems. Historically, Liberals had not fared well against an incumbent Labour administration (this could be seen with Jo Grimond in 1966, Jeremy Thorpe in 1970 and David Steel in 1979). Kennedy, the first Liberal Democrat to lead his party against a sitting Labour government, thus faced problems. And it was a novel problem. As Alan Leaman had written in the *Independent*, Kennedy was an opposition leader essentially campaigning for the re-election of the government.[37]

The Liberal Democrat manifesto, *Freedom, Justice, Honesty* was launched on 15 May. The party confirmed its pledge to raise £3 billion a year by putting a penny on the basic rate of income tax and to introduce a new top tax rate of 50p in the pound on incomes over £100,000. Major investment pledges for health, education and public services were also confirmed. In higher education, the manifesto promised to end tuition fees throughout the United Kingdom. On the constitution, the party repeated its commitment to proportional representation, promised to lower the voting age to 16, replace the House of Lords with a directly elected Senate and support disestablishment of the Church of England. On Europe, support for the euro was repeated. Other pledges included changes to the asylum laws and the creation of a Department of Rural Affairs. Although many of these policies were not new, the manifesto as a whole offered a wide-ranging package of progressive reforms.

The party, fielding 639 candidates in mainland Britain, fought an energetic and well-organised campaign.[38] Although fighting on a nationwide front, the party's fortunes largely rested on the 47 seats it was defending and the 20 Conservative seats vulnerable in the event of a Tory 'meltdown' or renewed tactical voting (the party manifesto had been shrewdly pitched not to frighten Conservatives too much and to encourage Labour tactical voting).

Not surprisingly, there was much discussion in the press of this subject of tactical voting during the campaign. Back in September 2000 there had been talk of a secret Blair–Kennedy pact to oust Tories. Seats such as Wells, Yorkshire East, Teignbridge and so on were mentioned. Early in the campaign, Liberal-held Lewes was mentioned in the local *Sussex Express* as one such case, while in Conservative-held Dorset West a tactical voting website was set up by rock singer Billy Bragg.

There was little doubt that the Liberal Democrats (and Charles Kennedy in particular) ran a good campaign. Kennedy had added to his stature in a way no other party leader had managed, to emerge '*victor ludorum*' of the hustings, declared Anthony Howard in *The Times*.[39] Liberal Democrat confidence grew during the campaign as opinion poll ratings increased to the 16–18 per cent band achieved in the 1997 campaign and hopes grew that the disarray in the Conservative ranks would add to the Liberal Democrat tally of seats. The defection of John Lee, a former Conservative junior minister, also helped morale, while the creation of five new Liberal Democrat peers in the dissolution honours brought the party strength in the Lords to 66.[40]

With a highly organised and energetic campaign, nothing dented Labour's commanding lead in the opinion polls – it remained the firmest favourite at the bookmakers since election betting first began. And so it proved, for the outcome of the 2001 election was in many ways a repeat performance of 1997. There was a Labour landslide, a Conservative debacle and a result to delight the Liberal Democrats (see Table 19.10).

In terms of seats won, the results were very similar to 1997. The Labour total fell slightly, the Conservatives made a net gain of just one seat, while the Liberal Democrats gained eight and lost two. One of the most marked features of the election was the fall in turnout to 59.3 per cent.

The Liberal Democrats had much to celebrate. Leading the party in his first election as leader, Charles Kennedy saw the tally of Liberal Democrat seats rise to 52 (the best result since the 1929 election when Lloyd George was leader). Although the party lost two seats (Taunton and the Isle of Wight) it made some sensational gains from the Conservatives. These gains included not only Teignbridge (a key Liberal Democrat target seat) but also quite remarkable gains in Ludlow, North Norfolk and Guildford. Its only gain from Labour was in Chesterfield. The full list of gains is shown in Table 19.11.

Table 19.10

	Seats	Gains	Losses	Total Vote	% of Vote
Labour	413	2	8	10,740,168	40.7
Conservative	166	9	8	8,354,460	31.7
Liberal Democrat	52	8	2	4,815,249	18.3
SNP	5	0	1	464,314	1.8
Plaid Cymru	4	1	1	195,892	0.7
Others	19	7	7	1,795,109	6.8

Table 19.11   Lib Dem Gains in the 2001 General Election*

Constituency	Majority	% Majority	Second Place
Cheadle	33	0.1	Con
Chesterfield	2,586	5.8	Lab
Dorset Mid and Poole North	384	0.9	Con
Guildford	538	1.1	Con
Ludlow	1,630	3.8	Con
Norfolk North	483	0.9	Con
Teignbridge	3,011	5.1	Con

* Note: This table excludes Romsey, a Conservative seat in 1997 but won in the by-election of May 2000.

Meanwhile, Liberal Democrats could also celebrate that many of the seats won by a narrow margin in 1997 were now held with very large majorities. In the four seats of Winchester, Torbay, Kingston and Surbiton, and Somerton and Frome, the combined Liberal Democrat majority in 1997 was 954. In June this was transformed to 35,744. The result in Kingston and Surbiton was little short of a landslide.[41] This consolidation could be seen across the country – from Lewes in Sussex to Harrogate in Yorkshire – even if it came on the back of a very low turnout.[42] There were other causes to celebrate. For the first time since before 1945, the party had won seats in Norfolk, Shropshire and Derbyshire.[43] And, again for the first time since before 1945, the party had returned an MP for every region of England, as well as in Scotland and Wales. Perhaps the most remarkable individual constituency result of all was Guildford, where the Conservative (an Old Etonian merchant banker from outside the constituency) was the first to lose the seat since 1906. Few had expected true-blue Guildford, the heart of the Surrey stockbroker belt, to desert the Conservatives.

Liberals could congratulate themselves that in all seven constituencies where sitting Liberal Democrat MPs had retired, the seats had all been held. And in the south-west of England, following the capture of Teignbridge, half the seats in Devon and Cornwall now returned Liberal Democrats. Equally important was the fact that the Liberal Democrat *share* of the total vote had increased – up 2 per cent to almost 19 per cent. At last, the Liberal Democrats had reversed the slide of the previous four general elections. Liberal Democrats tended to improve their share of the vote in 2001 in areas (such as London and the East Midlands) where they had previously been weakest. In Scotland they could take comfort that their share of the vote (16.1 per cent, up 3.8 per cent) had now overtaken the Conservatives (15.5 per cent, down 2 per cent). But there were also some less satisfactory aspects of the 2001 general election. There was some weakening of support in Liberal Democrat seats such as Hereford and Newbury which did not augur well for the future. There was also a further slide in old areas of strength, such as by-election seats won (for example Ribble Valley, Christchurch and Eastbourne). These no longer seemed recoverable. Perhaps more worrying was the number of Liberal Democrat hopefuls in 2001 that had not been taken. Of the 15 best hopes of victory from the Conservatives, only three were won.[44]

Nor had Liberal Democrats made much progress against Labour. Apart from victory in Chesterfield, the party failed to take Birmingham Yardley or Bristol West. There were strong swings to Liberal Democrats from Labour in some inner city areas and old working-class strongholds, but these seats still remained Labour, often with huge majorities.[45] The Liberal Democrats could also be worried by the results from the local elections, held the same day. The party suffered a net loss of 99 seats together with the loss of its two county councils (Devon and Somerset).

20
An Effective Opposition: 2001–2005

The general election of June 2001, the first of the new century and the first in which Charles Kennedy had led his party into battle, had left the party with 52 seats. If, for Labour and the Conservatives at a national level, the 2001 election had to some extent been a repeat of the 1997 contest, for the Liberal Democrats it had been an outstanding success. Not least, it had been a personal triumph for Charles Kennedy.

In the wake of the election, Liberal Democrats could take stock of their position. Looking to the future, they could take considerable comfort that they now had more apparently 'safe' seats than at any time since 1929. No less than 15 seats had majorities of 20 per cent or over. Of these, five had majorities of over 25 per cent. Also the party had narrowly missed winning a swathe of Conservative-held seats, 15 in all, now vulnerable in the event of a 5 per cent swing to the Liberal Democrats.

At the same time, it had to be conscious that many of its own seats were vulnerable, particularly to a revival of Conservative fortunes. There were 19 Liberal Democrat seats vulnerable to a 5 per cent swing to the Conservatives.

Despite these possible future problems, there could be little doubt that, in the wake of the June 2001 election, the Liberal Democrats were at an exciting moment in their history. Never in recent times had their prospects looked nationally so promising. They had 52 MPs at Westminster, a strong voice in the reformed House of Lords (where they held the balance of power) and a share in government in both Wales and Scotland. They also had a strong presence in local government and a growing voice in the European Parliament.

The election also gave Kennedy a new-found authority and a mandate of his own to refashion the party. Kennedy was quick to reshape the Liberal Shadow Cabinet in the aftermath of the election. Five younger

MPs were promoted to frontline roles: Evan Harris was given a major role as Health spokesman and Mark Oaten and Ed Davey were also promoted.

The composition of the party Kennedy led was also changing. In the parliamentary party at Westminster there were 14 new MPs, seven of whom had gained seats.[1] This tally included three new women MPs, including Patsy Catton at Cheadle and Sue Doughty who had won Guildford.

At the grassroots the party was also changing. The party activists of the new century were a quite different breed from a generation ago. From the caricature image of sandal-wearing, bearded eccentrics obsessed by the minutiae of electoral reform, a survey reported in the *Guardian* had found a very different 'typical' Liberal Democrat – white, male, middle-class, highly educated and relatively elderly.[2] Over half (55 per cent) were men and nearly half (42 per cent) had a degree.

After the 2001 election, the real problem for the Liberal Democrats was that, with Labour safely re-elected for a second term, the party might simply disappear from the news, awaiting the luck of a by-election in a favourable seat. External events in September 2001 were to change all this.

Within a few months of the 2001 election, political circumstances changed forever, not just in Britain but across the globe. The terrorist attack on America on 11 September 2001 was not only to lead to the global 'war on terror' and the attacks on Afghanistan and Iraq, it was to lead in terms of internal British politics, to a new direction for the Liberal Democrats as a focal point for criticism of the Blair Government's overtly close pro-Bush, pro-American stance and its decision to invade Iraq.

This was in the future. Coincidentally, 11 September was the date fixed to announce the suspension of the Joint Cabinet Committee, first formed back in 1997 under Ashdown. Its passing was not much lamented and the suspension of collaboration with Labour freed Kennedy for his path of effective opposition.

The 2001 Liberal Democrat autumn conference met in the shadow of the 9/11 attacks. In debating the terrorist attacks, although Kennedy spoke of being a 'candid friend' of Bush, he rejected warlike rhetoric and urged caution on issues such as counter-terrorism measures and ID cards. With the Conservatives having elected Iain Duncan Smith, a right-winger, as leader, Liberal Democrats were in optimistic mood. Lord Rennard spoke of doubling the party's representation and overtaking the Conservatives.[3] However there were sharp divisions over such issues as private finance in health care and a policy commission, under the economist and MEP Chris Huhne, was established to report on the issue. Equally fierce was the conference debate on ways of increasing the tally of Liberal Democrat women MPs (only five out of 52).

An unexpected recruit to the parliamentary party came with the defection of the dissident Labour Shrewsbury MP Paul Marsden – a left-winger who had fallen out with his party over Afghanistan and anti-terror legislation. His defection eventually did the Liberal Democrats little good.[4] Ironically, the Liberal Democrats had supported the military campaign to oust the Taliban in Afghanistan.

As 2002 began, there was repeated discussion of the need for a new Liberal Democrat strategy for the Parliament. How best should the party cash in on Tory disillusion? How should the party position itself on relations with Labour, or policy issues such as tax? In December 2001, following Iain Duncan Smith's election as Tory leader, a group to woo disenchanted Conservatives was established by Baroness Nicholson, along with Hugh Dykes and Bill Newton Gunn, all former Conservative candidates. But to move the party forward, the party needed the tonic of a by-election success.

Liberal Democrat hopes of gaining momentum on the back of their 2001 victories with further by-election successes during Blair's second term were not helped by the low number of contests. Only 17 had taken place between 1997 and 2001, now only six were to fall vacant between 2001 and 2005 (the lowest number ever recorded for a four-year parliament).

The first by-election, held on 22 November 2001 in Labour-held Ipswich, saw the Liberal Democrats come close to forcing the Conservatives into third place (even though the Liberal Democrat effort had been somewhat muted).[5] The second by-election, on 14 February 2002 in the very safe seat of Ogmore in South Wales, saw Labour comfortably hold the seat, with Plaid Cymru a poor second, the Liberals third and the Conservatives fourth (squeezing in ahead of a Socialist Labour candidate). In the absence of significant by-election contests, the local elections of 2 May 2002 provided the first nationwide test of the political barometer since the June 2001 general election. The Liberal Democrats achieved a remarkably good percentage of the national vote (27 per cent) and a small net gain of councillors (36), compared to 325 Labour losses and 218 Conservative gains. But there were swings and roundabouts for the Liberal Democrats. They gained Eastbourne, but lost Harrogate. They won Kingston but lost neighbouring Richmond. In the large cities, they gained Norwich but lost Sheffield. There was a noticeable Liberal Democrat advance in some inner city areas of London, such as Southwark, Lambeth, Islington and Haringey, as well as in Hull.

The issue of Kennedy's drinking habits came to a sudden limelight during an interview with Jeremy Paxman on *Newsnight* when the presenter repeatedly asked the Liberal Democrat leader about his alcohol intake, including a claim that he drank whisky by the bottle. Paxman later apologised and many viewers were clearly unhappy by the personal nature of this questioning.[6]

Before the autumn 2002 party conference, with the Conservatives under Iain Duncan Smith down to 28 per cent in the polls and clearly floundering, several of Kennedy's younger MPs urged him to seize the opportunity presented by this Conservative weakness. Some criticised him for not showing greater urgency or ambition. Kennedy responded with an important speech at party conference declaring that his party, for so long the third party in British politics, could now overtake the Conservatives. Kennedy also used an emergency statement to the Brighton conference to warn of the 'extreme uncertainties and undoubted dangers' of military action against the Iraqi dictator Saddam Hussein. It was a clear indication of his scepticism of US claims over Iraq.

Kennedy also intervened in an internal row over party rules to ensure more women would be elected among its MEPs in 2004 by favouring a woman among the top two candidates in the list system of proportional representation used in the European elections.

A key item of business at the Brighton conference was the party's new document on public services – *Quality, Innovation and Choice*. It was exactly the sort of policy which divided Liberals into two factions. One was the modernisers, represented by Mark Oaten and the Liberal Future organisation, with their emphasis on diversity of provision. The other was the group led by Evan Harris, and the Beveridge Group, who supported even larger spending on roughly similar services.[7]

Other items being debated included a call to reject ID cards and proposals to relax the law to allow persons aged over 16 to buy pornographic material and to relax the licensing costs for sex shops (a decision on this was postponed). Conference also heard from Jim Wallace, the Scottish Deputy First Minister, that proportional representation would be introduced into local elections in Scotland from 2007. The Brighton conference also saw a toughening of party policy towards violent offenders and strongly urged the Government to start campaigning for the euro.

Overall, the party conference had gone well. 'A very worthwhile week for Kennedy and his comrades', declared *The Times*.[8] The sentiment was echoed by *The Economist*. With the party conference behind them, Liberal Democrats at Westminster could be well content at the party's continued good poll ratings (around 20–22 per cent during November, higher and steadier than at such an early stage in any previous parliament).

The Liberal Democrats thus began 2003 in optimistic mood. Kennedy's upbeat New Year message was echoed in the opinion polls, which showed a collapse in confidence for Iain Duncan Smith, the Conservative leader, and which revealed Liberal Democrat support now rising to its highest level (25 per cent) for almost a decade (with growing support among the under 40s), Kennedy's own personal ratings were climbing. These poll findings had been reflected in municipal by-elections (from May to December 2002, of 163 contests, the Conservatives had a net loss of six – their worst performance since 1995).

Meanwhile, domestic politics was increasingly overshadowed by Iraq. The decision of Charles Kennedy to join the mass anti-war march in London on 15 February 2004 exhilarated the radical wing of the party.[9] It was a defining moment, setting the tone for the rest of the parliament. Kennedy was the only major national party leader to oppose an imminent war on Iraq. More and more of Kennedy's time came to be devoted to Iraq as the prospect of war grew closer. His closest confidant was foreign affairs spokesman Menzies Campbell (who was receiving treatment for cancer at this time).

Opposition to the war, however, brought its problems. As Kennedy insisted there were circumstances in which his party might not support British troops being sent into battle, he was met with Labour and Tory jeers in the Commons. Meanwhile on 25 February all 53 Liberal Democrat MPs signed an amendment calling for the UN inspectors in Iraq to be given more time and refusing to support military action unless sanctioned by a UN resolution and a vote in the House of Commons.

A first casualty of the Liberal Democrat position was their popularity in the polls once war began.[10] From 26 per cent in late February support was down to 20 per cent just four weeks later. Kennedy's own personal rating also fell. Among senior Liberal Democrats critical of Kennedy over Iraq was Paddy Ashdown who attacked him as 'a position taker, not a position maker'.[11] Other developments, meanwhile, were taking place within the party. On 12 February, in the contest for Deputy Leader following the retirement of Alan Beith, Sir Menzies Campbell was elected over his main challenger, Malcolm Bruce.

By the start of the 2003 spring conference the Liberal Democrats could be happy with several favourable factors, if mourning the death of Roy Jenkins. The 2003 spring conference at Torquay saw a toughening of Kennedy's position on the euro as the party debated the paper *The Future of Europe* as well as debating measures to encourage more women to stand for parliament and to devolve more Whitehall power to local level. Kennedy's tempering of enthusiasm for the euro was seen by some as another strategic shift on policy. Meanwhile, as the situation in Iraq deteriorated with a bloody counterinsurgency campaign and no evidence of any banned weapons programmes (and seemingly little prospect of finding any) public opinion began increasingly to favour the Liberal Democrats' position on the war.

In the local elections of May 2003, Liberal Democrats saw some gains in inner city areas with ethnic minority communities (particularly Muslims) where the party had campaigned vociferously against the war and on tuition fees and a pledge to cut council tax. The Liberal Democrats gained 12 councils (including Bournemouth, Chesterfield and Durham City) for the loss of seven. Their net gains of seats totalled 174 (compared to 757 Labour losses and 526 Conservative gains). Most impressive of all for the Liberal Democrats was their share of the vote – at around 30 per cent, their best ever tally. Among individual councils to fall to the Liberal Democrats were Torbay, Shepway (in Michael Howard's own territory of Folkestone), Windsor and Maidenhead (the constituency of Conservative Party Chairman Theresa May), and Waverley (the Surrey base of Virginia Bottomley). Away from the headlines a trend was discernible: Liberal Democrats did best where, at council level, they were seen as a party of opposition (particularly against Labour in such cities as Birmingham and Bristol). Where they had come to be seen as part of the local establishment (as in Sheffield and Hull) they slipped back (just as they had in parts of London in 2002). They also slipped back in wealthy rural areas after their recent gains. Equally, one of the most striking features of local council composition was the almost complete disappearance of the Conservatives as a major force (or indeed any force at all) in the big cities. There were no councillors elected as Conservatives in Newcastle, Manchester or Liverpool and only one in Sheffield.

If the Liberal Democrats had polled very impressively in the local elections, in the second elections for the Scottish Parliament and Welsh Assembly their performance was distinctly patchy. The Liberals were basically asking the electorate in Scotland to give them a mandate for a further period of coalition with Labour, but emphasising that their position as coalition partners had enabled them to restrain Labour's centralising tendencies, bring about the abolition of upfront student tuition fees and deliver free care of the elderly. The outcome, as predicted, produced another Labour–Lib Dem coalition.[12] The 13 seats won on the first-past-the-post system by the Lib Dems are set out in Table 20.1.

Table 20.1   Liberal Democrat seats in the Scottish Parliament: 2003

		% Share	% Share 1999
11	Argyll and Bute	35.13	34.89
10	Caithness, Sutherland and Easter Ross	36.65	41.07
5	Orkney	45.71	67.39
7	Ross, Skye and Inverness West	43.13	32.90
1	Shetland	46.14	54.47
12	Edinburgh South	32.07	–
6	Edinburgh West	43.34	36.46
2	Fife North East	46.03	37.00
4	Aberdeen South	45.88	32.57
3	Aberdeenshire West and Kincardine	46.00	35.92
9	Gordon	38.07	–
8	Roxburgh and Berwickshire	41.22	40.61
13	Tweeddale, Ettrick and Lauderdale	26.96	–

These constituency seats won disguised the fact that in many areas of Scotland, such as Glasgow and parts of the industrial belt, the Liberal Democrats had become squeezed into fourth or even fifth place, behind Labour, the SNP and various Socialist candidates.

During the campaign both the Liberal Democrats and Labour had ruled out saying who their coalition partners might be. Both parties had avoided attacking each other and had focused on what they had achieved. Although the outcome produced a renewal of the partnership, there were differences. This time round the coalition negotiations involved wide consultation and resulted in a 14,000-word document. Both parties were aware that, with turnout down and support for both coalition partners down on 1999, the threat from the SNP remained ever-present. In fact both coalition partners, now Nicol Stephen and Jack McConnell, enjoyed a good working relationship (even if not as close as that between Donald Dewar and Jim Wallace).

Meanwhile in Wales the Liberal Democrats, in coalition with Labour since October 2000, had campaigned with commitments to cutting class sizes and extending free care for the elderly. Their first task was to hold on to the six seats they had won in May 1999 (when they were the smallest party). The outcome gave the Liberal Democrats six seats, Labour 30 and the Conservatives 11. This time there was no need to form a coalition.

By the summer of 2003, the leadership of Charles Kennedy was once again causing concern among his colleagues and unwelcome publicity in the media. Whether it was the backlash against his stance on Iraq or problems in Wales, colleagues complained that he had lost focus, appearing introverted, unhappy and lacking in ideas. He had broken with Labour but appeared rudderless. He was criticised as lacklustre.[13] There were renewed attacks over his alleged drinking, but by early September, *The Times*[14] spoke of a defiant Kennedy, facing up to his demons, who had returned from the summer break in more buoyant mood. Certainly, not just Kennedy, but also the party, needed a tonic to revitalise it. It was to come, most unexpectedly, with the by-election in Brent East caused by the death of the sitting Labour MP.

The contest, on 18 September, was the first by-election since Ogmore some 19 months earlier. Brent East was a seminal by-election. The constituency was hardly promising Liberal Democrat territory. The party started the contest in third place (10.6 per cent in 2001) with no local council strength. Yet the outcome was a Liberal Democrat triumph. Relentless Liberal campaigning began the day of the former Labour MP's funeral. A million leaflets were delivered. Kennedy made several early well-publicised visits. In a constituency where crime was an issue, Labour's candidate was attacked as the Brussels-based candidate from millionaire's row (he was an MEP who lived in wealthy Weybridge). Sarah Teather, by contrast, was a young local candidate (a policy analyst for a cancer charity) with a popular touch. Labour had also gravely miscalculated by delaying the by-election until the autumn.

In a bitterly fought and increasingly dirty contest, Sarah Teather overturned a 13,000 Labour majority to capture the most ethnically-diverse seat in England with a 1,118 majority (to become the youngest MP in the Commons).[15] On a swing of 29 per cent to the Liberal Democrats, Labour had lost its first by-election in 15 years. For the Conservatives, who had been second in 2001, their relegation to third place with just 3,368 votes was a humiliation. A mixture of low turnout (just 36.4 per cent), growing opposition to the Iraq War and growing disillusion with the Blair administration all, no doubt, contributed to the result. But for the Liberal Democrats, the outcome was a terrific tonic on the eve of their party conference.

The Brighton conference of autumn 2003, held against this encouraging background, approved plans for a local income tax of around 3.5p in the pound to replace council tax – arguing that 70 per cent of people would be paying less. More controversial was the motion to abolish the monarchy and replace the Queen with an elected Head of State – proposed by the Youth and Student wing of the party. The party also discussed proposals to make 11-year-olds study sex education. More hard-line policies on crime were also proposed in the document *Payback not Layback*.

Not surprisingly, Conservatives reacted with fury to what they saw as a leftward Liberal Party. Iain Duncan Smith declared: 'Blair is soft on soft drugs; Kennedy is soft on hard drugs too. He wants higher taxes, weaker asylum rules, less burglars in prison and an end to our national currency. He is not a throwback to old Labour. He is a hangover.'[16]

Not surprisingly, Charles Kennedy enjoyed a good conference (he had committed himself wholeheartedly to campaigning in Brent East) and Liberal Democrat ratings rose in the opinion polls. It was against this background that in October the Liberal Democrat leader chose to make a radical reshuffle of his leading party spokesmen, with Vince Cable taking on the Treasury role and Mark Oaten handling Home Affairs. It was quickly interpreted as a political shift to the right – with the replacement of Matthew Taylor as chief Treasury spokesman by the free marketeer and ex-Shell chief economist, Vince Cable (and with David Laws as his number two).[17] In policy terms it was soon reflected by plans to reduce Whitehall budgets and abolish the DTI rather than increase taxation generally. Others saw the reshuffle as a clever balancing act, a blend of experience and youth, with Matthew Taylor earmarked as chairman of the parliamentary party and architect of the next election manifesto. The sharper edge of the new team reflected the coming battles as the European elections of June 2004 (and the next general election itself) approached. It was, declared *The Economist* a new, more muscular liberalism.

In October 2003, the Liberal Democrats faced a renewed bout of turmoil in the Conservative Party. On 29 October Iain Duncan Smith lost a confidence vote among Conservative MPs. Michael Howard rapidly emerged as a unity candidate and was elected unopposed on 4 November. Conservative fortunes began to revive.

On 18 November, in what was styled an Alternative Queen's Speech, Kennedy outlined a programme of legislation: it included a referendum on the euro, a new voting system for Westminster, the merging or scrapping of Whitehall departments, axing of tuition fees, devolving control of schools to local councils and the replacement of the council tax with a local income tax.

With the Conservatives equipped with a new leader in Michael Howard, some commentators predicted that 2004 would being a return to a more traditional two-party politics.[18] Indeed, the first months of 2004 revealed some Liberal Democrat problems. On 23 January Jenny Tonge, the MP for Richmond Park, was sacked from her front-bench position as spokesperson for Children after standing by remarks in which she said she would consider becoming a suicide bomber if forced to live like the Palestinians. Kennedy said her comments were unacceptable.[19] Further speculation about Kennedy was fuelled in March by his absence from the Budget debate and Prime Minister's Questions, which was blamed on an upset stomach. Menzies Campbell deputised at 12 minutes' notice at Prime Minister's Questions, Vince Cable responded to the Budget Statement.

More damaging unfavourable publicity surrounded the Southport conference in March. The press emphasised how ill Kennedy appeared. Friends conceded his appearance was awful, he was perspiring almost uncontrollably and his hands shook violently. His speech, emphasising 'tough liberalism' was overshadowed by talk of a plot to replace him with his deputy, Menzies Campbell.[20] Conference decisions such as approval to ban smoking in public places received little attention. Meanwhile, in the polls, Liberal Democrat support was fluctuating wildly. Against this background, attention focused on preparing for the local, European and London elections of 10 June 2004.

With a combination of local elections (delayed by the outbreak of foot and mouth disease) and elections to the European Parliament, the voting on 10 June 2004 took on the aspect of a nationwide referendum on the government. The local election results produced much encouragement for the party, with Kennedy declaring them the best ever for the Liberal Democrats, and clearly delighted with the impressive gains in Labour's heartlands. Overall, the party gained 151 seats, the Conservatives 232 and Labour lost 468. The Liberal Democrats doubled their seats in Newcastle (from 24 to 48) to wrest control of the council from Labour. Elsewhere, the Liberal Democrats became the largest party in Leeds, Rochdale and Burnley as well as making significant gains in such North West metropolitan districts as Manchester, Bolton and Sefton. Although the Liberal Democrat national share of the vote was marginally down (from the 30 per cent of 2003 to 29 per cent in 2004) they were still in second place and their gains at Labour's expense were impressive. A less comforting aspect of the results for the Liberal Democrats was the sign of a Conservative recovery in such areas as Winchester and Cheltenham.

In the contest for Mayor of London, there was some disappointment at the relatively poor showing of Simon Hughes. In the first count, Labour's Ken Livingstone easily came first (685,541 votes, 36.7 per cent), the Conservative Steve Norris second (542,423, 29.0 per cent) and Simon Hughes trailing with 284,645 (15.2 per cent). In the second round, Livingstone won easily. Although the Liberal Democrat share of the vote was up, it was a disappointment after the euphoria of Brent East. His campaign never really took off and clear political ideas were lacking. His chances of becoming party leader seemed to have slipped.

However, the gloss was taken off the local election successes when the European election results revealed a substantial upsurge for UKIP, thoroughly spoiling the Liberal Democrat party. For the EU parliament, with 78 seats at stake following the EU enlargement of May 2004, all MEPs were elected under a 'closed-list' regional system of proportional representation. England was divided into nine regions, whilst Scotland, Wales and Northern Ireland each constituted a region.

The most significant aspect of the result was the surge in support for the Eurosceptic UKIP and bad results for both Conservative and Labour. In England, UKIP secured third place in terms of votes and took 12 seats (with around 17 per cent of the vote). The Liberal Democrats, although increasing their percentage vote compared to 1999, and adding two to their tally of MEPs, had been forced into fourth place. A more detailed analysis by English region gives an indication of Liberal Democrat support (see Table 20.2).

Table 20.2

	Lib % Vote + Place	*+/– 1999*	*% UKIP 2004*
Eastern	14.00 (4th)	+ 2.05	19.61*
East Midlands	12.94 (4th)	+ 0.17	26.05*
London	15.32 (3rd)	+ 3.66	12.34
North East	17.78 (3rd)	+ 4.28	12.16
North West	15.92 (3rd)	+ 4.18	11.74
South East	15.33 (3rd)	+ 0.02	19.53*
South West	18.34 (3rd)	+ 1.89	22.56*
West Midlands	13.74 (4th)	+ 2.46	17.49
Yorkshire and the Humber	15.55 (3rd)	+ 1.15	14.54

* UKIP in second place

Despite the humiliation of fourth place in several regions in England, the Liberal Democrats had some successes when Fiona Hall became their first MEP in the North East (hitherto barren territory for the party). They also held on to their seat in London and in Yorkshire/Humberside. Lord Rennard was able to claim it was the only one of the three main parties not to be losing support. Meanwhile in Scotland, although remaining in fourth place with 13.1 per cent of the vote, their share was up from 9.8 in 1999. They returned one MEP (Elspeth Attwooll). In Wales, the Liberal Democrats sank to fifth place (with UKIP usurping fourth place) with 10.47 per cent of the vote (up from 8.19 in 1999) but again no MEP.

These elections were swiftly followed by two by-elections in normally safe Labour seats (Leicester South and Birmingham Hodge Hill) where Labour decided to hold by-elections as soon as possible (on 15 July) in an attempt to prevent the Liberal Democrats having a long period to organise an effective campaign.

The Leicester South by-election offered an interesting contest. The seat might have seemed fairly safe Labour territory with a majority of 13,243 in 2001. But the Liberal Democrats had taken minority control of the council the previous year. Some of the old housing estates (as in the Saffron Lane area) now elected Liberal Democrat councillors. Moreover the city had a vibrant Asian community which was likely to be strongly against the Iraq War as well as a thriving university electorate. The Conservatives had also lost much ground locally since their heyday a generation ago.

The Liberal Democrats were first to select a candidate in Parmjit Singh Gill, a 37-year-old local authority information officer, who was a local councillor and had contested the seat in 2001. Both UKIP and Respect had polled well in the Euro-elections in Leicester, further complicating the electoral arithmetic. Meanwhile Labour selected Sir Peter Soulsby, their former Leader of Leicester City Council. The Liberal Democrats were the bookmakers' favourites from the start. The Labour campaign soon became aggressive and dirty (Parmjit Singh Gill was shown shaking hands with a transsexual and leaflets asked 'Is this the man you want as your MP?'). Poster sabotage was rife.

The outcome was a sensational Liberal Democrat victory, a majority of 1,654 on a swing of 21.46 per cent with turnout at 41.6 per cent.[21] Although Iraq and the Butler Report was deemed a major issue, the *Guardian* reported that local issues (over bus passes and closure of post offices) were the real factor.[22] Leicester South gave the party its 55th MP and the first from an ethnic minority background.

In a sense, the outcome in the Hodge Hill by-election in Birmingham was an even more dramatic result. If George Galloway's Respect Party had not taken over 6 per cent of the protest vote, the Liberal Democrats would have won here. The constituency (once known at Stechford), with its deprived streets of council terraces and boarded up shops in east Birmingham had only a short three-week campaign (which probably saved Labour). It was not a nice contest. Defending an 11,618 majority Labour adopted a bare-knuckle attack on the Liberals. There were suggestions of a secret Conservative-Liberal deal.[23] *The Times* noted that Labour's campaign against the Liberal Democrats was both nasty and aggressive. The outcome saw Labour's majority slashed from 11,618 in

2001 to a meagre 460 – a swing of 26 per cent to the Liberal Democrats on a lowly turnout of 37.9 per cent. The Conservatives were a poor third, whilst Respect polled 1,282 votes.[24] These polls, taken with the June contests, were highly significant. In both by-elections, the Conservatives had been forced into third place on a reduced share of the vote. Despite fighting two crucial by-elections simultaneously, the Liberal Democrats had triumphed. It was heady stuff.

In the aftermath of these by-elections, the Liberal Democrat position was now stronger than at any time in Kennedy's leadership. The party, so long seen as challengers in Conservative-held seats, were now seen as the 'natural challenger' in many Labour-held strongholds as well. Commentators agreed, somewhat belatedly, that the party possessed both policies and politicians. As Matthew Parris wrote in *The Times*,[25] for a small party the Liberal Democrats could boast a range of original and undoctrinaire politicians – Ed Davey, David Laws and Mark Oaten were singled out along with Steve Webb. Ideas were certainly not in short supply. The publication in early September 2004 of *The Orange Book: Reclaiming Liberalism*, edited by Paul Marshall and David Laws, aroused considerable debate on the philosophy of the party on the eve of the party conference. The volume was an important collection of essays about the future policy direction of the Liberal Democrats, written by some of the party's brightest and youngest modernisers, MPs and MEPs – mostly centre-right economists. The main ideas put forward were seven-fold:

1. radical reform of the health services to introduce greater choice;
2. a vision of Britain in a liberal Europe;
3. a rebirth of local democracy, local accountability and local innovation;
4. a radical new approach to Britain's prison system;
5. new proposals to liberalise the economy, dismantling trade barriers and abolishing the DTI;
6. a rethink on proposals to support family life;
7. a new, funded pensions settlement.

The mixed reception of *The Orange Book*, particularly by sceptics on the social liberal wing of the party, provided the backdrop to the autumn conference at Bournemouth. This took on an added importance as it seemed likely to be the last before the next general election (and indeed so it proved). Kennedy, backed by consistently good opinion polls for the party, took the opportunity to use the occasion to target potential Labour voters, a theme pursued in the 12-page pre-election manifesto document (published on 14 September) and entitled *Freedom, Fairness and*

Trust. The manifesto struck a distinctly different note from *The Orange Book* (it was little wonder that *The Times* spoke of two Liberal Democrat conferences in the same week). Abandoning the previous position of higher taxes for all, taxes would now increase only for those at the top of the earnings scale as part of a wealth redistribution programme. Other commitments, replacing council tax with local income tax and a pledge to add £25 per week to the state pension for those aged over 75, were all to feature strongly when the general election campaign was waged. It was, declared the *Independent*, a cogent and considered manifesto.[26] Most commentators agreed it was Kennedy's most successful conference as party leader. Against this background, attention now turned to the forthcoming Hartlepool by-election.

The Hartlepool by-election, caused by the resignation of Peter Mandelson on his appointment as a European Commissioner, was eagerly awaited for its evidence that the Liberal Democrats could follow up their sensational victory in Leicester South in a constituency bordering that of Tony Blair. The constituency, part of the rock-solid Labour heartland, had a 14,571 majority in 2001. The Liberal Democrats chose Jody Dunn and threw everything into the campaign (Charles Kennedy himself visited the constituency six times). UKIP had polled strongly here in the June 2004 elections and this was a complicating factor if Liberals wanted a united anti-Labour vote. The town, battered by post-industrial decline, had received much help in the way of urban regeneration. With a largely white electorate with only 500 or so Muslim voters, the contest centred less on the Iraq War than on local issues – the threat to Hartlepool's hospital, greater toughness on crime and vandalism, etc. The Liberals poured in their foot soldiers to make the contest a nail-biter.

The result was a narrow Labour victory, by 2,033 votes after a massive 18.8 per cent swing to the Liberal Democrats (and with the Conservatives forced into fourth place by UKIP, the first time since 1945 this had happened to the official opposition).[27]

It had been a bitter contest and Labour breathed a sigh of relief at retaining the seat. It was a moral victory for the Liberal Democrats (the swing was only marginally less than the 20 per cent achieved in Leicester South in July), but Iraq was a less dominant issue here. It remained to be seen if (as Labour claimed) the Liberal by-election bandwagon had been halted in Hartlepool.

In fact, no further by-elections occurred before the general election. Meanwhile the Liberal Democrats could assess whether they had lived up to their promise to be an effective opposition to Labour. Effective opposition there had certainly been during the lifetime of the 2001 to

2005 Parliament. On a wide variety of issues, such as Iraq, top-up fees, tax, health, civil liberties, transport and immigration, Liberal Democrats voted at Westminster against Labour. The growing disenchantment with Labour can be seen in Table 20.3, which shows how often Liberal Democrats supported Labour in the division lobbies.

Table 20.3   Percentage of Occasions Liberal Democrats Vote with Labour

Year	%
2001/2	71
2002/3	68
2003/4	68
2004/5	66
2005/6	29

Source: Mark Oaten, *Coalitions* (2006), p. 282.

Although Liberal Democrats criticised the 'unconditional support' the Conservatives had given Labour over the 'war on terrorism', their partners in protecting liberal values were increasingly the Conservatives.

Much of this Liberal opposition to Labour took place in the House of Lords. In the session ending November 2002, the party had played a part in inflicting no less than 57 defeats on the Government. Its emergency anti-terror legislation alone had suffered seven defeats by early December 2001. One such Liberal Democrat achievement in the Lords was to help those supporting the right of homosexual and unmarried heterosexual couples to adopt children win an unexpected victory (by 215 to 184 votes, a majority of 31, on 5 November 2002). On this occasion Liberal Democrats had pulled out all the stops to ensure a Government victory and face down the Conservatives.

As the May 2005 general election approached, increasing attention was paid by the Liberal Democrats to their attack on Labour-held seats as the party cast itself as the 'real Opposition' to the Government on Iraq, ID cards and the council tax. A target list of Labour seats was drawn up.[28] Kennedy's pre-election timetable was scheduled to target Labour seats. Speeches and visits were closely coordinated with his key front-bench team. The Liberal Democratic manifesto for the election was drafted by Matthew Taylor. It was essentially a ten-point plan, careful to include only one tax increase (a top rate of income tax of 50p in the pound for those earning over £100,000 per annum). Its main proposals included free eye and dental tests; abolition of top-up fees for university students; free long-term personal care for the elderly (already introduced in Scotland);

cleaner transport and energy; a commitment of £1.5 billion to reduce class sizes; a £100 a month pension increase for the over-75s (guaranteeing a basic state pension of £167.05 for couples, £109.45 for single persons) with future increases linked to earnings); a pledge that Britain must never again support an illegal military intervention; and a commitment to replace council tax with local income tax (to be collected via the Inland Revenue). This latter commitment was not helped by a stumbling performance by Kennedy at the manifesto launch (the morning after the birth of his child).

Although the Liberal Democrats campaigned as the 'Real Alternative', the most frequently emphasised campaign issue was opposition to the Iraq War (and this clearly found a response, particularly among younger voters and students). In the media, the party enjoyed the endorsement of the *Independent*.

Meanwhile the party's electoral strategy in the campaign centred on two particular targets – the so-called 'decapitation strategy' aimed at leading Conservatives who faced very strong Liberal Democrat challengers and, at the same time, a guerrilla campaign to snatch Labour-held seats seen as vulnerable to the anti-Iraq War sentiment (such as Rochdale) and (often) with a strong student population (as in Bristol West and Manchester Withington) or where the party had made strong local government gains (such as Watford, Luton and Norwich). Left-wing Labour disillusion was reflected in the defection during the campaign of a hardened Bennite Labour left-winger, Brian Sedgemore, to the party (no doubt frightening off a few potential Conservative converts in the process).

The outcome of the May 2005 election saw the Liberal Democrats win 62 seats, gaining 16 and losing 5. This was their best result in over eighty years (since the 'Free Trade' election of December 1923). The party had polled 5,982,000 votes, around 22 per cent of the total (below its share in 1983 and 1987). Some of the Liberal Democrat gains, particularly from Labour, were unexpected and exhilarating (they took Manchester Withington, 106th on their target list of seats and Hornsey and Wood Green, 77th on their list). To these could be added Cardiff Central, Dunbartonshire East and Birmingham Yardley. Against the Conservatives however, they fared less well. Here, their most unexpected gain was Solihull (56th on their target list). Other gains from the Conservatives only amounted to two other seats (Taunton and the sprawling Westmorland and Lonsdale constituency of Tim Collins). In marked contrast Liberals had taken 12 seats from Labour (these gains concentrated on seats with a large student or academic vote). There were five losses to the Conservatives – these were Guildford, Newbury, Ludlow, Weston-super-Mare, and West Devon and Torridge. Table 20.4 gives the full list of gains and losses.

Table 20.4 Liberal Democrat Gains and Losses: May 2005

Constituency	Won From	Swing to Lib Dem
(a) Gains		
Birmingham Yardley	Labour	8.8
Bristol West	Labour	8.4
Cambridge	Labour	15.0
Cardiff Central	Labour	8.7
Ceredigion	Plaid Cymru	6.0
Dunbartonshire East	Labour	7.4
Falmouth and Camborne	Labour	9.5
Hornsey and Wood Green	Labour	14.6
Inverness, Nairn, Badenoch and Strathspey	Labour	6.0
Leeds North West	Labour	9.6
Manchester Withington	Labour	17.3
Rochdale	Labour	7.7
Solihull	Conservative	10.0
Taunton	Conservative	0.7
Westmorland and Lonsdale	Conservative	3.5

Constituency	Swing
(b) Losses (all to Conservative)	
Devon West and Torridge	3.9
Guildford	0.9
Ludlow	4.1
Newbury	5.5
Weston-super-Mare	2.5

To put these gains and losses in perspective, the net gains of the party were ten compared to 26 in 1997 and six in 2001. Even more important, the Liberal Democrats had proved, as in 2001, that they could still win seats from an incumbent Labour Government.

The most noticeable Liberal Democrat failure was its inability to capture those Tory-held seats which formed its so-called 'decapitation' policy – designed to claim the scalps of such figures as David Davis (Home Affairs Spokesman, Haltemprice and Howden), Theresa May (Maidenhead) and Oliver Letwin (Dorset West). These seats, and other hoped-for Conservative targets (except for Westmorland and Lonsdale) stayed stubbornly Conservative, perhaps aided by voter perception of the Liberals as more left-wing in 2005 than 2001. Moreover, even some Liberal Democrat gains had been by the slenderest of majorities, with four seats won with majorities under 300 votes (Romsey, Solihull, Westmorland and Lonsdale, and Ceredigion – gained from Plaid Cymru).

On the other hand, the Liberal Democrats had come within a whisker of considerably increasing their gains from Labour. Table 20.5 indicates these six nearest misses.

Table 20.5   Liberal Democrat Near-Misses in Labour Seats

Constituency	Labour % Majority
Aberdeen South	3.2
Oxford East	2.3
Watford	2.3
Islington South and Finsbury	1.6
Edinburgh South	0.9
Edinburgh North and Leith	5.0

The picture in Wales and Scotland also deserves analysis. In Wales, whilst Jenny Willott took Cardiff Central from Labour with a 5,593 majority and Mark Williams wrested Ceredigion from Plaid Cymru, total Liberal Democrat representation was only four. In Scotland, the Liberal Democrats had cause to celebrate, gaining two seats and increasing their share of the vote by 6.4 per cent to over 22 per cent (their best performance in over eighty years). The Liberal Democrats were now the second biggest party in Scotland in terms of Westminster votes as well as seats.

If the Liberal Democrat performance nationally is analysed by votes cast rather than seats won, some important trends are revealed. The Liberal Democrats increased their share of the vote in 543 of the 625 seats they contested. Their best increase in *share* of the vote by regions was Scotland (6 per cent up on 2001) and the north of England (up 6.1 per cent). In marked contrast their smallest increase compared to 2001 was in their hitherto strongest regions (SW England, up only 1.3 per cent, SE England, up 1.7 per cent).

In types of constituency, Labour lost most heavily in the seats it was defending where Liberal Democrats were a strongly-based challenger (although after 2005 there were still only ten seats where Liberal Democrats were less than 10 per cent behind Labour). Again, in marked contrast, Liberal Democrats seemed to hit a ceiling in the Conservative-held marginals which they hoped to take – particularly with the so-called decapitation strategy seats but also in hopefuls such as Wells which the party had long targeted. One interesting reflection on the nationwide appeal of the party was that only one deposit was lost (in the Blaenau Gwent constituency).

In the wake of the election, Liberal Democrats could console themselves that the electoral system had again worked to discriminate against them. On average, a Labour MP needed only 26,858 votes to get elected, a Conservative 44,241 and Liberal Democrat 98,484. Liberal Democrat reaction to the results was mixed. Exhilaration in some cases at some outstanding victories, but overall disappointment. After a fundamentally uneven performance, the 2005 election seemed an opportunity lost not the breakthrough that might have been.

21

From Kennedy to Clegg: 2005–2010

The five years from the general election of May 2005 to the general election of May 2010 can be divided into three main phases: the first was the final period of Kennedy's leadership, culminating in his resignation in January 2006 after a growing revolt against him. The second phase can best be called the Campbell interlude, lasting from his election as leader in March 2006 to his abrupt resignation in October 2007 against a background of plunging party support in the opinion polls. The third phase was the leadership of Nick Clegg, who was narrowly elected leader in December 2007 over Chris Huhne.

In the immediate aftermath of the election, at least for those unaware of Kennedy's mounting personal problems, the Liberal Democrats seemed to have some cause to celebrate. Not only had the party won its most seats since 1923, and made some exceptionally good gains from Labour, but also the composition of the party was younger than their rivals and their 'safe' seats were increasing in number. Moreover, the party was now in second place in 189 seats – 106 of them held by Labour. In addition, never in living memory had the Liberals had representation from the major cities of London, Southampton, Bristol, Birmingham, Manchester, Leeds and Sheffield. And Liberal Democrats were the second party in Scotland.

Youth was very much a feature of the new Liberal Democrat intake (three MPs were under 30, 39 under 50 and the average age was 46.4 compared to 52.7 for Labour and 49.9 for the Conservatives). Jo Swinson (at 25) became the youngest MP in the UK by taking Dunbartonshire East from Labour (and the former youngest, Sarah Teather, had narrowly retained Brent East). Also newly-elected was Julia Goldsworthy, the 26-year-old victor in the three-way marginal of Falmouth and Camborne. These were three of ten women Lib Dem MPs. At long last the tally of Liberal Democrat women MPs was increasing.

In the post-election reshuffle (a job which Kennedy never found easy) Steve Webb was appointed Health Spokesman (to give the party a clearer focus on reformist policies for the National Health Service), Ed Davey was moved to become Education spokesman (Davey had been behind the plans for a local income tax) and David Laws (co-editor of the *Orange Book*) promoted to Work and Pensions (in preparation for the coming battle in parliament over incapacity benefit). Three senior figures (Menzies Campbell, Vince Cable and Mark Oaten) stayed in their posts. Of the 20 newly-elected MPs, six were given junior front-bench appointments (and thereby upsetting some overlooked longer-serving figures). Kennedy had found jobs for Nick Clegg (a foreign affairs spokesman) and Chris Huhne (deputy Treasury spokesman). The party eventually elected Paul Holmes as Chair of the Parliamentary Party.

A first priority was to clear the decks for a complete policy review. Critics had argued that the party manifesto had been more of a shopping list of pledges than a coherent philosophy. Kennedy quickly announced this review on 9 May, paving the way for the party to ditch some of its tax proposals. Some Liberal Democrats feared the party had lost potential support with its plans to replace the council tax with a local income tax and its proposed 50p top rate of tax on incomes of more than £100,000 per annum. This argument came most vocally from those opposed to the party positioning itself as a left-wing alternative to Labour (it was all part of the debate on social or economic liberalism). The policy review was also to focus on Europe and nuclear energy (particularly party opposition to nuclear power), pensions policy and environment.

The question of party finance, in particular money received from donors, gave the Liberal Democrats some unpleasant publicity when it was revealed on 24 May that the party treasurer, Reg Clark, had resigned back in February in a furious row over the party's decision to accept around £2.4 million in donations from Michael Brown, a Scottish benefactor based in Majorca. Lord Razzall acted as interim party treasurer. The gifts by Brown were made by a British-based company, 5th Avenue Capital Partners, whose registered address was in London. Many were unhappy that the party had used a legal 'loophole' to accept this money – the biggest donation in the history of the party.[1] (The Liberal Democrats spent over £5 million in the 2005 election, compared to £3 million in 2001.)

Against this unwelcome publicity, an important boost for the Liberal Democrats came with the result from the Cheadle by-election in July (caused by the untimely death of the sitting Liberal Democrat Patsy Calton). In the first proper by-election of the new Parliament, and faced with a major and aggressive Conservative effort to recapture the seat, the Liberal Democrats fielded Mark Hunter, leader of Stockport Council. The party retained the seat with a majority of 3,657 with a swing of 2.8 per cent to them on a 55 per cent turnout. The Labour candidate lost his deposit. The major beneficiary of this victory was Kennedy himself who had sorely needed a victory amid what was seen as a period of drift and lack of leadership. This sense of drift, and a growing mood of introspection, seemed to have taken a firm hold of the party. For those who knew what the real problem was, it was all too clear: Kennedy's alcoholism. His drinking habits had been a talking point since his election in 1999. He had strenuously denied a drinking problem in the famous interview with Jeremy Paxman in July 2002. In March 2004 the Liberal Democrat leader again insisted on TV that he did not have a drink problem. During 2004 he was also directly confronted on the issue by four senior MPs. Many believed his excruciating performance when launching the Liberal Democrat 2005 election manifesto was also related to his drinking. To head off the ever-increasing murmurings, Kennedy needed to deliver a strong performance at conference. Despite his embarrassment over the party conference's position on the future of the Royal Mail and other issues, Kennedy delivered a forceful and passionate closing speech – his best yet as leader.[2] But it was a speech lacking in specifics on particular issues and did nothing to resolve growing divisions between the modernisers and a more left-leaning old guard.

Against this background, the party had to fight the Livingston by-election caused by the death of former Labour Foreign Secretary, Robin Cook, on 6 August. The contest, held on 29 September, saw Labour retain the seat with a much-reduced majority over the SNP. The Liberal Democrat, Charles Dundas, came third and the Conservatives a poor fourth.[3] Events now moved rapidly concerning the Kennedy problem. The respite gained by his speech to the party conference was short-lived. A speech on 15 November to students at the London School of Economics proved to be an unlikely turning point. Kennedy appeared drunk to Liberal Democrat MP Julia Goldsworthy who was present. She asked colleagues what she should do. On 17 November, his unexplained cancellation of a railway journey to Newcastle (citing 'family reasons') brought the rumour mill into overdrive.

His position was not helped on 24 November when he admitted he had been wrong not to declare to the Commons authorities his free flights in a private jet leased by Michael Brown, the party's most generous benefactor. During November senior colleagues, including Campbell, had been planning to send a letter of no confidence to Kennedy, but this manoeuvre came to nothing. The single external event which brought the Kennedy problem to a head was the election of David Cameron as leader of the Conservative Party on 6 December 2005. The election of a telegenic Conservative leader, heralding a likely Conservative recovery in the opinion polls, focused attention on Kennedy's own position.

Events gathered pace rapidly. On 13 December his plea to senior colleagues in the Shadow Cabinet to rally behind him was rejected and he faced a strong 30-minute barrage of criticism of his leadership. The next day went better for Kennedy. After a strong performance at a crisis meeting of the parliamentary party, support seemed to have rallied behind him (although it was the obscure backbenchers not senior figures who gave support). But it was a brief respite. An opinion poll on 15 December showed that his popularity had nosedived by a third since the May elections. Meanwhile, Vince Cable was to organise another 'no confidence' letter. The following day Sir Menzies Campbell stated that Kennedy's position was 'not invincible' and that he would stand in any leadership contest if Kennedy stood down. On 21 December *Liberal* magazine established an online petition calling for Kennedy to resign. It rapidly attracted the signatures of 3,000 activists.[4]

By now Kennedy's position was coming to look unsustainable, even if he had escaped a pre-Christmas assassination. Barracked in the Commons by other parties, colleagues had lost patience with his below-par performance since the election. The press was openly speculating on who the leadership contenders were likely to be. MPs warned him that his departure was inevitable as Ming Campbell refused to support him in public. Kennedy could hardly sack his critics without making obvious the scale of the revolt against him. Kennedy's first tactical reaction was a disaster. He seemed to believe he could still salvage his leadership by challenging his rivals to stand against him in an immediate election. Senior figures were horrified at the prospect of a prolonged, damaging election that might well see the party washing its dirty laundry in public.

The end came suddenly. On 5 January (with ITN preparing to release a story about his alcoholism), Charles Kennedy admitted publicly that he was receiving treatment for alcoholism and urged a leadership election to end the speculation about his leadership. After this, Kennedy was a 'dead man walking'. His senior frontbenchers wanted his resignation, the leader of the party's MEPs said he was finished. On 6 January Ed Davey and Sarah Teather announced that 25 Liberal Democrat spokesmen would resign unless Kennedy quit. The brutal assassination ended on 7 January when Kennedy resigned the leadership.

In assessing the reasons for Kennedy's downfall, it is important not to forget the blame which was being attached to other senior figures in the party, including Campbell, who were part of a conspiracy and cover-up to hide their leader's alcoholism. This perhaps was as important as the imagined plotting or schemes so often mentioned.

Kennedy's detractors could point to many failings. Lack of attention to detail, a refusal to choose between Liberalism or market forces – tacking in between them, and so forth. He rarely led from the front, being often a chairperson rather than a leader. His supporters, on the other hand, stressed that he was in no way the amiable lightweight to be contrasted with 'Action Man' Ashdown (who had given Kennedy his first front-bench position). Where some saw weakness, others saw Kennedy as an adroit politician, keeping his party united and steering it to heights not achieved since Lloyd George. Others saw just missed opportunities. Nearly all agreed it was a sorry end to an unfortunate personal and political saga. Andrew Rawnsley wrote in the *Observer* that it was a 'sorry conclusion to the leadership of an active, talented and fundamentally decent man who did a great deal for his party'.[5]

Perhaps the best interim assessment of a gifted politician who may yet play a major future role is that given by his biographer:

> Charles Kennedy is an enigma. As leader of his party he was almost universally liked by his MPs in Parliament, but brutally deposed by them. He never had another job other than that of full-time politician at Westminster, yet felt himself an outsider in the House of Commons. He was known as vivacious, sociable, witty and was so in demand as a regular media performer he earned the soubriquet 'Chat Show Charlie', but in fact was a painfully shy and stubbornly private man with very few close friends.[6]

Hurst continued:

> He was blessed with a brilliant talent as a communicator, shrewd political judgement and an intuitive ability to read the public mind and yet, as leader of the Liberal Democrats, his public performances were frequently diffident, pedestrian and forgettable. He could rise to the most testing challenge, then lose his way when the pressure of external events subsided.

The turmoil in the party following Kennedy's resignation saw support for the party in the polls fall to its lowest level in five years (down three points to 16). The polls also revealed considerable sympathy for Kennedy. Two thirds of Liberal Democrat voters backed his original determination to stay on as leader and a half still backed him, even though he had lied in the past. Some figures, such as Lord McNally, Leader in the Lords, had warned against changing leaders prior to the May elections. But now that Kennedy had gone, the focus quickly moved to the candidates who might enter the field to succeed him and lead the party into the May elections.

The most likely leadership contenders following Kennedy's resignation were Sir Menzies Campbell, the Deputy Leader and a senior figure with long parliamentary experience and an easy patrician manner (the press saw him as the natural successor). There was also Simon Hughes, the party president, MP for Southwark and Bermondsey, and failed mayoral candidate for London (and defeated in 1999 by Kennedy), and Mark Oaten, the party spokesman on Home Affairs who was seen as a young moderniser and who clearly had leadership ambitions. Sir Menzies Campbell, a 64-year-old Scottish lawyer and a former champion sprinter (once dubbed the fastest white man in the world), was probably the party's best known figure nationally. He had become widely known as the party's Foreign Affairs spokesman during the Iraq War where he had argued a careful, moderate but incisive case against the war.

When nominations closed, the main challengers were joined in the fray by a fourth challenger, Chris Huhne, newly-elected MP for Eastleigh in 2005 but a former MEP and widely tipped for high office in the party (to his detractors he was Chris Who? and seen as fiercely ambitious). Those who had hoped for an uncontested election and a swift 'coronation' of Ming were disappointed.

The Liberal leadership election got off to an unfortunate start when Mark Oaten, having withdrawn from the race on 19 January because he claimed insufficient support from fellow MPs, abruptly resigned on 21 January as the party spokesman on Home Affairs. His career was engulfed in scandal when the *News of the World* revealed that he had engaged in an affair with a male prostitute. Other issues diverted attention from policy issues. Simon Hughes admitted he had hidden his sexual orientation for years, whilst Lord McNally (the Leader in the Lords) was revealed to have suffered from alcoholism.

As the contest developed, despite being little known by the public at large (and indeed by some Liberal Democrats outside the South East), Chris Huhne moved up as his momentum gathered pace. His stance was as a moderniser with strong green credentials. Although Menzies Campbell became favourite as Hughes' campaign stalled, Huhne's smoothly executed media appearances and platform of tough environmental taxes were well received. Simon Hughes' campaign continued to drift. Outside the party faithful (73,000 members were entitled to vote) the Liberal Democrat leadership campaign excited little interest.

Inevitably against this background, Sir Menzies Campbell was strongly favoured as a possible leader, given his political experience and potential to rebuild a party badly fractured by the Kennedy resignation. If the party wanted a safe pair of hands, Campbell seemed to fit the bill.

The challenge from Menzies Campbell soon looked unstoppable. He had the support of two former leaders in David Steel and Paddy Ashdown. The press speculated that younger MPs would rally round him if only to prevent Simon Hughes, who was portrayed as too left-wing, being elected. Ming himself, faced with a faltering campaign and poor performances at Prime Minister's Questions, stressed fighting poverty and tough action on green issues.

As if the Liberal Democrats did not have enough problems to occupy them, the onset of a by-election in the Labour held Scottish constituency of Dunbarton and West Fife caused a further headache. The constituency was not an easy one to fight. In May 2005 Labour had held the seat with an 11,452 majority and 47 per cent of the vote. Although the Liberal Democrats were in second place (with 20 per cent), the SNP were hard on their heels with 19 per cent. The Liberal Democrat candidate, Willie Rennie, had local connections (having grown up in the village of Strathmiglo in the constituency, where his family ran the village shop). Labour's campaign ran into difficulties – their candidate Catherine Stihler was criticised for not resigning as an MEP. Seven hundred redundancies had been announced at Rosyth in the heart of the constituency the previous month by a computer ink maker while the local issues of tolls on the Forth Road Bridge and hospital closures also lost Labour some support. Continued casualties in Iraq were also a campaign issue. Despite being in coalition with Labour in Edinburgh, the Liberal Democrats seemed to be harnessing the protest vote. The result was a sensation. The Liberal Democrats took the seat with 35.8 per cent of the vote and a majority of 1,800 on a swing of 16.2 per cent, taking their representation at Westminster to a new post-war high of 63. Labour's only comfort was the poor showing of the Conservatives who finished a dismal fourth (with 7.8 per cent) and whose result gave David Cameron little cheer. It seemed for the Liberal Democrats that the damage suffered by the Kennedy resignation was a lot less than the polls nationally had indicated. It marked a particular embarrassment for Labour's prime minister in waiting, Gordon Brown, who had a house in the constituency and whose own constituency of Kirkcaldy and Cowdenbeath was next door. For the campaign of Menzies Campbell, whose Fife constituency was also next door, there was talk of the 'Dunfermline dynamic' probably boosting his chances for the leadership. It would also boost the Liberal Democrat morale for their March spring conference in Harrogate.

On 2 March 2006, Sir Menzies Campbell was elected Leader of the Liberal Democrats, defeating his main opponent, Chris Huhne, by 8,069 votes in the second round. Simon Hughes was eliminated in the first ballot.[7]

It was clearly important for the newly-elected Leader to stamp his authority on the party in the choice of a new Shadow Cabinet (particularly after a somewhat lacklustre leadership campaign). The key figures in the new team were Vince Cable (remaining at the Treasury), Nick Clegg (promoted to Home Affairs) and Michael Moore (Foreign Affairs). Simon Hughes received the Constitutional Affairs portfolio, Chris Huhne was given Environment, Food and Rural Affairs. Julia Goldsworthy, a former economic adviser to the party, became the youngest senior front-bench spokesperson of any of the major parties (and was one of three women Liberal Democrat MPs promoted). Nick Harvey took over Defence while Alistair Carmichael was promoted to Transport.[8]

In the subsequent election for Deputy Leader of the party, Vince Cable was elected. A former chief economist at Shell, Cable had been shadow Treasury spokesman since 2003. He beat off two contenders, Matthew Taylor and David Heath.

In a sense, Campbell's task was three-fold. He had to restore stability and purpose to a party rocked by the Kennedy revelations; secondly he had to make the internal operations of the party more professional; and, thirdly, he had to prepare the party for an eventual general election.

Campbell also acted swiftly to give impetus to the need to modernise the party's internal organisation. The *Observer* reported that the party was about to receive a US-style facelift of techniques already imported by Labour and the Conservatives.[9] At the heart of this reorganisation was Ed Davey who was the key driver of the internal party reforms aimed at making the party more professional.

With Campbell's newly-appointed team in place and internal party reform underway, the most crucial and immediate task was the elections of 4 May 2006. These elections would be the first nationwide test of Liberal Democrat support under their new leader. These elections were equally a crucial test of support for the newly-elected Conservative leader, David Cameron. On a very bad night for Labour, the Conservatives secured their best result since 1992, thereby comfortably confirming the leadership of David Cameron. The party secured around 40 per cent of the votes cast and took several key councils, especially in London.

The results for the Liberal Democrats were more mixed. In a campaign fought on crime and green issues, their share of the national vote was 27 per cent, down 2 per cent from 29 per cent in 2004. They had a net gain of just one council and two councillors (having lost Winchester to the Conservatives, Islington and Milton Keynes to No Overall Control, but in turn taking Richmond from the Conservatives and wresting St Albans and South Lakeland from No Overall Control). They had also made useful gains in Cambridge and Oxford (becoming the largest party in both university towns) and could be pleased that no Conservatives at all had been elected in Manchester, Liverpool or Newcastle. The party notched up impressive gains of seats in parts of London – gaining 16 seats in Brent, 12 in Camden and 11 in Haringey.

The mixed publicity of these results was added to by the resignation on 4 May of Chris Davies, the leader of the Liberal Democrat MEPs for the previous 12 years.[10] The results were a blow to Campbell – even though he could justifiably argue that the results showed more about the standing of the party than his own standing as leader. In the wake of the local elections, and after 100 days as leader, the press was beginning to raise questions about Campbell's lacklustre performance. *The Times* critically remarked that Ming had indeed upgraded – to mediocre (although admitting that he was doing most of the right things to sharpen up his party in terms of policy, organisation and funding).[11] His problems at Prime Minister's Questions and his personal image difficulty refused to disappear, while there was the strategy dilemma of how to deal with the Conservative revival under David Cameron.

A major shake up of tax policies was heralded in June. However, a by-election victory was needed to give a stimulus to the Campbell leadership. It very nearly came when, following the May elections, polling took place in two parliamentary by-elections on 29 June. Campbell's critics were temporarily silenced by the by-election result in Bromley and Chislehurst. This safe suburban Conservative seat in SE London had been held by the Conservatives with a 13,000 majority in 2005. In the by-election, the Liberal Democrats came within 633 votes of victory, with Labour forced into fourth place behind UKIP.[12] There was a 14.3 swing to the Liberal Democrats.

With Campbell's position shored up by the result in Bromley, the party unveiled its tax and environmental proposals during August ready for debate at the forthcoming Brighton conference. The autumn conference, the first with Campbell as leader, served in part to establish his authority as leader and went some way towards moving the party in a more clearly defined direction, signalling a shift to attracting disaffected

Labour voters and targeting more Labour seats. The 'green' tax proposals were endorsed much to the leadership's relief. Essentially, this was a radical plan, bold and courageous, to cut income tax but still balance the books by penalising those who damaged the environment most. Tax cuts were aimed to make the system fairer (with reductions in lower rate taxes) paid for by increased taxation on air travel, changes in vehicle excise duty, a carbon tax to replace the climate change levy, reducing tax relief for higher rate payers from 40 per cent to 20 per cent and so forth. Conference however took issue over the abandonment of the 50p rate for the highest earners.

Despite his performance at party conference, doubts remained on Campbell. The position was well summarised on the eve of the conference by Andrew Rawnsley:

> Sir Menzies, elected on the basis that a steady pair of hands was the best replacement for a shaky pair of hands, has struggled to make an impact with the public. Before he got the top job, he was the most assured performer in the Lib Dem line-up. He oozed authority and credibility. This was his main recommendation for the leadership.[13]

Rawnsley continued:

> In the top job, he has seemed ill at ease and unsure of himself except when he is on the territory of foreign affairs. He has been helped by one by-election victory and one near-miss during his seven months as leader, but he has been wounded by polls suggesting that voters still preferred Kennedy drunk to Campbell sober.

After the party conference, and particularly in the first months of 2007, the Liberal Democrats faced opinion polls showing the Conservatives gaining in strength with Labour at its worst since the general election. The *Independent* noted that, though Liberal Democrat support was up at 20 per cent in February, this improvement was not matched in Campbell's personal ratings. Earlier, *The Times* had spoken of a 'publicity drought' for the party and a sense of frustration among Campbell's colleagues. But most in the party knew that it was crucial for the party – and for Campbell – to do well in the local elections in May.

The elections of 3 May, 2007, held the same day as the voting for the Welsh Assembly and Scottish Parliament, were an important indicator of the political mood of the country – and a nationwide gauge of Liberal Democrat support after over a year of Ming Campbell's leadership.

The outcome produced heavy Labour losses (around 500 seats, but not as many as predicted), the Conservatives under David Cameron gained 880 and the Liberal Democrats suffered a net loss of nearly 250. There was a net loss of four councils. These were mixed results. The Liberal Democrat councils of Bournemouth (where local rubbish collections were an issue) and Torbay were lost, but they gained Hull (hitherto a long-time safe Labour council), Rochdale and Eastbourne. They were at best mixed results for the Liberals and once again brought renewed murmurings over Campbell's leadership.

In the voting for the third elections for the Scottish Parliament, the results for the Liberal Democrats were again mixed. The party won 11 constituency seats outright and five more on the Top-Up system. These 16 seats left them in fourth place behind the Conservatives (with 17), Labour with 46 and a resurgent SNP with 47. The Greens won two. Although the Liberals polled well in such seats as Dunfermline West and parts of Edinburgh (with strong swings from Labour) they were frequently in fourth place, squeezed by the SNP and Labour juggernauts. There were distinct swings to the SNP from the Liberals in a swathe of seats from Aberdeen South to Roxburgh and Berwickshire.[14] Clearly, if the Liberal Democrat–Labour coalition had plenty of policy achievements, it failed to reap any electoral benefits for the party.

Given that the SNP was the largest single party, the Liberal Democrats (although in a sense still the kingmakers) quickly ruled out continuing their partnership with Labour. Nicol Stephen quickly accepted that the party with the most seats should govern. Given the SNP's insistence on putting an independence referendum to the voters in 2010, no coalition with the Nationalists was possible. On 16 May Alex Salmond (the SNP leader) formed a minority government having given the Greens some concessions.

In the Welsh Assembly elections, Labour secured 26 seats but with its worst share of the Welsh vote for ninety years and Plaid Cymru increased its representation. The Liberal Democrats, with six seats (three constituency and three top-up) were firmly in fourth place behind the Conservatives with 12.[15] Only in six constituencies did Liberal Democrats manage to secure second place – Ceredigion (a Plaid Cymru stronghold), Merthyr Tydfil and Rhymney (a Labour fortress), Newport East (missed by only 875 votes), Pontypridd, Swansea East and Swansea West. In all, the voting in May had produced mixed fortunes for Campbell and his party. Further events were to exacerbate these worries. A week after these elections, Tony Blair announced that he would resign as Prime Minister on 27 June. The new Prime Minister, Gordon Brown, made various attempts to woo senior Liberal Democrats into taking posts in his administration – notably an offer of the Northern Ireland Secretaryship to Paddy Ashdown (an offer which was declined). Nothing came of various other offers, but these events, combined with falling opinion poll ratings, did nothing to help the party.

With a new Government in place, and with the Conservative Shadow Cabinet also reshuffled, in July 2007 Campbell reshuffled his own shadow team, but leaving the major figures in place. Even before the 2007 autumn party conference, there had been mutterings about the quality of Ming Campbell's leadership, but a positive and forthright speech at conference temporarily quelled these rumblings. However, when the intense media speculation about a snap late autumn general election (which the government had done nothing to dampen down) abruptly ended in fiasco with Gordon Brown's declaration that there would be no early poll, the leadership question suddenly became an issue again (particularly as it now seemed likely that there would be no election before 2009 at the earliest).

On Friday 12 October, Simon Hughes urged Campbell to 'up his game'. There was fevered press speculation over the leadership during the weekend of 13–14 October. On Monday 15 October, Vince Cable, the Deputy Leader, admitted the leadership was 'under discussion'. The same evening Campbell abruptly and dramatically announced his resignation 'with immediate effect' and headed back to Scotland without elaborating his reasons. He had become the first victim of the non-election. Vince Cable took over as Acting Leader. The resignation rocked the party and led to some immediate recriminations and also speculation of a plot. Some MPs reacted with anger and disgust.[16] Amongst Campbell's supporters, some blamed fractious dissidents eager to propel a leadership contest – this was widely seen as a reference to Huhne's supporters (some of whom were in open rebellion after the collapse in the polls).

Why, then, did Campbell resign? There were two immediate factors, several other longer term ones. The immediate factors were the precipitate fall in Liberal support in the polls (down to 11 per cent) coupled with the fact that a general election might be two or three years away. Allied to this (and Campbell stressed this factor) was the constant media attention to Campbell's age and appearance. Having sought the advice of his closest supporters (such as Jim Wallace) Campbell probably concluded that a protracted struggle would not serve the party well. In that sense it was his friends not his enemies who caused him to quit. Campbell was right not to soldier on (he would in any case be 70 in 2010). The example of Kennedy attempting to defy the odds was too recent – and the damage to his party would have been lasting. Probably Campbell (aided by his wife Elspeth) made his own decision to call time. Campbell only admitted his anger and frustration at the 'cloying blanket' of questions concerning his age.

Commentators differed on Campbell's virtues. The *New Statesman* declared that Campbell was a decent, honourable man whose instincts were invariably sound. *The Times* referred to the exit of an honourable man as the short-lived Ming dynasty ended. Not so the *Spectator* which saw that, despite his easy patrician air, he was grossly overrated, pompous and clueless, at sea in domestic politics. Many, like Vince Cable, paid tribute to the respect, affection and gratitude the party had for him.

How had Campbell's resignation left the party? It left the party, as indeed had the 2005 election and the departure of Kennedy in 2006, with worrying questions about its future strategy. Opponents argued the party was slipping into irrelevance, trying to occupy a centre ground already occupied by both major parties. It was nevertheless, a sad but necessary departure. The surprise was the timing of the resignation, not that it happened. It was not that he was too old. He was too old-fashioned, or, put differently, if Charles Kennedy was too drunk, Ming Campbell was too sober. Though curiously, as Ming himself reflected in his autobiography, his resignation turned into a canonisation.

The resignation had left the party facing a leadership election less than two years since Kennedy's departure. The first to declare his candidature officially was Chris Huhne, the 53-year-old MP for ultra-marginal Eastleigh (where he had first entered Westminster in 2005). An outsider who had rapidly gained support in the 2006 leadership contest, he had performed well as Environment Spokesman. Seen by some as intellectually aloof (a product of Magdalen College, Oxford) he was a former economics journalist and also an MEP. He started the contest as underdog and avoided comments that his supporters had undermined Campbell.

His main rival was seen as Nick Clegg (a friend of Huhne and also a former MEP). Born in 1967 in Buckinghamshire, with a half-Russian father and a Dutch mother, he had been educated at Westminster School (just like Chris Huhne) and had gone on to Cambridge. He had made history in 1999 when he was elected as a Liberal Democrat MEP for the East Midlands – the first Liberal parliamentarian in that region since 1931. He gave up his Brussels post to concentrate on Westminster, winning the Sheffield Hallam constituency in 2005 with over 50 per cent of the vote. Clegg had held back from contesting the leadership in 2006, but was promoted to Shadow Home Secretary by Sir Menzies Campbell. He was seen as future leadership material by such figures as Paddy Ashdown.

Clegg's confession of his leadership ambitions at a fringe meeting at the 2007 party conference had earned him a sharp rebuke from Lady Elspeth Campbell, but had probably not harmed his chances.

He had a very strong campaign team. Danny Alexander was his campaign manager and he commanded almost half the Liberal Democrat front-bench team and a sizeable majority of the parliamentary party. Senior figures to announce their support included an enthusiastic Lord Ashdown, Lord Razzall, Ed Davey, David Laws and Norman Lamb. Some former Huhne supporters, such as Greg Mulholland and Steven Williams also switched to Clegg. Both Kennedy and Campbell kept their counsel. When nominations closed on 31 October, the contest remained a two-horse race to be decided by the party's 55,000 members. There was a surprise that such figures as David Laws, Susan Kramer, Ed Davey or Steve Webb (from the more radical wing) had ruled out fighting.

It was very soon apparent that the leadership campaign was as much about personality as policy. The similarities between the candidates seemed far more obvious than the differences. If Huhne stressed he was anti-establishment, anti-Trident, pro-green and forward-looking, Clegg urged the party to modernise and break the stifling grip of two-party politics. Not even Clegg's keenest supporters could argue that he waged a good leadership campaign. It was widely seen as lacklustre, with little attempt to take the battle into Huhne's camp. Huhne showed more grit and attracted more publicity (especially over the 'Donorgate' donations scandal hitting Labour) but the real star of the leadership election period was the acting leader Vince Cable (whose memorable wisecrack that Gordon Brown had gone from Stalin to Mr Bean made some members wish his hat had been in the ring). Certainly, the party's ratings in the opinion polls began to climb at this time.

The campaign, which attracted only limited interest from the media, was only enlivened when the debate turned personal as Huhne labelled Clegg a 'flip-flopper' in terms of policy and had quickly to deny any involvement with a dossier branding his opponent as 'Calamity Clegg'. During the campaign the defection of a sitting Liberal Democrat MEP to the Conservatives attracted publicity of a negative sort. Sajjad Karim, the Euro MP for the North West of England, declared himself impressed by Cameron. At the close of the leadership campaign the Conservative leader, David Cameron, seemed to 'reach out' to the Liberal Democrats with an appeal to form a 'progressive alliance' with Conservatives and even Greens against Labour. Cable, Clegg and Huhne quickly dismissed the idea, sensing that it was mischief-making.[17]

Huhne's supporters claimed during the campaign that they were narrowing the gap on the perceived favourite. And so it proved. Clegg was declared winner on 18 December by the narrowest of margins. Of the 41,465 votes cast (around 64 per cent of those eligible to vote), Clegg took 20,988 (50.62 per cent) and Huhne 20,477 (49.38 per cent), a winning margin of just 511 votes. With less than two thirds of the party members voting, and with a wafer-thin majority, it was hardly a convincing mandate for Clegg. But it was just enough, even though turnout was down by 10,000 since Campbell's election in 2006.

On 20 December Nick Clegg unveiled his new front-bench team. His defeated leadership rival, Chris Huhne was given the pivotal position of Home Affairs spokesman. Vince Cable, who had performed exceptionally well as interim leader, remained Deputy Leader and economics spokesman. Ed Davey, the former chief of staff to Sir Menzies Campbell, replaced Michael Moore at foreign affairs (Moore was demoted to International Development). David Laws retained his Schools and Children brief but also became public services supremo. Among other changes Danny Alexander was promoted to Work and Pensions (with additional responsibility for drawing up the manifesto), Steve Webb (from the left of the party) moved to Environment, Norman Baker went to Transport, Julia Goldsworthy to Communities and Local Government, Sarah Teather to Business and Enterprise and Lembit Öpik to Housing. New to the front bench were such figures as David Howarth (shadow Solicitor General), Stephen Williams (Innovation, Universities and Skills) and Willie Rennie (chair of parliamentary campaigns). Jeremy Browne, a rising star and close Clegg ally, became Cable's number two on the Treasury team. Tim Farron was appointed to a new post as Countryside spokesman.

Although there was a 30-strong 'cabinet' (expanded from 23, with 29 of the 63 Lib Dem MPs having places in the front-bench team), in fact there were really six 'key' figures looking after the economy, home affairs, foreign affairs, public services, the environment and family. The swift reshuffle was seen by some a shift to the right, with demotion for Michael Moore and Steve Webb, though promoted, relieved of his responsibility for drafting the party election manifesto. The new team also found a place, of sorts, for Charles Kennedy, giving him an overview role on Europe.[18] In fact the enormously large Shadow Cabinet of 29 members was nearly half the parliamentary party.

Thus, in January 2008, the Liberal Democrats entered a new year with a new leader and a new team. David Laws, the newly-appointed head of public service reform, declared that 2008 would be the 'year of living dangerously' for the Liberal Democrats as they were led in a radical and daring direction. Clegg's New Year address emphasised his opposition to ID cards (he was already on record as stating that he would risk jail in his opposition to them).

On one thing all commentators agreed. Clegg and his party would face testing times over the coming months. Essentially, the party faced its second re-launch in two years against a background of poor opinion polls – 12 per cent in October 2007 (a record low) and 16 per cent in November and December. Clegg clearly needed to establish his own distinctive voice over a party that had been evenly split in the leadership election.

In January 2008 Clegg made an initial important move with the creation of a commission to carry out a 'root and branch' review of the party headed by Chris Bones, the Principal of Henley Management College. The first major dilemma to face the new leader concerned Europe, with parliament due to vote on ratification of the Treaty of Lisbon. Here Clegg faced a problem inherited from his predecessor. In an attempt to paper over internal party divisions, Campbell had promised that the parliamentary party would vote for a referendum on the principle of whether Britain stayed in or out of the EU but not for a referendum on approval of the Lisbon Treaty. Clegg turned this somewhat inconsistent and bizarre position into a vote of confidence in his leadership.[19] The situation turned into near farce. To begin with, when the Liberal Democrat amendment for an in/out referendum was not called, the party staged a much-publicised walkout at Westminster, pushing the party into the spotlight. Then, under orders to abstain over the motion for a referendum on the Lisbon Treaty, Clegg faced a rebellion. Three front-bench spokesmen defied him and resigned (these were Tim Farron (Countryside), Alistair Carmichael (Scotland and Northern Ireland) and David Heath (Justice). Ten more Liberal Democrat MPs (including some junior spokespersons) joined the rebellion. The MPs joining the rebellion came from a wide variety of constituencies, some where Euroscepticism was strong and their own majorities slender (as in ultra-marginal Somerton and Frome, or where fishing communities were strongly sceptical as in Orkney and Shetland and parts of the South West). The strength of the rebellion reflected the fact that the Liberal Democrats, once the most pro-European of all British parties, now had a vocal Eurosceptic element.

The debate fiasco seemed to commentators to suggest that Clegg's honeymoon was more of a one-night stand and added to criticism of a lacklustre start to his leadership. In the wake of all this, Clegg's keynote speech at the imminent Liverpool spring party conference needed to reassert his authority, silence any critics on NHS reform and set out a clear policy vision.

On the prospect of joining a post-election coalition, Clegg insisted in his speech that a constitutional shake-up, a 'new type of government' would be a prerequisite for any cooperation by the Liberal Democrats. He spurned talk of forming a coalition. The commitment to seek tax cuts and to reduce individuals' bills rather than boost public services was an important departure. It seemed to mark a shift from the party's social democratic position of the last decade.[20] If the Liberal Democrats would often justifiably complain about their lack of coverage in the media, the revelations of Nick Clegg's amorous activities in his earlier days certainly attracted the spotlight. His revelation that he had had 30 lovers in the past quickly gained him the nickname Cleggover.[21]

The local elections of May 2008 were the first test of Liberal Democrat fortunes under Nick Clegg's leadership (as they were of Gordon Brown's first months in office). The results turned out to be an unmitigated disaster for Labour and a triumph for the Conservatives (symbolised by the victory of Boris Johnson as Mayor of London). Against this background, with the Conservatives resurgent, there was relief for the Liberal Democrats that they managed not only a small net increase of 34 in their tally of seats won but also forced Labour narrowly into third place in terms of share of the national vote (for only the second time in the history of the Liberal Democrats, who took 25 per cent to the 24 per cent of Labour). The party could also be pleased with the capture of a number of councils, including Burnley (for the first time ever), St Albans, Hull and Sheffield (a prized target since Nick Clegg's own constituency was in the city).[22] Less cause for celebration was the loss of such councils as West Lindsey and Pendle. In addition, the party came within one seat of gaining overall control in Oldham, Cheltenham and Warrington. It had also consolidated its position as the largest party in Cardiff, Sefton and NE Lincolnshire (as well as becoming the largest party in Derby, Exeter and Wrexham). In Wales, where Liberal Democrats contested 437 of the 1,262 seats, they missed capturing Cardiff (although remaining easily the largest party), but picked up seats in Swansea, Merthyr and Rhondda Cynon Taft.

In the contest for Mayor of London, which attracted much attention as Labour's Ken Livingstone vied with Boris Johnson, the Liberal Democrats came a poor third with 9.8 per cent of the vote.[23] For Brian Paddick, campaigning on a 'greener, safer London', the result was a disappointment.[24] The results for the elections to the Greater London Assembly were also deeply worrying. Nowhere returned a Liberal Democrat by the first-past-the-post system. In the Liberal Democrat area of most strength, the South West Constituency, the party was a weak second (26.5 per cent to the Conservatives' 40.8 per cent). In Lambeth and Southwark, similarly,

Liberal Democrats were a poor second (22.7 per cent to Labour's 37.2 per cent). In no other seat could the party even secure second place. The final GLA result was Conservatives 11 seats, Labour 8, Liberal Democrats 3 (a net loss of two), Greens 2 and BNP 1. Overall, the local election outcome was something of a relief for Clegg. The mildly positive result could easily have been so much worse. But the forthcoming Crewe by-election was a different story.

With the Conservatives riding the crest of a wave after the local elections, and with Labour desperate to retain the seat amidst the ongoing turmoil over the abolition of the 10p tax rate, the Crewe and Nantwich by-election on 22 May was not an easy contest for the party. In 2005 the Liberal Democrats were in third place with 18.6 per cent of the vote, the Conservatives trailing the veteran sitting Labour MP, Gwyneth Dunwoody by 7,078 votes. Although only the 165th most winnable seat in the list of Conservative target seats, the unpopularity of Labour nationally meant that the seat was much more winnable for them than Labour's 7,000 majority might suggest.

The constituency, famous for its major railway junction, divided into two distinct halves – the more Conservative Nantwich and the well-heeled villages nearby, and the traditionally Labour Crewe. The Liberal Democrats had no real local power base in either. Their campaign began poorly when the candidate they had already selected was replaced.[25] On a 58.2 per cent turnout the Conservatives polled 20,539 votes, Labour 12,679 and the Liberal Democrats 6,040. There was a 17.6 per cent swing from Labour.

The outcome was a highly significant Conservative victory ending a 26-year period when they had failed to win a seat from another party at a by-election.[26] For the Liberal Democrats, a poor result was made worse by the obvious momentum of the Conservative advance.

In many respects, the subsequent Henley by-election caused by the resignation of the Conservative Boris Johnson after his victory in the contest for Mayor of London, was a golden opportunity. The party was already in a strong second place, and Labour was no longer a real political force. It was essentially affluent Conservative territory (such as Henley itself and Goring) with commuter suburbs for Reading that ought to have offered good Liberal Democrat prospects. But, after the Crewe and the May local election upsurge, the Conservatives were riding high. The outcome saw the Conservatives easily retain the seat with a 10,116 majority over the Liberal Democrats whose share of the vote rose only minimally (up 1.84 per cent to 27.85 per cent), a minute swing of 0.1 per cent from the Conservatives. Although Labour fell to fifth place, the real losers were the Liberals. Given that they had plenty of time to prepare for the contest, and that it was exactly the sort of southern English seat in which they were the natural challenger, it was a salutary reminder of the problems facing the party. It was 'an astonishing repulsion of the Lib Dem challenge' according to the *Guardian*, in a seat where the party had deployed all its formidable by-election black arts.[27]

The next two by-elections, both in Scotland, were infinitely worse. On 3 July Nicol Stephen resigned as Labour MP for Glasgow East, one of the toughest, most run-down, poverty-stricken, socially-deprived constituencies in the whole of the country. Male life expectancy here was 63, joblessness pockets hit 50 per cent. It was soon dubbed the by-election from hell. Normally a rock-solid Labour constituency, almost part of its birthright, it proved fertile recruiting ground for the Nationalists in the by-election. On 24 July the SNP won a historic victory, with a narrow 365 majority over Labour. The hapless Liberal Democrats came in a lowly fourth place, with a mere 3.35 per cent of the vote.[28] The Liberal share of the vote had fallen from 11.9 per cent in 2005, a 75 per cent fall and the party was even pushed into fifth place by the Conservatives. The sequence of bad by-election contests continued with Glenrothes, the Labour stronghold in central Fife in which the Liberal Democrats had come third in 2005 with 12.6 per cent of the vote. In the struggle between Labour and the SNP, with Labour emerging victorious, the Liberal Democrat vote collapsed on 6 November to a humiliating 2.6 per cent of the vote and fourth place behind even the Conservatives. This result was all the more galling as the party had won nearby Dunfermline West back in February 2006.

These by-election contests had rather overshadowed the election of a new leader of the Scottish Liberal Democrats. Tavish Scott was elected on 26 August. Born in 1966 he had been the MSP for Shetland since 1999. Also rather neglected was the revamp of the party structure initiated by Clegg – 'an attempt to seize control from the committee men', according to one source.[29] The 2008 autumn conference, the first which Nick Clegg would address as party leader, was an important event. Clegg needed both to demonstrate that the party was united behind him and also take it along the road he had decided to travel – it was to be a conference of repositioning.

The party – as *The Economist* noted – was also fighting the danger of being sidelined to anonymity.[30] Clegg put on a good performance, attacking Cameron as juvenile and the Labour Government as the 'living dead'. But the animated and impressive speech did little to attract long-lasting press notice as the media was swamped by the speculation over Gordon Brown's position. The party was successfully re-branded as tax cutting, with £20 billion in savings across Whitehall identified to fund a 4p reduction in basic rate tax (and to fund the party's own priorities). This was not without protest from the left of the party. The media also seized on the apparent shift in the party towards a more Eurosceptic stance on Europe, ditching its hard-line pro-European position.[31] It was welcomed by those, as in south-west England, who found it an election-eering handicap, but bitterly denounced by such Lib Dem MEPs as Chris Davies. Although Clegg had positioned the party as redistributive, and attacked Cameron as the 'Andrex Puppy' of British politics, in truth many felt the party was now more akin to doing a deal with the Conservatives rather than Labour. On balance, Nick Clegg had achieved a pretty good conference result – a good week at the end of a good year, declared *The Times*.[32] But there was little uplift in the opinion polls.

Meanwhile the election later in the year for the presidency of the party, to find a successor to Simon Hughes, came as something of a relief for the party establishment. There was a three-cornered contest between Ros Scott (former leader of Suffolk County Council and the Liberal Democrat spokeswoman on Communities and Local Government in the Lords), Lembit Öpik (the somewhat flamboyant MP for Montgomeryshire perhaps best known for his engagement to one of the Cheeky Girls) and Chandila Fernando. Ros Scott secured an easy victory with 20,736 votes (72 per cent) to 6,247 (21.7 per cent) for Lembit Öpik and 1,799 (6.3 per cent) for Chandila Fernando. Turnout was 47.8 per cent of the party's 60,000 membership. The press reported that privately Clegg's senior allies were mounting a stop-Öpik campaign.[33] Meanwhile, some unwelcome publicity arose when the *Sunday Mirror* gave details of a conversation heard by one of their reporters in which Nick Clegg apparently made some pretty disparaging remarks about his senior colleagues. Some he appeared actually to dislike, others were dismissed as not up to the job.[34]

Following these well-publicised indiscretions, financial problems returned to trouble the party once again in December 2008. One of the party's biggest donors, Lord Jacobs, resigned in protest over the party's 'timid' tax policies. A party member since 1972, and a Liberal Democrat peer since 1997, he was believed to have donated around £1 million over the past 20 years.[35] This defection was doubly unwelcome following the conviction *in absentia*, of a former previous large donor.

Meanwhile, the opinion polls only grudgingly began to revive from the dismal showings earlier in the year. In terms of winners in 2008, it was Vince Cable, the party's economic guru, who had captured the public imagination.[36] Described by the *Daily Telegraph* as 'the sage of the credit crunch', his prescient warnings about the housing market bubble and the coming banking crisis gave his words great authority. Wistfully, many in the party conceded that he was 'the best leader the party never had'. If Cable was having a good recession, Clegg was only having a mixed one.

In the opinion polls, the New Year failed to raise Liberal spirits. The first opinion poll of 2009 gave Cameron's Conservatives a seven-point lead over Labour with the Liberal Democrats stuck around 15 per cent (even though speculation about a possible hung parliament had increased attention on the Liberal Democrats). On 8 January Clegg took the opportunity to reshuffle some of his front-bench team. Simon Hughes became the new Energy and Environment spokesman, David Howarth moved to Justice, David Heath (who had resigned over the Lisbon Treaty) moved to Shadow Commons Leader, Jenny Willott moved to Families (replacing Susan Kramer who left the front bench to head the campaign against the expansion of Heathrow) and Steve Webb moved to Work and Pensions. In two other appointments, Lynne Featherstone was given charge of the party's online campaigning and John Sharkey (Clegg's adviser on strategic communications) became Deputy Chairman of the party's general election campaign. There was also speculation that senior Labour figures were attempting to line up Sir Menzies Campbell as the next Speaker of the Commons (although any such scheme was to be overtaken by events following the expenses scandal).[37]

As 2009 opened, British politics was dominated by two themes: the erosion of Labour support witnessed in the opinion polls (down to 28 per cent in February, with the Liberal Democrats on 22 per cent) and the growing realisation that in the changed fiscal and economic situation after the credit crunch old policies and old commitments would have to be reviewed.

As far as the polls were concerned, the New Year opened on a fluctuating note. The *Guardian*/ICM poll, published on 27 January 2009, gave Liberal Democrats 16 per cent, down four points compared to January 2008. However, another poll registered 22 per cent Liberal Democrat support. Meanwhile, an *Evening Standard* poll for London constituencies gave the Liberals only 13 per cent, down from 22 per cent in 2005 (suggesting five Liberal Democrat seats in the capital could be lost in a general election).

Of more immediate concern for the party was the changed economic climate of a Britain mired in recession. As commentators talked of a 'new age of austerity' Clegg called in February for government spending cuts of £20 billion (to be funded by barring middle-class families from claiming tax credits, ending the child trust fund and scrapping road building projects). By the spring, Clegg had gone further in repositioning party policy. He had now formally abandoned the party's short-lived pledge to go into the next general election promising tax cuts, given the drastic deterioration in the public finances.[38]

In this uncertain political and economic climate, the first really major test of the national political temperature would take place in June with the European and municipal elections. As the run-up to the 4 June elections approached, it was revealed that Labour MPs disillusioned with Gordon Brown's leadership had held private talks with the Liberal Democrats about the possibility of defecting.[39] The revelation, made by former leader Lord Ashdown, disclosed that some senior Labour figures were prepared to leave the party because they feared it could lurch to the left after a general election defeat. A figure of between 6 and 12 Blairite defectors was mentioned. It all seemed very reminiscent of the split that led to the emergence of the SDP in the early 1980s. However, nothing came of these reports.

Meanwhile, the elections of 4 June presented a difficult test for the Liberal Democrats. Although there were local elections for 27 county councils and a clutch of unitary authorities, the biggest test of public opinion would be in the voting for the European Parliament. At the previous European elections, back in 2004, the party had been forced into fourth place behind UKIP (see p. 270). Now, with the country in recession, the Labour Government in seeming disarray and a general election due at the latest by June 2010, it was vital for the Liberal Democrats to make an impact.

However, another factor had entered the equation. The parliamentary expenses scandal dominated the political scene in the early summer of 2009. A series of allegations embroiled senior figures of all parties as juicy revelations of moats, mortgage fiddles, flipping of homes and almost any excuse to filch money emerged.

The Liberal Democrats did not escape completely. Their former leader, Sir Menzies Campbell, claimed nearly £10,000 expenses for luxury home furnishings, including scatter cushions, a king-sized bed and a loo brush. Similarly, Richard Younger-Ross, the MP for Teignbridge, claimed over £4,300 for mirrors, hi-fi and home décor. Many were smaller, often fairly trivial claims – from Julia Goldsworthy's leather rocking chair to Chris Huhne's fluffy dusters and Charles Kennedy's brace of toffee-coloured teddy bears (apparently an 'error'). Also embroiled were some Liberal Democrat peers. Baroness Tonge, for example, seemingly billed the taxpayer for a second home in central London and then rented it out to an MP after being made a peer.

Also caught up in this scandal was the Speaker of the Commons, Michael Martin. The Liberal Democrats, and Clegg in particular, defied traditional conventions and increased the pressure on the Speaker to step down – citing his dogged defence of the status quo when drastic and radical reform was urgently needed.[40] As a motion of confidence in the Speaker was being prepared, Liberal Democrats very publicly withdrew their support from him. He duly resigned.[41]

The effect of the expenses scandal could be seen first in the opinion polls and then in the June local and European elections. Labour support slumped to new lows. An ICM/*Sunday Telegraph* poll on 31 May showed the Conservatives on 40 per cent, Liberal Democrats on 25 per cent and Labour trailing in third place on a mere 22 per cent, its lowest showing since 1987. Yet the previous day a Populus poll for *The Times* showed the Liberal Democrats on 15 per cent. The electorate seemed to be in volatile mood, with support for the smaller parties fluctuating wildly.

The outcome of the local elections was mixed. In some areas of previous strength, there were reverses. Thus in the county councils Liberal Democrats suffered a net loss of 19 seats in Devon, 8 in Somerset and 5 in Oxfordshire. These were partly offset by gains in Cumbria (6 seats), Essex (4), Hertfordshire (3), Lancashire (6), Leicestershire (3), Nottinghamshire (4) and West Sussex (5) – mainly a trickle of gains from Labour's collapse.[42]

Overall, although the Liberal Democrat share of the vote easily surpassed Labour, the local election results were something of a disappointment, an opportunity missed. The party lost its power base in the South West, losing control of both Somerset and Devon and failing to take the new unitary authority in Cornwall. Partly the losses in the South West could be put down to the anti-incumbent factor (and also to the hostility to the EU in some areas). Nonetheless these results boded ill for the parliamentary seats the party would be defending in the 2010 general election.

This relatively poor result was repeated when the votes were counted in the European elections. Here the outcome gave the Conservatives 25 seats, Labour 13, UKIP 13, the Liberal Democrats 11, the BNP 2, Greens 2 and Nationalists 2 in Scotland and 1 in Wales. Even more remarkable than the tally of seats was the distribution of votes cast compared to 2004: the Conservatives took 27.1 per cent (up 1 per cent), UKIP 16.5 per cent (up 0.3 per cent), Labour 15.7 per cent (down no less than 6.9 per cent), Liberal Democrats 13.7 per cent (down a disappointing 1.2 per cent), Greens 8.6 per cent (up 2.4 per cent) and the BNP 6.2 per cent (an increase of 1.3 per cent). In Scotland the SNP vote rose slightly, Plaid Cymru in Wales decreased marginally. Turnout was 39 per cent. Forty per cent of the overall vote had been won by parties not represented in the Westminster Parliament.

Labour's share of the vote, at 15.7 per cent, was its worst in any post-war poll. The party was beaten into second place by a resurgent UKIP with 13 MEP seats. The Liberal Democrat results – one additional MEP, but fourth place nationally in terms of votes – were more mixed. Back in 2004 the party had played down its pro-EU stance (partly from pressure in some constituencies, partly from the UKIP threat) and garnered votes on its anti-Iraq War policy. In 2009, the Liberal Democrats had no such popular appeal. Hence a closer examination of the regional voting showed some very worrying features of the party's performance (see Table 21.1).

Table 21.1 The 2009 European Elections: Results by Region for the Liberal Democrats

	Seats Won	Share of Vote	Position
North East	1	17.6	3rd
South West	1	17.2	3rd
North West	1	14.3	4th
South East	2	14.1	3rd
East of England	1	13.8	3rd
London	1	13.7	3rd
Yorkshire & The Humber	1	13.2	4th
East Midlands	1	12.3	4th
West Midlands	1	12.0	4th
Scotland	1	11.5	4th
Wales	0	10.7	5th

In no region had the party won more votes than any other party. In no region was it even in second place. Its best result (in terms of votes) was in the North East (17.6 per cent where it came third), its worst result was Wales (a lowly 10.7 per cent of the vote and fifth place, with not a single MEP returned). In the South West, a traditional stronghold, the party was in third place with 17.2 per cent of the vote. In five areas (Yorkshire and the Humber, the East Midlands, the West Midlands, the North West and Scotland) the party was in fourth place.

Why had the party not fared better? Although not disastrous, the results were disappointing. Clearly, if the party had once garnered a major protest vote, other parties were now successfully chasing the disillusioned voter. Four out of every ten votes cast went to parties not represented at Westminster – and hence not damaged by the expenses scandal. Moreover, UKIP was clearly a potent force in EU elections where electors were not returning MPs to Westminster. The Liberal Democrats were learning the bitter lesson that they were not the only home for protest votes in a multi-party system.

After the 4 June local and European elections, two further by-elections provided difficult tests for the Liberal Democrats. Norwich North, presented an awkward challenge. This seat, where the sitting highly-popular MP Ian Gibson had precipitated a by-election over the expenses scandal, required a 5.6 per cent swing for the Conservatives to win. The Liberal Democrats had been a relatively poor third (unlike neighbouring Norwich South where the party was a strong second) and had not polled well in the 2009 local elections.[43]

Ian Gibson, caught up in the expenses scandal, was summarily ordered by the Labour Party to stand down, without a chance to appeal over what many of his constituents saw as a borderline issue.[44] In the European elections both Greens and UKIP had done well in the area. The Liberal Democrat campaign made little impact (despite April Pond, a charismatic candidate) and most commentators believed the Labour vote in a fairly traditional Labour seat would stay at home rather than defect.

In the event, the outcome of the first by-election in the wake of the expenses scandal was a lacklustre result for the Liberal Democrats, whose share of the vote fell from 16.2 per cent to 13.97 per cent. The Conservatives won the seat with a 7,348 majority on a swing of 16.5 per cent from Labour, whose vote collapsed, although the absolute Conservative vote was down.[45] It seemed many Labour voters, disillusioned with the treatment of their former MP Ian Gibson, had indeed simply stayed at home, sickened by the sleaze issue. However UKIP (11.83 per cent, up from 2.4 per cent) and the Greens (9.74 per cent, up from 2.7 per cent) both registered their best-ever performance in a by-election for Westminster.

There were several worrying factors for the Liberal Democrats: the strong swing to the Conservatives was almost the same as that evidenced in Crewe, although the pattern was different: the anti-Labour protest vote, far from coming to them, had gone to minor parties such as UKIP, the Greens and even the BNP. Moreover the lack of progress in a Labour-held seat did not augur well for the party's strategy of attacking such seats in industrial England at the general election. Some Liberal Democrats could argue that Norwich North had always been a hard-fought seat where the battle had traditionally been between Conservative and Labour, but given that the party was in a good second place in neighbouring Norwich South the result was still a worrying disappointment.[46] The party was not capitalising on the anti-politics mood after the expenses scandal.

Indeed, on the eve of the 2009 autumn party conference at Bournemouth (the last before the 2010 general election), there were signs that not all was entirely well with the party. It was reflected in party finance and party membership, in disappointing election results and stagnant poll support. Over the year, party membership had suffered a 10 per cent loss, down now to around 60,000. Meanwhile, party income in 2009 was reported to be £5.5 million, against expenditure of £6 million. The party's financial reserves had halved to £460,000 from £1.1 million in 2007. The party was clearly struggling financially to cover its costs, especially if contributions to the pension fund were factored in. On this basis there was a loss of £670,000 in 2008.[47]

The party had also received unwelcome publicity during the summer of 2009 with two defections to the Conservatives – the barrister Chamali Fernando (who had attempted to run as Liberal Democrat candidate for Mayor of London in 2007) and her brother Chandila Fernando (who had run unsuccessfully to become President of the party in 2008).[48] This came on top of the defection of the Liberal Democrat candidate for Chelsea and Fulham, Norsheen Bhatti, in April.

In the higher echelons of the party, where some had criticised Cowley Street for lack of innovation and near paralysis, major changes had also taken place. Lord Rennard, the Chief Executive of the party since 2003, was replaced by Chris Fox (there had been some reports of disagreements between Clegg and Rennard).

With lacklustre local election and disappointing European results, It was not surprising that some blamed Nick Clegg for this atmosphere of malaise. This was hardly fair. In fact, as *The Economist* noted, Clegg had often led the way, but not the polls. He had spoken effectively and forcefully on the campaign for fairer treatment of Gurkha veterans, he had taken a lead on the monitoring of G20 police behaviour, he had led criticism of Michael Martin (The Speaker) and had generally handled the expenses scandal well.

But it was true few people were sure what he stood for. He was eclipsed in the political limelight by Vince Cable as the guru of the crash. Prior to the autumn party conference, on 22 July the party had issued its document *A Fresh Start for Britain*. With its concern over levels of government debt, some political commentators saw this as a shift in the party's fiscal policy to a position nearer the Conservatives – moving to consider tax rises and a cut in public sector pay because of the economic crisis.

It was against this background that Clegg began repositioning his party's place in the political spectrum and also accelerating the party's change in electoral strategy to an assault on Labour. Certainly, Clegg urgently needed to redefine his party's message. Where was the future of the party to lie in a very changed political climate?

To some extent this was done with the publication by the think-tank Demos of *The Liberal Moment*. This pamphlet effectively set out a clarion call for the Liberal Democrats to replace Labour by becoming the progressive party of the Left. Writing in *The Times*, Clegg was to declare:

> So the real choice at the next election is not the old red-blue/blue-red pendulum of British politics. It is between yellow and blue. A choice between a liberal movement – led by the Liberal Democrats – that is attracting disaffected progressive voters from a Labour Party which will take years to recover, if at all; and a Conservative Party that parrots the language of change to maintain the status quo.[49]

So what change of electoral strategy would the Liberal Democrats adopt in these circumstances when the general election came? It seemed now as if the plan was essentially to be on the defensive in the south of England against a revived Conservative Party, but to attack a weakened Labour Party in the industrial seats of the North and Midlands. To some extent this reversal of Liberal Democrat electoral strategy had already taken place. Whereas in 1997 and 2001 most of the party's gains were in southern England from the Conservatives, in 2005 the picture had been different. The party lost five seats to the Conservatives whilst gaining three – but in addition taking nine seats from Labour. In the 2008 local elections this trend could be seen with Liberal Democrat success in Burnley, Hull and Sheffield and advances in Derby and Oldham.[50]

There were obvious problems with this strategy. There was the simple one of arithmetic. Out of the 100 most winnable seats for the Liberal Democrats, only 17 were in northern England (whereas 48 were in the Conservative-held south of England). Even more important, this strategy would hardly help the Left – simply replacing Labour MPs with Liberal Democrats would not help a united progressive future. Although there were 52 constituencies where Liberals were nominally second to Labour, many of these were hopeless cases.

It was against this background that the party faced its annual conference. The outcome of the 2009 Bournemouth party conference was a disappointment. 'Missing the Liberal Moment' declared *The Times* which pointed to old divisions surfacing again.[51] Fractious, lacklustre and troublesome were words frequently used by commentators. Party conferences in the past had been rebellious and this continued the tradition. Nick Clegg's call for 'savage' cuts to reduce the national debt, the possible abandonment of the pledge to abolish university tuition fees and a somewhat botched announcement of a tax on homes worth over £1 million by Vince Cable all stoked up murmurings of discontent. It seemed Cable (hitherto held in almost saintly regard by the party) had failed to consult widely before floating the idea. In any case, those MPs representing wealthy constituencies were unlikely to see the proposal as a vote winner.

There were, however, positive aspects. The party took a major initiative in debating the war in Afghanistan following a warning from Paddy Ashdown and Nick Clegg that the Taliban would not be beaten without a major change in strategy. Conference subsequently passed a motion calling for just this. There were also important decisions on requiring Liberal Democrat councils to cut their carbon emissions by 10 per cent in 2010.

If the official theme of the conference had been 'A Fresh Start for Britain' the outcome was hardly a fresh start either for Clegg or the party. With Clegg committed to targeting child benefit and public sector pay and pensions, there was clear disaffection from some on the left of the party.

The first by-election after the Bournemouth conference (and another contest related to the expenses affair) came in Glasgow North East following the resignation of the Speaker, Michael Martin, on 21 June.[52] It was an unattractive constituency for the Liberal Democrats (and a very unwelcome contest for Labour given the SNP's earlier by-election triumph in nearby Glasgow East). SNP attempts to move a writ for an early contest failed and the by-election was not held until 12 November.

In 2005 no Liberal Democrat or Conservative had fought the constituency which the Speaker had held with a 10,134 majority over the SNP, with Socialist Labour in third place. Given that the constituency adjoined Glasgow East (won by the SNP in the by-election of 24 July 2008), this was in every way a hopeless seat for the Liberal Democrats. It was a seat with the second highest premature mortality rate and a male unemployment rate among the highest in Scotland; and the estates of Possil and Milton with their crime and poverty. The outcome was an unexpectedly comfortable Labour victory with an 8,111 majority over the Nationalists on a lowly turnout (less than a third of the electorate voted). The Liberals came sixth with an abysmal 474 votes (2.3 per cent of those cast).[53] It was among the worst Liberal Democrat results ever.

On 30 November Nick Clegg unveiled a range of tax proposals – including a reduction of tax relief on high value pensions and a pledge that no income tax would be paid on the first £10,000 of income earned

– but most attention centred on the U-turn over the proposed 'mansion tax'. Under the new proposals, properties valued at over £2 million would incur a 1 per cent charge – not the 0.5 per cent charge on properties over £1 million proposed earlier.

With the advent of 2010, the general election now dominated the political scene. Nick Clegg effectively launched the party's election campaign on 11 January. Warning that 'the world has changed' he announced the shelving of previous party pledges on the extension of free childcare, free personal care for the elderly and the 'citizen's pension'. Clegg also confirmed that tuition fees would now be ended over a six-year period. Even though pledges amounting to £18 billion of spending had been axed, the details of how the Liberal Democrats would meet their commitment to halve the deficit over four years were not given. Clegg also sidestepped the vexed issue of what his party would do in the event of a hung parliament, but he did emphasise the need to break up the biggest City banks, close tax loopholes for the richest and questioned the principles of 'economies of scale' in business. Unlike many politicians, at least Clegg had broken his party's promises before, not after, an election.

There was a curious development from Labour early in 2010. On 2 February Gordon Brown proposed a raft of constitutional reforms including the news that MPs would shortly vote on whether there should be a referendum (to be held by October 2011) on switching to the alternative vote (AV) electoral system for Westminster elections. It was, as Chris Huhne the Lib Dems' Home Affairs spokesman commented, something of a death-bed conversion.

There were other aspects of the announcement that prompted much speculation. Was it an attempt to woo the Liberal Democrats in the event of a hung parliament? And if Brown believed in the AV system, why announce the proposals only three months away from a May general election when the Constitutional Reform and Governance Bill had no chance of becoming law? On 9 February the Commons voted 365 to 187 in favour of a referendum – with strong opposition from the Conservatives and some backbenchers. If this was Brown's commitment to 'new politics' some cynics found it remarkably similar to the old discredited politics. The election was to be very much fought against this background. The appearance of the Legg Report back in October 2009 had ensured that the unsavoury expenses scandal and the image of the 'rotten parliament' were still very much in people's minds.

In a further development on 15 February 2010 the *Guardian* reported (prematurely as it turned out) that the Liberal Democrats were planning to rule out forming a coalition with either the Conservatives or Labour if the coming election produced a hung parliament. Instead, the Liberal Democrats would forgo any Cabinet posts, but focus on winning support for four key demands:

1. investment of extra funds in education for disadvantaged children;
2. tax reform aimed at taking a million out of tax while requiring capital gains and income to be taxed at the same rate;
3. a rebalancing of the economy in a greener direction;
4. constitutional reforms to ensure a fairer voting system and a democratically elected House of Lords.

These would be the proposals which, over time, a minority government would have to deliver.

The spring 2010 party conference, held in Birmingham, provided the launch pad for the forthcoming general election. The party unveiled its somewhat unwieldy theme 'Change that works for you, Building a fairer Britain', and Clegg reiterated the four key planks on which the Liberal Democrats would campaign: fairer taxes, ensuring children get a fair start in life, a fairer, greener economy together with open and transparent politics.

However, the party was more opaque than transparent over what it would do in the event of a hung parliament (to which the polls now pointed). Clegg insisted it was the 45 million voters, not the Liberal Democrat leader, who would be kingmaker. He again emphasised that the electorate would, when the polls closed, leave one party with a moral majority – but whether that was in seats won or votes cast was left very unclear. As political analysts sought to see if Clegg was positioning his party to the right or left, some were driven to conclude that the party was going both ways at once (as indeed it had to in order to woo potential Conservative voters in the South and potential Labour converts in the industrial North). Certainly, the danger of creating a very divisive split with either the radical or the more conservative elements in his party always remained if the election left the party holding the balance of power.

22
Voting for Deadlock:
The General Election of May 2010

The general election of May 2010 proved to be an extraordinary affair. Both the campaign itself and the hung parliament which it produced provided the heady stuff of high political drama. Curiously, however, when the election was finally called for 6 May, the contest got off to a somewhat subdued start with the Liberal Democrats trailing well behind in the opinion polls.

Most of the proposals in the Liberal Democrat manifesto, launched on 14 April, had been well flagged in advance. The party pledged to cut spending more slowly than either the Conservatives or Labour. The heart of their message was to 'hardwire fairness' into society. Much prominence was given to the pledge that those on incomes below £10,000 would pay no tax, class sizes in schools would be reduced and (eventually) tuition fees scrapped. To pay for these measures there would be a £2 billion banking levy and a £12 billion curb on tax concessions and loopholes.

It was not the manifesto which galvanised the campaign but a new feature of British elections: the TV debate. On 15 April the first of the three television debates featuring the three main party leaders (the first-ever such debate in British electoral history) utterly transformed the election campaign. A sterile even rather boring campaign became galvanised. The main factor was the polished, personable and persuasive performance of Nick Clegg (he went, in his own words, from terrified to terrific). The result was a dramatic, almost seismic upsurge in Liberal Democrat support in the opinion polls. In some, the party overtook Labour to come in neck and neck alongside the Conservatives. Some even put the Liberals in first place. On the basis of projections from all these polls, no party would win an outright majority, a hung parliament would ensue and the Liberal Democrats would hold the balance of power. Clegg would be kingmaker, electoral reform could be achieved and British politics would be transformed. It was all heady stuff and 'Cleggmania' entered the political vocabulary. It seemed as if the fresh appeal of Clegg had tapped into a deep vein of anti-politics, the simmering anger and resentment at sordid expenses scandals, obscene bonuses for bankers and the staleness of the old two parties. It was, as *The Economist* called it, the granola-eaters' revenge.[1] But was it (as some like Lord Ashdown feared), merely a spasm? Would the balloon burst as quickly as it had appeared? The second television debate confirmed this was no momentary infatuation. Despite fiercer attacks Clegg again performed confidently and appealingly. Both Labour and Conservatives responded to this new factor.

The Conservatives now switched part of the thrust of their attack away from Brown to Clegg. Parts of the right-wing press launched rabid and often scurrilous attacks on Clegg, none of which really found their mark. Labour also responded belatedly to the threat now posed by the Liberal Democrats (accusing Clegg of arrogance and hostility after he had signalled he would not prop up a discredited Gordon Brown).

The final television debate failed to burst the Liberal bubble. At times slightly sidelined, and perhaps losing some of his novelty and shine, Clegg still gave as good as he got (albeit under pressure on issues such as immigration and Europe). Cameron was judged the winner, Brown the loser. But with the Labour campaign faltering and the Conservatives seemingly regaining some momentum, the polls were now giving conflicting figures for the Liberal Democrats. In some, the party was still neck and neck with the Conservatives, in others it had slipped well back into third place behind Labour.

A significant media boost for the Liberal Democrats came with the declaration of support on 1 May from the *Guardian*, strongly praising the party's commitment to electoral reform. The same day *The Times* switched its support from Labour to the Conservatives (which it had not supported since 1992). On 2 May the *Observer* also came out strongly in support of the Liberal Democrats.

In the final days of the campaign, three senior Labour figures argued the case for tactical voting for the Liberal Democrats to keep out the Conservatives. The Cabinet Minister, Peter Hain (interviewed by the *Independent* and himself a former Liberal) even foresaw the merits of a four-year 'partnership government' with the Liberal Democrats.[2] Ed Balls, the Children's Secretary and a close confidant of Gordon Brown and Tessa Jowell, the Olympics Minister, also hinted at tactical support for Liberal Democrat candidates. These overtures were denounced by the party leaders as Brown called for the maximum party vote. At the same time, the Liberal Democrats widened their attack on Labour-held seats (in such constituencies as Liverpool, Wavertree, Glasgow North, Lewisham, Durham and Redcar) with a hitherto solid Labour tradition. As polling day neared, financial turmoil in Europe following the Greek debt crisis, and wild stock market gyrations, all seemed to show the need for a clear mandate from the election. After such an unpredictable campaign it was hardly surprising the outcome was exactly the opposite.

The outcome of the election was the first hung parliament since February 1974. The votes cast are shown in Table 22.1. For the Conservatives, it was an impressive result. The party had gained 100 seats, losing only three. But this net gain of 97 (the highest since 1931) was not enough to secure an overall majority. The Conservatives had won more seats and more votes than any other party. Nationally, the overall swing was calculated at 5.0 per cent from Labour to Conservative and 1.4 per cent from Liberal Democrat to Conservative (although there were a host of extraordinarily divergent swings, not just from region to region but from constituency to constituency).

Table 22.1 The May 2010 General Election Result*

	Seats	*% Vote*	*Votes*
Conservative	306	36.1	10,706,647
Labour	258	29.0	8,604,358
Liberal Democrats	57	23.0	6,827,938
SNP	6	1.7	491,386
Plaid Cymru	3	0.7	165,394
Others	19	9.6	2,857,915

* excluding Thirsk and Malton which polled later due to the death of a candidate

For Labour, the party gained only three seats (two from by-election losses) but lost 94, a net loss of 91. It was the biggest swing against Labour since the 1930s, but not quite the catastrophe that had at times seemed likely. The Liberal Democrats finished with 57 seats, over 6,825,000 votes and a national share of 23 per cent. After the heady optimism engendered by the campaign and their support in the opinion polls, the result was in many ways a bitter disappointment. The party gained only eight seats and lost 13 compared to 2005. Its 23 per cent share of the vote was barely above its 2005 level. In terms of swing, there had been a 1.4 per cent swing to the Conservatives from the Liberal Democrats, but a 3.6 per cent national swing from Labour to the Liberal Democrats. The seats gained by Liberal Democrats (compared to 2005) included a handful from Labour (Bradford East, Brent Central, Burnley, Norwich

South and Redcar) and the former Conservative-held seats of Eastbourne and Wells. These seats were, to say the least, a mixed bunch. To offset these gains the Liberal Democrats suffered some wide-ranging losses. These losses included Camborne and Redruth, Chesterfield, Cornwall South East, Dunfermline West, Harrogate and Knaresborough, Hereford and South Herefordshire, Montgomeryshire, Oxford West and Abingdon, Richmond Park, Romsey and Southampton North, and Winchester (the former constituency of Mark Oaten).

The three most prominent Liberal Democrat casualties were all to the Conservatives: Evan Harris in Oxford West, Susan Kramer in affluent Richmond Park (defeated by the millionaire Zac Goldsmith) and the ebullient Lembit Öpik in the rural Welsh Montgomeryshire constituency.

As a result of these gains and losses (and MPs who had retired), there were 11 new Liberal Democrat MPs. The newcomers to the Liberal Democrat ranks included Stephen Lloyd at Eastbourne and, most unexpected of all, Simon Wright in Redcar. There were only seven women Liberal Democrat MPs (down from ten). This compared to 48 Conservative and 81 Labour out of a total of 142 in the new Commons. No less than 40 per cent of Liberal Democrat MPs had been educated privately – reinforcing the male, middle-class image of the party. It was an election of extraordinary diverse behaviour. Swings were extremely volatile. Thus Guildford, the top target in the Liberal Democrats' sights to take from the Conservatives, produced a 7,782 Conservative majority. Yet the party won Wells, nineteenth on its target list. Against Labour, the Liberal Democrats failed to take the ultra-marginal Edinburgh South yet took Redcar (the most unlikely of all the Liberal Democrat gains) on a swing of 21.8 per cent. The voters were clearly refusing to follow a set pattern. At times the outcome seemed more like a giant by-election. Some examples of this diversity of swing are given in Table 22.2.

The same phenomenon was to be seen against Labour. There were large swings to the Liberal Democrats, from Ashfield to Pontypridd, but in part matched by swings in the opposite direction (as at Chesterfield or Edinburgh West).

In terms of regions, the South West (and particularly Cornwall) produced mixed results. Hampshire also saw two seats lost. There was no breakthrough in Wales or Scotland (indeed Scotland produced in May 2010 an exact replica of the 2005 result). Whilst there were scattered gains from Labour in the North (one in Lancashire, one in Yorkshire and one in the North East) there was no new solid phalanx of Liberal Democrat territory. In the regions there were no great marked changes in Liberal Democrat support – up 2.2 per cent in both the East Midlands and Yorkshire/Humberside – but down 3.8 per cent in Scotland (where Labour put up a resilient performance). The Liberal Democrats picked up more lower-middle-class support than in 2005 but lost support among unskilled workers and the unemployed.

Table 22.2   Swings from Con to Lib Dem, Lib Dem to Con

Constituency	Swing
(a) Over 4 per cent swing (to Lib Dems)	
Westmorland and Lonsdale	11.06
Sheffield Hallam	6.86
Bosworth	5.87
Leeds North West	5.44
Cheltenham	4.33
Carshalton and Wallington	4.26
(b) Over 7.5 per cent swing (to Con)	
Montgomeryshire	13.15
Orpington	12.19
St Ives	10.39
Cornwall South East	9.13
Winchester	9.09
Berwick-upon-Tweed	8.29

Despite the loss of some important seats, the Liberal Democrats still retained some pretty impregnable strongholds in 2010. Their greatest percentage of the vote (over 55 per cent) was in Orkney and Shetland (61.97), Westmorland and Lonsdale (60.01), Bath (56.6), Yeovil (55.71) and Norfolk North (55.48). In all, the party had 15 seats with majorities over their nearest challengers of over 7,500 votes.

On this calculation, their seven entrenched power bases (all with majorities over 10,000), were Sheffield Hallam (Nick Clegg's seat, 15,284), Ross, Skye and Lochaber (Charles Kennedy's constituency, 13,070), Yeovil (13,036), Westmorland and Lonsdale (12,264), Twickenham (Vince Cable's south-west London seat, 12,140), Norfolk North (11,626), Bristol West (11,366) and Bath (11,183). In terms of swing required to unseat the sitting Liberal Democrats, the six safest seats are (with per cent majorities over second place candidates): Orkney and Shetland (51.3), Ross, Skye and Lochaber (37.5), Sheffield Hallam (29.8), Bath (25.2), Westmorland and Lonsdale (23.8) and Norfolk North (23.4).

One very obvious problem with the Liberal Democrat safe seats is that they do not fit a very homogeneous pattern. They range from rural Scottish and Welsh seats (Ross, Skye and Lochaber, Ceredigion) to middle-class suburbs (Twickenham, Kingston and Surbiton, Leeds North West, Sheffield Hallam) to inner city areas (Bermondsey and Old Southwark). As against these Liberal Democrat strongholds, the party finds itself with a fair number of seats with wafer-thin majorities and very vulnerable to any swing against them at the next general election. There are 15 Liberal Democrat seats with majorities of less than 3,000 over their nearest opponents. Five seats have majorities of under 1,000 (Solihull, 175; Dorset Mid and Poole North, 269; Norwich South, 310; Bradford East, 365 and Wells, 800). Of the 15 most vulnerable Liberal Democrat seats, the Conservatives are second in nine, Labour in six. These six seats where Labour are challenging will be key Labour targets at the next election.[3]

Any squeeze or pincer movement against the Liberal Democrats by both Conservative and Labour could produce substantial losses. The single most disappointing aspect of the results was the failure to make gains from Labour. After Labour's 13 years in power, the Liberal Democrats gained only four seats held by Labour at the dissolution. Two were won with the narrowest of majorities (Norwich South and Bradford East) whilst Redcar was clearly the result of very local factors (the huge 21.8 per cent swing to the Liberal Democrats was the largest swing in any seat and must have been closely linked to the decommissioning of the local Corus steel plant with 1,600 redundancies).

Most frustrating for the Liberal Democrats was that some of the highest swings to them from Labour were in seats that were hopeless cases (17.2 per cent in Ashfield, 16.9 per cent in Merthyr Tydfil and Rhymney, 14 per cent in Barnsley East). There were numerous examples (not least in inner city areas and South Wales) of substantial swings to the Liberal Democrats that just fell short of giving them victory. Table 22.3 sets out the electoral frustration for the party.

To add insult to injury, in just the seats which Liberal Democrats hoped to win from Labour, there were frustratingly small (or no) swings – as in Edinburgh South, Islington South and Finsbury, Aberdeen South and Edinburgh North and Leith. If the strategy of winning seats in the industrial North had thus largely failed (the Liberal Democrats gained no new parliamentary seats in Manchester, Liverpool, Hull or Newcastle), the party also faces the dilemma of where its next electoral thrust must be directed. Will it be against Labour, or the Conservatives, or both?

The May 2010 election has left the Liberal Democrats as very strong challengers in 20 seats where the newly-elected MP has a majority of under 3,000. It is symbolic of the Liberal Democrat dilemma that ten of these are Conservative-held and ten Labour-held (see Table 22.4).

Table 22.3   Examples of Major Swings from Labour to Liberal Democrat*
(by order of swing)

Constituency	Swing	Result
Redcar	21.80	Lib Dem gain
Ashfield	17.20	Lab hold
Merthyr Tydfil and Rhymney	16.92	Lab hold
Barnsley East	14.02	Lab hold
Pontypridd	13.30	Lab hold
Hull North	12.18	Lab hold
Burnley	9.58	Lib Dem gain
Salford and Eccles	9.43	Lab hold
Sheffield Heeley	9.23	Lab hold
Newport East	8.35	Lab hold
Stoke Central	8.33	Lab hold
Bradford East	7.57	Lib Dem gain
Sheffield Central	7.36	Lab hold

* excluding Brent Central (complicated by earlier by-election)

Table 22.4   The 20 Liberal Democrat Hopefuls (listed in order of majority in 2010)

Constituency	Majority	Won By
Camborne and Redruth	66	Con
Oldham East and Saddleworth	103	Lab
Sheffield Central	165	Lab
Oxford West and Abingdon	176	Con
Ashfield	192	Lab
Edinburgh South	316	Lab
Truro and Falmouth	435	Con
Swansea West	504	Lab
Newton Abbot	523	Con
Chesterfield	549	Lab
Hull North	641	Lab
Rochdale	889	Lab
Harrogate and Knaresborough	1,039	Con
Montgomeryshire	1,184	Con
Watford	1,425	Con
Newport East	1,650	Lab
Edinburgh North and Leith	1,724	Lab
St Albans	2,305	Con
Hereford and Herefordshire South	2,481	Con
Weston-super-Mare	2,691	Con

Although overshadowed by the general election, the local elections held the same day also produced very disappointing results for the Liberal Democrats, most particularly in the big cities where the party had recently been either in control or had a strong presence.

Voting took place in May 2010 for all the 32 London boroughs, 36 metropolitan authorities and 20 unitary authorities. Nearly 16,000 candidates were contesting 4,222 seats. Most of these seats were last fought in 2006, when Labour had done extremely badly.

This time round, Labour gained over 400 seats, and made a net gain of around 15 councils. The Conservatives and Liberal Democrats each lost around 120 seats. This much-needed boost for Labour included the capture of Liverpool from the Liberal Democrats. In both Rochdale and Sheffield, the party lost power. The Liberal Democrats had hoped to take seats and control in parts of London, but here again it was a bad night. The Conservatives gained Richmond and Liberal Democrats lost heavily in such areas as Islington and failed to make inroads elsewhere.

Against this background of numerous failures and limited successes, how had the Liberal Democrats really performed? It was, declared the *Guardian*, a decent but disappointing result.[4] The electoral system had worked once more against the party (it took 119,000 votes to elect a Liberal Democrat, 34,000 to elect a Conservative and 33,000 to elect a Labour MP). The press, by and large, had been voraciously hostile in their attempts to do down the party. As the *Guardian* summarised the election:

> ...Through the campaign, the Liberal Democrats looked set to be the chief beneficiaries of the nation's rage against the old politics. For the first time in a generation, the third force dared to hope that it would break the mould. In the event that did not happen, and they ended the evening with fewer MPs than they had at the start.[5]

The final paradox of an extraordinary election was thus, for the first time since 1992, the party had suffered a net loss of seats. But the electoral arithmetic now left Nick Clegg a more than willing kingmaker holding the balance of power. It was an election the Liberal Democrats had both lost and won.

23
Consenting Adults:
The Liberal–Conservative Coalition

The outcome of the May 2010 election left no party with an overall majority in the Commons. During the campaign, Clegg had repeatedly emphasised that the party with the most seats and most votes after the election should have the first chance to attempt to form a government. The May 2010 election clearly gave that position to the Conservatives under David Cameron.

But the electoral arithmetic of the May 2010 election left a very complicated position. The Conservatives were short of a majority (and would be even with the tacit support of smaller parties such as the DUP from Northern Ireland). On the Labour side, a deal with the Liberal Democrats would also not produce a majority (even if Plaid Cymru, the solitary Green MP and the Northern Ireland SDLP were brought in to bolster any pact). There was a real deadlock. For those (and there were many) who thought the Liberal Democrat natural instincts would be to do a deal with Labour, it was a very difficult time. As Paddy Ashdown said, it was a peculiar form of torture – our instincts go one way, the mathematics the other.

It was against this background that coalition negotiations began. Events moved swiftly. Early on the Friday morning at 4.30 a.m., as the results were still coming in, Nick Clegg and Gordon Brown were reported to have had an angry telephone exchange as the initial wrangling to form a coalition began. Later that same Friday morning Clegg stated that he would talk to the Conservatives first, reiterating that he believed the party with the most votes should have the chance to form the next government. Clegg did not, however rule out a deal with Labour. Brown stated he would welcome talks with the Liberal Democrats, but accepted they should talk first to the Conservatives. As the final results came in on the Friday the paradox of the situation became clear. With less seats than in 2005, Clegg was very much the kingmaker.

On Saturday 8 May Clegg held a morning meeting to sound out his MPs. With the parliamentary party broadly supporting him, that evening Cameron and Clegg engaged in key negotiations on forming a coalition. The next day the Conservative and Liberal Democrat negotiating teams met for a full Sunday of negotiations at the Cabinet Office. On the Liberal Democrat side, the four members of the negotiating team were Chris Huhne, Danny Alexander (a key ally of Nick Clegg), Andrew Stunell (with a long track record of overseeing negotiations at council level over pacts and coalitions) and David Laws, the MP for Yeovil and Shadow Education spokesman. On the Conservative side the negotiators were William Hague (the former party leader and currently Shadow Foreign Secretary), George Osborne, Oliver Letwin (the party's policy chief) and Ed Llewellyn, Cameron's chief of staff. As the negotiating team conducted its work, thousands of protesters calling for electoral reform marched past Westminster.

The Conservative–Liberal Democrat negotiating teams resumed their work at 8.00 a.m. on Monday 10 May. Meanwhile, as the negotiations were underway with the Conservatives, many Liberal Democrats still hankered after a deal with Labour. Formal talks began.[1] There was talk of a 'traffic-light coalition' (red, yellow and green) of Labour, Liberal Democrats and Greens (a solitary Green MP, Caroline Lucas, had been elected for Brighton Kemptown). However, the obstacles to such an alliance (dubbed 'a coalition of the losers' by its opponents) were manifold. There was the issue of Gordon Brown himself, where Clegg was on record as saying he would not prop up a Brown-led administration – and the personal chemistry between the two men was unfriendly. But even when Brown dramatically said he would quit as Labour leader (on Monday 10 May) he also stated that he wanted to remain to oversee the transition. He repeated his desire to work with the Liberal Democrats. It was clear this unprecedented move was prompted by fears of a Liberal–Conservative coalition emerging (fears which prompted Shirley Williams to warn against coalition with the Conservatives that same evening). Ironically it encouraged the Conservatives to make more concessions. The climax came on 11 May. The Liberal Democrats were informed that the Conservative MPs were prepared to put aside party interests by agreeing to a referendum on electoral reform and that the time had come for the Liberals to decide. The die was cast after a 25-minute phone call between Clegg and Cameron. That evening the parliamentary party supported Clegg's decision. Also that same evening Brown resigned as Prime Minister, with David Cameron succeeding him.

As the details of the agreement became known, and the composition of the new Cabinet was announced (with Nick Clegg exalted to the post of Deputy Prime Minister), many commentators were surprised that there had been no greater opposition from senior Liberal Democrats. Ashdown, Steel and Shirley Williams were all thought to be wary (or downright opposed) to a Conservative alliance. Sceptics in the Commons were believed to include such leading figures as Charles Kennedy, Simon Hughes, Vince Cable and Sir Menzies Campbell (who was on friendly personal relations with Gordon Brown). In the media both the *Guardian* and the *Observer* clamoured for the Liberal Democrats to seize a historic moment and turn to Labour in a progressive alliance. And Liberal Democrats at the grassroots were bombarding such figures as Simon Hughes with e-mails on the need for electoral reform.

The final act in cementing the Liberal–Conservative Coalition now needed to take place. A special Liberal Democrat conference was called for 16 May to consider the coalition deal. In an article in the *Observer* that morning Charles Kennedy explained why he was unable to support the deal, arguing that formal coalition with the Conservatives would wreck for ever plans for a progressive centre-left alliance in British politics.[2]

However, Kennedy's appeal (which might have struck a strong chord with the traditional radical left-wing rank-and-file party membership) was not reflected in support at the meeting. Clegg was able to declare that, after just five days as Deputy Prime Minister, there would now be no ID cards, no third runway at Heathrow airport, no child detention and no fingerprinting in schools without parental consent. Clegg's appeal triumphed. Of more than 1,500 delegates, apparently only a dozen or so were opposed outright. It was a seemingly overwhelming endorsement, but in fact it was qualified by a series of motions passed by the party activists reaffirming the Liberal Democrat manifesto pledges where they differed from Conservative policy and urging the leadership to stay true to these key policies.[3] In the end, though, Nick Clegg had got the support he wanted – David Steel's appeal to 'head over hearts' perhaps caught the mood of the delegates. And most delegates preferred to back Clegg to do the right thing.

Why then had the Liberal Democrats finished in alliance with the Conservatives rather than Labour? In retrospect, it was clear that too many obstacles existed for any agreement with Labour. The voters had pretty decisively shifted from New Labour after 13 years in power. The electoral arithmetic would not produce a stable government with a workable majority (it would have been a coalition of losers). Any Labour promises of electoral reform simply could not be guaranteed to get through parliament. Even more importantly, Labour itself was deeply divided on the way forward.

Leading Labour figures opposed to any Liberal Democrat deal included the Justice Secretary, Jack Straw (who argued the party should go into opposition), David Blunkett (who accused the Liberal Democrats of behaving like harlots) and former Home Secretary John Reid (who believed it would be self-destructive for both parties).

It is possible that Clegg had all along decided to take the Conservative route, but this remains conjectural. He certainly played both sides off against each other, but this was hardly unexpected. The party had tried hard to talk business with Labour. Clegg had met Brown on three occasions (once with Mandelson present). It seems that Clegg found the Conservatives more willing and flexible than expected to do a deal (and Clegg's personal chemistry with Cameron was good).

On the Conservative side, there were indeed strong arguments for a Liberal Democrat deal. Expediency was high among them. For Cameron, it would create a safe Commons majority, at the same time neutralising his own right-wing and criticism of the election campaign. It would reassure the financial markets. As the cuts came and reduction of the deficit gathered momentum, it would not just be the Conservatives who would suffer any electoral backlash – the Liberal Democrats were in the business of administering pain as well. And if things fell apart, the Conservatives would probably be in a far stronger position than the Liberal Democrats to fight another general election – perhaps virtually eating up their coalition partners in the process.

In the political excitement after the election, it was overlooked how many agreements in fact already existed at local council level between Conservative and Liberals. A strong coalition existed in Birmingham and other deals had broadly worked well. Ironically, the May 2010 local elections, with their Labour gains, ended the existing alliances in St Helens, Camden, Brent and Southwark.

In terms of reaching a deal nationally on policy issues with the Conservatives, there was in fact already a fair degree of common ground – on education reform, creating a low-carbon economy, reform of the political system, decentralising power, protecting civil liberties, abolishing plans for ID cards and so forth. The real problem was in the 'red line' issues neither party could give way on. The initial agreements were fleshed out before a final published version of the deal was made public. Inevitably, there had to be compromises. On the Conservative side, Cameron agreed to bring forward a referendum bill for a national vote on the alternative vote (AV) system (this was as far as the Conservatives would go on a tricky issue with their backbenchers). On tax, the Conservatives agreed to move towards the Liberal objective of lifting earnings up to £10,000 out of income tax. Conservative plans to increase the inheritance tax threshold were shelved (whilst the Liberal Democrat 'mansion tax' was likewise ditched). On Europe, there would be no further transfer of powers to Brussels and both parties agreed not to join the euro during the coming parliament. On education the Conservatives signed up to a 'pupil premium' to help children in disadvantaged schools (the scrapping of tuition fees was not mentioned). In defence, the renewal of Trident would go ahead (the Liberal Democrats had wanted this scrapped). In health Liberals secured their policy of elected health boards, whilst the Conservatives lost on replacing the Human Rights Act with a British Bill of Rights. Political reforms (apart from the AV referendum) included a commission to reform the House of Lords and a vote on fixed-term parliaments and a 55 per cent dissolution threshold (by June this latter proposal had run into trouble).

On immigration the Liberal Democrats lost their key proposal of a regional points-based immigration system and an amnesty for illegal immigrants in the UK for more than ten years. On the environment, whilst the Liberal Democrats agreed to drop their opposition to a new generation of nuclear power stations, the Conservatives agreed to replace air passenger duty with a per flight duty (a Liberal Democrat plan). Some minor surprises (not in either manifesto) included a crackdown on sales of cheap alcohol and anonymity for defendants in rape cases. Despite all efforts, some issues could not be resolved (29 reviews and four commissions were set up on outstanding contentious issues).

The full details of the Coalition Agreement reached by the Conservatives and Liberal Democrats were set out in a 32-page document published on 20 May. The task of implementing this deal fell to the Coalition Government, with Liberal Democrats now back at the Cabinet table for the first time since the ending of Churchill's wartime coalition in 1945.

Five Liberal Democrats became members of the Coalition Cabinet: Nick Clegg became Deputy Prime Minister and Lord President of the Council (with special responsibility for political and constitutional reform); Vince Cable became Secretary of State for Business, Enterprise and Skills (having apparently not wanted to work under George Osborne at the Treasury); Chris Huhne became Secretary of State for Energy and Climate Change; David Laws became Chief Secretary to the Treasury (with a key role in carrying out cuts in public expenditure and reducing the national debt);

and finally Danny Alexander, one of Clegg's most trusted advisers, became Secretary of State for Scotland (a post with relatively light duties since devolution).

At Minister of State level, the six Liberal Democrat appointments were Steve Webb at Work and Pensions (an unlikely colleague for Iain Duncan Smith), Lord McNally at Justice, Nick Harvey with responsibility for Armed Forces, Jeremy Browne at Europe, Sarah Teather as Minister of State for Children and Families and Paul Burstow as Minister of State for Health. Among other posts David Heath became Deputy Leader of the Commons (under Sir George Young) and Lynne Featherstone became Minister for Equalities. Lord Wallace of Tankerness became Advocate General for Scotland, Norman Baker became Parliamentary Under-Secretary at Transport and Ed Davey held the same rank in Vince Cable's Department. Alistair Carmichael became Deputy Chief Whip in the Commons and Lord Shutt in the Lords. Overall, Clegg had exercised good judgement (or so it seemed) in appointing a balanced team from different wings of his party.

The immediate tasks of the new Coalition were both many and pressing. There were three key priorities before Parliament rose for the Summer Recess: they were the Public Spending Review (on 24 May), the Queen's Speech (on 25 May) and the Emergency Budget set for 22 June.

The Government's legislative programme, as set out in the Queen's Speech on 25 May, was to be based on the principles of 'freedom, fairness and responsibility'. The Speech contained 22 bills and one draft bill. There were few surprises. There was a bill on electoral reform, to give the public the right to decide whether the first-past-the-post system should be ditched in favour of the alternative vote. Plans for Identity Cards would be scrapped, the Home Information Packs (HIPs) abolished, the number of quangos slashed and a Social Responsibility Bill would ban the sale of alcohol below cost price. Under the Academies Bill, all schools (including primaries) would be allowed to gain academy status, removing the need for local authority approval. There were proposals to make the police more accountable. Political reform featured strongly, with plans for 'recall' of MPs, fixed-term Parliaments and the redrawing of constituencies in the interests of fairness. Immigration from outside the EU was to be capped. Major welfare reforms were planned and an Office for Budget Responsibility created.

This was a full programme. It now remained to be seen whether backbenchers from either wing of the Coalition would flex their muscles as the Bills went through Parliament. And how would the voters react to the advent of a Liberal–Conservative Coalition? In the first *Guardian/*

ICM poll to be published after the election, most voters were shown to be supporting the coalition. The poll, carried out after the coalition government had put forward its constitutional reform proposals, showed 59 per cent of voters approving the decision to form a coalition government (with 81 per cent of Conservative voters approving the deal). Overall support was strongest in the South (68 per cent in favour) and weakest in the North and Scotland (48 per cent).[4] The poll showed support for the Conservatives at 39 per cent (2 up on the general election), Labour on 32 per cent (also up 2 per cent) and the Liberal Democrats on 21 per cent (down 3 per cent, but higher than in many pre-election ICM polls). The first real poll took place on 27 May in the delayed contest for the Thirsk and Malton constituency (where the UKIP candidate had died during the general election campaign). If recent events had confounded the political pundits, it was little wonder the voters of Thirsk and Malton showed similar evidence of confusion. The poll in this normally Tory area of north Yorkshire was marked by fairly lively exchanges between the Conservatives and Liberal Democrats at local level, regardless of their parties having joined together in the national coalition. The result was a very comfortable Conservative victory, with the Liberal Democrats a good way behind in second place.[5]

On Saturday 29 May an unexpected crisis hit the new Coalition Government. The *Daily Telegraph* published damaging allegations concerning David Laws in regard to his expenses claims for rent. Laws apologised and offered to repay the money he had received – around £40,000. By that evening, Laws had rightly decided to quit his Cabinet post – the most rapid Cabinet resignation in modern British history. It was a personal tragedy for Laws and an unwelcome disaster for the new Government. Danny Alexander was quickly shifted to become Chief Secretary to the Treasury, whilst Michael Moore (the MP for Roxburgh, Selkirk and Peebles) became Secretary of State for Scotland. The new kind of politics promised by Clegg had been hit by a very old kind of political scandal.

The affair weakened the Coalition. Danny Alexander was seen as a somewhat inexperienced figure for Chief Secretary to the Treasury, while the competent Michael Moore had never been first choice as Scottish Secretary. Clegg had opted to play safe. It was all a warning of how an unexpected crisis could derail plans. The parliamentary party faced a rather different affair on 9 June, following the resignation of Vince Cable as Deputy Leader of the party on 26 May in order to devote more time to his Cabinet post as Business Secretary. Simon Hughes declared his candidacy for the Deputy Leadership almost immediately, claiming he would be the conscience of the party in these turbulent times. He had the backing of Vince Cable. His only rival turned out to be Tim Farron, fresh from an excellent result in the Westmorland and Lonsdale constituency. The contest was narrowly won by Simon Hughes.

A pivotal test for the new Coalition – and for the Liberal Democrat input into its policies – came with the Emergency Budget introduced by the Chancellor, George Osborne, on 22 June. As Clegg realised, this would be the one issue above all others that would test the credibility of the Coalition.

The Budget, described as the most austere since the Second World War, was designed to attack the large government fiscal deficit. The Chancellor called it a progressive Budget from a progressive alliance. Although there were clear signs of Liberal Democrat input (as with the £1,000 increase in the personal allowance for Income Tax from April 2011) the most contentious measure was the increase in VAT to 20 per cent from January 2011. Since the Liberal Democrats had campaigned against a VAT increase during the election (and had warned voters of a 'Tory VAT bombshell'), the party was very open to accusations of hypocrisy. The Liberal Democrats argued that, with the public finances apparently worse than expected, unavoidable measures had to be taken.

Four Liberal Democrat MPs, led by Andrew George, tabled an amendment to the proposed VAT rise and two Liberal Democrat MPs, Bob Russell and Mike Hancock, voted against the Government in the first back-bench revolt of the Parliament. Their actions clearly reflected widespread unease among grassroots activists (such as Richard Grayson, the Vice-Chair of the Federal Policy Committee) at the way the Coalition was going.

Moreover, it now became much easier for Labour critics of the Coalition to portray Clegg as a 'dumb waiter' or as 'Mr Cameron's poodle' who had sold his party in return for office. Certainly, if the Conservative–Liberal Democrat marriage was still there, the honeymoon period was quite clearly over (and in the opinion polls, Liberal Democrat support sagged, with 22 per cent saying they were much less likely to vote for the party because of its VAT U-turn and a further 26 per cent saying they were somewhat less likely).

At the heart of the Coalition Agreement, at least as far as the Liberal Democrats were concerned, was the promise of a referendum on electoral reform. In a widely-anticipated announcement, Nick Clegg outlined a series of reforms on 5 July. The proposed measures included a referendum on whether to replace first-past-the-post by the alternative vote (AV) (with the referendum held on 5 May 2011, the same date as voting for the Scottish Parliament, Welsh Assembly and English local elections). It was also proposed to reduce the number of MPs from 650 to 600 by having constituencies with approximately the same number of voters (the Western Isles and Orkney and Shetland were exempt from this).

The proposals produced an immediate outcry. Many Conservative backbenchers were firmly opposed to any changes in the voting system (and particularly objected to a referendum on the same day as other elections were taking place). Cameron himself, it was confirmed, would not support a change to the first-past-the-post system. With many Labour backbenchers at best lukewarm (and others firmly opposed both to AV and to a reduction in the number of MPs on the lines proposed) the proposal seemed likely to face a heated passage through Parliament.

Moreover, advocates of proportional representation could hardly enthuse over a measure which was not in essence at all proportional (except insofar as the proportion of Liberal Democrat MPs might increase in a general election).[6] Indeed, Clegg himself had once called AV a 'miserable little compromise'. In the coalition with the Conservatives, it was all that was on offer.

Thus, as the MPs left Westminster on 29 July for the Summer Recess, and after the fast-moving and seismic events of May 2010, few commentators could look ahead with any certainty to the likely contours of the new political landscape. There were plenty of questions to be asked, but few were prepared to give answers. How long would this ground-breaking Coalition last? Would the Cabinet survive without resignations? Would the respective Conservative and Liberal Democrat backbenchers remain loyal?

Liberal Democrats could reflect that in the fifty years since the spectacular onset of the Liberal revival in the 1962 Orpington by-election, the party had made perhaps the longest wilderness march in modern British political history. Now, in May 2010, it seemed the Liberal moment had arrived. In the somewhat unexpected result of the general election Clegg had opportunely led his (albeit reduced) parliamentary army back into government. But the Liberal Democrats need to be prepared. The Coalition euphoria may not last. Unpopularity may replace novelty. Backbenchers may precipitate rebellions. Cabinet unity may not survive. And in those circumstances, the next election may be a far more difficult task than May 2010, not least if the party is assailed from both sides.

For both Conservatives and Liberals, and most especially for David Cameron and Nick Clegg personally, the new coalition offered great potential but also very great danger. Historians of the Liberal Party are only too aware of what has happened to the party in some previous coalitions, not least in the 1930s. Divisions and recriminations have been followed by calamity. If that was to happen now, there will be a second even stranger death of Liberal England to be written.

Appendix I

Major Holders of Liberal Party Office, 1900–1988[1]

Party Leaders[2]

February	1899	Sir Henry Campbell-Bannerman
April	1908	Herbert Henry Asquith[3]
October	1926	David Lloyd George
November	1931	Sir Herbert Samuel
November	1935	Sir Archibald Sinclair
August	1945	Clement Davies
November	1956	Joseph Grimond
January	1967	Jeremy Thorpe[4]
July	1976	David Steel[5]

Leaders in the House of Lords

1900	Earl of Kimberley		1931	M. of Reading
1902	Earl Spencer		1936	M. of Crewe
1905	M. of Ripon		1944	Vt Samuel
1908	E. (M) of Crewe		1955	Ld Rea
1923	Vt Grey		1967	Ld Byers
1924	Earl Beauchamp		1984	Lady Seear

Chief Whips in the House of Commons

1900	H. Gladstone		1932	W. Rea
1905	G. Whiteley		1935	Sir P. Harris
1908	J. Pease		1945	T. Horabin
1910	Master of Elibank		1946	F. Byers
1912	P. Illingworth		1950	J. Grimond
1915	J. Gulland		1956	D. Wade
1919	G.Thorne		1963	E. Lubbock
1923	V. Phillipps		1970	D. Steel
1924	Sir G.Collins		1976	G. Smith
1926	Sir R. Hutchinson		1977	A. Beith
1930	Sir A. Sinclair		1985	D. Alton
1931	G. Owen		1987	J. Wallace[6]

Chief Whips in the House of Lords

1896	Ld. Ribblesdale		1949	M. of Willingdon
1907	Ld. Denman		1950	Ld. Moynihan
1911–22	Ld. Colebrooke		1950	Ld. Rea
1919	Ld. Denman		1955	Ld. Amulree
1924	Ld. Stanmore		1977	Ld. Wigoder
1944	Vt. Mersey		1984	Ld. Tordoff[7]

National Liberal Federation, 1900–36

Chairman of Committee		*Secretary*	
1900	(Sir) E.Evans	1893	(Sir) R. Hudson
1918	Sir G. Lunn	1922	F. Barter
1920	A. Brampton	1925	H. Oldman
1931	R. Muir	1930	H. Oldman and W. Davies
1933	R. Walker	1931	W. Davies
1934	M. Gray		

Treasurer			
1901	W. Hart	1923	Sir R. Hudson
1903	J. Massie	1927	Sir F. Layland-Barratt
1907	R. Bird	1934	P. Heffer
1910	F. Wright		

Liberal Party Organisation, 1936–88

Head

1936	W. Davies (Secretary)
1952	H. Harris (General Director)
1960	D. Robinson (Directing Secretary)
1961	P. Kemmis (Secretary)
1965	T. Beaumont (Head of Liberal Party Organisation)
1966	P. Chitnis (Head of Liberal Party Organisation)
1970	E. Wheeler (Head of Liberal Party Organisation)
1977	H. Jones (Secretary-General)
1983	J. Spiller (Secretary-General)

Chairman of Executive Committee

1936	M. Gray
1946	P. Fothergill
1949	Ld. Moynihan
1950	F. Byers
1952	P. Fothergill
1954	G. Acland
1957	D. Abel
1959	L. Behrens
1961	D. Banks
1963	B. Wigoder
1965	G. Evans
1968–69[8]	J. Baker

Treasurer

1937–50	Sir A. McFadyean	1962–66	Sir A. Murray
1937–41	P. Heffer	1963–65	T. Beaumont
1941–47	Ld. Rea	1966–67	J. Thorpe
1942–47	H. Worsley	1967–68	L. Smith
1947–53	Ld. Moynihan	1968–69	J. Pardoe
1950–58	W. Grey	1969-72	Sir F. Medlicott
1950–52	Vt. Wimborne	1972–77	P. Watkins
1953–62	Sir A. Suenson-Taylor	1977–83	Ld. Lloyd of Kilgerran
	(Ld. Grantchester)	1977–83	M. Palmer
1955–59	P. Fothergill	1983–86	Sir H. Jones
1959–62	Miss H. Harvey	1983–86	A. Jacobs
1959–60	P. Lort-Phillips	1986–88	C. Fox
1961–62	J. McLaughlin	1986–88	T. Razzall[9]
1962–65	R. Gardner-Thorpe		

Chairman

1966	Ld. Byers	1973	K. Vaus
1967	T. Beaumont (Ld.)	1976	G. Tordoff
1968	Ld. Henley	1980	R. Pincham
1969	D. Banks	1983	Mrs J. Rose
1970	R. Wainwright	1984	P. Tyler
1972	C. Carr		

Appendix II

Major Holders of Liberal Democrat Office, 1988–2010[1]

Party Leaders

1988	Paddy Ashdown	2006	Sir Menzies Campbell
1999	Charles Kennedy	2007	Nick Clegg

Deputy Leaders

1988	Alan Beith	2006	Vince Cable
2002	Sir Menzies Campbell	2010	Simon Hughes

Chief Whips in the House of Commons

1987	J. Wallace[2]	2001	A. Stunell
1992	A. Kirkwood	2006	P. Burstow
1997	P. Tyler	2010	A. Carmichael

Leaders in the House of Lords

1988	Ld. Jenkins	2004	Ld. McNally
1997	Ld. Rogers	2010	Ld. Shutt
2001	Lady Williams		

Party Organisation[3]

President

1988–90	Ian Wrigglesworth	1999–2004	Lord Dholakia
1990–94	Charles Kennedy	2004–08	Simon Hughes
1994–98	Robert Maclennan	2008–	Baroness Ros Scott
1998–99	Baroness Maddock		

General Secretary/Chief Executive

1988–89	A. Ellis	1999–2003	H. Rickard
1989–98	G. Elson	2003–09	Lord Rennard
1998–99	Ms E. Pamplin	2009	C. Fox

Appendix III[1]

The Liberal Vote, 1918–2010[2]

Election	Candidates	Unopposed Returns	MPs Elected	Forfeited Deposits	Total Votes	% of UK Total
1918	421	27	163	44	2,785,374	25.6
1922	477	10	115	31	4,080,915	28.3
1923	457	11	158	8	4,301,481	29.7
1924	340	6	40	30	2,931,380	17.8
1929	513	0	59	25	5,308,738	23.6
1931	118	5	37	6	1,506,630	7.2
1935	161	0	21	40	1,443,093	6.8
1945	306	0	12	76	2,252,430	9.0
1950	475	0	9	319	2,621,487	9.1
1951	109	0	6	66	743,512	2.6
1955	110	0	6	60	722,402	2.7
1959	216	0	6	55	1,640,761	5.9
1964	365	0	9	52	3,101,103	11.2
1966	311	0	12	104	2,327,533	8.5
1970	332	0	6	184	2,117,638	7.5
1974 (Feb)	517	0	14	23	6,063,470	19.3
1974 (Oct)	619	0	13	125	5,346,800	18.3
1979	577	0	11	284	4,313,804	13.8
1983[3]	633	0	23	11	7,781,764	25.4
1987[3]	633	0	22	25	7,339,912	22.6
1992[4]	632	0	20	11	5,999,384	17.8
1997[4]	639	0	46	13	5,242,947	16.8
2001[4]	639	0	52	1	4,815,249	18.3
2005	639	0	62	0	5,982,045	22.0
2010	631	0	57	0	6,836,824	23.0

The National Liberal Vote 1931–66

Election	Candidates	Unopposed Returns	MPs Elected	Forfeited Deposits	Total Votes	% of UK Total
1931	41	7	35	0	809,302	3.7
1935	44	3	33	0	866,354	3.7
1945	49	0	11	0	737,732	2.8
1950	55	0	16	0	985,343	3.4
1951	55	0	19	0	1,058,138	3.7
1955	45	0	21	0	842,113	3.1
1959	39	0	20	0	765,794	2.7
1964	19	0	6	0	326,130	1.2
1966	9	0	3	0	149,779	0.5

Appendix IV

Liberal By-Election Victories since 1945[1]

Date	Constituency	From	To	Swing
27 Mar 1958	Torrington	Con. −27.7	Lib. +38.0	32.0
14 Mar 1962	Orpington	Con. −21.9	Lib. +31.7	26.8
24 Mar 1965	Roxburgh	Con. −4.2	Lib. +10.3	7.3
26 Jun 1969	Ladywood	Lab. −33.4	Lib. +30.6	32.0
26 Oct 1972	Rochdale	Lab. −10.5	Lib. +11.9	11.2
7 Dec 1972	Sutton	Con. −26.4	Lib. +38.9	32.7
26 Jul 1973	Isle of Ely	Con. −24.9	Lib. +38.3[2]	31.6
26 Jul 1973	Ripon	Con. −20.2	Lib. +30.4	25.3
8 Nov 1973	Berwick	Con. −11.0	Lib. +18.0	14.5
29 Mar 1979	Edge Hill	Lab. −28.1	Lib. +36.8	32.5
22 Oct 1981	Croydon N.W.	Con. −18.5	Lib. +29.5	24.2
26 Nov 1981	Crosby[3]	Con. −17.2	SDP +33.9	25.6
25 Mar 1982	Hillhead[3]	Con. −14.5	SDP +19.0	16.8
24 Feb 1983	Bermondsey	Lab. −37.5	Lib. +50.9	44.2
14 Jun 1984	Portsmouth S.[3]	Con. −15.7	SDP +12.2	14.0
4 Jul 1985	Brecon	Con. −20.5	Lib. +11.3	15.9
8 May 1986	Ryedale	Con. −17.9	Lib. +19.8	18.9
26 Feb 1987	Greenwich[3]	Lab. −4.4	Lib. +27.8	16.2[4]
18 Oct 1990	Eastbourne[5]	Con. −19.0	Lib. Dem. +21.1	20.1
7 Mar 1991	Ribble Valley	Con. −22.4	Lib. Dem. +27.1	24.8
7 Nov 1991	Kincardine & Deeside	Con. −10.0	Lib. Dem. +12.7	11.4
6 May 1993	Newbury	Con. −29.0	Lib. Dem. +28.3	28.4
29 Jul 1993	Christchurch	Con. −32.1	Lib. Dem. +38.6	35.4
9 Jun 1994	Eastleigh	Con. −26.5	Lib. Dem. +16.3	21.4
27 Jul 1995	Littleborough & Saddleworth	Con. −18.6	Lib. Dem. +2.6	11.6
4 May 2000	Romsey	Con. −4.0	Lib. Dem. +21.2	12.6

Postscript. From 2001 to the general election of May 2010, the Liberal Democrats captured three seats: Brent East (18 September 2003), Leicester South (15 July 2004) and Dunfermline and West Fife (9 February 2006). All these gains were from Labour.

Appendix V

Liberal Democrat Seats (after May 2010)

Constituency	Majority	% Majority
Aberdeenshire West and Kincardine	3,684	8.15
Argyll and Bute	3,431	7.58
Bath	11,183	25.24
Bermondsey and Old Southwark	8,530	19.10
Berwick-upon-Tweed	2,690	7.00
Berwickshire, Roxburgh and Selkirk	5,675	11.58
Birmingham Yardley	3,002	7.35
Bradford East	365	0.90
Brecon and Radnorshire	3,747	9.65
Brent Central	1,345	2.97
Bristol West	11,366	20.54
Burnley	1,818	4.34
Caithness, Sutherland and Easter Ross	4,826	16.78
Cambridge	6,792	13.55
Cardiff Central	4,576	12.66
Carshalton and Wallington	5,260	11.46
Ceredigion	8,324	21.76
Cheadle	3,272	6.23
Cheltenham	4,920	9.32
Chippenham	2,470	4.72
Colchester	6,982	15.13
Cornwall North	2,981	6.36
Devon North	5,821	11.34
Dorset Mid and Poole North	269	0.57
Dunbartonshire East	2,184	4.55
Eastbourne	3,435	6.59
Eastleigh	3,864	7.20
Edinburgh West	3,803	8.19
Fife North East	9,048	22.58
Gordon	6,748	13.83
Hazel Grove	6,371	15.18
Hornsey and Wood Green	6,875	12.49
Inverness, Nairn, Badenoch and Strathspey	8,765	18.61
Kingston and Surbiton	7,560	13.24
Leeds North West	9,103	20.93
Lewes	7,647	15.27
Manchester Withington	1,894	4.21

continued

Constituency	Majority	% Majority
Norfolk North	11,626	23.41
Norwich South	310	0.65
Orkney and Shetland	9,928	51.32
Portsmouth South	5,200	12.60
Redcar	5,214	12.43
Ross, Skye and Lochaber	13,070	37.52
St Austell and Newquay	1,312	2.78
St Ives	1,719	3.74
Sheffield Hallam	15,284	29.89
Solihull	175	0.32
Somerton and Frome	1,817	3.00
Southport	6,024	13.77
Sutton and Cheam	1,608	3.31
Taunton Deane	3,993	6.87
Thornbury and Yate	7,116	14.76
Torbay	4,078	8.29
Twickenham	12,140	20.33
Wells	800	1.43
Westmorland and Lonsdale	12,264	23.82
Yeovil	13,036	22.81

Appendix VI
The Continuing Liberal Party

The 'continuing' Liberal Party was launched in 1989 by those party members unhappy with the merger with the Social Democrats. Although small, it continued to contest elections throughout the 1990s and after. In the 1992 general election the 'continuing' Liberal Party contested 73 seats.[1] It polled 64,744 votes in all (an average of 887 votes, or 1.7 per cent in its 73 seats). Its best result (8.3 per cent) was, not surprisingly, achieved by Michael Meadowcroft in Leeds West.[2] The party also managed to come ahead of the Greens in 18 of 31 contests. In the local elections of May 1992, having fought 56 seats, the party could claim seven county councillors and three metropolitan district councillors. In the local elections of 1993, the party successfully defended five county council seats, fighting 56 in total in the local contests. A similar pattern of scattered local successes was repeated in May 1994 (in such areas as Liverpool, Exeter and Peterborough). A more significant opportunity arose with the European elections of June 1994 when the 20 Liberal Party candidates polled around 100,000 votes, an average of 5,000 each (just under 3 per cent). Of these candidates, David Morrish polled the highest vote (14,621 in the Devon and East Plymouth constituency).

This pattern of scattered pockets of strength continued late into the 1990s. After the 1996 local elections, Liberals retained representation on such councils as Liverpool (2 seats), Exeter (3), Peterborough (3), Slough (3) and Wyre Forest. For the 1997 local elections, 74 seats were fought, but these contests were overshadowed by the general election held the same day. The party fielded 55 candidates in the May 1997 general election, polling a total of 45,166 votes (an average 821 votes per seat, 1.7 per cent). However, two deposits were saved and the party also achieved one second place. By far the best result was in Liverpool West Derby where the party came in second place, ahead of the Liberal Democrats, Conservatives and Referendum Party, polling 9.6 per cent of the vote. Other relatively good results included Bethnal Green and Bow (6.6 per cent), Slough (3.9 per cent) and Wolverhampton North East (3.8 per cent).[3]

As the new century began, and 12 years after the Liberal Party had resolved to continue with an independent existence, the party still had councillors on such local authorities as Liverpool, Peterborough, Slough, Exeter and Guildford. In the general election of June 2001 a few candidates were put forward, in such seats as Exeter and Leeds West. None was elected, although in Liverpool West Derby the Liberal took second place with 14.89 per cent of the vote, forcing the Liberal Democrat candidate into third place.

In 2005, with a handful of candidates, the party obtained a creditable result in Liverpool Wavertree. In the May 2010 election, the party took 9.3 per cent of the vote in Liverpool West Derby, leaving the Conservative in fourth place.

Bibliographical Note

There is no authoritative comprehensive history of the Liberal Party from the Victorian period to the present day. There are, however, a mass of monographs and detailed studies of particular periods and particular themes. It is hoped this list will point the student to some of the more important articles and studies. In addition to the books mentioned below, two works of reference are of particular relevance. These are C. Cook and B. Keith, *British Historical Facts, 1830–1900* and D.E. Butler and G. Butler *Twentieth-Century British Political Facts, 1900–2000*. Both books contain a mass of biographical, electoral and statistical material.

For the Victorian Liberal Party, a basic starting-point is J. Vincent, *The Formation of the Liberal Party, 1857–1868* (London, 1966). For the general background of Liberalism, there is R.B. McCallum, *The Liberal Party from Earl Grey to Asquith* (London, 1963) and also J.L. Hammond and M.R.D. Foot, *Gladstone and Liberalism* (London, 1959). A modern study with a broad chronological coverage is Alan Sykes, *The Rise and Fall of British Liberalism, 1776–1988* (London, 1997). Also of considerable value is T.A. Jenkins, *The Liberal Ascendancy, 1830–1886* (London, 1984).

The 1867 Reform Act is covered by M. Cowling, *Disraeli, Gladstone and Revolution* (Cambridge, 1967). A useful specialist article on the 1868 election is A.F. Thompson, 'Gladstone, the Whips and the General Election of 1868', *English Historical Review*, LXIII (1948). There is much useful material in D. Southgate, *The Passing of the Whigs, 1832–1886* (London, 1962).

On Gladstone himself, an excellent one-volume study can be found in R. Jenkins, *Gladstone* (1995). Other studies include H.C.G. Matthew, *Gladstone, 1809–74* (1986) and *Gladstone, 1874–98* (1995), while shorter works include E. Feuchtwanger, *Gladstone* (1975) and P. Stansky, *Gladstone* (1979). There is a valuable detailed study in J.P. Parry, *Democracy and Religion: Gladstone and the Liberal Party, 1867–75* (1986).

For the period after 1874, there is much relevant material in D.A. Hamer, *Liberal Politics in the Age of Gladstone and Rosebery* (Oxford, 1975). The origins and development of the National Liberal Federation are covered by B. McGill, 'Francis Schnadhorst and Liberal Party Organisation', *Journal of Modern History*, March 1962.

A detailed account of the Midlothian campaign has been written by R. Kelly, 'Midlothian: A Study in Politics and Ideals', *Victorian Studies*, IV, 2 (1960). The crucial period of the Home Rule crisis is superbly covered by A.B. Cooke and J. Vincent, *The Governing Passion: Cabinet Government and Party Politics in Britain, 1885–1886* (Brighton, 1974). The problem of Liberal Reunion is covered by M. Hurst, *Joseph Chamberlain and Liberal Reunion: The Round Table Conference of 1887* (Newton Abbot, 1967). For Joseph Chamberlain's career, see P. Fraser, *Joseph Chamberlain; Radicalism and Empire* (London, 1966). Liberal strength and weakness in general elections can be clearly followed in M. Kinnear, *The British Voter: An Atlas and Survey since 1885* (London, 1968). This book is of value for every election from 1885 to 1966.

Among the detailed specialist studies of Gladstone during this later period, there are R.T. Shannon, *Gladstone and the Bulgarian Agitation, 1876* (London, 1963), M. Barker, *Gladstone and Radicalism: The Reconstruction of Liberal Policy in Britain* (Brighton, 1975) and D.M. Schreuder, *Gladstone and Kruger: Liberal Government and Colonial Home Rule* (London, 1969). On the Irish question, there is J.L. Hammond's 1938 classic *Gladstone and the Irish Nation*, new ed. (1964). A useful specialist article is F.S.L. Lyons, 'The Irish Question and Liberal Politics, 1886–1894', in *Historical Journal*, XII (1969).

On the Liberal Unionist revolt, see B. Goodman, 'Liberal Unionism: The Revolt of the Whigs', *Victorian Studies*, December 1959; and P. Fraser, 'The Liberal Unionist Alliance: Chamberlain, Hartington and the Conservatives, 1886–1904', *English Historical Review*, LXXVII (1962). Rosebery's career is covered by R.R. James, *Rosebery* (London, 1963). There is much useful material in another important study of this period, H.C.G. Matthew, *The Liberal Imperialists* (Oxford, 1973). Morley is well covered by D.A. Hamer, *John Morley: Liberal Intellectual in Politics* (Oxford, 1968). On Morley, see also S. Koss, 'Morley in the Middle', *English Historical Review*, LXXXII (1967). Much the best account of the Newcastle Programme, and the internecine warfare of the party in the 1890s, is to be found in P. Stansky, *Ambitions and Strategies: The Struggle for the Leadership of the Liberal Party in the 1890s* (Oxford, 1964). Two useful regional studies are Kenneth O. Morgan, *Wales in British Politics, 1868–1922* (Oxford, 1963) and J.G. Kellas, 'The Liberal Party in Scotland, 1876–1895', *Scottish Historical Review*, XLIV (1965).

For the whole period after 1895, there is much of use in R. Douglas, *The History of the Liberal Party, 1895–1970* (London, 1971) – a book sympathetic to the party and even more sympathetic to Free Trade. A reliable life of Campbell-Bannerman is the solid if unexciting account by J. Wilson, *Campbell-Bannerman* (London, 1972). The Liberal Party's involvement in South Africa is well covered by J. Butler, *The Liberal Party and the Jameson Raid* (Oxford, 1968). There is also H.W. McCready, 'Sir Alfred Milner, the Liberal Party and the Boer War', *Canadian Journal of History*, II (1967). See also P.D. Jacobson, 'Rosebery and Liberal Imperialism, 1899–1903', *Journal of British Studies*, XIII (1973). An important survey is M. Bentley, *The Climax of Liberal Politics: British Liberalism in Theory and Practice, 1868–1918* (1987).

The revival of Liberal fortunes after 1900 is well detailed in M. Craton and H.W. McCready, *The Great Liberal Revival, 1903–6* (Hansard Society pamphlet, 1966). The agitation over the 1902 Education Act is very ably discussed by S.E. Koss, *Nonconformity in Modern British Politics* (London, 1975). The Liberal Party's relationship with the Labour Representation Committee is well covered in two articles: F. Bealey, 'The Electoral Arrangement between the L.R.C. and the Liberal Party', *Journal of Modern History*, December 1956 and the same author's 'Negotiations between the Liberals and the L.R.C. before the 1906 election', *Bulletin of the Institute of Historical Research*, XXIX (1956). The 1906 election is ably discussed in A.K. Russell, *Liberal Landslide: The General Election of 1906* (Newton Abbot, 1973).

The period from 1906 to 1914 is extremely well covered by a variety of books and articles. There is much material in P. Rowland, *The Last Liberal Governments: The Promised Land, 1905–10* (London, 1968). The best short study of Campbell-Bannerman's premiership is J. Harris and C. Hazlehurst, 'Campbell-Bannerman as Prime Minister', *History*, XV (1970). The most succinct study of Asquith, a model of a concise yet authoritative biography, is S.E. Koss, *Asquith* (London, 1976). There is also R. Jenkins, *Asquith* (London, 1964) and C. Hazlehurst, 'Asquith as Prime Minister', *English Historical Review*, LXXXV July 1970). Two specialist articles are J.E. Tyler, 'Campbell-Bannerman and the Liberal Imperialists (1906–8)', *History*, XXIII (1939) and C.C. Weston, 'The Liberal Leadership and the Lords' Veto, 1907–1910', *Historical Journal*, XI, 3 (1968).

The definitive biography of Lloyd George has been done by John Grigg (Harmondsworth, 2002). There is much of value in P. Rowland, *Lloyd George* (London, 1976), but Kenneth O. Morgan, *Lloyd George* (London, 1974) is a masterly summary. The same author's *Lloyd George Family Letters, 1885–1936* (Cardiff, 1973) is an illuminating source. A highly readable, if now outdated account with some fascinating anecdote, is Frank Owen, *Tempestuous Journey: Lloyd George, his life and times* (London, 1954). Equally entertaining on the struggle with the House of Lords is R. Jenkins, *Mr Balfour's Poodle* (London, 1954).

Liberal social reform is covered by H.V. Emy, *Liberals, Radicals and Social Politics, 1892–1914* (Cambridge, 1973) and by Bentley B. Gilbert, *The Evolution of National Insurance in Great Britain* (London, 1966). On foreign policy, much useful material can be found in A.J.A. Morris, *Radicalism against War, 1906–1914* (London, 1972). See also the same author's volume of essays, *Edwardian Radicalism, 1900–1914* (London, 1974).

The definitive account of the 1910 elections and the constitutional crisis is in N. Blewett, *The Peers, The Parties and the People: The General Elections of 1910* (London, 1972). For the period from 1910 to 1914 there is also P. Rowland, *The Last Liberal Governments: Unfinished Business, 1911–1914* (London, 1971). The suffragette question is covered by D. Morgan, *Suffragists and Liberals* (London, 1975). The question of the rise of Labour and the downfall of the Liberal Party has generated one of the major historical debates of our time. G. Dangerfield, *The Strange Death of Liberal England* (London, 1935) can be safely left alone. It is a highly impressionistic account and at times highly misleading. T. Wilson, *The Downfall of the Liberal Party, 1914–1935* (London, 1966) emphasises the importance of the First World War. P. Clarke, *Lancashire and the New Liberalism* (Cambridge, 1971) is an important book whose conclusions need to be tested for other parts of the country. An approach which hardly fits the older arguments is C. Cook, 'Labour and the Downfall of the Liberal Party', in A. Sked and C. Cook, *Crisis and Controversy: Essays in honour of A.J.P. Taylor* (London, 1976); H. Pelling, *Popular Politics and Society in Late Victorian England* (London, 1968) contains useful material. For the mining areas, see R. Gregory, *The Miners in British Politics* (Oxford, 1968). For an older article, see L. Noonan, 'The Decline of the Liberal Party in British Politics', *Journal of Politics*, February 1954.

The period of the First World War is again very well covered. A.J.P. Taylor, *Politics in Wartime* (London, 1964) is stimulating. The studies already cited by Trevor Wilson and Stephen Koss are all useful. C. Hazlehurst, *Politicians at War* (London, 1971) seems as much concerned with rivalries between historians. Specialist articles of importance are B. McGill, 'Asquith's Predicament, 1914–1918', *Journal of Modern History*, XXXIX, 3 (1967); S. Koss, 'The Destruction of Britain's Last Liberal Government', *Journal of Modern History*, XL, 2 (1968), C. Hazlehurst, 'The Conspiracy Myth', in M. Gilbert, *Lloyd George* (Englewood Cliffs NJ, 1968) and E. David, 'The Liberal Party Divided', *English Historical Review* (1972). For the 'Coupon' arrangements, see T. Wilson 'The Coupon and the British General Election of 1918', *Journal of Modern History* (1964).

For the inter-war period, the basic starting point is T. Wilson, *The Downfall of the Liberal Party* (London, 1966). This can be supplemented by C. Cook, *The Age of Alignment: Electoral Politics in Britain, 1922–1929* (London, 1975), which contains much material on party organisation and municipal politics as well as on electoral strength. For a personal view of high politics, see M. Cowling, *The Impact of Labour, 1920–1924* (Cambridge, 1971). The 1922 election is covered in M. Kinnear, *The Fall of Lloyd George: the Political Crisis of 1922* (London, 1973). A succinct discussion of the Coalition Liberal Party can be found in K. Morgan, 'Lloyd George's Stage Army', in A.J.P. Taylor (ed.), *Lloyd George: Twelve Essays* (London, 1971). On the philosophy of the party, see J. Campbell, 'The Renewal of Liberalism: Liberalism without Liberals', in G. Peele and C. Cook (eds) *The Politics of Reappraisal, 1918–1939* (London, 1975) and M. Bentley, 'The Liberal Response to Socialism, 1918–29', in K.D. Brown (ed.), *Essays in Anti-Labour History* (London, 1974). A very useful source is T. Wilson (ed.), *The Political Diaries of C.P. Scott* (London, 1970). Two specialist studies are R. Dowse, 'The Entry of the Liberals into the Labour Party, 1910–1930', *Yorkshire Bulletin of Economic and Social Research*, XIII, 2 (1961) and K. Morgan, 'The Twilight of Welsh Liberalism: Lloyd George and the Wee Frees, 1918–35', *Bulletin of the Board of Celtic Studies*, XXII, Pt 4 (May 1968). The 1929–31 period lacks a detailed Liberal study. Trevor Wilson's book remains useful, but see also R. Skidelsky, *Politicians and the Slump: The Labour Government of 1929–31* (London, 1967). There is no major study of the Liberal Party in the 1930s. Some material can be found in C. Cook, 'Liberals, Labour and Local Elections', in G. Peele and C. Cook, *The Politics of Reappraisal 1918–1939* (London, 1975). On the 1935 election, see C.T. Stannage, *Baldwin Thwarts the Opposition* (London, 1980). Also important for the earlier inter-war period is M. Bentley, *The Liberal Mind, 1914–1929* (1977).

Also for the inter-war period, three useful recently-published studies are David Dutton, '1932: A Neglected Date in the History of the Decline of the British Liberal Party', *Twentieth-Century British History*, XIV (2003); Garry Tregidga, *The Liberal Party in South West Britain since 1918: Political Decline, Dormancy and Rebirth since 1918* (Exeter 2000) and also his article 'Turning of the Tide? A Case Study of the Liberal Party in Provincial Britain in the late 1930s', *History*, 92, 3 (July 2007).

The Liberal Leader Sir Herbert Samuel has an excellent biographer in Bernard Wasserstein, while for a useful biography of Sir Archibald Sinclair, see Gerard J. de Groot, *Liberal Crusader: The Life of Sir Archibald Sinclair* (London 1993).

For the neglected history of the National Liberals, who eventually fused into the Conservative Party in the post-war period, see David Dutton, *Liberals in Schism: A History of the National Liberal Party* (London, 2008).

For the Second World War, see R. Douglas, *History of the Liberal Party, 1895–1970* and P. Addison, 'By-Elections of the Second World War', in C. Cook and J. Ramsden (eds), *By-Elections in British Politics* (London, 1997). This book has material on successive Liberal by-election revivals right up to the 1997 general election.

The post-1945 period is short of serious studies of the Liberal Party. There is useful material in J. Rasmussen, *Retrenchment and Revival: a Study of the Contemporary Liberal Party* (London, 1964). Highly readable is A. Watkins, *The Liberal Dilemma* (London, 1966). For the period from 1959 to 1970, see the outline by C. Cook, 'The Liberal and Nationalist Revival', in D. McKie and C. Cook, *The Decade of Disillusion: British Politics in the Sixties* (London, 1972). All the Nuffield election studies (which David Butler has participated in) have relevant material; and there is also material in D.E. Butler and D. Stokes, *Political Change in Britain* (London, 1969). On contemporary developments see V. Bogdanor (ed.), *Liberal Party Politics* (Oxford, 1983). A useful short study is John Stevenson, *Third Party Politics since 1945* (Oxford, 1993). Also of value are Roy Jenkins, *A Life at the Centre* (London, 1991) and David Steel, *Against Goliath: David Steel's Story* (London, 1989). Other studies, with material on the birth and progress of the Liberal Democrats, include I. Bradley, *The Strange Rebirth of Liberal Britain* (London, 1985) and D. Maclver (ed.), *The Liberal Democrats* (Hemel Hempstead, 1996). The definitive study of the Social Democratic Party is to be found in I. Crewe and A. King, *The Birth, Life and Death of the Social Democratic Party* (Oxford, 1995). On the Ashdown years there is extensive material in P. Ashdown, *The Ashdown Diaries I, 1988–97* (London, 2000), and *The Ashdown Diaries II, 1997–99* (London, 2001). The European elections of June 1999 are fully analysed by D. Butler and M. Westlake, *British Politics and European Elections 1999* (London, 2000).

With the new century has come a spate of publications, both general surveys of the Liberal Democrats and more specialist studies. For general surveys there is useful material in Roy Douglas, *Liberals: The History of the Liberal and Liberal Democrat Parties* (London, 2005) and also David Dutton, *A History of the Liberal Party in the Twentieth Century* (Basingstoke, 2004). A detailed published study of the party at its roots can be found in Patrick Seyd and Paul Whiteley, *Third Force Politics: Liberal Democrats at the Grassroots* (Oxford, 2006). Also of importance is Andrew Russell and Edward Fieldhouse, *Neither Left nor Right? The Liberal Democrats and the Electorate* (Manchester, 2005).

On the 2005 general election (which had produced the party's best result since 1923) see Pippa Norris and Christopher Wlezien (eds), *Britain Votes, 2005* (Oxford, 2005), Andrew Geddes, *Britain Decides: The UK General Election 2005* (London, 2005) and the standard Nuffield study by Dennis Kavanagh and David Butler, *The British General Election of 2005* (Basingstoke, 2005). One aspect of Liberal Democrat thinking in the new century can be followed in Paul Marshall (ed.), *The Orange Book: Reclaiming Liberalism* (London, 2004). On the Liberal Democrat policy towards alliances with other parties for the Scottish Parliament and Welsh Assembly, see Mark Oaten, *Coalitions* (London, 2006).

With very few archives yet available for the history of the Liberal Democrats, there is a dearth of scholarly monographs or articles. However, the first issue of *Political Quarterly* in 2007 (Vol. 78, No. 1) was devoted to a detailed study of the party and should be consulted. In addition, any researcher on the Liberal Democrats will need to be aware of the rich material available in the *Journal of Liberal Democrat History* (published since 1993 by the Liberal Democrat History Group).

Among more popular biographies and autobiographies, the career of Charles Kennedy (with much material on his leadership and downfall) is covered in Greg Hurst, *Charles Kennedy: A Tragic Flaw* (London, 2006). For the earlier Ashdown years there is his autobiography, *A Fortunate Life: The Autobiography of Paddy Ashdown* (London, 2008) and for Menzies Campbell, see his own *Menzies Campbell: My Autobiography* (London, 2008).

Notes

1   The Liberal Tradition

1. M. Cowling, *1867: Disraeli, Gladstone and Revolution* (Cambridge, 1967), p. 100.
2. Ibid., p. 301.
3. Ibid., Appendix II, p. 344.
4. D. Southgate, *The Passing of the Whigs* (1962), p. 333. See also A.F. Thompson, 'Gladstone's Whips and the General Election of 1868', *English Historical Review*, LXIII (1948), pp. 12–24.
5. J. Vincent, *The Formation of the Liberal Party* (1966), p. 52.
6. John Morley, *William Ewart Gladstone*, 3 vols (1903).
7. Ibid., I, 928.
8. Southgate, *The Passing of the Whigs*, p. 347.
9. H.T. Hanham, *Elections and Party Management: Politics in the Time of Disraeli and Gladstone* (1959), p. 114.
10. Morley, *Fortnightly Review*, February 1874.
11. Hanham, *Elections and Party Management*, p. 119.
12. Ibid., pp. 349 ff.
13. Considerable historical debate has centred around the origins of the National Liberal Federation. Ostrogorski connected the rise of the NLF directly with the desire of local Liberals from 1868 to organise the minority vote and win all three Birmingham seats. But, as Herrick points out, Liberalism was strongly established in Birmingham before 1868, and was given the impetus to organise itself efficiently as much by the importance of party in municipal elections and by the presence of organised Nonconformity in the city as by the provisions of the 1868 Act. See F.H. Herrick, 'The Origins of the National Liberal Federation', *Journal of Modern History* (1945).
14. R. Spence Watson, *The National Liberal Federation, 1877–1906* (1907), pp. 6 ff.
15. B. McGill, 'Schnadhorst and Liberal Party Organisation', *Journal of Modern History* (1962).
16. Watson, *The National Liberal Federation*, pp. 12–13. The Constitution of the National Liberal Federation appeared to be reasonably democratic. The Council, consisting of representatives of the Federated Associations and all Liberal Members of Parliament, met annually. The number of delegates each association might send was apportioned in accordance with the electorate of the constituency.
17. Hanham, *Elections and Party Management*, p. 30.
18. R. Kelly, 'Midlothian: A Study in Politics and Ideas', *Victorian Studies*, IV, 2 (1960).
19. As McGill has shown, the main benefit of the NLF efforts cannot be interpreted, as Schnadhorst claimed at the time, in terms of seats gained wherever the NLF was active. This was not true. But the NLF's organisation had been invaluable in dissuading Liberals from standing against each other so that the activities

of the NLF were a constant background to Liberal success rather than a major
cause of it.

20. In its final form the Bill extended the comprehensive occupancy franchise
from the boroughs into the counties. At the same time, all parliamentary
boroughs of fewer than 15,000 inhabitants were disfranchised; boroughs
with a population of 15,000–50,000 were reduced to single-member seats,
and this principle also extended to the counties and big cities, which were
all divided into single-member constituencies. These provisions were the
result of a compromise between Liberal and Conservative leaders after the Bill
was at first rejected by the Lords. This rejection had given the NLF another
opportunity for a mass protest and demonstration.

21. McGill, 'Schnadhorst and Liberal Party Organisation'.

2 Liberalism in Eclipse

1. B. Goodman, 'Liberal Unionism: The Revolt of the Whigs', *Victorian Studies*
(December 1959).
2. D.A. Hamer, *John Morley: Liberal Intellectual in Politics* (Oxford, 1968), p. 198.
3. R. Spence Watson, *The National Liberal Federation, 1877–1906* (1907), pp. 84 ff.
4. Hopes of a reconciliation in the party collapsed with the failure of the 1887
Round Table Conference. For this episode, see M. Hurst, *Joseph Chamberlain
and Liberal Reunion: The Round Table Conference of 1887* (Newton Abbot, 1967).
5. See P. Stansky, *Ambitions and Strategies: The Struggle for the Leadership of the
Liberal Party in the 1890s* (Oxford, 1964).

3 The Liberals in Opposition: 1900–1906

1. Herbert Gladstone's memorandum of 13 March 1903 is printed in full in
F. Bealey, 'Negotiations between the Liberal Party and the Labour Representation Committee before the General Election of 1906', *Bulletin of the Institute
of Historical Research*, XXIX (1956), p. 269 f.
2. For this contest, see R. Douglas, *The History of the Liberal Party, 1895–1970*
(1971), pp. 71–3.
3. For the 1906 election, see A.K. Russell, *Liberal Landslide: The General Election
of 1906* (Newton Abbot, 1973), *passim*.
4. See Jesse Herbert to Herbert Gladstone, 16 February 1906, quoted in Douglas,
History of the Liberal Party, p. 76.

4 The Liberal Ascendancy: 1906–1910

1. Lord Ponsonby's notes on Campbell-Bannerman in Francis W. Hirst, *In the
Golden Days* (1947), p. 259, quoted in José F. Harris and Cameron Hazlehurst,
'Campbell-Bannerman as Prime Minister', *History*, 55:185 (Oct. 1970),
pp. 360–383.
2. Gladstone to Campbell-Bannerman, 21 January 1906, quoted in Harris and
Hazlehurst, 'Campbell-Bannerman as Prime Minister'.
3. J.P. Alderson, *Mr Asquith* (1905), p. 268, quoted in Harris and Hazlehurst,
'Campbell-Bannerman as Prime Minister'.

4. For a detailed discussion on this theme, see A.J. Dorey, 'Radical Liberal Criticism of British Foreign Policy, 1906–1914', unpublished DPhil thesis (Oxford, 1964), pp. 120–2.
5. See C. Hazlehurst, 'Asquith as Prime Minister', *English Historical Review* (1972), p. 513.
6. J.A. Hobson, *The Crisis of Liberalism* (1909), p. xii, quoted in Hazlehurst, 'Asquith as Prime Minister', p. 514.
7. Quoted in P. Rowland, *The Last Liberal Governments: The Promised Land, 1905–10* (1968), p. 243. This is a detailed and excellent account of this period.
8. For details of the January 1910 election, see M. Kinnear, *The British Voter: An Atlas and Survey since 1885* (1968). See also N. Blewett, *The Peers, The Parties and The People: The British General Elections of 1910* (1972).

5 The Crisis of Liberalism: 1910–1914

1. See C. Hazlehurst, 'Asquith as Prime Minister', *English Historical Review* (1972), p. 523.
2. Labour fielded only 56 candidates in December 1910, 22 fewer than in January. Labour returned 42 members, gaining five seats (Fife West, Bow and Bromley, Sunderland, Whitehaven and Woolwich) but losing three (St Helen's, Wigan and Newton), all in straight fights with Conservatives. As in January, the party's independent strength was conspicuously absent. The great bulk of the 42 members had been returned without Liberal opposition, some of these running in harness in double-member seats (with the Liberal almost invariably polling more votes than Labour).
3. See R. Douglas, *The History of the Liberal Party, 1895–1970* (1971), pp. 55–6.
4. T. Wilson, *The Downfall of the Liberal Party* (1966), pp. 16–17.
5. R. McKibbin, *The Evolution of the Labour Party* (Oxford, 1975), p. 84.
6. R. Gregory, *The Miners in British Politics, 1906–14* (Oxford, 1968), p. 171.
7. For the North East Derbyshire contest, see Douglas, *History of the Liberal Party*, pp. 80–2.
8. Gregory, *The Miners in British Politics*, p. 117.
9. For Midlothian, see Douglas, *History of the Liberal Party*, p. 83.
10. McKibbin, *Evolution of the Labour Party*, p. 80.
11. Philip Snowden, *An Autobiography* (1932) pp. 217–18.
12. George Dangerfield, *The Strange Death of Liberal England, 1910–14* (New York, 1961).
13. McKibbin, *Evolution of the Labour Party*, p. 236. For a critique of Dangerfield, see also H. Pelling, *Popular Politics and Society in Late Victorian England* (1968), pp. 102–3.

6 Liberals at War: 1914–1918

1. Henry to Gladstone, 5 September 1914, Gladstone MSS, BM Add. MSS 46,038, f.99, quoted in C. Hazlehurst, 'Asquith as Prime Minister', *English Historical Review* (1972).
2. Asquith Papers, Box XXVII, ff. 162–3, quoted in Roy Jenkins, *Asquith* (1964), p. 360.

3. C. Addison, *Four and a Half Years* (1934), I, p. 35.
4. E.R. Cross to Lloyd George, 30 May 1915, Lloyd George Papers, D/20/1/6.
5. Lloyd George's proposal, though gaining the support of John Redmond and also of leading Ulster Unionists, soon foundered on the opposition of Lansdowne and Walter Long. On this issue, the Conservatives in the Cabinet were totally split.
6. For a fuller discussion of the crisis, see Lord Beaverbrook, *Politicians and the War, 1914–16*, pp. 287–534. See also C. Hazlehurst, 'The Conspiracy Myth', in Martin Gilbert (ed.), *Lloyd George* (Englewood Cliffs NJ, 1968).
7. Hazlehurst, 'The Conspiracy Myth'.
8. Churchill was eventually brought back in July 1917 – as Minister of Munitions.
9. T. Wilson, *The Downfall of the Liberal Party* (1966), p. 104.
10. *Liberal Magazine* (1917) quoted in Wilson, *Downfall of the Liberal Party*, p. 106.
11. For details of these debates, see E. David, 'The Liberal Party Divided', *English Historical Review* (1972).
12. R.B. Haldane to E.S. Haldane, 2 March 1917, quoted in Wilson, *Downfall of the Liberal Party*, p. 104.
13. The Military Service Bill became law on 18 April 1918. However, the Coalition Government never actually applied its provisions to Ireland.
14. M. Kinnear, *The British Voter* (1968), p. 70.
15. C. Cook and J. Ramsden, *By-Elections in British Politics*, p. 17.

7 A Party Divided: 1918–1923

1. K.O. Morgan, 'Lloyd George's Stage Army', in A.J.P. Taylor (ed.), *Lloyd George: Twelve Essays* (1971), p. 247.
2. See M. Kinnear, *The British Voter* (1968), pp. 88–91.
3. See Chris Cook, *The Age of Alignment*, pp. 43–5.
4. Quoted in M. Kinnear, *The Fall of Lloyd George: The Political Crisis of 1922* (1973).
5. See P. Thompson, *Socialists, Liberals and Labour: The Struggle for London* (1967).
6. See Chris Cook and John Ramsden, *By-Elections in British Politics* (1973).
7. Kinnear, *The Fall of Lloyd George*, p. 201.
8. T. Wilson, *The Downfall of the Liberal Party* (1966), p. 243.
9. *Lloyd George Liberal Magazine*, June 1923, p. 697.
10. For the by-elections of this Parliament, see Chris Cook and John Ramsden, *By-Elections in British Politics*, pp. 44–8.

8 Revival and Decline: 1923–1926

1. A.J.P. Taylor, *Beaverbrook* (1972), p. 219.
2. M. Cowling, *The Impact of Labour* (Cambridge, 1971), p. 346.
3. Much the best discussion of the main speeches of the Liberal leaders is to be found in R. Lyman, *The First Labour Government* (1957), pp. 42–52.
4. See Chris Cook, *The Age of Alignment* (1975), pp. 180–96.
5. Ibid., p. 252.

6. See Chris Cook and John Ramsden (eds), *By-Elections in British Politics* (1973), pp. 44–71.
7. T. Wilson (ed.), *The Political Dairies of C.P. Scott* (1973), entry dated 27 November 1924.
8. For the details of these discussions, see R. Douglas, *The History of the Liberal Party, 1895–1970* (1971), pp. 181–3.
9. T. Wilson, *The Downfall of the Liberal Party* (1966), p. 276.
10. Fisher's diary, 16 September 1923, H.A.L. Fisher Papers, quoted in Wilson, *Downfall of the Liberal Party*, p. 276.
11. For these pacts, see Cook, *The Age of Alignment*, p. 294.
12. Wilson, *Downfall of the Liberal Party*, p. 318.
13. See Lloyd George's speech at the National Liberal Club, 5 April 1927, quoted in Wilson, *Downfall of the Liberal Party*, p. 315.

9   Lloyd George Again: 1926–1931

1. The intrigues and negotiations of these months are well detailed in both Douglas and Wilson. See R. Douglas, *The History of the Liberal Party, 1895–1970* (1971), pp. 188–97.
2. Particular opposition was aroused by the proposal to end the private ownership of agricultural land by converting farmers into 'cultivating tenants' under the supervision of county committees.
3. R. Skidelsky, *Politicians and the Slump* (1967), p. 521.
4. D.E. Butler, *The Electoral System in Britain since 1918*, 2nd ed. (Oxford, 1963), p. 181.
5. T. Wilson, *The Downfall of the Liberal Party* (1966), p. 345.
6. R. Douglas, *History of the Liberal Party*, p. 203.
7. *Liberal Magazine*, September 1929.
8. Wilson, *Downfall of the Liberal Party*, pp. 349–50.
9. These four clashes were in Ashford, East Dorset, Nuneaton and the Western Isles.

10   Dissension and Decline: 1931–1945

1. R.H. Bernays, J.A. Leckie, W. McKeog, J.P. Maclay. As a compensation one former Liberal National (A.C. Curry) came over with Samuel.
2. With the exception of Gwilym Lloyd George, who remained as Minister of Fuel and Power.
3. J.S. Rasmussen, *Retrenchment and Revival* (1964).
4. Lloyd George himself died in March 1945, having previously been elevated to the House of Lords as Earl Lloyd-George of Dwyfor.

11   A Party in the Wilderness: 1945–1956

1. See Chris Cook and John Ramsden, *By-Elections in British Politics* (1973), pp. 191–2.
2. *Westminster Newsletter*, August 1945, quoted in J.S. Rasmussen, *Retrenchment and Revival* (1964), p. 209.

12 The Sound of Gunfire: 1956–1967

1. David Butler and Richard Rose, *The British General Election of 1959* (1960), p. 233.
2. 'What Kind of Third Party', *New Society*, 26 January 1967.

13 The Thorpe Leadership: 1967–1976

1. Hugo Young, 'The Liberal Candidates', *Sunday Times*, February 1974.
2. For a detailed discussion of this period, see D. Butler and D. Kavanagh, *The British General Election of October 1974* (London, 1975), pp. 49–50.
3. Cyril Smith subsequently did resign, on the ground of ill health, after the immediate crisis had subsided. He was succeeded by Alan Beith, the MP for Berwick-upon-Tweed.

14 Pacts and Alliances: 1976–1983

1. After the party assembly vote supporting the renewal of the pact, Cyril Smith resigned as Liberal spokesman on employment.
2. V. Bogdanor (ed.), *Liberal Party Politics* (1983), p. 94.
3. The Liberals were 3,882 votes behind the Scottish Nationalists in the Highlands and Islands constituency and 13,414 behind the Conservatives in the North East Scotland seat.
4. *The Economist*, 15 May 1982.

15 A Tale of Two Leaders: 1983–1987

1. *The Economist*, 16 May 1987.
2. The full results were: (Ryedale) Lib. 27,612; Con. 22,672; Lab. 4,633 (Lib. maj. 4,940); (West Derbyshire) Con. 19,896; Lib. 19,796; Lab. 9,952; Others 637 (Con. maj. 100).
3. *Liberal News*, September 1986.
4. *Daily Telegraph*, 11 December 1986.
5. *Daily Telegraph*, 28 February 1987.
6. For details of the Alliance candidates and votes, see p. 331.

16 Merger Most Foul: 1987–1988

1. *Liberal News*, 3 July 1987.
2. Total excludes 170 intentionally spoilt papers; 162 marked abstention.
3. A second amendment, defeated by 228 votes to 115, called upon the national committee, as soon as any merger terms eventually agreed were known, (i) to put such terms to the members in a second ballot, giving each member the choice as to whether they wished to join the merged party or continue as a member of the SDP; (ii) to transfer the premises of the party to the majority; (iii) to divide all other assets or liabilities in proportion to the members' wishes expressed in the second ballot; and (iv) to appoint an independent arbitrator

to determine who might be properly regarded as representative of the two options for these purposes, and to resolve any areas of disagreement.

4. *Independent*, 31 August 1987.
5. *Sunday Telegraph*, 30 August 1987.
6. A proposal that the team should consist of David Steel, the party's President and Chairman and eight people elected by the Assembly, was preferred to a team composed entirely of elected people. A total of 571 voted for the first option and 527 for the second.
7. Eight Liberal negotiators were elected by the Assembly to join Adrian Slade, the party President, Tim Clement-Jones, the Chairman, and David Steel's nominee, Alex Carlile, MP for Montgomery, in the merger talks with the Social Democrats. The eight were Alan Beith, the Liberal Deputy Leader, Des Wilson, the retiring President, Rachel Pitchford, Chair of the Young Liberals, Tony Greaves, head of Liberal publications, Andrew Stunell, Michael Meadowcroft, former MP for Leeds West, John MacDonald, and Peter Knowlson. In addition, there were representatives from the Welsh and Scottish Liberals.
8. *Guardian*, 19 December 1987.
9. *Guardian*, 14 January 1988.
10. *Guardian*, 14 January 1988.
11. *Observer*, 17 January 1988.
12. This was on the motion to hold a ballot to approve, by a simple majority, a resolution to incorporate the Liberal Party with the SDP into the Social and Liberal Democrats.
13. Carried by 2,059 votes to 275.
14. For details of this, see *The Times*, 25 January 1988.
15. Although the vote was more than 80 per cent in favour of merger, and thus constitutionally the margin was sufficient not to require a ballot, it was according to Shirley Williams 'right and proper' to hold such a ballot.
16. In addition, there was a minuscule total of 126 abstentions.
17. In addition, 125 abstained and 132 spoiled their ballot papers.

17   A New Agenda: 1988–1992

1. *Guardian*, 15 September 1990.
2. *Guardian*, 6 April 1992.

18   Voting for Change: 1992–1997

1. Patrick Wintour, *Guardian Political Almanac, 1992–93*, p. 35.
2. *The Times*, 20 September 1993.
3. Ibid.
4. Accusations of racism were alleged over the actions of some Liberal Democrats in Tower Hamlets – an East End of London inner city area. The matter had come to public attention when the British National Party (BNP) won the Millwall ward by-election in September. See p. 219.
5. The councils gained by Liberal Democrats in May 1994 were Bath, Colchester, Congleton, Eastleigh, Kingston-on-Thames, Mole Valley, Rochford, St Albans, Winchester and Worthing.

6. A major exception to Liberal Democrat advances in the inner city areas was Tower Hamlets. Having controlled the borough for eight years, the Liberals lost 22 seats to Labour, their representation on the 50-seat council slumping to a derisory seven. This was a clear consequence of the bitter wrangling discussed earlier (see p. 219).
7. On the same day as Eastleigh, polling took place in four Labour strongholds (Dagenham, Barking, Bradford South and Newham North East). Here the only real excitement was in Newham North East where Alec Kellaway, the Liberal Democrat, defected to Labour during the campaign.
8. *Guardian*, 25 June 1994.
9. Ibid.
10. *The Times*, 21 September 1994.
11. *Guardian*, 6 May 1995. Chichester, as the *Guardian* noted, had been Conservative since it was built by the Romans in AD 70 and made Tunbridge Wells seem like Islington.
12. *Liberal Democrat News*, 26 May 1995.
13. *Independent*, 28 May 1995.
14. See *Guardian*, 27 May 1995. A local Liberal Democrat–Conservative pact had existed on Rochdale metropolitan council since 1992.
15. *The Times*, 14 September 1995.
16. *Guardian*, 18 September 1995.
17. Patrick Wintour, *Guardian*, 18 September 1995. On a call by Young Liberals for the gay age of consent to be lowered to 16, and for 16-year-olds to be able to become MPs, no vote was taken.
18. *The Economist*, 23–29 September 1995.
19. Although, as *The Times* noted rather unkindly, she would not mingle altogether comfortably with the open-toed sandal wing of the party. *The Times*, 2 January 1996.
20. *Daily Telegraph*, 22 January 1996.
21. *The Times*, 25 September 1996.
22. *The Times*, 30 October 1996.
23. For example, Liz Lynne (MP for Rochdale), Sir Cyril Smith and Chris Davies (MP for Littleborough and Saddleworth). See *The Times*, 23 November 1996 and 29 December 1996. They were joined by David Alton (see *The Times*, 20 January 1997).
24. In the constituency 81 per cent of the electorate were home owners, 74 per cent were car owners and 46 per cent were in professional or managerial jobs. There were, apparently, more ponies per capita than in any other constituency. *Sunday Telegraph*, 2 February 1997.
25. *Guardian*, 3 May 1997. For similar comments, see Peter Riddell in *The Times*, 29 April 1997.

19   Living with Labour: 1997–2001

1. *Daily Telegraph*, 23 July 1997.
2. The five senior Liberal Democrats on the committee were Paddy Ashdown, Alan Beith, Menzies Campbell, Lord Holme and Robert Maclennan.
3. *The Times*, 22 September 1997.
4. *Observer*, 21 September 1997.
5. *Sunday Telegraph*, 28 November 1999 and *Guardian*, 29 November 1999.

6. Ashdown kept records of this meeting in a code which apparently referred to Blair as OMF (Our Mutual Friend) and the coalition plan as TFM (The Full Monty). Other persons present were Peter Mandelson and Jonathan Powell, Blair's chief of staff.
7. The dispute centred around 55 unfranked ballot papers.
8. The only other by-elections of 1997, in Uxbridge and Paisley South, had proved barren territory.
9. The amendment said that if three-quarters of the executive or parliamentary party did not support closer co-operation, the issue would be put to Conference. If two-thirds of Conference did not support it, the issue would go to a ballot of the membership requiring a simple majority.
10. Liberal Democrats had some ground for optimism. Of 25 local councillors defecting to them in the previous year 19 had come from Labour (*Sunday Telegraph*, 19 April 1998).
11. *The Times*, 11 May 1998.
12. *The Times*, 4 September 1998.
13. *Guardian*, 30 October 1998.
14. It came as even more of a surprise to those who believed what he said at the celebrations to mark his tenth anniversary as leader in July 1998: 'I intend to lead this party through this Parliament, through the next election and into the next government, if that's all right with the rest of you.'
15. *Guardian*, 21 January 1999.
16. For this version, see *Daily Telegraph*, 17 November 1999. Tony Blair had apparently been told of Ashdown's decision in mid-1998.
17. Liberal Democrats also did well in areas near to Sheffield such as Chesterfield and Doncaster.
18. The Liberal Democrats also nearly unseated Labour's Sir Peter Soulsby in Crown Hills. The new composition of Leicester Council was Labour 30, Liberal Democrats 16 and Conservatives 10.
19. Plaid Cymru took such seats as Rhondda, Islwyn and Llanelli.
20. The idea of a coalition between Labour and the LibDems in Scotland had been developed at a meeting held at Lord Irvine's house in West Hampstead in late 1995 with Ashdown and his advisers on one side and Tony Blair, Robin Cook, Donald Dewar and Peter Mandelson on the other. According to Donald Macintyre's biography of Mandelson, the summit was 'lengthy and amicable...lubricated by some of Lord Irvine's excellent claret' (*Sunday Telegraph*, 9 May 1999).
21. Education had been a prominent plank in the Scottish Liberal Democrat manifesto, in particular a £100 million 'Schools 2010' building programme, the recruitment of extra teachers and (most vexed of all for Labour lo accept) the scrapping of student tuition fees.
22. *Guardian*, 14 May 1999.
23. Turnout in England was highest in the South West (27.8) and South East (24.7), lowest in the North West (19.1), North East (19.6) and in Yorkshire and the Humber (19.7). At 30 per cent, turnout in Wales was relatively high.
24. The full result was Labour 6,361; Liberal Democrat 4,068; Conservative 1,618. The Labour candidate, Hilary Benn was the son of Tony Benn.
25. *The Times*, 29 July 1999.
26. *The Times*, 2 August 1999.

27. His well-publicised £50 bet that the LibDems would only win two seats in Europe in 1994 enhanced his reputation for not taking politics seriously.
28. Indeed, one Liberal grandee, when asked if Kennedy would be the next David Steel, replied 'No, he's more interested in politics than David was'.
29. *Guardian*, 24 September 1999.
30. Ibid.
31. *The Times*, 8 January 2000.
32. *Independent*, 7 January 2000.
33. *Independent*, 9 August 2000.
34. In nearly 500 municipal by-elections held between summer 1999 and April 2001, Liberal Democrats lost 37 seats and gained 49.
35. *The Times*, 19 March 2001.
36. Kennedy met Blair on 20 March 2001, producing speculation that a deal on PR in the future was not entirely dead.
37. *Independent*, 9 August 2000.
38. The only English constituency not contested was Wyre Forest, where the Liberal Democrats stood down to support local doctor Richard Taylor in his campaign against hospital closures.
39. *The Times*, 5 June 2001. See also the editorial in *The Times* 'The Right Voice', 31 May 2001. Even the *Daily Telegraph* agreed (6 June 2001).
40. The new Liberal Democrat peers were Sir Paddy Ashdown, Robert Maclennan (the former party president) and three former MPs (Richard Livsey, Ray Michie and Ronnie Fearn).
41. The 56 majority of 1997 became a 15,676 majority, a swing from Conservative to Liberal Democrat of 15.9 per cent. The majority in Torbay (once known as Torybay) rose from just 12 in 1997 to 6,708.
42. Examples of swing from Conservative to Liberal Democrat can be found in Lewes, Eastleigh, Hazel Grove, Northavon, and Harrogate and Knaresborough.
43. Shropshire had not returned a Liberal since 1923; Norfolk and Derbyshire had been barren Liberal territory since 1931.
44. Seats in this target list 'missed' by the Liberal Democrats included Wells, Totnes, Bridgwater, Dorset West and Orpington.
45. For big swings in Labour areas, see Hornsey and Wood Green (13.2 per cent), Holborn and St Pancras (8.3 per cent), Newcastle East and Wallsend (8.5 per cent), Durham City (7.8 per cent) and Blaydon (7.5 per cent). The highest swing (in St Helen's South of 14.3 per cent) was where a Conservative defector had been parachuted in to a safe Labour seat.

20   An Effective Opposition: 2001–2005

1. This total included Viscount Thurso, the first peer elected a Liberal MP in living memory.
2. *Guardian*, 20 September 1999.
3. *The Economist*, 29 September 2001.
4. During the 2005 election, he switched sides again.
5. Labour polled 11,881 votes, the Conservatives 7,794 and the Liberal Democrats 6,146 on a turnout of 40.1 per cent. The Liberal Democrats polled more votes than in the general election and on a lower turnout.
6. *Daily Telegraph*, 19 July 2002.

7. *The Times*, 23 September 2002.
8. *The Times*, 27 September 2002; *The Economist*, 28 September 2002.
9. Chris Huhne was on the march. Neither Menzies Campbell nor Nick Clegg marched and were apparently angered at Kennedy's participation.
10. *The Times*, 28 March 2003.
11. *The Times*, 23 April 2003.
12. The result was: Labour 50; SNP 27; Conservatives 18; Liberal Democrats 17; Others 17.
13. *The Times*, 30 June 2003.
14. *The Times*, 6 September 2003.
15. The figures were: Liberal Democrats 8,158; Labour 7,040, Conservative 3,368.
16. *The Times*, 23 September 2003.
17. *Guardian*, 13 October 2003. Other significant changes included the appointments of Paul Burstow to Health, Malcolm Bruce to Trade and Industry and Sandra Gidley as spokesperson on older people and women.
18. *The Times*, 6 January 2004.
19. *The Times*, 24 January 2004.
20. *The Times*, 22 March 2004, 29 March 2004.
21. The main party figures were: Liberal Democrat 10,274; Labour 8,620; Conservative 5,796; Respect 3,724.
22. *Guardian*, 16 July 2004.
23. It was suggested that the Conservatives would wage only a weak campaign, in return for Lib Dem help to wrest control of the city council from Labour.
24. The main figures were: Labour 7,451; Liberal Democrat 6,991; Conservative 3,543; Respect 1,282.
25. *The Times*, 17 July 2004.
26. *Independent*, 20 September 2004.
27. The main figures were: Labour 12,752; Liberal Democrat 10,719; UKIP 3,193; Conservative 3,044. Turnout was 46 per cent.
28. Among the targets mentioned were Leeds NW, Bradford North, Falmouth and Camborne (where the party was third), Newcastle Central, Cardiff Central and the new seat of Dunbartonshire East. The list even targeted seats with large Labour majorities such as Oxford East (10,344) and Islington South (7,280) but deemed winnable in the changed climate.

21   From Kennedy to Clegg: 2005–2010

1. This money easily dwarfed other important donors such as Carrousel Capital (£290,000), the Joseph Rowntree Reform Trust (£250,000) and Alpha Health Care (£100,000).
2. The party leadership was defeated not only on the part-privatisation of the Post Office but on an increase in membership subscriptions and on curbing the rise in the EU budget.
3. The figures for the major parties were: Labour 12,319; SNP 9,639; Liberal Democrats 4,362; Conservatives 1,993.
4. *The Times*, 30 December 2005.
5. *Observer*, 8 January 2006.
6. Greg Hurst, *Charles Kennedy: A Fatal Flaw* (2006).

7. The full figures in the first round were: Campbell 23,264; Huhne 16,691; Hughes 12,081. In the second round the figures were Campbell 29,697 (58 per cent); Huhne 21,628 (42 per cent).

8. Campbell also appointed Norman Lamb as his Chief of Staff and Lord Kirkwood of Kirkhope as his 'political counsellor'.

9. *Observer*, 5 March 2006.

10. His resignation followed an attack by Davies on the 'influence of the Jewish lobby' in politics in an intemperate outburst in an exchange of e-mails. Sarah Ludford replaced him as acting leader.

11. *The Times*, 9 June 2006.

12. The figures were: Conservative 11,621; Liberal Democrat 10,988; UKIP 2,347; Labour 1,925. In the Blaenau Gwent contest the same day, the Liberal Democrats finished a lowly fourth, but still ahead of the Conservatives.

13. *Observer*, 17 September 2006.

14. Some examples of large swings from Liberal Democrats to SNP include Aberdeen South (11.2), Gordon (10.7), Argyll and Bute (9.2), Roxburgh and Berwickshire (9.4) and Aberdeenshire West and Kincardine (8.5).

15. The Welsh Assembly figures were: Labour 26; Plaid Cymru 15; Conservatives 12; Liberal Democrats 6; Others 1. The three constituency seats won were Brecon and Radnorshire, Cardiff Central and Montgomeryshire.

16. Mike Hancock MP apparently told the BBC: 'I think he was shafted by a complete shower of shits.' Frontbencher Norman Baker added: 'I think a decent man deserved better than that.'

17. *Observer*, 16 December 2007.

18. Sir Menzies Campbell was given responsibility for carrying out a review of Britain's future military capability.

19. It was, as *The Times* observed, such a tangled position it would put a contortionist to shame. *The Times*, 8 March 2008. It was unclear why Clegg had not simply allowed his MPs a free vote on the issue rather than have a three-line whip to abstain.

20. *Guardian*, 10 March 2008.

21. The boast was in an interview with *GQ* magazine.

22. In Sheffield, once dubbed the Socialist Republic of South Yorkshire, the party won six seats to take outright control with 45 of the 84 council seats.

23. The figures (first preference votes) for the major parties were: Conservative 1,043,761 (43.2); Labour 893,877 (37.0); Liberal Democrat 236,685 (9.8); Green 77,374 (3.2); BNP 69,710 (2.9). Turnout was 45.3 per cent.

24. The Liberal Democrat candidate for Mayor of London was an openly gay former police commander in London (and once known as the 'Cannabis Cop'). He had defeated rivals Chamali Fernando and Fiyaz Mughal to secure the nomination.

25. The displaced Marc Godwin, it seemed, was deemed rather too much beard and sandals.

26. The previous occasion was Mitcham and Morden in 1982.

27. *Guardian*, 28 June 2008. Some criticised the party for choosing Stephen Kearney, a candidate from Plymouth rather than Susan Cooper, a local Oxfordshire councillor.

28. The figures for the main parties were: SNP 11,277; Labour 10,912; Conservative 1,639; Liberal Democrat 915. The swing from Labour to SNP was 22.53 per cent. Turnout was 42 per cent.
29. *The Times*, 16 July 2008.
30. *The Economist*, 20–26 September 2008.
31. Vince Cable, with Clegg's full blessing, dropped the commitment to hold a referendum on Euro entry.
32. *The Times*, 18 September 2008.
33. *The Times*, 17 September 2008.
34. *Sunday Mirror*, 30 November 2008. The conversation was overheard on a flight from London to Inverness. Steve Webb and Julia Goldsworthy all came in for criticism.
35. *The Times*, 8 December 2008. Most of the fortune amassed by Lord Jacobs came from his involvement with the British School of Motoring.
36. Vince Cable was born in 1943. A special adviser to the Labour leader John Smith. Chief Economist at Shell. Liberal Democrat MP for Twickenham after 1997. Treasury Spokesman, 2003. Interim Leader after Campbell's resignation.
37. *The Times*, 9 January 2009.
38. *Financial Times*, 27 March 2009.
39. *Daily Telegraph*, 2 May 2009.
40. *The Times*, 15 May 2009.
41. In the contest to elect a new Speaker, the Liberal Democrat Alan Beith secured only 55 votes (leaving him in 5th place) in the first round. He subsequently withdrew.
42. Another bright spot was the unitary authority of Bristol, where the party now had 36 seats to the 17 Conservative and 16 Labour.
43. The figures in 2005 were: Labour 21,097; Conservatives 15,638; Liberal Democrats 7,616; Greens 1,252; UKIP 1,122; Independent 308. Labour majority 5,459 (11.6 per cent)
44. *Independent on Sunday*, 19 July 2009.
45. The outcome was: Conservatives 13,592; Labour 6,243; Liberal Democrats 4,803; UKIP 4,068; Greens 3,350 (9.74 per cent); BNP 941. Turnout 45.7 per cent.
46. April Pond, 'a local Norfolk businesswoman to the core', unfortunately possessed a moat in her property which may not have helped her campaign.
47. *Independent*, 31 July 2009. Duncan Greenland, the party treasurer, was clearly right to stress that it was vital for the party to raise its fund-raising capability.
48. *Independent*, 16 July 2009.
49. *The Times*, 17 September 2009.
50. *The Times*, 13 August 2008.
51. *The Times*, 24 September 2009.
52. This was the first time since 1695 that a Speaker had effectively been ousted from office.
53. The result was: Labour 12,231 (59.4 per cent); SNP 4,120 (20 per cent); Conservatives 1,075 (5.2 per cent); BNP 1,013 (4.9 per cent); Solidarity 794 (3.9 per cent); Liberal Democrats 474 (2.3 per cent). The Greens polled 332. Other minor parties polled less than 300 votes. Turnout was 32.97 per cent.

22   Voting for Deadlock: The General Election of May 2010

1. *The Economist*, 24 April 2010.
2. *Independent*, 4 May 2010.
3. The six Liberal Democrat seats most vulnerable to Labour (with majorities in parenthesis) are: Norwich South (310); Bradford East (365); Brent Central (1,345); Burnley (1,818); Manchester Withington (1,894) and Dunbartonshire East (2,184).
4. *Guardian*, 8 May 2010.
5. *Guardian*, 8 May 2010.

23   Consenting Adults: The Liberal–Conservative Coalition

1. The Labour negotiating team included Lord Mandelson and Lord Adonis.
2. *Observer*, 16 May 2010. Scottish Liberal Democrats had particular reasons to be wary of a Conservative embrace since they faced elections to the Scottish Parliament in May 2011.
3. *Guardian*, 17 May 2010. Issues of most concern were the scrapping of tuition fees, protection of the Human Rights Act and radical electoral reform.
4. *Guardian*, 25 May 2010. Overall, 54 per cent of those questioned thought the Coalition would change Britain for the better.
5. The full figures were: Conservatives 20,167; Liberal Democrats 8,886; Labour 5,169; UKIP 2,502; Liberals 1,418. Conservative majority, 11,281.
6. One estimate gave the Liberal Democrats 79 MPs under this system at the 2010 election. *The Times*, 6 July 2010.

Appendix I

1. Source: D.E. Butler and G. Butler, *Twentieth-Century British Political Facts, 1900–2000* (1999).
2. All were Liberal 'Leaders in the House of Commons'. Sir H. Campbell-Bannerman from 1899 to 1908 and H. Asquith from 1908 to 1926 were the only 'Leaders of the Liberal Party'.
3. After Asquith's defeat at the 1918 General Election, Sir Donald Maclean was elected leader of the Parliamentary Party but resigned his post on Asquith's return to the Commons in March 1920.
4. Jeremy Thorpe resigned on 10 May 1976. Jo Grimond became caretaker leader.
5. With the formation of the Social and Liberal Democratic Party, Steel ceased to be Liberal leader and became interim joint leader of the new party until July 1988.
6. Continued in office as first SLDP Chief Whip.
7. Continued in office as first SLDP Chief Whip.
8. In 1969 this post was combined with the Chairmanship of the party.
9. Continued in office as Treasurer of Liberal Democrats.

Appendix II

1. Principal Source: D.E. Butler and G. Butler, *British Political Facts since 1979* (2006).
2. Continued in post as Chief Whip.
3. Source: D.E. Butler and G. Butler, *British Political Facts since 1979* (2006).

Appendix III

1. Source: F.W.S. Craig, *British Parliamentary Election Statistics* (Glasgow, 1968).
2. Including both Liberal and National Liberal candidates in 1922, and Independent Liberals in 1931.
3. Includes the Social Democrat wing of the Alliance, 1983 and 1987.
4. Social and Liberal Democrats in 1992, 1997 and 2001.

Appendix IV

1. This table does not include those seats retained at by-elections (e.g. Montgomery, Truro, or the re-run Winchester contest of November 1997).
2. The party did not stand at previous election.
3. Won by SDP wing of Alliance.
4. Swing is from Lab. to SDP. The swing from Con. to SDP was 23.6 per cent.
5. The first by-election victory of the Liberal Democrats.

Appendix VI

1. Source: *Liberal News* (28), May 1992. After Leeds West, other good results were David Morrish in Tiverton (3.8 per cent), Kath Lappin in Knowsley North (3.3 per cent) and Mark Austin in Medway (3.0 per cent).
2. Ibid.
3. *Liberal News*, May 1997.

Index

Compiled by Sue Carlton

9/11 terrorist attacks 261

Afghanistan, war in 261, 262, 306
Alexander, Danny 292, 293, 318, 322,
   323
Alliance of Liberal and Social
   Democrats 1, 168–87
alternative vote (AV) system 243, 253,
   307, 321, 322, 325
   see also electoral reform;
   proportional representation
anti-terror legislation 262, 274
Ashdown, Paddy 1, 198, 205, 206–9,
   214–15, 219, 225, 226–31, 238
   becomes party leader 201–2
   and European election results
      (1989) 204
   and 1992 election 212, 214
   and Bosnia 214
   Cabinet reshuffle (1994) 223–4
   and 1997 election 233, 234, 238
   and cooperation with New Labour
      239, 240, 241–4, 249–50, 261
   resigns from party leadership 244,
      248
   criticism of Kennedy 264
   support for Menzies Campbell 285,
      291
   offer of Northern Ireland
      Secretaryship 290
   support for Clegg 292
   and disclosure about defections 300
   and war in Afghanistan 306
   and alliance with Conservatives
      (2010) 317, 319
Asquith, Herbert Henry 1, 24, 28,
   36–8, 62, 64, 91
   and war in South Africa 31–2, 34,
      79
   and Liberal League 33
   and social reform 36, 46–8

and Free Trade 36, 91–2
as Chancellor of the Exchequer 38,
   41
becomes prime minister 44–5
and 1910 January election 48–9,
   51
and 1910 December election 52–3
and Franchise Bill (1912) 54
and Home Rule 55–6
during First World War 62–72
and Coalition 64
and conscription 65–7
relations with Lloyd George 66–7,
   88, 89, 91, 95–6, 97, 99, 100,
   104, 105
resignation from Coalition (1916)
   67–9
and relations with Labour 81
and lack of leadership 82, 96–8
and 1922 election 85, 87
and support for Labour 94–6
and 1924 election 103
and Russian Treaty 100–1
death of 106

Baldwin, Stanley 89, 90–1, 92, 95,
   101, 111, 114, 115, 119
Balfour, Honor 125
Balfour, James Arthur 24, 37, 38, 39,
   42–3, 53
Ballard, Jacquie 249, 251
Ballot Act (1872) 8
Beith, Alan 154, 167, 198, 202, 223,
   229, 240, 252, 264
Bell, Martin 232
Beveridge, Sir William 126–7
Birrell, Augustine 41, 43, 67
Blackpool Assembly (1988) 195,
   197–8
Blackpool Conference (1990) 205

Blair, Tony 213, 221, 224, 228, 238, 268
  and cooperation with Liberal Democrats 228–9, 230, 232, 239, 240–4, 261
  announces resignation 289
Bonar Law, Andrew 55, 64–5, 67–8, 71, 72, 73, 77, 83, 84, 87
Bright, John 3, 5, 7, 16, 17, 22
Brown, Gordon 285, 289–90, 307, 310, 317, 318
Brown, Michael 280, 281
Bruce, Malcolm 224, 249, 251, 264
by-elections 23, 29, 32, 34, 35, 36, 37, 43, 45–6, 48, 56–60
  inter-war years 78, 80–1, 83, 86, 87, 89, 97, 98, 99, 107–8, 111, 113, 118–20, 123
  during Second World War 125–6, 129
  post-Second World War 129, 133–5
  during Grimond leadership 1, 137–8, 139–41, 143–4
  during Thorpe leadership 147, 148, 149–50, 151, 152–5, 156, 161–2, 163
  during Steel leadership 163, 165, 166
  during Alliance with Social Democrats 169–72, 176–9, 181, 182–5
  during Ashdown leadership 201, 203, 204, 205–6, 213, 215–16, 218, 219, 226–7, 232, 234, 241, 248
  during Kennedy leadership 252, 254–6, 262, 271–2, 273, 281
  after 2005 281, 285, 287, 296–7, 303, 306

Cabinet Committee 239, 242, 243, 244, 261
Cable, Vince 268, 269, 282, 286, 292–3
  takes over as Acting Leader 290
  as economic guru 298–9, 304
  and tax on homes 306
  as Business Secretary 321, 323
Callaghan, James 163–4, 165

Cameron, David 282, 286, 287, 292, 297, 298, 310
  becomes prime minister 319
  and coalition with Liberal Democrats 318–19, 320, 326
  and electoral reform 320–1, 325
Campbell, Menzies 224, 238, 240, 249, 252, 264, 269, 279, 284–91
  urges Kennedy to resign 281, 282
  and leadership contest 284–5
  elected party leader 286
  resigns 290–1
Campbell-Bannerman, Sir Henry 24, 34–44
  army reforms 28
  becomes party leader 29, 30
  and war in South Africa 30–4
  and Home Rule 37
  as prime minister 37–44
Carmichael, Alistair 286, 294, 322
Chadwick, Bill 256
Chamberlain, Austen 83
Chamberlain, Joseph 10, 11, 16, 17, 18, 19–24
  and Education Bill 8
  as president of NLF 13
  unauthorised programme 19, 20
  and Home Rule Bill 21–3, 24
  and National Radical Union 23
  and war in South Africa 30, 31
  Tariff Reform 36
Chamberlain, Neville 124
Changing Britain for Good 208
Cheadle by-election (2005) 280–1
Christchurch by-election (1993) 215–16, 234
Church of England 8, 256
Churchill, Winston 36, 45, 69
  as Under-Secretary at the Colonial Office 41, 44
  and New Liberalism 46
  and conscription 65
  in 1918 Coalition Cabinet 76
  and 1922 election 86
  opposition to support for Labour 94
  and 1923 election 97
  forms government (1940) 125, 126
  offers Conservative–Liberal coalition 133

Clegg, Nick 279, 280, 286, 291–6,
    297–300, 304–10
  elected party leader 293
  criticism of Michael Martin 301,
    304
  and 2010 election result 316,
    317–18
  and coalition with Conservatives
    318–26
Coal Bill (1929) 111–12
Coalition Liberals 72, 74, 76, 77–9,
    82–5, 86–7, 88
community politics 149–50, 151–2,
    154, 166, 219
conscription 65–7, 70
Conscription Bill (1916) 66
Cook, Robin 231–2, 281
Corrupt Practices Act (1883) 18
council tax 265, 267, 268, 273, 274,
    275, 280
Criminal Law Amendment Act (1871)
    9
Curragh Mutiny 56

Davey, Ed 261, 272, 280, 282, 286,
    292, 293
Davies, Clement 133, 134–5
decapitation strategy 275, 276, 277
Dewar, Donald 247
Disraeli, Benjamin 5, 8, 10, 11, 12, 14
Dunbarton and West Fife by-election
    (2005) 285
Duncan Smith, Iain 261, 262, 263,
    264, 268

Eastbourne by-election (1990) 205–6
Eastleigh by-election (1994) 222–3
Education Act (1902) 33, 34, 36, 37,
    43
Education Bill (1870) 8
Education Bill (1906) 43
electoral reform 231, 239, 241, 243,
    253, 261, 309, 310, 318–19, 320
  referendum on 324
  see also alternative vote (AV)
    system; proportional representa-
    tion
Employers' Liability Bill (1886) 24
euro 256, 263, 264, 265, 268, 321

European Assembly Elections Bill
    (1977) 164
European elections
  1984 177
  1989 203–4
  1994 213, 220–2
  1999 239, 244, 247–9
  2004 263, 268, 270
  2009 300, 301–2, 303
  and electoral reform 165, 229
expenses scandal 300–1, 302, 303,
    304, 306, 307, 310, 323

Facing up to the Future 218–19
Falklands War (1982) 170
Farmers' Alliance 14–15, 17, 20
Farron, Tim 293, 294, 324
Featherstone, Lynne 299, 322
Finance Bill (1909) 48
First World War (1914–18) 62–75
Foster, Don 249, 250
Franchise Act (1885) 18
Franchise Bill (1884) 18
Franchise Bill (1912) 54
Free Trade 36, 38–9, 46, 49, 65, 90–2,
    97, 102, 120, 123
  see also general election, 1923
Freedom, Fairness and Trust 272–3
Freedom, Justice, Honesty 256
Freedom in a Liberal Society 255
The Future of Europe 264

Gang of Four 168, 170, 172, 175, 188,
    189, 226
general elections
  1868 2, 5–6
  1874 10–11
  1880 15–16
  1885 19–20
  1886 23
  1892 25–6
  1895 28, 29
  1900 32–3
  1906 39–40, 42
  1910 (January) 48–50
  1910 (December) 52–3, 57
  1918 (coupon election) 72–5, 76
  1922 85–7

1923 (Free Trade election) 91–4, 96, 97, 174
1924 102–3
1929 108–10
1931 115–16, 117
1935 120–2
1945 127–8, 129
1950 131–2
1951 132–3
1955 134–5
1959 138–9, 143
1964 142–3
1966 143, 144–6, 147
1970 150–1
1974 (February) 1, 155–7
1974 (October) 159–61
1979 165–7
1983 171–4
1987 185–7
1992 208–12, 213–14
1997 233–7
2001 256–9, 260
2005 274–8, 279
2010 309–16
General Strike (1926) 105
Gibson, Ian 303
Gidley, Sandra 254
Gladstone, Herbert 20, 35, 37, 38, 42, 56, 79–80, 91
Gladstone, William Ewart 2–3, 4
  and 1868 General Election 5–6
  and disestablishment of Irish Church 5, 7
  Cabinet (1868) 6–7
  and dissension in Party 7–9, 22
  dissolution of Parliament (1874) 10
  withdrawal from leadership (1875) 11
  re-entry into politics (1877) 14
  attacks on government foreign policy 14–15
  second ministry 15–17
  Cabinet (1880) 16
  and Home Rule for Ireland 17, 20–1, 22–3, 26
  and Franchise Bill 18
  third ministry 21
  split with Chamberlain 21–2

  and 1886 General Election 23
  fourth ministry 26
Goldsworthy, Julia 279, 281, 286, 293
Government of Ireland Bill (1912) 55
Grayson, Richard 252
Greater London Authority (GLA) 238, 254, 295–6
Grimond, Joseph 133, 136, 141–2, 143, 144, 159, 162
  and Suez crisis 136–7
  resignation as party leader 145–6
  and Lib–Lab Pact 165

Haldane, R.B. 41, 44
Hall, Fiona 270
Harcourt, Sir William 16, 26, 28, 29
Harris, Evan 261, 263, 312
Hartington, Marquis of 11, 14, 15, 16, 18, 21, 22
Hartlepool by-election (2004) 273
Harvey, Nick 229, 249, 250, 286, 322
'Hawarden Kite' 20–1
Heath, David 286, 294, 299, 322
Holme, Richard, Baron 207, 229, 232
Home Rule Bill (1886) 19, 21–3, 26
House of Lords 17, 42, 48, 52, 53–4, 55, 274
  reform of 25, 26–7, 49, 166, 205, 231, 256, 260, 308, 321
Housing (Homeless Persons) Bill (1977) 164
Hughes, Simon 171, 180–1, 224, 229, 234, 249, 251–2, 290
  and contest for Mayor of London 269
  and leadership contest 284–5, 286
  as Energy and Environment spokesman 299
  and coalition with Conservatives 319
  election as Deputy Leader 323–4
Huhne, Chris 261, 280, 307, 318, 321
  and leadership contests 279, 284, 286, 291, 292–3
Human Rights Act 321

ID cards 261, 263, 274, 294, 319, 320, 322
Import Duties Bill (1932) 117

Independent Liberals 74, 81–2, 85–8,
    96, 99, 125, 131
Iraq war 267, 271, 275, 285
    Liberal Democrat position on 261,
        263, 264–5, 274, 284, 302
Ireland 16–17
    conscription 70
    and Home Rule 17, 20–3, 25, 26,
        27, 37, 55–6
Irish Church, disestablishment of 5,
    6, 7
Irish Compensation for Disturbance
    Bill (1880) 17
Irish Land Bill (1870) 7–8
Irish Land Bill (1881) 17
Irish Land Purchase Bill (1886) 21
Irish University Bill (1873) 9

Jenkins Commission on Electoral
    Reform 241, 243
Jenkins, Roy 167–70, 176
    resigns as SDP leader 175
    and Liberal–SDP merger 188, 189,
        190, 198, 202
    and New Labour 230, 240
    death of 264

Kennedy, Charles 1, 238, 251–7,
    260–5, 266–7, 268–9, 272–3,
    279–83
    and Liberal–SDP merger 188, 190
    leadership campaign 249–50
    elected party leader 250–1
    and 2001 election 256–7, 260
    and alcoholism 263, 281, 282
    and intervention in Iraq 263, 264
    and 2005 election 274, 275
    resignation 282
Kilmainham Treaty (1882) 17
Kirkwood, Archie 238, 250
Kramer, Susan 254, 292, 299, 312

Labour Representation Committee
    (LRC) 34–5
Land and Nation League 106
Laws, David 272, 280, 292, 293, 318,
    321, 323
Liberal Action Group (later Radical
    Action Group) 125–6

Liberal Democrat Guarantee 227–8
Liberal Democrats
    relationship with New Labour
        238–59, 319–20
    and women MPs 262, 263, 264–5,
        279
    and donations scandal 280
    defections (2009) 304
    coalition with Conservatives
        317–26
Liberal League 33, 37
The Liberal Moment 305
Liberal National Party 89, 131
Liberal Party
    origin and development of 1–4
    organisation restructuring 11–12,
        13–14, 122, 130
    and pact with Labour (1903) 34–6,
        39–40
    relations with Labour 56–61, 112,
        113, 122–3
    and First World War 62–3
    local constituency pacts with
        Labour 101–2
    finance 120, 141, 150
        from Lloyd George 78, 91, 96, 99,
            101, 106, 108, 110–11, 130
    relations with Conservatives 131
    new constitution (1969) 150
    Lib–Lab Pact (1977) 163–5
    alliance with Social Democrats 1,
        168–87
    merger with SDP 188–200
Liberal Registration Association 11–12
Liberal reunion 88–9, 90–1, 95–6
Liberal Unionism 22, 25
Liddle, Roger 240
Liquor Licensing Bill (1872) 9
Littleborough and Saddleworth
    by-election (1995) 226–7
Livingston by-election (2005) 281
Lloyd George, David 1, 27, 45, 56
    and war in South Africa 32
    at Board of Trade 41, 44
    as Chancellor of the Exchequer 45,
        47, 56
    People's Budget 47–8
    and Marconi affair 55

and Coalition 64, 65, 69, 70, 83–4, 97
and conscription 65, 66
as Secretary of State for War 67
becomes prime minister 68–9, 71
as prime minister 69–87
and 1918 election 72, 74, 76
and reconstruction policy 76
and creation of 'Centre Party' 77, 79
finance for Liberal Party 78, 91, 96, 99, 101, 106, 108, 110–11, 130
resigns as prime minister 83
and 1922 election 85, 87
lecture tour of America 89
and free trade 90–1, 92
and Liberal reunion 90–1
and 1923 election 96
as Chairman of the Parliamentary Liberal Party 103
and General Strike 105
and Land and Nation League 106–7
and unemployment 106–7, 108
and Coal Bill 112
and cooperation with Labour 112–13
illness 114
and 1931 election 115–16
New Deal campaign 120
urges Chamberlain to resign 124–5
local elections
1906–08 43, 60
inter-war years 80, 123
post-Second World War 129, 133
1960s 140
1970 150
1980s 178, 184–5, 204
1990s 207, 225, 230, 244
after 2001 265–6, 286–7, 288–9, 295–6, 300, 301, 320

MacDonald, Ramsay 35, 59, 60, 94, 97–8
McKenna Budget (1916) 65
Maclennan, Robert 201, 202, 231–2, 240
becomes leader of SDP 190, 191
and Liberal–SDP merger 192, 195, 196–7, 200

Make a Difference 233
Mandelson, Peter 227, 240, 256, 273
Marconi affair 55
Marsden, Paul 262
Meadowcroft, Michael 180, 181, 194–5, 197, 214
Merchant Shipping Act (1906) 44
Meston Report (1936) 122
Moore, Michael 286, 293, 323
Moving Ahead 242

National Insurance Act (1911) 54
National Liberal Federation (NLF) 20, 27, 33, 106, 118, 122
formation of 11, 12, 13–14
and 1880 elections 15
and Irish Land Bill 17
and Irish self-government 22
increased influence of 24–5
reaction against 28
and Liberal reunion 88–9
National Radical Union 23
New Labour 213, 224, 227, 230, 232
relations with Liberal Democrats 238–59
Newbury by-election (1993) 215, 216
'Newcastle Programme' (1891) 24–5, 27
Newmarket by-election (1903) 34
Nicholson, Emma 213, 229–30, 262
Nonconformists 3–4, 8, 11, 25, 34, 43, 62, 227
Norwich North by-election (2009) 303
nuclear weapons 167–8, 169, 180–1, 195

Oaten, Mark 241, 261, 263, 268, 272, 284
Öpik, Lembit 293, 312
The Orange Book: Reclaiming Liberalism 272
Orpington by-election (1962) 1, 140
Owen, David 168, 175, 185, 188–92, 196–7, 198, 199–200, 202, 204–5

Palmerston, Henry John Temple, 3rd Viscount 1–2
Pardoe, John 161, 162, 166
Parliament Act (1911) 54, 55

Parliament Bill (1910) 52, 53–4
Parnell, C.S. 16–17, 20–1, 24, 25
Payback not Layback 268
Penhaligon, David 181
Plural Voting Bill (1914) 54
Port of London Authority Act 44
proportional representation 122,
164–5, 169, 171, 205, 208, 212,
214, 218, 224, 256, 325
and European elections 164, 239,
263, 270
in Scotland 263
see also alternative vote (AV)
system; electoral reform; regional
list system
Protectionism 70, 90, 92, 97, 113, 115

Quality, Innovation and Choice 263

Redistribution Bill 12–13
redistribution of seats 12, 72, 73, 234,
237
Reform Act (1832) 1, 2
Reform Act (1867) 1, 2, 12–13
Reform Bill (1866) 5
Reform Bill (1867) 2, 4–5, 6
regional list system 164, 165, 247
Rendel, David 249, 251
Representation of the People Act
(1918) 73
Representation of the People Bill
(1918) 72
Rodgers, William 168, 172
Romsey by-election (2000) 253–4
Rosebery, Archibald Primrose, 5th Earl
26, 27–8, 29, 31, 33, 36
Royal Commission on Euthanasia 240
Russell, Conrad 239–40
Russell, John, 1st Earl 2, 22
Russian Treaty 99–101

Samuel, Herbert 70, 106, 108, 112,
114–15, 116, 118–19, 120–1
Scotland, coalition 246–7
Scott, Ros 298
Scottish Parliament 238, 239, 244,
245, 246, 289
Second World War (1939–45) 124–6
Simon, Sir John 64, 65–6, 79, 81, 89,
94, 97, 105, 113–14

Smith, Cyril 152, 159, 161–2, 164–5,
226
Smith, John 213, 220, 221, 225
Social Democratic Party (SDP) 167–9,
175–6
merger with Liberal Party 188–200
Social and Liberal Democratic Party 1,
198, 199, 200
South Africa, war in 30–3, 34
Steel, David 143
coalition campaign (1974) 157
becomes party leader 162, 163
and Lib–Lab Pact 163–6
and Alliance with Social Democrats
168, 169, 175–6, 185, 187
and defence policy 180–1
and Liberal–SDP merger 188,
189–90, 192–3, 194–5, 197–8,
199–200, 201
and SLDP 202
retirement of 223, 224
support for Menzies Campbell 285
support for Clegg 319
Suez crisis 136–7

tactical voting 161, 183, 206, 210,
231, 234, 236, 254, 257, 310
Taff Vale decision 34, 44
Tariff Reform 36, 52, 56
Tax Pollution, not People 218
Taylor, Matthew 183, 225, 250, 252,
268, 274, 280, 286
Teather, Sarah 267, 279, 282
television debates (2010) 310
Territorial and Reserve Forces Act
(1907) 44
Thatcher, Margaret 163, 164, 167,
170, 184, 205, 223
Thorpe, Jeremy 138, 140, 147–8,
157–8, 159, 183
death of wife 151
and Scott affair 161, 162
resigns party leadership 162
Thurnham, Peter 231
Towards 1996 230
Trade Union Act (1871) 9
tuition fees 247, 256, 265, 268, 306,
307, 309
Tyler, Paul 238, 250

UKIP (UK Independence Party) 270, 271, 273, 300, 302–3
unemployment 46, 76, 99, 106–7, 112, 118, 171, 184, 216
    insurance/pay 54, 90, 119
University Test Act (1871) 8–9

Wales
    coalition 246–7
    Welsh Assembly 238, 244, 245–6
Wallace, Jim 180, 196, 197, 245, 247, 263
Wallace, William 232, 233

war on terror 261, 274
We Can Conquer Unemployment 107, 127
Webb, Steve 272, 280, 292, 293, 299, 322
Williams, Shirley 168, 169–70, 172, 188, 189, 190, 199–200, 202, 318, 319
Wilson, Des 180, 195, 196, 201, 208, 242
Winchester by-election (1997) 241

Young Liberals 120, 124, 148–9, 194